Benefit of Clergy in Colonial Virginia and Massachusetts

Peter Johnstone

University of North Texas

Cover images are in the public domain

Kendall Hunt
publishing company

www.kendallhunt.com
Send all inquiries to:
4050 Westmark Drive
Dubuque, IA 52004-1840

Copyright © 2015 by Peter Johnstone

ISBN 978-1-4652-4821-3

Kendall Hunt Publishing Company has the exclusive rights to reproduce this work, to prepare derivative works from this work, to publicly distribute this work, to publicly perform this work and to publicly display this work.

All rights reserved. No part of this publication may be reproduced, stored in a retrieval system, or transmitted, in any form or by any means, electronic, mechanical, photocopying, recording, or otherwise, without the prior written permission of the copyright owner.

Printed in the United States of America

Contents

Acknowledgments
Preface

Chapter One
The privilege: Legitimate immunity or legal farce

Establishing the privilege and early use 325-1066 A.D. 1

William I of England, *privilegium clericus* and the
beginning of a legal fiction 10

Henry II, Beckett and secular retrenchment 14

Chapter Two
Clerical status, the "Neck Verse" and secularization

The validity of *clericus* claimants and plea submission
before the secular courts 17

Extension of the privilege, the increase of capital crimes
and the influence of Henry VIII 22

The Stuarts: Transportation and exportation of *privilegium
fori* to the Colonies 32

Chapter Three
Benefit of clergy in Colonial Virginia

Settlement and early law 37

Transportation and benefit of clergy 45

Criminal courts and the rule of law in Virginia 49

Chapter Four
English law in Virginia: Local variances in the application of *clericus*

Clericus and non-*clericus* crimes 59

Benefit of clergy in the Virginia courts: Establishing a framework for permitting the plea 71

The availability and quality of court records 75

The use of the clergy plea by white males 79

Clergy claims by women 88

The 1732 act and use of clergy by Negroes 90

Unsuccessful pleas and clergy by implication 96

Clergy under American common law 103

Chapter Five
Benefit of clergy in Massachusetts

Establishing a justice system 107

Original charters and early laws 120

Criminal courts and the role of lawyers 126

Chapter Six
Due process and clergy in the northern colony

Law as a union with God 131

Massachusetts court records 133

Benefit of clergy cases before the Massachusetts courts 135

Cases of implied use of clergy 145

Special cases 151

The Boston Massacre clergy case 153

Chapter Seven
Abolition of benefit of clergy in America

Shrugging off the veneer of ecclesiasticism 157

The end of the legal anomaly 162

Appendix One

Lawes Divine Morall and Martiall, &c. 165

Appendix Two

The Massachusetts Body of Liberties 249

Appendix Three

The Laws and Liberties of Massachusetts 270

Index 319

PREFACE

Benefit of clergy existed in the English-speaking world for almost fifteen hundred years. Subsequently it has been referred to as evil, a farce and a queer old legal anomaly. At its worst it permitted members of the church immunity from prosecution before secular courts for the crimes of murder, robbery, rape and a suite of other felonies. At its best it saved women, children and the poor from the gallows for the most minor of thefts. The life and history of benefit of clergy is a fascinating insight into the development of the common law and the relationship that members of the church had with the society they served. Over time the benefit became available to first-time offenders regardless of their station in society in exchange for a sentence of transportation to the American colonies. The criminal courts of England attached an indentured servitude to benefit pleas, resulting in thousands of men and a few women and children being sent to Virginia to service the labor pool needed to make Virginia the financial success its London backers had hoped for. Within a short period of time benefit of clergy became an established part of the legal system of the colony to the extent that it was possible to claim benefit of clergy in Virginia and be transported away to the West Indies. Further north the motivation for colonization differed. The early arrivals to Massachusetts were familiar with benefit of clergy, but their enthusiasm for wholesale adoption of English common law was tepid. Notwithstanding these reservations, the practicality of having a mitigatory plea that was known to all members of the community meant that the written law could appear to embrace religious severity but in practice could be applied with leniency when appropriate.

There is, as of writing this preface, one scholarly book dedicated to the topic of benefit of clergy. Leona Gabel's 1923 doctoral thesis was fortunately converted into a monograph and published in 1928 as *Benefit of Clergy in England in the Later Middle Ages*. Since her work there have been a couple of dozen scholarly articles and an entertaining unreferenced read by George Dalzell, *Benefit of Clergy in America*, published posthumously in 1955. I am deeply grateful to Dr. Gabel and Mr. Dalzell for introducing me to a topic that has become a passion.

Benefit of Clergy in Colonial Virginia and Massachusetts explores the development of the clergy plea and its journey from London to colonial Virginia and Massachusetts. Virginia because the uptake of "clergy" was of immediate and practical use to a colony founded on the basis of entrepreneurship and business. Massachusetts because it was absorbed into the fabric of the legal system for very different reasons than Virginia and was utilized with much disdain until forced upon the colonials towards the end of the seventeenth century only to rise up again, ironically as a defense for English soldiers during the Boston Massacre trial.

This book represents a modest attempt to bring to the fore a fascinating and much understudied area of social and legal history. In writing this work I have been forced to look further back in history to unravel the intrigue and complexity of the benefit of clergy during its most dynamic period; the end of the thirteenth century through to the mid-sixteenth. That has become the focus of what will be a second book in my future.

In 1969 Leona Gabel wrote the introduction to the second printing of her work. She lamented that so little had been written on the topic during the forty years that had passed since the first edition. She concluded, "Thus the last forty years have yielded little either to add to or modify our knowledge of the exercise of the privilege of clergy in England during the closing centuries of the Middle Ages. Clearly the last word on the subject cannot have been said!"[1] This book represents an attempt to fill part of the void, one piece of the discussion; benefit of clergy in two colonies. Mistakes are of course entirely my own and if I misquoted you I apologize.

As Leona Gabel inferred, there is indeed much more to be said. If my contribution stimulates in you the fascination and passion for this topic that Gabel and Dalzell have provided for me then you are about to begin a wonderful journey.

PJ.

Dallas. 2014.

---

[1] Gabel, L. *Benefit of Clergy in England During the Later Middle Ages*, 1969 Reprint, New York, Octagon Books, 1969. P. iv

Acknowledgments

I wish to express my sincere gratitude to Neil Davie. I also wish to thank Christine; for reading and then reading again. Thank you both.

Chapter 1. The privilege: Legitimate immunity or legal farce

Establishing the privilege and early use, 325-1066 A.D.

Privilegium fori, the "privilege of the legal forum" or venue for hearing, has been applied generally to describe a privilege that allowed trial before a particular court. Throughout history a number of denominations have been utilized by the Church; *Privilegium clericale, privilegium canonis,* benefit of clergy and *privilegium fori.*[1] In a broad sense throughout the early Middle Ages, imperial legislation[2] was viewed as subordinate to sacerdotal and in particular that members of the clergy should never be answerable to the laity.[3] Interpretation of the benefit is of itself problematic though, as the Church consistently viewed the privilege differently than did the secular courts. The ecclesiastical position has always been that temporal courts are not competent to hear matters involving clerics. The secular viewpoint is that it is not a privilege but a benefit; that is, the secular courts permit

---

[1] Strictly interpreted, the term *priveligium clericale* has broader meaning than Benefit of Clergy. Clergy extended to all laity; whereas privilege existed for a broad range of ecclesiastical matters justiciable at canon law. At common law the benefit exempted clerics from secular courts in certain criminal matters. At canon law the privilege was based upon the notion that the clergy could not be judged by the laity. The classic interpretation of p*rivilegium clericale* is Blackstone: "I. Clergy, the *privilegium clericale,* or in common fpeech *the benefit of clergy,* had it's origin from the pious regard paid by chriftan princes to the church in ity's infant ftate; and the ill ufe which the popifh ecclefiaftics foon made of that pious regard. The exemptions, which they granted to the church, were principally of two kinds: 1. Exemption of *places,* confecrated to religious duties, from criminal arrefts, which was the foundation of fanctuaries: 2. Exemption of the *perfons* of clergymen from criminal procefs before the facular judge in a few particular cafes, which was the true original and meaning of the *privilegium clericale.*" Blackstone, W. *Commentaries on the Laws of England : A Facsimile of the First Edition of 1765-1769,* Chicago, The University of Chicago Press, 1979. Book IV Public Wrongs Chapter the Twenty Eighth. On the BENEFIT OF CLERGY. pp 358-367. p. 358.

[2] E.g., Laws of Holy Roman Emperor Frederick II Statimus 1139 ad. I 33, C. de episc. I,3 www.newadvent.org/cathen/12437a. This is not to say that the burgeoning secular states were accommodating and there remained resistance to spiritual supremacy.

[3] C.f. Lea, H.C., *Studies in Church History,* London, Sampson Low, Son, & Marston, 1869 p.62 et sec.

clerics to have cases against them heard by the courts Christian so that the trial and punishment of the criminous clerk would result in being judged by his peers. In one case it is a clerical right and in another a benefit allowed by the secular law.[4]

"Touch not Mine anointed, and do My prophets no harm" is contained within the first book of Chronicles, chapter sixteen.[5] Literal interpretation of this text is the basis upon which the Christian Church held that the priesthood should not be held responsible before a secular tribunal; some commentators have viewed this as a prize the Church was loath to relinquish.[6] In 319 Roman Emperor Constantine afforded immunity from suit to all *clericus* and an exemption from all public duties as well so that clergy could focus exclusively upon the deity and "may devote themselves without any hindrance to their own law."[7] His

---

[4] Clergy achieved immunity from suit by Emperor Constantine's introduction of *Privilegium fori*. Tertullianus and Lactantius were both influential with regard to *privilegium*. http://www.tertullian.org/articles In 325 A.D. Pope Sylvester I decreed no layman should bring a charge against a clerk. *Constitutum est ut nullus crimen clerico andeat inferred…testimonium laici adversus clericum nemo recipiat.* Lea, supra p.65 note 6. The Edict of Clothar (614) and later Carlovingian laws confirmed the privilege and extended it to censure clerics appearing before civil tribunals (789). Initially the pope had no secular criminal jurisdiction other than degradation of the clerk before secular criminal trial. Attempts to exclude clergy from criminal trials was recorded in various early laws; e.g., King Wihtraed 690-725 A.D. held a clerk should be heard exclusively before four of his peers. For a chronology of early use c.f. Boyd, W.K. *The Ecclesiastical Edicts of the Theodosian Code*, New York, AMS Press, 1969. And see: Dalzell, R., *Benefit of Clergy in America*, Winston-Salem, NC, Blair Publishing, 1955. p. 11. Also Baker, N. F., Benefit of Clergy-A legal Anomaly, *Kentucky Law Journal* Vol. XV. No. 2 (Jan., 1927) pp. 85-115. p. 85 with regard to the *Codex Theodosianus* (319 A.D.).

[5] Psalms 105:15 and 1 Chronicles 16:22. This most famous penitential psalm originates from King David's admission of his affair with Bathsheba and prayer for forgiveness.

[6] Baker, supra. p. 85.

[7] Boyd, W. *The Ecclesiastical Edicts of the Theodosian Code*, New York, AMS Press, 1969. p. 73. Pollock, F. & Maitland, F. W., *The History of English Law Before the Time of Edward I* (2nd edition) Cambridge, Cambridge University Press, 1968. Vol.I. "The early history of clerical privileges on the continent of Europe [sic] is a long and dark tale and one that we can not [sic] pretend to tell." p. 453. They proceed to give a complete history with references for further reading. Poole, A. L., "Outlawry as a Punishment of Criminous Clerks" in *Historical Essays in Honour of James Tait*, (eds. Edwards, J.G., Galbraith, V.H., Jacob, E.F.) Manchester, 1933. pp. 239-246. p. 243 also provides evidence of the use

move permitted tonsured clerics to exemption from the secular courts in all matters.[8] It did not, however, preclude clerical involvement in the administration of the secular courts and various ranks of the clergy remained active participants in a range of secular trials for the following millennium. Some commentators have viewed this as a coup for the Church as it now had a formal stake in the justice of the laity during life and the afterlife.[9] The fourth century diocesan see had jurisdiction over all matters concerning its brothers[10] as well as the opportunity to make a considerable impact upon secular criminal justice[11] by providing confessional to capital criminals and sanctuary and asylum prior to abjuring the realm. In common with continental jurisdictions, English prelates commonly held ecclesiastic and high temporal office jointly.[12] A concomitant of clerical involvement in

---

of Benefit of clergy and see Von Bar, L. *A History of Continental Criminal Law*, Boston, Little Brown, 1916. Vol 6.

[8] 583. A.D. the Third Council of Orleans decreed that a clerk could not appear before a secular tribunal as plaintiff or defendant without episcopal consent.

[9] E.g. Lea, supra. p. 68.

[10] This was a time when the Roman influence was diminishing substantially across its entire Western empire and the vacuum of social order and cultural and intellectual heritage was in part filled by the Church. Legal authority has always been crucial to the development of nation states and institutions and this period of change presented the church with an opportunity to confirm the sanctity and privileged status of its members.

[11] Infra. Odo of Bayeux, also, for example. It was customary that bishops held high secular office as advisors to the king, personally as confessor and chief counselor as well as fiscally through the office of chancellor. This was recognized early on through the wergild system when in terms of financial compensation archbishops were valued at the same rate as an Anglo-Saxon prince, bishops the same as an earl (ealdorman) and priest with the thegn. Baker, supra, p.87. also see: Henderson, E. F., *Select Historical Documents of the Middle Ages*, London, George Bell & Sons, 1896. p.158. Bishops presided over both ecclesiastic and secular courts, the shire and moots courts for commoners and the Privy Council for matters involving peers.

[12] Demonstrated in the cases brought by William I against his brother and former regent Odo, Bishop of Bayeux in 1084 and by Rufus (William II) against William of St. Calais, Bishop of Durham for treason in 1088. In both cases each king made it very clear that he brought charges against the men not as clerics but as "brother and earl." Additionally there has been a long line of ecclesiastical Chancellors of England from the early Saxon period into the late seventeenth centuries. During the 14th century only five chancellors from a total of thirty-eight who served in this capacity throughout the century did not hold the joint bishopric and chancellorship. Pollock & Maitland, Vol. I. Pollock, F. & Maitland, F. W.,

public life was that it exempted clerics from giving evidence in secular court trials.[13] Throughout the early Middle Ages pontiffs held the view that kings and princes were subordinate and members of their flock; interdiction and excommunication being available to them to reign in errant monarchs. Blind obedience to the Catholic Church was expected of all men regardless of their status and canon law was regarded as supreme in many instances. For example, when King Stephen attacked Bishop Robert (Roger) of Salisbury an *exceptio spolii* was pled and the matter was dealt with before the courts Christian with the king personally appealing the matter before the pope.[14]

By the twelfth century blanket exemption from prosecution for all clergy had become a matter of discussion and discord between the monarchs of Europe and the Roman Catholic Church.[15] The Church was firmly of the view that the nature and scope of the work of the clergy meant that they were answerable exclusively to God and never to a secular authority or courts temporal. This was occasionally

---

The History of English Law Before the Time of Edward I (2nd edition) Cambridge, Cambridge University Press, 1968. Vol.I. p. 205.

[13] Boyd, supra, p. 100 "It was forbidden to force bishops to bear witness in criminal cases, a privilege which was extended in the Justinian law to an exemption from presenting any evidence in person."

[14] See Pollock, F. & Maitland, F. W., *The History of English Law Before the Time of Edward I* (2nd edition) Cambridge, Cambridge University Press, 1968. Vol.I. pp. 117-118. When Salisbury, his sons and nephews were all seized and imprisoned by King Stephen, an ecclesiastic council censored the king. Baker, supra, p. 91 and Pollock and Maitland, supra, p. 450-451.

[15] William the Conqueror's separation of the temporal and spiritual courts in 1072 caused significant changes to the balance of power that had existed in England between the church and state since Anglo-Saxon times. See Ogle, A., *The Canon Law in Mediaeval England: An Examination of William Lynwood's "Provinciale," in Reply to the Late Professor F.W. Maitland*, London, John Murray, 1912. p. 23 The Council of Rheims, 1049, at which England and Normandy were present and at the later Council of Lillebonne the bishops were unable to prevent extended lay ownership of some episcopal rights and temporalities. Morris, C. William I and the Church Courts, *The English Historical Review*, Vol.82. No.324 (Jul.1967.), pp. 449-463. Morris notes the evidence for Germany during this period has been studied by Hilling. p. 461 note 6. Of the situation in France and Germany and the "prolonged struggles" between the church and state see: Pollock & Maitland, *The History of English Law* Volume I, supra, pp. 124-125 and Williams, A., (ed) *Old Church Life*, London, William Andrews & Co, 1909. p. 19-20.

exacerbated by the appellate role the Christian courts performed during the Roman era in occupied territories. Submission to the judgment of an occupying force was never well received across Europe and the Church often acted as a mediator and then adjudicator in disputes that tested Roman law and local custom.[16] Increasingly the emerging monarchs of Europe were concerned at the sphere of the Church's secular and canonical judicial roles; they responded with varying degrees of force as they moved cautiously towards establishing regional power and the geneses of nation states.[17]

For the English monarchs during the Middle Ages the heart of the discussion was the matter of forfeiture of goods and chattels.[18] A convicted felon was typically not permitted to retain his goods and nor were his goods allowed to be passed over to his family. Upon conviction of a felony the goods, including land, reverted back to the crown. Initially this was not a matter of great contention as few clerics had great wealth but as the use of benefit began to increase and non-clerics were clearly circumventing the secular law, the crown became increasingly interested in the abuse of the privilege and its associated

---

[16] C.f. Lea, supra, pp. 71-72.

[17] It can be argued the move started with Charlemagne (crowned Holy Roman Emperor by Pope Leo III on December 25, 800) and establishment of the Holy Roman Empire, an event that hastened the decreasing role of the pope. This was exacerbated in 1054 by the crisis of the Church and the East-West schism and a reshaping of borders by the invasion by William the Conqueror in 1066 which became part of the general move towards the establishment of France, England, Portugal and Spain as nation states. Many books have been written that record the struggles between church and state during this era. For example see: Flora, P., Kulne, S., Urwin, D., *State Formation, Nation-Building, and Mass Politics in Europe; The Theory of Stein Rokkan*, Oxford, Oxford University Press, 1999.

[18] The Church claimed jurisdiction over spiritual dues, oblations, pensions, marriages, divorce and legitimacy. In a time when bastards could not inherit, but might be eligible to obtain clerical status, the crown and Church sought to make each other bring their law into accord with the other. The last words of a dying man were also contentious: the Church viewed final confession as having the same validity as a final will which of course had implications for who inherited goods and chattels or titles. The crown did not agree. c.f. Pollock & Maitland, supra, pp. 126-128.

lost revenue.[19] In England the matter ebbed and flowed over many centuries with each party gaining and losing ground; that is until the reign of Henry VIII when the benefit was retained but extended to all classes of men regardless of their association with the Church.[20] It is important to recognize that, although there were major disagreements over *privilegium fori*—most notably between Henry II and Beckett (1162-1170) and again between Henry VIII and Rome (1527-1534), the position of the church and crown was never as clear cut as being a simple divide of bishops and "popish" clerks against the king and laymen. After Henry VIII those who could claim their benefit increased greatly but the number of clergyable offences decreased significantly.

By the Edict of Clothar (Clothaire),[21] Paris 614, the *privilegium fori* was extended to criminal matters and matters concerning clerical

---

[19] Clerical immunity from civil suit existed since the conversion of Constantine. In criminal cases criminous clerks would be degraded and then handed over to the secular courts for trial. Secular law held that a convicted felon's property belonged to the crown and not the family of the convict. As clerks, especially bishops, gained estates, they were often some of the wealthiest members of society. Parish priests also accrued wealth through the collection of church taxes and payment from parishioners for extraordinary services such as: baptisms, weddings and funerals. The crown wished to treat the clergy in the same way as secular society and have access to the individual wealth of clerics upon criminal conviction or death.

[20] Pollock & Maitland, supra, p.133. observe that Blackstone's view is rather narrowly constructed. Also, "It was particularly unfortunate that Beckett's murder, coming at a time when interest in the contest was most intense, raised him to the position of martyr of the Church, for thereby Henry was forced to admit the right of the Church to the privilege of benefit of clergy." Baker, supra, p. 94. The murder of Beckett was a major event in English history by any proportions and it added considerable strength to the position of the clergy with regard to *privilegium clericus*. I am of the view that Henry VIII recognized that a diminution in the power and role of the clergy was to his benefit and he deliberately acted to remove privileged status from clergy by making numerous crimes non-clergyable. In many respects Henry was leveling the criminal trial playing field by letting all males claim the benefit and at the same time significantly restricting the offenses for which it could be applied to such an extent that the privilege was worthless. In effect he did not so much remove the privilege from the clergy as make many more crimes unclergyable to all. In support of this it has been suggested (and contested) in Holinshed's *Chronicles* that Henry VIII was responsible for the execution of 72,000 citizens during his thirty-eight year reign. It seems that many could claim the benefit and very few got it.

[21] Clothar II, (584-629) Merovingian King of the Franks, 613-629. The Edict of Clothaire II 614, c.4. confirmed the rights and privileges of the nobility (including clerics) to have criminal matters heard before their peers; for clerics the Christian forum. C.f. Murray, A.C., Immunity, Nobility and the Edict

debts. Over time criminal matters involving the clergy were brought exclusively before a courts Christian and so began a period of use and abuse by the clergy who manipulated the privilege to circumvent both civil and criminal liability. Ultimately this would culminate in the abolition of the benefit for clergymen but the extension of the legal fiction[22] for all men, and finally to all defendants, regardless of gender, race or social status. "Clergy" was a fiction in the sense that it was manipulated in the courtroom to ameliorate severe sanguinary laws between 1600 and abolition in 1827. Until the end of Edward III's reign in 1377 there is no evidence of benefit being anything other than a device to protect a particular class of society, *clericus*. With far greater use, though, benefit became an established vehicle through which the judiciary could soften the draconian aspects of the old common law and permit considerable latitude in the monetary value that juries placed upon property in order that a crime could be deemed clergyable rather than capital. As some commentators have noted, benefit may have been a mockery according to the letter of the law but it was certainly not such in terms of its practical application.[23]

In early history the term *clericus* had a relatively narrow construction; those tonsured and perhaps nuns.[24] Tonsuring was a prerequisite for

---

of Paris, *Speculum*, Vol. 69. No.1. (Jan., 1994), pp. 18-39. Boyd, supra, notes that under the Edict of Paris personal actions against clerics were now to be dealt with exclusively by the bishops court "a privilege more explicitly guaranteed in the Mantuan capitulary of 787" at page 117.

[22] "Very generally legal fictions were devised as means of evading or modifying laws, which, obstructive or oppressive as they might be in particular cases, could not be repealed," Cross, A.L. The English Criminal Law and Benefit of Clergy during the Eighteenth and Early Nineteenth Century, *The American Historical Review*, Vol.22. No. 3 (Apr., 1917), 544-565. p. 544.

[23] Cross, supra, notes that: "The method by which judges came to soften the rigor of the old penal code was largely by means of the fiction of benefit of clergy and various transparent distortions of fact by which they and juries made it apply." Ibid, p. 545.

[24] There is no evidence that I can find to support the use of benefit of clergy by nuns. This would follow as women were excluded from the clergy *per se* and once the privilege was extended to all women then nuns would have the same opportunity to utilize the benefit as all categories of lay persons. Contrast with "This exemption included all who had been tonsured and wore the ecclesiastical dress, and was shared in by monks and nuns." www.catholicity.com/encyclopedia/benefit_of_clergy.html

receiving the minor and major orders. Failing to appear *tonsure clericus* or *ornamentum clericale* resulted in the secular tribunal denying clerical status.[25] The value of being identified *clericus* did not escape secular criminals and increasingly they adopted pseudo-clerical attire when appearing before temporal justices.

> The increasing frequency of faked first tonsures,[26] forged Holy Orders, and the wearing of stolen clerical vestments placed an additional burden on the court's determination of clerkship and called for the institution of a new mode of proof, one that was less available to fakery and forgery...[27]

Blind men and bastards were never permitted clergy as they were *de facto* ineligible to become priests. It is conceivable though that a bastard or blind man who was able to speak Latin would be able to convince the temporal court that he was a cleric and demand that the ordinary receive him.[28] Offenses that were clergyable could become unclergyable either by royal decree, statute, or implied custom. For

---

Benefit was extended to women in larceny cases where the value of property stolen was not greater than 10 shillings by 21 Jac. I c.6 (1623) and to "any person" (men and women) by 3 W & M. c. 9 (1691). 15 years later the reading test was abolished.

[25] For priests the size of the tonsure was meant to replicate the size of the host. Some orders of tonsured monks, Carthusians and Trappists favored exposure of the entire crown.

[26] Gabel. L. *Benefit of Clergy in England in the Later Middle Ages*, New York, Octagon Books, 1929, p. 64. "A gaoler himself might confer a 'tonsure'!" Gabel cites the example of Robert de Neuby who acquired tonsure from his prisoner guard before appearing in court.

[27] Kendall, C., "Nooses and Neck Verses: The Life and Death Consequences of Literacy Testing" in Bizzell, P. (ed) *Rhetorical Agendas: Political, Ethical, Spiritual*, New Jersey, Lawrence Erlbaum, 2006. p. 100. Poole, A. L., 'Outlawry as a Punishment of Criminous Clerks' in *Historical Essays in Honour of James Tait*, (eds. Edwards, J.G., Galbraith, V.H., Jacob, E.F.) Manchester, 1933. pp. 239-246. p. 240 note 5 cites the capture of a man in 1221 at Kidderminster who pretended to be a deacon and afterwards confessed he was not an ordained cleric.

[28] "Nor could any man who had a physical disability which would prevent his becoming a priest. Blindness was not held such an impediment as long, that is, as the prisoner could speak Latin congruously." Bellamy, J. G., *Criminal Law and Society in Late Medieval and Tudor England*, New York, St. Martin's Press, 1984. p. 116.

example between 1276 and 1547[29] English law held that if a man married a widow or took a second wife after the death of the first any offence committed by him that was otherwise clergyable became *de facto* unclergyable. The reasoning was that, because the benefit applied only to clerks and canon law forbade bigamous marriage to a widow, any clerk committing bigamy was subject to degradation and therefore it was impossible to claim clergy.[30]

In Saxon England King Wihtraed (690-725) held "Let a priest clear himself by his holy sooth, in his holy garment before the altar, thus saying: 'Veritatem dico in Christo, non mentior.'"[31] King Alfred (871-901)[32] acknowledged a privileged status for the clergy[33] with the caveat that once tried before the bishop's court the guilty party would be returned to the king for disposition of sentence unless the convicted party's lord paid the wergild.[34] This was later to become an issue for

---

[29] In 1547 Edward VI enacted a statute that forbade Jews, Turks, blind men and pirates from claiming clergy regardless of the law concerning other users of the benefit. Egyptians and vagabonds had already been marginalized by Henry VIII in 1531 (22 Hen VIII, c.10).

[30] Three types of bigamy existed at canon law; true, interpretative and similar. C.f. www.newadvent.org/bigamy. And "By marrying a second time, or by marrying a widow, the clerk, who thus became *bigamus* forfeited his immunities:-this rule, promulgated by Gregory X., was at once received in England and a retrospective force, was attributed to it by a statute of Edward I." Statute 4 Edw.I. *De Bigamis*. Pollock and Maitland, supra, p.445.

[31] The Laws of King Wihtraed 690-725 A.D. Sec. 19 "Let a clerk clear himself with four of his fellows, and he alone with his hand on the altar, let others stand by, make the oath." www.fordham.edu/halsall/source/560-975dooms.asp.

[32] For the Laws of King Alfred 871-901 A.D. www.fordham.edu/halsall/source/560-975dooms.asp and further: Lee, F.N. *King Alfred the Great and Our Common Law* at www.dr-fnlee.org/docs6/Alfred/Alfred.pdf.

[33] Gabel, supra, p. 10 (Alfred's Laws c. 21).

[34] Wergild was a form of blood money based upon Nordic and early Anglo-Saxon laws that required the guilty party to a felony murder make financial payment to the victim's family. In certain instances part of the wergild was paid to the king and to the lord—these having lost, respectively, a subject and a vassal. The wergild was at first informal but was later regulated by law." www.britannica.com/EBchecked/topic/639839/wergild Alfred ordered a secular judged hanged for executing a cleric because the king's justice "must have known" he had no authority over clerks. White, E.J., Benefit of Clergy, *The American Law Review*, Vol. 46, (1912), pp. 78-94. p. 82 and Blackstone, supra, pp. 400-436 "Public Wrongs Book IV."

members of the clergy as it could be viewed as double jeopardy to be brought before a secular court, transferred to the courts Christian and then be returned to the temporal courts for sentence, presumably having been de-frocked by the bishop's court. The implicit rivalry this situation created between the jurisdictions was addressed by William the Conqueror when he ordered the separation of the courts, Christian and temporal, in 1072.[35] His approach was logical; after all, if the clergy wanted absolute immunity from temporal culpability why should the Christian courts assume any control over secular matters.

William I of England, *privilegium clericus* and the beginning of a legal fiction

William's ordinance[36] stated that the canonical courts would deal with matters *ad regimen animarum*. As Gabel has noted, what this effectively meant was two classifications of ecclesiastical involvement; spiritual cases and spiritual persons.[37] Spiritual *cases*[38] were justiciable on the basis of the nature of the offense and spiritual *persons* were to be brought before the courts Christian regardless of the offense. Matters that were regarded as spiritual cases would be those that were

---

[35] "From the above it is to be understood that a clergyman is not to be brought before the public courts either in a civil or criminal case, unless perhaps the bishop should not wish to decide the civil case, or unless he should, in a criminal case, degrade him". Gratian cap. Xlvii, IIa pars Dec, causa XI. Ix I. at www.catholicity.com/encyclopdedia/benefit_of_clergy. See also: Morris, C., William I and the Church Courts, *The English Historical Review*, Vol. 82. No. 324 (Jul., 1967), pp. 449-463.

[36] "William by the grace of God King of the English… I command, and by royal authority decree, that no bishop or archdeacon shall any longer hold, in the hundred court, pleas pertaining to the episcopal laws, nor shall they bring before the judgment of secular men any case which pertains to the rule of souls; but whoever shall be summoned, according to the episcopal laws, in any case or for any fault, shall come to the place which the bishop shall choose or name for this purpose, and shall there answer in his case or for his fault, and shall perform his law before God and his bishop not according to the hundred court, but according to the canons and the episcopal laws…" http://avalon.law.yale.edu/medieval/ordwill.asp.

[37] Gabel, supra, p.12.

[38] E.g. Simony, usury, sacrilege, heresy, fornication, matrimonial matters.

dealt with by the courts Christian regardless of the status of the offender, whether he be cleric or not. These would include, for example, heresy, simony, sacrilege, matrimonial issues and matters testamentary. Spiritual persons were those that were heard by the ecclesiastical courts due to the spiritual status of the defendant, most frequently the criminous clerk. However, far from preventing legal discord through his ordinance William inflamed it and brought into question the authority of the king over the Church to invoke legislation that questioned the ultimate authority of the deity over temporal laws. William's ordinance makes no specific reference to the immunity of clerics from appearance before the courts temporal but the Church was soon to interpret this to be the case and demand exclusive jurisdiction over criminous clerks.[39] Though William would not be alive to see his descendants grapple with the issue of the sovereignty of the common law, he was relied upon as an authority as the clergy used and abused the privilege over the succeeding five centuries, and the kings of England sought to reduce the scale and scope of the benefit throughout the realm. Benefit of clergy would eventually run out of control and then out of use; along the way it would be manipulated by the clergy and exploited by lay defendants with the tacit consent of juries and judges. The British monarchy would eventually formalize the legal fiction and extend the benefit to all classes of citizens, not just those in the United Kingdom but also all of its territories and colonies.

Fundamental to the application of *privilegium clericus* was defining who was a cleric. In England by the eighth century clerks were clearly divided into higher and lower orders. By the middle of the twelfth

---

[39] Lea, supra, pp. 180-183 argues that throughout France secular courts had authority to try criminous clerks and that papal juridical supremacy was not achieved without recourse to the threat of excommunication. This may be the case in respect of the early medieval period but could not be said of the supremacy of the Church in dealing with criminal religious matters once the grip of the Inquisition took place across Europe. C.f. Walker, C.H., The Date of the Conqueror's Ordinance Separating the Ecclesiastical and Lay Courts, *The English Historical Review*, Vol. 39. No. 155 (Jul., 1924), pp. 399-400.

century Henry II (1154-1189) attempted to limit the use of the benefit to those holding higher orders only.[40] Higher orders were defined as those holding the rank of subdeacon and above. This division would effectively exclude acolytes, porters, lectors, exorcists, cantors, curates and vicars from claiming benefit and only allow the major orders, subdiaconate, deaconate, presbyterate and episcopate, to have the privilege.[41] Unordained monks, nuns and friars were also no longer considered *clericus*.[42] Within the Church developed the distinction between religious people and lay people who served the Church. The religious were defined as: deacons, priests, monsignors, bishops, archbishops, cardinals and the Pope. Amongst this religious group are the three sacramental ordained positions: deacon, priest and bishop.[43] In 1267 by the Statute of Marlborough[44] Henry III reversed the direction that had been sought by his grandfather Henry II in the previous century when he, Henry of Winchester, extended the term *clericus* to all clergy; first tonsure (psalmist) and higher orders. During

---

[40] Immunity from secular prosecution applied to "all punishable acts except those against forest laws and non-fulfillment of feudal obligations." Assize of Northampton 1176. c. 4.5. and cited in Baker, supra, p.104.

[41] The Council of Trent (Dec 1545-Dec 1563) defined seven orders: priests, deacons, subdeacons, acolytes, exorcists, readers (lectors) and doorkeepers (*ostiarus*). This is not definitive (e.g., first tonsure has often been considered an "order"); also this may include cantors (*psalmistae*), fossarii (*fossores*), grave diggers, interpreters (*hermeneutoe*) and guardians of relics (*custodes martyrum*). There appear to have been consistent attempts throughout the centuries by the church to apply a very broad brush to the term "cleric" even to the point of it including a church "janitor" in 1462, Firth, C.B. Benefit of Clergy in the Time of Edward IV, *The English Historical Review*, Vol. 32, No. 126 (Apr., 1917), pp. 175-191, p. 180 citing British Museum Add. MS. 12195. f. 74.

[42] Monks and Friars were now classified as belonging to the minor orders of ostiary, lectorate, order of exorcists and order of acolytes. *Tonsurati* as previously discussed was a defining feature up to and throughout the fifteenth century.

[43] For a discussion and explanation of the term *clericus* see, Gabel. L. *Benefit of Clergy in England in the Later Middle Ages*, New York, Octagon Books, 1929. Chapter III The Term *Clericus*.

[44] 52 Hen. III. 1267. Henry III was recovering from recent internal turmoil (it was just two years since De Montfort's Parliament had been disbanded) and it is very likely that he knew extending *clericus* would achieve widespread approval from the bishops and in doing so bring a measure of stability to the realm. The Statute of Marlborough remains in force today.

this period it was first tonsure and *in habitu clericali* not literacy that determined clerical status.[45]

As use of *privilegium clericale* increased, it became necessary that rules were established to ensure that only those entitled to the privilege were invoking it.[46] Ecclesiastic dress was only one way of establishing credentials and this was open to abuse; tonsure too was easily achieved as the benefits of escaping the death penalty in lieu of purgation before the bishop's court were extremely attractive to a broad spectrum of criminals. To overcome the difficulty of determining genuine clerics from those attempting to escape the gallows, claimants were required to prove their clerical status by reading from a psalter or the bible. In a time when very few members of society were educated at all and literacy was a privilege of the Church and nobility, the reading test was a major obstacle to overcome. Fortunately for the lay criminal by the middle of the fourteenth century the same reading test was applied with a large degree of uniformity[47] thereby allowing the illiterate the opportunity to learn a bible passage verbatim and avoid the hangman's noose. The chance to avoid capital punishment was decided by a defendant's ability to quote Psalm 51, David's prayer for the remission

---

[45] 52 Hen. III. C.27 (18 Nov. 1267) and Poole, A. L., "Outlawry as a Punishment of Criminous Clerks" in *Historical Essays in Honour of James Tait*, (eds. Edwards, J.G., Galbraith, V.H., Jacob, E.F.) Manchester, 1933. pp. 239-246. p. 240. Should a criminous clerk fail purgation and he was outlawed. If he returned he suffered death as a layman. C.f. Poole, supra, p. 246.

[46] This was a challenge as by the end of the thirteenth century there were an estimated 9,500 parishes and in the region of 8,100 beneficed (those in receipt of temporalities) and 16,000 unbeneficed clerks. Additionally there may have been as many as 7000 nuns. The population of England was estimated to be at around 3 million during this time. Powicke, M., *The Thirteenth Century 1216-1307*, Oxford, Clarendon Press, 1953 pp. 445-447. For a thorough discussion see: "The maddeningly imprecise term of *clericus*" (p. 930) see: Turner, R. V., The *Miles Literatus* in Twelfth- and Thirteenth-Century England: How Rare a Phenomenon? *The American Historical Review*, Vol. 83. No. 4 (Oct., 1978) pp. 928-945.

[47] Gabel. supra, p. 76-77. I cannot find a definitive source that specifies a date at which there was a transition from any bible text to wholesale use of the *misère*. Certainly by the time that Edward III enacted legislation in 1351 to extend the benefit to the laity all records indicate that psalm 51 was in widespread use by the courts.

of sin. "Have mercy upon me, O God, according to Thy Loving kindness; according unto the multitude of Thy tender mercies, blot out my transgressions."[48] Not surprisingly the *Miserere mei Deus* became commonly known as the Neck Verse.[49] The transition from claiming benefit by tonsure or habit to the Latin reading test[50] was not achieved in a few years; rather more it grew over time until eventually literacy replaced all other modes of proof.[51]

Henry II, Beckett and secular retrenchment

Henry I had enacted legislation that would not permit an accusation against an ordained clerk to be heard other than before his bishop.[52] By the end of the twelfth century, however, disagreement over *privilegium fori* and the potential for "double jeopardy" provided the platform for the famous dispute between Henry II and Archbishop Thomas

---

[48] Williams suggests that "each prison had its own neck verse," Williams, A., (ed) *Old Church Life*, William Andrews & Co, London, 1909. p. 14. I am not able to confirm this assertion and the general view appears to be that psalm 51 was widely used throughout England; this is certainly the position proposed by Gabel, supra..

[49] The first recorded use of the reading test is gaol delivery Rolls 6 Edward I. a case involving the escape from prison by Thomas le Blake. Source. Gabel, supra. p. 65. Further examples of episcopal prison escapes are provided by McHardy, A.K., Church Courts and Criminous Clerks in the Later Middle Ages in *Medieval Ecclesiastic Studies in Honour of Dorothy M. Owen*, Woodbridge, Suffolk (UK), Boydell & Brewer, 1995. pp. 165-183, p. 173. Venues for *privilegium fori* sometimes referred to as *in foro ecclesiastico*, trials were at the discretion of the bishop (e.g., local churches, cathedral chapels and during formal consistory courts). C.f. Pugh, R.B., *Imprisonment in Medieval England*, Cambridge, Cambridge University Press, 1968. Chapter III imprisonment of clerks, Chapter VI bishop's prisons and Chapter XVIII monastic prisons.

[50] The exact date from which Psalm 51 was recited in English is not recorded. It was being used from at least the eighteenth year of Elizabeth I's reign onwards.

[51] By the mid fourteenth century the literacy test was the exclusive test for *clericus* C.f. Bellamy, Criminal Law, supra, p. 116. Rarely discussed there appears no legislative provision to non-Christian religions. Foreigners were permitted to use a bible in their own tongue. A curious allowance as genuine clerics, regardless of origin, would all presumably read, write and speak Latin.

[52] *Leges Henrici*. Hen I, 57 x. 9 Statutes of the Realm.

Beckett.[53] The controversy[54] resulted in Beckett's exile, murder and martyrdom; actions closely followed by a papal edict in 1215 banning the clergy from involvement in secular trials and restating the unique status of the clerical right to canonical jurisdiction. The implications of Henry II's Assize of Clarendon have been subject to much discussion over the centuries and it is generally accepted that it was not Henry's intention to abolish *privilegium fori* but rather more to curb the abuses of benefit and have criminous clerks returned to the secular courts for punishment after degradation (*degradatio*). Disagreement started when Henry II claimed the statutory[55] and cotumal heritage of his forefathers, and by inference the Edict of Clothar, for the contents of the Constitutions of Clarendon.[56] They provided for clergy accusation and plea in the secular court, trial, conviction and degradation (laicization of the cleric) at the bishops court followed by sentence and punishment in the temporal. In effect the constitutions promulgated at Clarendon Palace in January 1164 required that Archbishop Beckett agree to a range of measures that placed a considerable degree of ecclesiastical jurisdiction within the scope of temporal law.[57] For

---

[53] Numerous works relate to the great Beckett controversy. Chapter Six The Quarrel with the King, Barlow, F., *Thomas Beckett*, Berkeley, CA, University of California Press, 1990, pp. 88-197 is comprehensive. Also Staunton, M. *Thomas Becket and His Biographers*, Woodbridge, Suffolk, Boydell and Brewer, 2006. Chapter 9 Conflict pp. 97-128.

[54] It would seem that Beckett (Becket and de Becket)) and the king were on a collision course more than once (e.g., 1163 Beckett degraded a clerk and required him to abjure the realm. Henry II disputed Beckett's authority to do this and "maintained that exile was not a punishment which could be imposed by a priest but only by a ruler." Beckett responded that he represented God who was above all kings). Poole, supra, p. 239 also the de Broi incident, supra.

[55] E.g. William I Ordinance and Stephen I Charter 1136 (The Oxford Charter).

[56] Of No. IV., the Assize of Clarendon, Stubbs says "It is a legal document of the greatest importance to our legal history, and must be regarded as introducing changes into the administration of justice which were to lead the way to self-government at no distant time." Henderson, E. F., *Select Historical Documents of the Middle Ages*, London, George Bell & Sons, 1896. p. 3.

[57] The Council, held at Clarendon Palace hunting lodge Wiltshire, January 25, 1164, proposed 16 articles, infra. Many sought to curb Church jurisdictional dominance which had been growing since the lax monarchy of Stephen (1135-1154). The emphasis was to restrict the legal loophole of benefit of clergy which Henry viewed as being far too lenient and open to abuse. In particular Henry was offended by the idea that one man could be hanged and another escape all forms of meaningful punishment

Beckett this was the ultimate effrontery to *Nec enim Deus iudicat bis in idipsum*,[58] an open assault upon double jeopardy, the erosion of a renowned friendship and a physical and intellectual move from chancellorship to monastic orders and entrenchment of behalf of the clergy. Notably though Innocent III held the view that if an ordained clerk was to commit forgery of papal letters they should be degraded and then handed to a secular court for trial. This seems a very strong position to take and a complete move away from protecting one's brothers who were only answerable to God. Apparently forging the pope's papers was so serious that penance was insufficient even for a criminous clerk and they should face the death sentence. It is hard not to see this as being a case of double standards where on one hand the Church washes its hands of bloodletting and on the other views forgery of papal material so heinous the Church is incapable of dealing with the matter and passes over jurisdiction to the "inferior" secular courts.[59]

---

whatsoever. Beckett was of the view that degradation followed by secular trial was double jeopardy and unacceptable. What occurred at Clarendon was the starting point for the monumental events culminating in Beckett's death and martyrdom. The Clarendon cotumals make a number of references to degradation; degradation strips a cleric of office entirely and perpetually and by Innocent III c. viii, Decrim. Falsi, X, v, 20, all degraded clerks were to be handed to the secular courts for trial. Degradation does not, however, remove the cleric from the law of celibacy and recitation of Breviary. Bishops can degrade but only the Holy See may re-instate.

[58] "God himself does not punish twice." See: Maitland, F.W., Henry II and the Criminous Clerks *The Collected Papers of Frederic William Maitland*, Ed by H.A.L. Fisher, Cambridge, Cambridge University Press, 1911. Vol. 2. and Pollock & Maitland, supra, pp. 447 and p. 455. note 1.

[59] "This seems plain enough. Henry might well have said, "Here, at any rate, is an exception to your principle, and for my own part I cannot see that the forgery of a decretal—though I will admit, if you wish it, that it is wicked to forge decretals—is a much worse crime than murder, or rape, or robbery." Maitland, F. W., Henry II and the Criminous Clerks, The *English Historical Review*, Vol. 7. No. 26 (Apr., 1892), pp. 224-234. p. 232.

Chapter 2 Clerical status, the "Neck Verse" and secularization

The validity of *clericus* claimants and plea submission before the secular courts

More than one hundred years after Henry II, Edward II (1307-1327) promulgated legislation that required a felonious cleric to appear before the temporal court and once he had proved his clergy he was removed to the bishop's court, even if the clerk had made a confession of guilt before the secular tribunal.[1] By the reign of ECh 2dward III[2] (1327-1377) all clerks, secular and religious, were permitted to enjoy the protective privilege of the Church and claim benefit. The *Statute of Provisors of Benefices*[3] held that privilege was subject to proving satisfactorily to the secular court that the benefice was able to read. This 1350 legislation was quickly counterbalanced by Edward with

---

[1] 9 Edw. II. c.15, 16. If brought before the courts temporal a second time the cleric was permitted to claim benefit again upon production of their letters of ordination.

[2] During Edward III's reign the Bishop of Ely, Thomas de Lisle, engaged in a lifetime of organized crime, including murder, arson, kidnapping, extortion and fraud. See: Aberth, J. *Criminal Churchmen in the Age of Edward III: The Case of Bishop Thomas de Lisle*, University Park, PA, Pennsylvania State University Press, 1963. Also cleric Robert Colyson committed: deception, making false accusations against members of court, fraud and living off immoral earnings. For details: Bellamy, J., *Crime and Public Order in England in the Middle Ages*, London, Routledge, 1973. pp. 40-41. During 15 Edward IV (1461-1483) William Wodeward attacked a cleric brother and stole forty shillings from him. Sir Edward Hanyngton, deputy of the Bishop of Winchester, heard Wodeward read as a clerk and claimed him as clergy. Firth, supra, p.185. In 1536 or 1537 Robert Packyngton was allegedly murdered by priests for being outspoken against the clergy. It is thought that this crime was perhaps linked to the infamous Hunne and Standish affair that occurred early into Henry VIII's reign. Bellamy, J., *Strange, Inhuman Deaths: Murder in Tudor England*, Westport, Preager, 1930. p. 40. And Davis, J., The Authorities for the Case of Richard Hunne (1514-1515), *The English Historical Review*, Vol. 30, No. 119 (Jul., 1915), pp. 477-488, Milsom, S.F.C., Richard Hunne's Praemunire, *The English Historical Review*, Vol. 76, No. 298 (Jan., 1961), pp. 80-82. For a detailed discussion surrounding the entire Hunne, Standish and Blackfriars affairs see Skousen, L., *Redefining Benefit of Clergy During the English Reformation: Royal Prerogative, Mercy, and the State*. MA Thesis 2008 University of Wisconsin (Unpublished). pp. 44-54.

[3] 25 Edw III, St. 4. The creation of this statute was prompted by the plot of a servant, James Grame, to murder his master. Grame was hanged, drawn and quartered for this treason.

penal law of *Praemunire*, "the whole being directed against those who dares, in collusion with the Pope, to act against the rule and jurisdiction of the English Common Law."[4] *Sacerdotes a regibus honorandi sunt, non judicandi* may well have been the official position the English kings took but the reality was the Holy Fathers continued to regard the monarchy as sons.[5] Edward IV (1461-1483) favored the bishops in principle by confirming the courts Christian held exclusive jurisdiction over criminous clerks, and that establishing *clericus* was the exclusive preserve of the bishop's court.[6] 4 Henry VII c.16[7] addressed the issue of benefit being claimed repeatedly by the laity[8] by restricting use to once in their lifetimes. To ensure compliance beneficed laymen were branded on the brawn of the thumb; M for murder and T for theft and other crimes. No longer would recidivists be able to claim benefit twice. In 1496 Henry enunciated legislation to the effect that a lay person murdering their lord or master, "shall not have clergy upon conviction and will be executed as though he were not a clerk."[9] Elevated levels of protection for lords and masters was to remain in place throughout most of the history of benefit and also

---

[4] "The Pope is the Holy Father; the King his most beloved son; but he is a grown-up son, with an estate of his own to administer." Ogle, A., *The Canon Law in Mediaeval England: An Examination of William Lynwood's "Provinciale", in Reply to the Late Professor F.W. Maitland*, London, John Murray 1912. p.60.

[5] Ogle, supra, p. 65.

[6] Edward IV "Great Charter." For the most pertinent clauses see: Firth, C.B. Benefit of Clergy in the Time of Edward IV, *The English Historical Review*, Vol. 32, No. 126 (Apr., 1917), pp. 175-191 and Makower, F., *The Constitutional History and Constitution of the Church of England*, Vol. 2. London, Swan Sonnenschein, 1895 p. 403 Edward was not so keen to put his rhetoric into practice though as he stalled on application of the law. See Firth, supra, p. 180. Firth indicates the charter was enunciated during the first two years of Edward's reign.

[7] 4. Hen. VII c.13. 1467. This was the first piece of English legislation to implement branding.

[8] Clerics found guilty of assisting the illiterate in learning the misère were liable to an unclergyable felony charge. Baker, supra, p. 97 cites the example of the vicar of Round Church, Canterbury who was arraigned and tried by the secular court for providing instruction to the illiterate William Gore.

[9] 12. Hen. VII c.7.

travelled to America to ensure that slaves were not permitted to claim their benefit when tried for the murder of their owners.[10]

Sanctuary for criminous clerks grew successively also throughout the 15th and early 16th centuries until Henry VIII addressed the issue. Benefit of clergy, sanctuary and, for women, pleading the belly all represented opportunities for felons to escape the death sentence. Throughout the history of each there is a visible tendency to reduce and restrict the application of them by the crown. The period commencing with Henry VIII's reign and concluding with Elizabeth I's death in 1603 exemplifies how English monarchs used the criminal law to leverage authority and power; pardons decreased, they became the personal preserve of the monarch, benefit options decreased with the laicization of the plea, and pleading the belly was less successfully claimed than benefit generally.[11] Successfully pleading clergy[12] allowed the defendant

---

[10] Infra.

[11] Attractive as it is to place "Pleading the Belly" alongside benefit of clergy it would be incorrect to do so. Clergy avoided execution, pregnancy delayed it. The work of Kesselring, K., Abjuration and its Demise: The Changing Face of Royal Justice in the Tudor Period, *Canadian Journal of History*, Vol. 34, No. 3 (Dec., 1999), pp. 346-358, is important in this area as she poignantly demonstrates in her Appendix II referring to the use of Pleading the Belly, "Thus, of the women convicted, only 21 per cent escaped death, a percentage that compares unfavorably with the 57 percent of male convicts who used clergy and pardons to evade the gallows." p. 214.

[12] Gabel, supra, argues that as the lay courts were seeking greater control and authority over proceedings holding a trial was an important reflection of this. Importantly if there had been a secular trial the defendant's goods would become property of the crown until he was successful in his purgation. If there was no secular finding of guilt this did not occur. Perhaps it is a combination of both motives; implied power and revenue from goods held by the secular tribunal that made the crown favor this procedure. Gabel argues by the close of the fourteenth century the lay trial method had become prevalent and established procedure by the early fifteenth century. Gabel, supra, Appendix A lists cases showing the increase of lay trial procedure. Bellamy, *Criminal Law*, supra, p. 117-118. "…they must have been actually entering a plea and no longer merely requesting benefit and the presence of the ordinary. Confirmation of this turn of events seems to be provided by the evidence of gaol delivery rolls, where this 'lay plea', as it has been called, began to assume significant proportions from the end of the *thirteenth* century [my emphasis]." I believe that the gaol delivery rolls Bellamy is referring to are those of Edward I (1272-1307) (as provided by Gabel) when a total of 227 cases were recorded for the period. Noticeable increase in use is from Edward II's (1307-1327) reign and beyond when there is

to be claimed by the bishops ordinary[13] and be held, *clericus convictus*, pending appearance at the courts Christian.[14]

Until the reign of Edward II (1307-1327) there appears to have been at least a couple of ways that the actual plea of benefit was entered; most commonly the clerk would enter his plea immediately before the secular court and be claimed. An alternative involved the clerk standing trial, a "lay plea," and then at the conclusion of the trial and before sentence he would claim his clergy. The crown's motivation to secure a lay trial first was likely vested in the ownership of a convicted felon's property and the authority over criminal proceedings that this method implied. By the end of this century the lay trial method was prevalent.[15] Upon appearance at the bishop's court the clergyman had the opportunity to purge himself; that is to clear his name by swearing innocence and getting others from within the ecclesiastic community to swear his good name and innocence also. Understandably one of the major criticisms of benefit of clergy was that it facilitated a usurpation

---

evidence of a number of clerks waiting to claim *clericus* and only then, if convicted, by the secular tribunal. Bellamy, *Criminal Law*, supra, p. 119.

[13] The temporal judge asked the ordinary was the defendant *"Legit ut clericus?"* If the response was *legit* the prisoner was handed over to the bishop's commissary. In cases of *"non legit"* the defendant remained in the custody of the courts temporal for sentencing. The judge was permitted to explore the legitimacy of the ordinary's claim. If it was found erroneous the repercussions were twofold, from the lay court and the bishop. Bellamy, supra, cites two pertinent examples. pp. 120 and 166. (26 Edw. III. Year Books no. 19) and White, supra, p. 84 note 18. By sixteenth century the ordinary's responsibilities increased further as Chief Justice Fineux ruled claimed clerks awaiting spiritual trial were "lay prisoners" and therefore subject to the same conditions of imprisonment as secular prisoners. This had the effect of making the ordinary responsible, upon payment of a one hundred pound fine, that the prisoner did not escape, nor was granted bail and that he was held in conditions neither less nor more harsh than a prisoner in the secular system. *Year Books*, Trinity 15 Hen. VII nos. 1 and 10. McHardy, A.K., Church Courts and Criminous Clerks in the Later Middle Ages in *Medieval Ecclesiastic Studies in Honour of Dorothy M. Owen*, Woodbridge, Suffolk (UK), Boydell & Brewer, 1995. pp. 165-183, pp. 169-71.

[14] Laity confidence that the bishop's court would administer meaningful justice was rightly skeptical. Poole, supra, p. 105 "The notorious incompetence of the Church courts was one of the greatest evils in the judicial administration of the realm."

[15] Bellamy, supra, p.117-118.

of the law as clearly guilty clerics were able to avoid trial in the secular courts and then swear their innocence at canonical trial and be acquitted.[16] In those rare cases when a cleric was unsuccessful in purgation he might be found guilty and sentenced by the bishop. The Christian courts were prohibited from imposing a judgment of blood;[17] it was permitted, however, to impose a custodial sentence and a number of cases resulted in terms of imprisonment for clerics.[18] Referred to as "penance," this could amount to a degrading and then life imprisonment, a flogging or public humiliation.[19] The period of time between purgation and release was itself a potential ordeal and a number of clerics waited months and sometimes years from the time of being claimed from the temporal courts to purgation and release.[20] In order that bishops could accommodate criminous clerks it was

---

[16] So we introduce the terms compurgation and purgation. Compurgation refers to those who swear by oath of one's innocence. In the secular courts this was part of the Wager of War process. In the ecclesiastical courts it remained in use until the reign of Elizabeth I. Purgation was the process of the accused formally swearing his innocence. Outlawry and abjuration was a bar to purgation. During the time of Edward I (1272-1307) if a person was found guilty of a crime in the temporal courts his sentence could be that he was outlawed. Abjuration and outlawry were abolished by James I (1566-1625).

[17] Pope Innocent III's concern, resulting in the 4th Lateran Council's (1215) ban on clergy being involved in ordeals, was that trial by ordeal frequently involved the drawing of blood; by battle, by torture, by sentence. Before 1215, priests and bishops were often involved in ordeal trials. Preparation for ordeal was complex and involved the local priest in numerous sacramental activities (e.g., the Ordeal by Boiling).

[18] See Gabel, supra and Pugh, R.B., *Imprisonment in Medieval England*, Cambridge, Cambridge University Press, 1968. Chapter III "The Imprisonment of Clerks, Serfs, and Jews." Pugh states that as a result of the *pro clero* statute of 1352 "Perpetual penance came to be the statutory punishment for unpurged clerks." p.49. This legislation prompted Archbishop Simon Islip to issue an archiepiscopal mandate requiring proper dietary and living conditions for the imprisonment of clerics. McHardy, A.K., Church Courts and Criminous Clerks in the Later Middle Ages in *Medieval Ecclesiastic Studies in Honour of Dorothy M. Owen*, Woodbridge, Suffolk (UK), Boydell & Brewer, 1995. pp. 165-183 p. 166.

[19] Pugh, supra. p. 48. The imposition of a flogging or public humiliation is important as this becomes the most common method of imposing a criminal sanction against offenders in Colonial America and reflects the close association between Benefit of Clergy and what it was to become in application; a secular penal sanction.

[20] The longest serving prisoner, twenty-six years, was John Porter, charged with stealing two horses. Pugh, supra. p. 49. Further examples at: McHardy, supra, p.172. and Firth, supra, p. 187.

encouraged, and then required by law through the Constitutions of Archbishop Boniface in 1261,[21] that each diocese establish a prison.[22] Criminous monks and nuns were always an anomaly in the benefit discussion and their exact status fluctuated. In terms of imprisonment it existed for this class of cleric in a particularly unpleasant manifestation[23] as the offending party was typically incarcerated in a dungeon environment devoid of light or worldly company other than for periods of enforced divine attendance.[24]

Extension of the privilege, the increase of capital crimes and the influence of Henry VIII

Henry VIII moved quickly to restrict the use of benefit of clergy.[25] In 1512 he limited the use with exception to those in holy orders so that clergy was denied in cases of murder or robbery on the king's highway, murder or robbery inside an occupied house and committing any felony in churches.[26] Henry's anticlericalism was yet in the early stages

---

[21] Pugh, supra. p. 135.
[22] The first, 1216-1218, belonged to the Bishop of Worcester although a prison attached to the bishopric of Salisbury, 1200, is noted by Pugh, supra, p. 134 note 7.
[23] The exact number of examples of perpetual *clericale convictus* are few as recognized by Baker, supra p.101 and Pollock & Maitland, supra, p. 445.
[24] Pugh, supra. p. 376. Variations include: incarceration in windowless pits that are accessed by ladder, the wearing of chains, repeated floggings and, when a brother murdered another brother, the culprit faced perpetual solitary confinement with a diet of bread and water for life. The Church used the term immuration, *inter alia*, to describe a voluntary solitary confinement with access only to food and water and perhaps a line of sight to an altar. For an alternative use see: Pollock & Maitland, supra, pp. 444-445 and: Maitland, F. W., The Deacon and the Jewess; or; Apostacy at Common Law, *The Collected Papers of Frederic William Maitland*, Ed by H.A.L. Fisher, Cambridge, Cambridge University Press, 1911. Vol. I.
[25] Henry VIII's entire reign was marked by an increase in restrictive legislative measures. His parliaments were in session for just two years throughout his entire thirty-eight-year reign and yet they managed to pass one hundred fifty statutes that imposed financial penalties upon the English. Kesselring, K.J., *Mercy and Authority in The Tudor State*, Cambridge, Cambridge University Press, 2003. p. 25 and thirteen statutes relating to Benefit of Clergy, Skousen, supra, pp. 115-116.
[26] 4 Hen. VIII c.2.

of growth but would grow immensely as he approached the fight for his divorce and supremacy over the Church in his realm culminating in Reformation.[27] By the time Henry had finished with benefit of clergy it would bear no resemblance to a spiritual privilege whatsoever as it transformed into a lay privilege entirely.[28] By the twenty-third year of his reign clergy was denied to any lower order or lay person in cases of petty treason, willful murder, robbery from a holy place, robbery from a dwelling (whether occupied or not at the time), highway robbery and arson of a dwelling or grain barn.[29] Importantly 23 Hen. VIII c.1 also changed the manner in which a clerk was dealt with by the bishop's court in terms of sentencing. Upon enactment it became law that a clerk was not permitted purgation or to be set free by the bishop but was to "remain and abide in perpetual prison under the keeping of the ordinary."[30] Life imprisonment was avoidable though if the cleric could find sureties.[31] Buggery became a capital offense without clergy two years later as one of three statutes passed by Henry's Parliament of 1534.[32] The progressive move towards severely restricting the use of

---

[27] Ironically the Roman Catholic priests who had fought so hard for centuries to retain the *Privilegium fori* were now required to profess their allegiance to Henry. If a priest returned from abroad he had three days in which to do so or be hanged *without* benefit of clergy.

[28] For a thorough discussion see: Skousen, L., *Redefining Benefit of Clergy During the English Reformation: Royal Prerogative, Mercy, and the State.* MA Thesis 2008 University of Wisconsin (Unpublished).

[29] 23 Hen. VIII c.1. During this time many acts of parliament needed to be renewed, the alternative was to make an act perpetual. 23 Hen VIII was made perpetual 32 Hen. VII c.3 (1540).

[30] 23 Hen. VIII c. I *Statutes of the Realm.* p. 390.

[31] Bellamy, *Criminal Law*, supra, p.141 and Skousen, supra, p. 72 citing Bellamy suggest the amount of surety was eighty pounds. As Skousen notes the source for this figure is not given. Life imprisonment was of course only applicable to those below the rank of sub-deacon as Henry's previous legislative moves had removed all benefit privileges from the lower orders.

[32] 25 Hen. VIII c.6. This session also made piracy unclergyable and buggery justiciable by magistrates; effectively a further erosion of the ecclesiastical power as it removed the crime from religious to secular. With regard to the buggery act "A determined historian could interpret the Act as an overt attack on monks just two years before Cromwell began inspecting monasteries for their dissolution" Skousen, supra, p. 79. 27 Hen. VIII c. 7 also removed right of clergy from servants who stole 40 shillings or more of value. The changing role of the ecclesiastic courts is presented by Rodes, R. E., *Lay Authority and Reformation in English Church: Edward I to the Civil War*, Notre Dame, The University of Notre

benefit by all classes of persons culminated in Henry's legislation of 1536 when it became the law that those in holy orders "shall henceforth be subject to the same penalties as those who are not...any provision or exception specified in any of the said acts, or any other usage or custom of this realm, to the contrary thereof notwithstanding."[33]

Benefit of clergy had always been limited to those offenses that attracted the death penalty[34] but what the Henrician statutes achieved was an expansion of the "lay plea"[35] to a general secularization of benefit of clergy at the same time as an erosion of the elite status of ordained clerics to the claim, and a general diminution of the number of offenses for which clergy could be claimed. The courts temporal had long taken the view that purgation was a mere ritual that facilitated criminous clerks to commit numerous felonies with impunity.[36] As

---

Dame Press, 1982, pp. 197-211. and Bellamy, J.G. *The Criminal Trial in Later Medieval England: Felony Before the Courts From Edward I to the Sixteenth Century,* Toronto, University of Toronto Press, 1930.

[33] 28 Hen. VIII c.I "An Act that Abjurers in certain cases shall not have Clergy." The act held: sanctuary could only be claimed once, if a felon in sanctuary committed a felony the sanctuary would be revoked, roving felons would henceforth be tried by lay magistrates, and offenses committed in churches, cemeteries and church grounds, the king's highway, occupied dwellings, arson of granaries or buildings nearby were all now unclergyable. Any defendant who refused to enter a plea would not be permitted to claim their clergy after trial. Crucially those offenses listed as being within Holy Orders henceforth shall "stand and be under the same peins [sic] and dangers for the offences contained in any of the said statutes and be used and ordered to all intents and purposes, as other persons, not being with Holy Orders." 28 Hen. VIII c. 1. *Statutes of the Realm,* p. 480. Under this legislation the only class of offenders now fully privileged were peers of the realm. 33 Hen. VIII c. 1-c.14 denied clergy to "persons practicing witchcraft or enchantment and to those making prophecies upon coates of arms badges etc" White, supra, p. 88.

[34] With the exception of treason which historically was never clergyable. A distinction between types of treason was introduced, however, in 1352 when "high treason" was defined as treason against the king's person and lesser treasons such as those against your master or husband. The title "petty treason" was first used in statute, 25 Edw. III s. 6. c. 4. The *De Clero* statute permitted benefit for petty treason. Generally a felony was a crime that attracted the death sentence or loss of limb.

[35] Bellamy, *Criminal Law*, supra, p. 118.

[36] There are many examples of clerics purging themselves for heinous crimes and receiving nominal sentences. The case of Philip de Broi, canon of Bedford, particularly irked the king when in 1166, having been charged with murdering a knight, de Broi purged himself and was released. The evidence against de Broi was so strong, however, that royal judge Simon Fitz Peter ordered a new trial. De Broi

Cross noted with typical vitriol, "The proceedings in the episcopal court were usually a sham, a 'blasphemous farce.'"[37] This is of course not entirely accurate and the bishop's court had always made due deference to legalistic manner and form that embraced the solemnity of the law. The problem for the secularists was that purgation so rarely failed and consequently even when genuine clerics were afforded their benefit it was extremely rare that they were ever found guilty of an offense. Therefore it would follow that if the benefit was at best a mitigatory mechanism to ensure that the death penalty was applied less frequently and all first-time felons were permitted a second chance (and a branding) then why would a legal system support the continuation of immunity for just one section of society. Henry VIII accommodated this by opening up the benefit for all male citizens but at the same time extended the number of unclergyable crimes. He had given with one royal hand and taken away with the other. Clerics would now be subjected to branding[38] alongside any literate layman.[39]

---

was so furious he lashed out verbally against the Fitz Peter. The king heard of this and took the rebuke personally. The Bishop of Lincoln became so concerned by the publicity that he returned de Broi to the ecclesiastic court, removed his prebend and gave him further penance. Henry II considered this yet another example of clerical abuse and added further weight to his attempts to rein in the clergy at Clarendon. *Materials for Life of St. Thomas* (Rolls Series), i. 12, 13, iii. 45; From: "Houses of Austin Canons: The Priory of Newnham," *A History of the County of Bedford:* Volume I (1904), pp. 377-381. http://www.british-history.ac.uk/report.aspx?compid=40039.

[37] Arthur Lyon Cross, The English Criminal Law and Benefit of Clergy during the Eighteenth and early Nineteenth century, *The American Historical Review*, Vol. 22 No. 3 (Apr., 1917) pp. 544-565. p. 553.

[38] Branding criminous lay clerks remained popular on both sides of the Atlantic. England abolished the practice in 1779. 19 Geo III. C. 74. Adams, M., Bonner, H.B., Foote, G.W., Roberts, H., Collison, J., & Salt, H. *Humanitarian Essays: Being Volume III of "Cruelties of Civilization,"* London, William Reeves, 1897. p. 7 appears to be accurate whereas the entry by Burtsell, R.L. suggesting that branding was abolished under George IV is rather difficult to follow and may be incorrect. Burtsell's entry is found at www.catholicity.com supra.

[39] Per 32 Hen. VIII c.3 provided those in holy orders were subject to branding as lay clerks. It cannot escape the reader that the discussion so far is located within the privilege as it pertains to adults; clerics, nuns, monks, peers, lay men and lay women. Given that children were subject to the criminal law and the doctrine of *doli incapax* was in its legal infancy throughout this entire period one might also include

Edward VI radically altered the limitations his father placed upon the benefit of clergy through the Act of Repeals.[40] This act indicated a monarch who wanted to achieve harmony with his subjects through obedience and respect rather than fear. It also probably reflected the influence that his advisors, Somerset and Northumberland, succeeded in exerting upon the young king who was only nine years of age when crowned.[41] Murder, poisoning, burglary of an occupied dwelling, highway robbery, horse theft and stealing from churches, refusing to plead and challenging more than twenty jurors peremptorily remained unclergyable. All other felonies now reverted back to clergyable status as they had before his father's reign. The act went further though in its third section in repealing all new felonies created by statute since 1509. Edward was also clearly seeking to establish a new cordiality with the house of lords as he extended benefit of clergy for any felony[42] to all peers of the realm regardless of whether they could read or not.[43] What

---

children in the discussion. A fascinating article on the subject was written by Neil Postman in *Childhood Education* March/April 1985 pp. 286-293 where he explains that if children survived to beyond seven years of age they were viewed as adults in medieval society; they were "miniature adults." He then rightly explains that it was the Catholic Church that introduced the idea of seven years of age as being the point at which a child knows right from wrong and should therefore be held accountable for their actions. This helps to explain why it is that children of seven years of age and above are given capital sentences and were, by implication, if literate, also eligible to claim their clergy. He concludes that *ipso facto* Benefit of Clergy had the effect of producing the most literate class of criminals in history. On the point of literacy McHardy, supra, p.182 supports Postman's contentions in concluding, "However, what finally brought the privilege of benefit of clergy into disrepute was neither the lax procedures of the Church, nor the crown's search for new areas of jurisdiction, and certainly not a lessening of the Church's vigilance in defence of its rights. The most serious challenge to this ecclesiastical liberty was mounted by those changes in society which led to the numbers of those, outside holy orders, *who could read.*" (My emphasis).

[40] 1 Edw. VI c. 12.

[41] Edward VI reigned from the age of nine years until his death, aged fifteen (1547-1553). His advisors were his uncle the Duke of Somerset and Lord Protector and two years later the Duke of Northumberland. Both men were keen on achieving religious reform and may well have influenced Edward and his legislative reforms.

[42] Other than murder or poisoning.

[43] Of significant benefit to peers as any trial would be held exclusively before other peers. Additionally beneficed peers were not subject to any loss of inheritance or "corruption of blood." Interestingly this provision created a completely new class of "clergy" in that the peers had neither to be literate or

the "repeals" also did was permit clergy to those committing bigamy.[44] The words of the statute themselves are of note, "divers and sundry times" because they give a more contemporary gloss on the word bigamy implying that it was not only marrying again once widowed in the traditional sense but also marrying another when currently married to a first wife. As shall be discussed in later chapters the early American colonists in the biblical north chose to follow the established historical interpretation of bigamy when making this a non-clergyable death penalty offense. In Edward's case it was probably a concession to the number of clergy who were known to have wives and mistresses.[45] Further statutory provisions during Edward's reign removed benefit from soldiers[46] who left military employment without permission;[47] buggery became a death penalty offense without benefit of clergy again[48] and in doing so firmly established this crime as being of

---

entered into holy orders. Peeral benefit claims by women were tested in the matter of the Duchess of Kingston who bigamously married the Duke while still wife to the Earl of Bristol. Though eligible for *pares curiae* Kingston failed to convince her peers that she held the benefit and was found unanimously guilty by all 119 lords at Westminster Hall on April 20, 1776. She abjured the realm to retire to Russia under the protection of Catherine the Great. See: Lovell, C.R., The Trial of Peers in Great Britain, *American Historical Review*, Vol. 55. No.1. (Oct., 1949), pp. 69-81 and Dalzell, supra, pp. 20-21 and R v Chudleigh, Duchess of Kingston 168. E.R. 175, 1776 I. Leach. 146.

[44] The Church viewed bigamy differently than secular law in part due to the requirement of clerical celibacy. It was first addressed in 1274 as a Canon of the Second Council of Lyons where a clerk's marriage to a widow was decreed bigamous. For married clerks committing a felony other than bigamy Boniface VIII required they wore clerical dress and were tonsured. There were three obstacles to claiming a clerk for the ordinary after 1274; if he is bigamous, married but not properly dressed and tonsured, or he has been previously degraded. Cheney, C.R. The Punishment of Felonious Clerks [sic] *The English Historical Review*, Vol. 51. No. 202 (Apr., 1936), pp. 215-236.

[45] C.f. Bellamy, *Criminal Law*, supra. p. 48-149.

[46] Returning soldiers and wandering vagabonds were problematic for centuries due to successive wars with European neighbors. It became practice to apply a whipping to wandering soldiers. Vagabonds were subjected to a branding of "V" or "F" for fraymaker. Dalzell, supra, p.19.

[47] 2/3 Edw. VI. C.2.

[48] It had become clergyable under 25 Hen. VIII c. 6. This act was now repealed under 2/3 Edw. VI c.29.

temporal jurisdiction and riotous behavior was now deemed to be a felonious offense without benefit of clergy.[49]

Few matters relating to benefit of clergy were addressed through Marian legislation. Mary did repeal her brother's "Act of Repeals"[50] in part because Edward's act had removed the right of the Church to try matters of sexual misconduct. Her provisions did not, however, alter the newly created privilege extended to the peerage. Three further Marian acts relating to benefit were promulgated but these were all of a minor nature; most notable was her inclusion of accessories before the fact into the realm of those who could not claim their clergy for petty treason, murder, highway robbery and those other crimes as defined by the original statute of 23 Henry VIII.[51]

Perhaps not surprisingly Elizabeth I repealed some of her Catholic sister's attempts to re-establish ecclesiastic juridical authority. Her Act of Supremacy, 1559,[52] implied a reversion back to her brother's position with respect to the clergyability of bigamy. A subsequent law of 1567 permitted clergy for one offense. Henceforth an offender

---

[49] 3/4 Edw. VI c.5. Designed to curb recent groups of roving criminals from organized attacks of poaching, theft from fishponds and dovecotes and thefts from barns, grain houses and dwellings. Whereas Edward had repealed all of the new unclergyable felonies created by his father he was now creating a new unclergyable felony himself.

[50] 1/2 Philip & Mary c.8.

[51] 4/5 Philip & Mary c.4. extended non-clergyable to accessories before the fact for: petty treason, murder, highway robbery, burglary from an occupied dwelling, arson of a house or grain barn, failing to plea, peremptory challenges of more than twenty jurors. Per 23 Hen. VIII c.I (and repealed by 1 Edw. VI c.12). 23 Hen. VII. c.I. also dealt with the distinction between murder and manslaughter for the purposes of benefit of clergy. Murder, murther, being committed by "malice prepensed" was felonious homicide beyond the protection of clergy. Henry also succeeded in reducing the options for sanctuary and abjuration for clerics. As Kesselring noted, "It has been frequently noted that benefit of clergy and benefit of sanctuary were analogous practices," Kesselring, K., Abjuration and its Demise: The Changing Face of Royal Justice in the Tudor Period, *Canadian Journal of History*, Vol. 34, No. 3 (Dec., 1999), pp. 346-358 at p. 356 Much of this additional double blow, reducing sanctuary and self-imposed exile, was achieved under the same statues as those restricting benefit of clergy such as 23 Hen. VIII, c. I, Hen. VIII, c. 11, 27 Hen. VIII, c.4 and 28 Hen. VIII, c. 17.

[52] 1 Elizabeth c.1.

charged with multiple offenses could not transfer clergy across when arraigned on separate occasions. One benefit could not serve more than one offense.[53] The most notable act introduced by Elizabeth was 18 Elizabeth c. 7 which severed the relationship between the criminous lay cleric and the ordinary.[54] Henceforth once benefit had been claimed, "The farce of delivering the released convict to the ordinary, or episcopal office, was disused, and he was imprisoned at the discretion of the judge for a period not exceeding one year."[55] As a result of this act all cases other than those involving *bona fide* Anglican clergymen would be tried before the royal justices. As well as removing the diaconal representative from the secular proceedings, other than in cases of establishing the true claim to clerical status of those in holy orders, it also confirmed that the punishment process was entirely temporal. Clerics were now permitted to claim benefit once,[56] then face the death sentence for a subsequent felony. Elizabeth proceeded to promulgate fourteen further acts that removed clergy from a number of specific offenses,[57] including the new unclergyable felonies of repeating slanderous tales about the queen[58] and embezzlement of military supplies.[59] Overall Elizabeth followed the trend started by her father in increasing the number of felonies and decreasing the number of those clergyable. She also confirmed the secularity of the matter and fully

---

[53] 8 Elizabeth c.4.
[54] This act also made carnal knowledge with a female less than 10 years of age a felony without clergy 18. Eliz. C.7 Sec. 4 and permitted an alien the privilege of reading from a book in his own language and from his own country. Baker, supra, p.103.
[55] Lea, supra, p. 190 per I Mary Sees I cap I & 5.
[56] Handing over a *clericus legit* was sometimes referred to as *absque purgation*, without purification, implying the clerk was still to be dealt with as a criminal before a lawful tribunal.
[57] C.f. Bellamy, *Criminal Law*, supra p. 154.
[58] 23 Elizabeth c. 2.
[59] 31 Elizabeth. C.4. and c.12. C.5. of the same act made accessories before and after felony of horse stealing non-clergyable.

moved clergy into the courts[60] temporal as a matter of literacy rather than anointed status.[61]

The late Tudor period marks a critical point in the history of the benefit of clergy as it is during this era a prominent decrease in the use of benefit occurs across society generally. Although literacy had increased nationally and the reading test was being applied more meaningfully, the number of non-clergyable felonies had increased considerably. But a more significant factor started to appear, one which would frame the use of clergy for the remainder of its history, in England and very soon in the American colonies. From this point forward juries started to reduce[62] the monetary value of the items stolen thereby mitigating automatic imposition of the death sentence.[63] Although this was a gradual move and one that only came to fruition after the impact of the Enlightenment took full effect, perhaps unknowingly the English juryman, in allowing the substitution of monetary value to the clergyable threshold,[64] was fashioning future custodial reform: plea bargaining and a range of case disposition that would rely upon alternative punitive sanctions rather than execution or disfigurement.[65] Juxtaposed with this manipulation of the criminal law was a

---

[60] Skousen, supra, p. 110 writes "Although it was not abolished, the exemption was permanently altered. The lay version survived and became a more prominent social tool than before, while clergy lost their unlimited immunity along with their monasteries."

[61] For Tudor era numbers see Bellamy, *Criminal Law*, supra, p.156. contrast Alexander. M., who proposes in one Exeter assize 134 prisoners were indicted; 17 of those were hanged, 15 were pardoned and just 11 claimed their benefit and were branded.
http://www.sourcetext.com/lawlibrary/underhill/03.htm.

[62] December 1730 Stephen Gay stealing goods valued at one penny; a gold ring, eleven guineas and thirty-five shillings in money. Cross, supra,. pp. 562-63. Note 45 p. 128 Lea, supra, cites hundreds of examples and refers to authority for more than twelve hundred specific cases of jury value manipulation.

[63] Items to the value of one shilling or greater were *de facto* felonies and attracted the death sentence or a one-time benefit plea.

[64] Thefts involving goods valued at greater than five shillings dropped from 25 per cent of all property cases down to seven per cent after the enactment of 39 Elizabeth c.15. Bellamy, *Criminal Law*, supra, p.163.

[65] Bellamy, *Criminal Law*, supra, asserts that during Elizabeth's reign members of the judiciary knowingly ignored legislation on occasions. C.f. p.158.

burgeoning explosion in population and pending, massive, crime waves throughout the seventeenth and particularly eighteenth centuries. It is perhaps this phenomenon that aided in the retention of benefit, as it would appear at first blush that benefit should have died a natural death soon after the Tudors. It did not; in fact, the legal fiction clung on for another two hundred years. As the secularization of benefit of clergy gained momentum alongside a general decriminalizing of many felony offenses by juries so the judiciary exercised unfettered dexterity in applying a benefit sentence; not infrequently the standard branding[66] was substituted for ear cropping, whipping or a period of public humiliation. Interestingly as the idea of sending criminals to America rather than executing them in London gained royal approval it was only a short step to also applying transportation[67] to clergy "sentences." Either way thousands of English criminals were exported to Virginia, thousands more left England to avoid religious suppression and by mistake and poor navigation ended up in Massachusetts, leading to both colonies warmly embracing the application of benefit style sentencing with widespread variety for criminal and religious miscreants.

During the reign of Elizabeth I the population of England doubled. This had considerable implications for her successor, James I, whose subjects were in dire need of food and legitimate employment. The Stuart era was one of religious, political and social instability.[68] Initially

---

[66] Branding was traditionally imposed in the courtroom and with a hot iron. Over time this became merely symbolic (e.g., "In the eighteenth century, moreover, it became the practice in Virginia, in some cases at least, to use an 'Iron scarcely heated,' thus rendering the whole business a 'Piece of absurd Pageantry.'" Friedman, L., *Crime and Punishment in American History*, New York, Basic Books, 1993, p. 44.

[67] Transportation is first found in statute 31 Car. 2 c.2 (1679). Under 4 Geo I. C. 11 (1717) felonious clerks were to be transported for a minimum of seven years.

[68] C.f. Levack, B.P. *The Formation of the British State: England, Scotland, and The Union, 1603-1703*, Oxford, Clarendon, 1987. Sharpe, J.A., *Early Modern England: A Social History. 1570-1760*, London, Arnold, 1987. Lockyer, R. *The Early Stuarts*, Paris, Lavoisier, 1989. Notestein, W. *The English People on the Eve of Civilization 1603-1630*, New York, harper, 1954.

few but increasingly throughout the century Englishmen and women sought alternative life options in the New World.[69] Conterminously one solution to increasing domestic crime was to supply the commercial venture known as Virginia with an indentured or criminal workforce. Benefit of clergy was transitioning from the original model; a privilege given to the Church, to one of a benefit to all men that would allow them to avoid the scaffold.[70]

The Stuarts: Transportation and exportation of *privilegium fori* to the Colonies

Tudor criminal justice had increasingly manipulated benefit to be a secular sentence manifest in benefit branding. The Stuarts took matters further, literally and metaphorically, by substituting benefit for a sentence of transportation so that "By about 1600, this old device [benefit of clergy] had been twisted into a wondrous new shape."[71] James I inaugurated the process[72] by order of commission;[73] the first

---

[69] This number was very few initially. The first shipload of entrepreneurs that headed for Virginia numbered just 127 men. Farther north the driving force was different as men and women together left England for the opportunity of a new religious freedom in Massachusetts, Plymouth and the puritan colonies.

[70] "...to reprive and stay from execucon such and soe many persons as nowe stand attainted or convicted of or for any robberie or felonie, (willful murder rape witchcraft or Burglarie onlie excepted) Whoe for strengthe of bodie or other abilities shall be thought fit to be ymploied in forraine discoveries or other services beyond the Seas" Smith, A.E., The Transportation of Convicts to the American Colonies in the Seventeenth Century, *The American Historical Review*, Vol. 39, No.2 (Jan., 1934), pp.232-249. p. 234 taken from Patent Roll, C. 66/2043, *in dorso*.

[71] Friedman, supra. p. 43.

[72] James I was the first monarch to implement transportation through the process of reprieve for felonious lay clerks. Prior to 1614/1615 James had approved legislation that denied clergy to "one who stabs another who has not first struck him, and the stab results in death within 6 months, though malice aforethought cannot be proven." 2 Jac. I. c. 8. (1604).

[73] January 24, 1614/1615 permitted the King or a minimum of six members of the privy council to reprieve a convicted felon and find them suitable for transportation. Felons returning before completion of the time limit, or if they refused to go in the first place, would make the reprieve null and void. Patent Roll C.66, supra.

"reprieved" criminous clerks were transported two days after his commission took effect.[74] James was also responsible for granting benefit of clergy to women convicted of larceny of goods to the value of greater than twelve pence and less than ten shillings. Upon claiming their clergy they were to be branded and could be imprisoned "not over a year."[75] Charles II excluded "great, known and notorious thieves" from clergy but provided that upon conviction they may be transported "into any of his Majesty's dominions in America, there to remain, and not to return."[76] Between the years of 1655 and 1699, 4431 convicted benefit felons were pardoned and transported.[77]

The first formal move towards transportation in lieu of the death penalty occurred in January 1615 when King James I directed justices to reprieve criminals convicted of clergyable crimes "upon condition of

---

[74] The first cohort of seventeen men was handed over to Sir Thomas Smith, governor of the East India Company. Initially it was left to Smith to decide on the destination of the convicts. The commission was renewed by royal decree in 1617, 1622, 1626, 1628 and 1633. Smith, supra. pp. 234-236.

[75] 21 Jac. I. c. 6. "whereas by the laws of this realm the benefit of clergy is not allowed to women convicted of felony, by reason whereof many women do suffer death for small causes, Women convicted of felonious taking of money or goods above value of 12 pence and under 10s., or being accessory, it not being burglary or highway robbery or private stealing from person, *shall have clergy as men do,* [my emphasis] and be branded and may be imprisoned not over a year." Since the time of the Conqueror England had set grand larceny at a monetary value of twelve pence; the sum estimated needed to keep a person in food and heat for eight days and had traditionally been the set figure that delineated a larceny felony from a misdemeanor. This was still the same figure upon succession by James I and consequently the likelihood of receiving the death sentence for a case of low value theft was ludicrously high. Increasingly judges and juries sought to address this anomaly by devaluing the amount to a clergyable status. Dalzell, supra, p. 38 supplies a delightful sample of judicial manipulation with his examples of where a heifer was held not to be a cow, a colt not a horse and a drake not a duck citing King v Cook 168 E.R. 155.174, 168 E.R. 917 and Rex v Holloway 171 E.R. 1131.

[76] 18 Car. 2. c. 3 (1666).

[77] Smith, supra. p. 238. It is of note that this timeframe covers not only the restoration of the monarchy, Charles II, in 1660 but also the period of the Lord Protector(s) 1653-1658, indicating that the utility of transportation and the established basis of benefit of clergy were appreciated by both the monarchy and the short-duration commonwealth.

transportation."[78] Interestingly this direction captured a broad swathe of felons under sentence of death as well as branded recidivists eligible to be hanged. This move by James introduced an alternative to established penal practice throughout the realm and commenced the beginning of an entirely new penology.[79] Transportation was, at this time, optional and no condemned man was required to accept the offer.[80] For the next thirty years transportation warrants were issued personally by the king, then Cromwell, until such time as an act of parliament was introduced.[81] Once transported to the new colonies benefit was integrated into its legal systems by allowing those who had claimed benefit in London to claim it again in Virginia and Massachusetts; but with branding, cropping and public humiliation and in isolated circumstances to transportation from Virginia to the Caribbean. Over the course of the next 150 years it would be possible to claim the benefit in London and then again be within clergy if found guilty of a felony in the New World.

---

[78] Dalzell, supra, p. 46. Further change took place in 1655 when convicts were transported by the method of conditional pardons. The first recorded instance being August 2, 1655. Patent roll C66/2912, no. 3. C.f. Smith, supra. p. 237.

[79] A number of factors merged such as the burgeoning merchant classes and their ability to influence the legislative, the power of the Guilds of London, and as the century progressed the desire of the Restoration monarchy to achieve a new purpose and harmony within the kingdom alongside the opportunities presented to rebuild the capital after the Great Fire all combined a number of obvious and subtle forces to make sentencing options reform a major component of seventeenth-century legislation.

[80] Some elected to hang instead of face transportation; such were the concerns and unknown elements surrounding what life would be like as an indentured servant in the colonies. Prisoners were also known to elect not to claim their clergy as they preferred to have the matter "put on the country." Baker, supra, pp. 99-100.

[81] 18. Car. II. C.3. Applied exclusively to the northern counties of Cumberland and Northumberland. It deprived cattle thieves of the choice of death or transportation and directed judges to "sentence" benefit thieves to transportation. 22 & 23 Car. II c.7; 3 Stat.L. 354 (1670) extended transportation to those committing arson of corn stacks, theft of ammunition and cloth from racks. Under these acts the convicted felon could still exercise a constitutional right to the death penalty. The last recorded use of 23 Car. II. C.7. was in 1763 when two felons from the county of Hampshire were transported for "stealing cloth from the rack" July 12, 1763. Public Record Office Assizes 23/5 Smith, supra. p. 233.

In 1679 Charles II signed the Habeas Corpus Act[82] that built upon the old established writ from *Magna Carta* and created an option of transportation for any felony. In 1706,[83] the literacy test was abolished and the absurdity of illiterate laity claiming they were clerics was finally a part of legal history.[84] Henceforth a manifest inability to quote the Neck Verse was no longer a bar to making a false claim of cleric privilege before a secular court of law.[85] Optional transportation ended in 1717[86] when George I substituted branding and release for transportation for clergyable offenses and transportation in lieu of execution for unclergyable offenses.[87] In one respect "transportation clergy"[88] extended the severity of the law as it exiled felons who had

---

[82] 31 Car. II. c.2.

[83] 5 Anne. c. 6 s.6. (1706) "If any person be convicted of a felony for which he should have his clergy, he shall not be required to read, but shall be punished as clerk convict as if he had read like a clerk." 12 Anne. c. 7 (1713) increased the financial tariff from 10s. to 40s. The English monetary system was of course legal tender in the American colonies and Massachusetts followed English law when "Massachusetts enacted that persons who had previously been convicted of two thefts of property valued at 40s., should upon third conviction of theft of property valued at three pounds, be subject to capital punishment without benefit of clergy" Mass. Charter (1759) 283. Hall, J., *Theft, Law and Society* (2 ed), Indianapolis, Bobbs-Merrill Company, 1935. p.125 n.36.

[84] Firth, supra, p.191 referring to the benefit said "Clerical immunities in the fifteenth century give a clear example of that straining at a gnat and swallowing a camel, which has been in all ages the peculiar temptation of an official hierarchy." Baker, supra, p. 100 called it a "farce." Pollock & Maitland, supra, p. 435 refer to it as a "fiction," Friedman, supra, p. 43 refers to that "curios legal fiction" as one of the "quaintest habits of the common law" and Poole, supra, p.245 wrote that "Compurgation was like the ordeal 'little better than a farce'" and White, E.J., Benefit of Clergy, *The American Law Review*, Vol. 46, (1912), pp. 78-94. p. 78 viewed it as nothing but mere "fantastic quibble." Cross, supra. p. 565 called it "That queer old exemption."

[85] 4 George I (1717). Beattie, supra, p. 474-475. "It is almost certainly the case that most offenders could have been denied clergy on the grounds of their illiteracy had the courts insisted, 'Were it not for the favour of the Court,' it was said in 1652, 'not one in twenty could save their lives by reading.'" Citing March, J., *Amicus Reipublicae*, 19 May 1652, quoted by Veall, D., *The Popular Movement for Law Reform, 1640-166*, Oxford, Clarendon, 1970. p.4. n.4. Benefit of Clergy was abolished in England 7 and 8 Geo. IV. C. 28. s.6. (1827).

[86] 4. Geo. I.

[87] 7 years for larceny and 14 years for non-clergyable offenses. Dalzell, supra, p. 52.

[88] 19 Geo. 3. c.30. (1779) In response to 1776 and the Declaration of Independence: "Offenders sentenced to transportation shall be transported beyond the seas elsewhere than America. This act also abolished branding with the substitution of a fine or whipping, s. 3. It also brought prison ships to the

previously got off with a branding. It also lessened the severity of the law, though, as it allowed capital crime felons to avoid Tyburn.

During the seventeenth century England expanded statutory sentencing options through the jury, the bench,[89] pardons and transportation warrants.[90] This legal dexterity was soon imitated in Virginia[91] and Massachusetts so that within one decade of their establishment these colonies would apply benefit of clergy broadly to a range of criminal and biblical capital and non-capital offenses. What had started in Europe as a uniquely ecclesiastic privilege had transformed into a secular benefit that was now so integrated into English culture and legal practice that it was readily exported and subsumed into the American colonies until such time as they were able to create their own American common law.

Thames whereby convicts could be sentenced to one to five years of labor on board a prison ship in lieu of transportation. s.27. Transportation to Australia commenced in 178:. "Between 1787 and 1857 more than one hundred thousand convicts were transported there." Hall, supra, p. 113-114.

[89] Through judicial discretion which had grown increasingly during the Stuarts. Also, 15 Geo. 2. C. 27 (1742) introduced fines for a first conviction of theft of wool or cloth, imprisonment for a second conviction and transportation for a third. Beattie, supra, p.476 shows Surrey courts in 1665 offering felons the option of transportation for clergyable offenses as well as instances of felons who were denied clergy being transported.

[90] "It has been shown that over the seventeenth century there was a decided decline in several counties (and apparently nationally) in both the absolute number of felons hanged and the proportion of accused felons eventually brought to the gallows." Beattie, J., *Crime and the Courts in England 1660-1800*, New Jersey, Princeton University Press, 1986. p. 469. By 1776 England was exporting two thousand convicts to the colonies each year. Hall, supra. p.113.

[91] The General Court of Virginia enacted a law in 1670 to stop the crown sending desperate villains as it presented a "danger to the colony." The "law" was not challenged in Westminster and was allowed to stand. This was in fact followed by a privy council order, supra, that confirmed the Virginian law that "no felon or other condemned persons shall be sent or transported from hence to his majesty's said Colony of Virginia" Acts of the Privy Council (Colonial) vol. 1. p. 553 See: Beattie, supra, p. 479.

Chapter 3. Benefit of clergy in Colonial Virginia

Settlement and early law

From 1607 to 1624 Virginia was ruled by an entity known as the Virginia Company of London.[1] Established to promote entrepreneurship and wealth for its investors, it was financed by private individuals to explore and exploit the territory known as Virginia. The Virginia Company[2] existed for eighteen years and during this time operated under three charters. The first one hundred twenty-seven men to arrive in Jamestown in 1607 needed significant support and financial investment to help them establish a colony and consequently the Virginia Company was established as a monopoly with policies that retained control over all assets, all economic transactions and ownership of all labor.[3] Labor was to be controlled through rigid discipline and coercion and not financial incentives and rewards.[4] Initially private ownership of land was prohibited. The Virginia Company relented in part and in 1613 it granted every settler a

---

[1] It is not uncommon to see this body referred to as the London Company, the Virginia Company of London and the Virginia Company. E.g. Dalzell, G.W. *Benefit of Clergy in America*, Winston-Salem, Blair, 1955, the London Company and Scott, infra, the Virginia Company and Chittwood, O.P., *Justice in Colonial Virginia*, New York, Da Capo, 1971. The original charter stated London Company but very soon after formation Virginia Company was utilized in commercial and legal documents.

[2] Created by Royal Charter April 11, 1606. It was believed, inter alia, there were "mines and many other rich commodities." Bereton, J., "A Brief and True Relation" (London, 1602) at p. 32 in Fitzmaurice, A., The Civic Solution to the Crises of English colonization, 1609-1625 *The Historical Journal*, Vol. 42. No.1 (March, 1999), pp. 25-52.

[3] From this first cohort seven men were appointed to be the Council of Virginia. The names were placed in a sealed box and opened April 26, 1607. For names and details see: Chitwood, supra. p. 10.

[4] C.f. Nelson, E. *The Common Law in America, Vol. I. The Chesapeake and New England 1607-1660*, Oxford, Oxford University Press, 2008. Esp. Chapter 1. Seven of the original one hundred twenty-seven nominated as the Council. Their authority, legislative, executive and judicial, was supreme.

small parcel of land[5] to promote growing of produce and to stimulate the establishment of families in the colony.

From the outset the legal system was part common law and part local improvisation designed to support the needs of investors rather than individuals; for example, settlers were prohibited from trading with the native population, on pain of death,[6] and in one instance a court based its findings upon Leviticus and ordered a man who murdered his wife to be burnt to death.[7] Without the opportunity to engage in local trade the predominantly male settlers had few chances of accruing financial stability and a future. Consequently, drunkenness and general lawlessness were a problem.[8] Theft of company property was commonplace and with the food shortages experienced during the early years theft of produce and livestock from the company was frequent. Life was harsh and vulgar. The response was brutal coercive laws that provided for the death penalty in abundance. The period of deputy-governorship by Thomas Dale[9] from 1611 to 1616 is considered by many

---

[5] In 1618 the London Company started the "headright" system of allowing 50 acres of land to anybody who transported himself or another to Virginia. This built upon 50 acres of land available to anyone, already in Virginia, who would subscribe to purchasing twelve pounds and ten shillings worth of company stock. Nelson, supra, p. 18.

[6] Nelson, supra. p.14.

[7] Scott, A. P. *Criminal Law in Colonial Virginia*, Chicago, University of Chicago Press, 1930. p. 139. And Perry, G., "Observations Gathered Out of a discourse of the Plantation of the Southerne Colonie in Virginia by the English, 1606," p. 60 in Jordan, D., & Walsh, M., *White Cargo: The Forgotten History of Britain's White Slaves in America*, New York, New York University Press, 2007.

[8] For a fascinating list of petty offenses and punishments (e.g., modesty in dress and carrying a firearm to church) c.f. Scott, supra. pp. 143-145. Private persons found drunk were dealt with by the parish minster on the first occasion and the courts subsequently. One commentator reports that up to half an entire congregation might be drunk at services. See; Richards, J., Samuel Davis and the Transatlantic Campaign for Slave Literacy, *Virginia Magazine of History and Biography*, Vol. 111. No. 4. (2003) pp. 333-378. p. 358. Overall the laws pertaining to public morals were revised four times in the fifteen years between 1690 and 1705. Scott. Supra. p. 288.

[9] Sir Thomas Dale was appointed deputy governor in 1611 and is credited with penning *Articles, Laws, and Orders, Divine, Politique, and Martiall for the Colony in Virginia*. See: Konig, D. T., Dale's laws' and the Non-Common Law origins of criminal justice in Virginia, *The American Journal of Legal History*, Vol. 26. No. 4 (Oct.1982), pp. 354-375.

commentators[10] as an example of extreme harshness and his "laws" contained some of the most draconian legislative provisions ever seen in the colony. However, as was the case in London, capital offenses rarely attracted the death sentence as this depleted the sparse colonial workforce. It soon became the practice that amercements, whipping,[11] ear cropping and a variety of mutilations were applied as substitutes for execution. Extended periods of servitude were also applied as a criminal sanction. Religious laws were wrapped into a general legal code[12] so that blasphemy,[13] sodomy, adultery, rape and theft all attracted the death sentence.[14] During the first twenty years of its existence Virginia was a primitive place and its pioneers suffered great hardships both natural and those imposed by agents of the Virginia Company. In 1624 King James I dissolved the Virginia Company; he recognized the vast financial opportunities and was concerned at the uncontrolled and independent expansion of the settlement, and for the remaining period until the American Revolution Virginia was a royal province under direct control of the English crown.[15] Royal proclamation did not yet guarantee due process, as Edward Sharpless

---

[10] E.g. Dalzell, supra. pp. 96-97, Scott, supra, p. 8., Nelson, supra, p. 14.

[11] Traditionally set at a maximum of thirty-nine lashes. Only the General Court could impose more. Hoffer & Scott, infra. p. lxxi.

[12] Known as Lawes Divine, Morall, and Martial. See: Konig, Thomas (1982). Dale's Laws' and the Non-Common Law Origins of Criminal Justice in Virginia. *The American Journal of Legal History* Vol. 26 No. p.354. and Virginia Foundation for the Humanities, *Lawes Divine, Morall and Martiall*, Encyclopedia Virginia available at: www.encyclopediavirginia.org/Lawes_Divine_Morall_and_Martiall.

[13] Under Dale's laws a second offense of blasphemy was to have the tongue pierced with a bodkin. Other moral offenses were subject to whippings and ear cropping and tying the neck and heels together, every night for one month. Chitwood, supra. p. 14.

[14] Nelson, supra. p. 16.

[15] In practical terms this meant greater scrutiny over the running of the colony and the power to make laws and apply them vested in a governor appointed directly by the king. Charles I stated that the government of Virginia should 'depend immediately' upon himself. Scott, A.P. *Criminal Law in Colonial Virginia*, Illinois, University of Chicago Press, 1930, p. 13.

found out in May 1624 when he was pilloried and then had his ears removed without an indictment, jury trial or appeal process.[16]

During the seventeenth century American colonial law developed piecemeal. Judges were frequently called to serve without any formal legal training; they literally learned the law as they applied it. They were typically unpaid and qualified lawyers too were extremely rare. In Virginia the limited population of educated gentlemen meant that opportunities to learn and build the law into a cogent body of rules and procedures were hampered by a number of factors.[17] Whereas in the Virginia Company era, Virginia was a legal experiment largely left to its own devices by London, now that the colony was a royal province the impact of the established common law was far greater but never absolute. What emerged was a natural fusion of laws from England that were adjusted and applied to suit local needs. Although the colony probably never had absolute power to enact legislation, it frequently did so and unless particularly offensive to the practices in London the Virginians were left to utilize their own laws across the territory. In 1619 the first Assembly met; this body comprised the governor, councilors and burgesses,[18] who sat together as a legislative body and a criminal court, referred to as the General Court.[19] It comprised the

---

[16] Sharpless was clerk to the crown's Council of State and obeyed a lawful royal command. Local officials of the Virginia Company were not supportive of orders Sharpless implemented and conducted a quick trial and sentencing without any formalities before the new royal proclamation could be put into effect. Nelson, supra. p. 20-21. On the same day another defendant was sentenced to having his tongue bored through with an awl and summarily outlawed. Nelson, supra. p. 21.

[17] As late as 1760 Patrick Henry was admitted to the Virginia bar having read law for just six weeks. Source Dalzell, supra. p. 86. C.f. a substantial list of sources regarding the paucity of legal knowledge. Dalzell, supra. p. 88.

[18] For records of the court and legislative proceedings 1620-1926 see: McIlwaine, H.R., *Legislative Journals of the Council of Colonial Virginia in Three Volumes*, Richmond, VA MCMVXII and McIlwaine, H.R., *Minutes of the Council and General Court of Colonial Virginia 1622-1632, 1670-1676 With Notes and Excerpts from Original Council and General Courts Records into 1683, Now Lost*, Richmond, VA. MCMXXIV.

[19] Unlike the English Privy Council and House of Lords the highest court of Virginia did not comprise any professional judges. Overtime the court members did make purchases of law books from England

governor and two representatives from each county. These deputies were known as Burgesses. The assembly had authority to create and pass laws and act as a trial court for loss of life or limb felonies that occurred within the colony. The burgesses also sat as an appellate court for matters appealed from the county courts. From this period onwards it became one of the main bodies for creating and applying the criminal law. The constitutionality of the acts created were never fully tested; they were subject to veto by the governor and in theory confirmation or disapproval by the Privy Council in Westminster. In practice it was never really clear as to whether or not laws enacted by the Assembly were always applicable. For example if a law was contested the deciding body was the Privy Council. In reality it could take years for a decision from Westminster so in the meantime the Assembly laws were applied even if it later transpired they were deemed inapplicable. Conversely, the force of English statutes upon the colony was crucial, particularly with regard to matters such as benefit of clergy and pleading the belly that provided such useful mitigatory mechanisms against centuries of sanguinary legislation. As for the Virginian legal community, it sought to know whether all English laws enacted before 1607 were applicable or only those promulgated after 1607. As these uncertainties were worked through, the legal system had to operate on a daily basis as defendants were brought to trial for a variety of felonies, clergyable and unclergyable. The first boatload of immigrants to Virginia comprised a mixed bag of society but did include at least thirty-five gentlemen who would have been able to read and therefore apply the benefit reading test. The initial charter captured the "rights and liberties of Englishmen" and included a specific reference to benefit of clergy but restricted its use to manslaughter only.

---

and they met regularly to share legal knowledge and learning. Hoffer, P.C. & Scott, W.B., (eds) *Criminal Proceedings in Colonial Virginia [Records of] fines, Examination of criminals, Trials of slaves, etc., From March 1761[1711] to [1754] [Richmond County, Virginia]*, American Historical Association, Washington, D.C., University of Georgia Press, 1984. p. xx. The court sat in Jamestown until the end of the seventeenth century when it moved to Williamsburg. Chitwood, supra. p. 37.

Interestingly this made some crimes that were clergyable in England unclergyable in Virginia; for example adultery and incest now attracted the death sentence.[20]

- Responsibility for examining suspects to determine the appropriate course of action, no action, misdemeanor or felony trial, was vested in the local magistrates.[21] This mirrored the position in England since enactment of the Marian statute of 1554[22] and remained in place until Virginia created an examining court[23] in 1705.[24] Unlike the court system in England, which continued to require the plaintiff to incur the cost of bringing a criminal prosecution, the colony of Virginia bore the cost of felony prosecutions. Under the 1705 provisions, the colony also formalized the common practice of offense reduction so that, rather than having to involve a justice and jury in the manipulation of monetary values to downgrade a felony to a misdemeanor, in Virginia judicial discretion was expressly accommodated.[25] Oyer and terminer[26] courts had existed in England since the end of the thirteenth century. They were established as a mechanism to receive defendants from the custody of gaols and to hear, determine and sentence in cases of serious felonies. By the seventeenth century English felony trials were heard before an assize justice on circuit, and justices of the peace, magistrates, no longer heard any matters dealing with the loss of life or limb. Virginia copied this model and operated the oyer and terminer

---

[20] It would have been remarkably hard to commit these crimes since the first immigrants were exclusively male. As Dalzell comments these instructions might well reflect the view that James I was "The wisest fool in Christendom" Dalzell, supra. p. 95.

[21] Initially known as commissioners Virginian justices of the peace were local freemen, and men of influence and ability. Most had no formal legal training and may not have had extensive education either. C.f. Chitwood, supra. pp. 74-107.

[22] 1 and 2 Philip and Mary 1554-1555. C.13 and 2 and 3 Philip and Mary, c.10. Legislation that required magistrates to interrogate suspects and obtain written testimony in suspected felony cases.

[23] Also referred to as the "Called Court." Rankin, infra, p. 54.

[24] Hoffer & Scott, supra. p. xxxvii.

[25] Hoffer & Scott, supra. p. xliii.

[26] To "hear and determine."

courts. However, in addition to hearing serious criminal cases, this court also heard matters relating to slaves.[27] Trials were public and much like the English criminal trial, notoriously speedy. Convictions depended to some extent upon venue. Following English precedent, defendants could either "put themselves upon the country" before a local jury of twelve men, elect trial before a panel of justices at oyer and terminer or be judged summarily. Slaves were not permitted to elect trial venue until 1732 when benefit of clergy was extended to them. This was not before some outrageous examples of bias, presumably brought about by irrational fear among the white community, where the idea of injecting fear into the black community extended beyond death. In one instance a slave died before his trial for alleged murder. His body was exhumed, quartered, decapitated and placed on display at strategic locations much the same as occurred in England for notorious criminals.[28] Although never considered a punishment as seen in the previous chapter, benefit of clergy was certainly construed as one by the Old Bailey as judges substituted the death sentence for clergy and branding[29] or transportation. In Virginia the same can be said; it was never *de facto* a sentence, but was clearly utilized as such with the adoption of the entire suite of corporal punishments seen in England being applied across the colony, whether a formal claim of benefit was entered or not. Just as eighteenth-century England moved progressively towards a culture of making more crimes capital

---

[27] The status of blacks had deteriorated progressively throughout the seventeenth century from 1660 onwards. So much so that by 1690 blacks were no longer regarded as servants but had now been reduced to chattels. This shift in definition brought many matters previously dealt with locally before the assize courts. The procedure was that when a slave was suspected of a felony the sheriff would inform the justices who applied to the governor for a commission of oyer and terminer. The court then met and its commission was read by the clerk before proceedings commenced. For a relevant case see: Janey (an Indian slave) tried for murder of his master. 2/22/1700. McIlwaine, supra. p.41.

[28] Hoffer & Scott, supra. p. lxxii.

[29] For the origins of branding see: Bellamy, J., *Criminal Law and Society in Late Medieval and Tudor England*, New York, St. Martin's Press, 1984. Chapter 6. and Sawyer, J.K., "Benefit of Clergy" in Maryland and Virginia, *The American Journal of Legal History*, Vol. 34. No. 1 (Jan., 1990), pp. 49-68. p. 54.

offenses[30] so too Virginia successively applied more severe sentences; disfigurement accounted for one-third of all felony sentences between 1714 and 1733.[31]

One fundamental difference between the powers of the legal institutions of Virginia compared with those in England was in relation to ecclesiastical laws. In Virginia the common law, civil and criminal, was subsumed into courts of general practice, canon law too was brought into these courts so that distinctions between areas of jurisdiction were never subject to the power battles experienced in England during the preceding six hundred years. English legal practice was from the outset a reference point for Virginia but it was trimmed and modified locally to suit the needs of a territory in development so that, for example, masters were not permitted to whip Christian white servants naked without an order from a justice, a blacksmith was sentenced to death for threatening a member of the Virginia council and John Davis was pilloried for forgery, a capital offense in England.[32] Most curious was the case against Evan Ward in 1675. He was tried for the murder of Jonathan Button and found guilty then acquitted and banished from Virginia as the court could not find the body of the deceased.[33] To utilize the English law made sense to the colonists; it was what they were familiar with and the common law was sufficiently

---

[30] E.g. The Waltham Black Act. 9. Geo. I. c.22. 1772.

[31] Source. Hoffer & Scott, supra. p. lxxii Non-acquittals increased also during this period. Figures for the oyer and terminer Courts cited by Hoffer & Scott are drawn from Schwartz, P.J., *Slave Criminality and the Slave Community: Patterns of Slave Assertiveness in 18th Century Virginia*, unpublished paper. Note 142. p. xlviii.

[32] Hening, W. W., *Statutes at large: being a Collection of all the Laws of Virginia*, Richmond, VA, Franklin Press, 1823. Vol. I. pp. 255, 440 and Chitwood, supra, p.82. A further example of the localization of law and procedure was that Litigants typically started suit proceedings by bill procedure rather than writ. There was a far greater reliance upon statute rather than common law, so much so that by 1657 all former Virginian laws were repealed and a new code of 130 sections was introduced. Preamble to Law of March 13, 1657/58 Hening. Statutes I at 432. Blacksmith Reade was sentenced to death for "giving bad language" to council president Ratcliffe. Chitwood, supra. p.12. Note **6**. For John Davis see: *Virginia Gazette* Oct.20, 1738. p.3.

[33] McIlwaine, supra. p. 428. Evan Ward convicted of murder 10/12/1675.

established that it already had a set of rules and doctrines that were adequate to serve the region. In those instances where English law did not deal satisfactorily with an issue local laws were created to fill the lacuna. For England this arrangement made sense also as it did not have a large standing army in place in Virginia nor a complex system of courts and judges paid by London. Local volunteers who had education and possessed a rudimentary knowledge of the law sufficed for both local and English needs. Fiscal and natural resources restricted the development of a complex government structure in Virginia and the domestic gentry were given a degree of latitude to create policies and laws that ensured the territory functioned.[34] England was keen to see a venture that might enhance trade and domestic profits after a period of expensive war with Spain but there were not crown funds available to support the enterprise.[35] The new colonists arrived to a settlement that was susceptible to attack by local Indians, poor geographical location, swamp and lack of drinking water and disease, culminating in the period referred to as "Starving Time."[36] Benefit of clergy was naturally incorporated into the legal framework; it was familiar and it worked.

Transportation and benefit of clergy

Deportation of criminals to America began in 1618 as a substitute for hanging. It served the same purpose as benefit of clergy in that it spared the convict from capital punishment but it was to some extent

---

[34] C.f. Nelson, supra. p.41.

[35] C.f. Hatch, C.E. *The First Seventeen Years: Virginia 1607-1624*, Charlottesville, University of Virginia press, 1957. 10th Printing 1991. The Project Gutenberg E Book. www.gutenberg.org.

[36] Earle, C.V., "Environment, Disease, and Mortality in Early Virginia" in *The Chesapeake in the Seventeenth Century: Essays on Anglo-American Society*, Tate, T.W., & Ammerman, D. L., (Eds) Chapel Hill, UNC Press, 1979. Re 'Starving Time' c.f. Chitwood, supra. p. 13. Also James I had inherited debts of £400,000 and soon accrued personal debts of £80,000 pounds due to his own lifestyle. By 1605 his wife, Anne of Denmark, had spent £40,000 on clothes. C.f. Somerville, J.P. The Government of James I at www.faculty.history.wisc.edu/sommerville .

an improvement as it brought convict labor to Virginia. Given the dual benefits of getting rid of London's criminals and supplying labor to the Virginia Company transportation was quickly applied to capital and clergyable offenses. As a result of increasing crime rates and the number of offenses that attracted the death sentence on January 24 1615 James I directed members of the Privy Council to reprieve felons, other than murderers, rapists and burglars,[37] for employment beyond the seas.[38] In creating this order James was modifying existing benefit practice and law to make clergyable crimes subject to deportation, a stark move away from the branding that had become commonplace since the changes introduced by Henry VIII. The process for transportation reprieve was straightforward. At the end of the court sessions a list of those eligible was submitted to the Privy Council. A royal pardon was issued and the convicts were formally handed over to merchant speculators for transportation. This form of deportation remained optional for convicts until 1718 when legislation was introduced that permitted the court to order transportation for offenses within benefit of clergy and capital crimes reprieved upon condition of transportation.[39] Transportation was provided by government contractors who received a crown subsidy for providing the shipping services. Shipping contractors were free to negotiate the convict's final destination[40] depending upon the local market value of the servitude contract.[41]

---

[37] Highway robbery and arson were added as unclergyable for transportation in 1621.
[38] Dalzell, supra. p.46.
[39] 4. Geo. I. c. 11. 1717. Fourteen years transportation for unclergyable crimes. Seven years for clergyable crimes in lieu of whipping or branding.
[40] England possessed twenty-five American colonies by 1700. Twelve on the mainland and thirteen were "sugar islands" in the Caribbean.
[41] Dalzell, supra. p. 50. A four-year servitude contract was sold for approximately double the cost of shipping the convict. Longer contracts attracted considerably higher returns for the ship's captain. Sales were conducted port-side upon arrival. Life sentences were very rare. One example is William Duell who in 1740 was sentenced to life exile after he came to life on the dissecting table at Surgeons Hall, London having survived his hanging. Dalzell, supra. p. 52

The labor shortage in Virginia was so acute by 1611 that deputy-governor Thomas Dale petitioned the king for convicts.[42] The response was not immediate; only five were sent from Newgate[43] in 1618, one hundred followed the year after. Capital punishment had never brought atonement for a serious crime; it merely disabled some offenders and attempted to terrify others into a life of legal compliance. Transportation was different, it removed dangerous miscreants from English society and it confirmed the monarch's love for his subjects through the generous application of deportation pardons. Locally, public whippings and hangings were becoming raucous affairs and always exposed the crown to the risk of demonstrations if the defendants were popular or the method of punishment was disapproved of[44] so that a growing dissatisfaction with penal options after 1660[45] saw an inevitable increase in the use of clergy transportation to the Americas. The courts were caught between the crown and public opinion and had few alternative penal measures available to them before transportation; hanging or a symbolic branding for clergyable crimes. A disinclination on behalf of the courts to send more and more felons to the gallows reflected the courts' sensitivity to the increase in laws that attracted the death sentence. Manipulating benefit of clergy to open up transportation was an attractive option for judges, juries, the crown and the general public.[46] For convicts it provided an opportunity to avoid capital punishment or, for those transported as a substitute for benefit, it meant the chance of a new start and a new identity in Virginia after the period of servitude

---

[42] In 1611 Dale took 300 "disorderly persons" with him from England. Hall, J., *Theft, Law and Society* (2nd edition) Indianapolis, Boobs-Merrill, 1935. p. 112. Note 6.

[43] Newgate prison was the central prison in London that held defendants awaiting trial and convicted felons before execution or deportation.

[44] C.f. Beattie, J.M., *Crime and the Courts in England 1660-1800*, New Jersey, Princeton University Press, 1986. P. 469.

[45] Beattie, supra. pp. 468-483.

[46] Transportation was not the only departure from branding or hanging. For alternatives see: Beattie, supra. p.470-471

had been completed. However, a new start was not always an easy sell to convicts who previously had got off with a branding; increasingly the courts found ways of not accepting benefit though so that horse thieves, highway robbers and larcenists could be lawfully deported.[47] By 1670, the manipulation of benefit was so established it was formalized in statute.[48] By the end of the eighteenth century, the number of convicts sentenced to transportation had increased significantly[49] and now included women as well. This caused its own problems as fit healthy young males were a boon to the labor pool in Virginia, but women were not. By the 1660's Virginian sentiment towards convict labor had changed. After the Restoration the number of loose and disorderly[50] persons being sent to the colony had increased and established Virginians were now keen to put a stop to the trade and leave benefit as a lawful plea within the colony but not have it applied in London as a means of deporting unwanted criminals *en masse* to America.[51] In 1670 the Assembly introduced a law that attempted to prohibit the influx of "jail-birds" to Virginia.[52] The law was effective from January 20 1671 and first used to prevent an English

---

[47] E.g., Judges were not accepting the recitation of Psalm 51 or they disputed the ordinary's claim with the threat of a fine if the ordinary were found to claim fraudulently. Recidivists had little option as a branding was clear evidence of previous crime and transportation was the only life-saving option. Beattie, supra. p.474-475.

[48] 22. Chas II, c.5. s.4 (1670). If convicted and transportation was refused they hanged.

[49] Beattie, supra. p.482. As early as 1676 Virginia had passed a penal statute forbidding transportation into the colony. This was disallowed by the crown as an infringement of English law. Dalzell, supra. p. 66.

[50] C.f. Bruce, P.F. *Economic History of Virginia in the Seventeenth Century*, New York, Macmillan. Vol. I. Chapter XI at www.archive.org/details/economichistory.

[51] There are no records that I am aware of that give an exact figure with regard to the total number of convicts deported to Virginia between 1618 and 1776. Dalzell cites a source for around 20,000 for Virginia and Maryland combined. Dalzell, supra. p.79.

[52] Hening, supra. Vol II. p. 510

sea captain from landing his cargo of felons.[53] England strongly resisted such attempts and held any such legislation as void.[54]

Criminal courts and the rule of law in Virginia

The first reorganization of Virginia took place in 1609 when the appointed governor was given authority to administer the law. Officially the laws of England were supreme; in practice a body of local laws developed alongside English law and the two were applied. Various local courts were created over the next one hundred fifty years, but the basic framework of General Court[55] being supreme remained in place until after the Revolution.[56]

Locally, justices of the peace held jurisdiction similar to that of magistrates in England; they heard all criminal matters involving larcenies to the value of less than twenty English shillings.[57] In Virginia the jurisdiction of these local courts extended to the entire county and as a result these courts were referred to as county courts. By 1619 there were eight shires operating county courts in Virginia.[58] The justices were appointed by the governor;[59] their sentencing authority was

---

[53] Mr. Hugh Nevitt. Source: Bruce, P.A. supra.

[54] C.f. Dalzell, supra. p. 66. and Butler, J.D. British Convicts Shipped to American Colonies, *American Historical Review*, Vol 2, No. 1 (Oct. 1896), pp. 12-33.

[55] Criminal sittings were sometimes called the "Session of General Jail Delivery of Criminals." Rankin, H. F., Criminal Trial Proceedings in the General Court of Colonial Virginia, *The Virginia Magazine of History and Biography*, Vol.72. No.1. Part One (Jan., 1964), pp. 50-74. p. 55.

[56] Scott, A.P., *Criminal Law in Colonial Virginia*, Chicago, University of Illinois Press, 1930. Chapter III The System of Courts. pp. 41-49.

[57] Excepting that English justices of the peace never heard matters relating to slavery or game laws.

[58] Warrosouyoake, Accomac, James City, Charles City, Elizabeth City, Charles River, James City River and Warwick. Originally called shires they adopted the term county in 1619. C.f. Chitwood, O.P., *Justice in Colonial Virginia*, Baltimore, Johns Hopkins Press, 1905.

[59] Prior to 1626 justices were referred to as commissioners. Each county had between eight and twenty justices.

confined to the imposition of short terms of imprisonment, fines or whipping,[60] additionally they were permitted to issue warrants of arrest[61] and raise the hue and cry.[62] Appeals were rare and lay to a single judge sitting at the General Court.[63] One explanation for the lack of appeals is that, much like the practice in England where juries manipulated benefit of clergy by lowering the monetary value of items stolen to ensure the defendant was not subject to the death penalty, so too the Virginian justices were able to reduce the offense[64] to within their jurisdiction, hear the matter and dispense summary justice. Few defendants would argue against a misdemeanor conviction rather than a felony.[65] Furthermore, as many local justices also sat as burgesses[66] at the General Court, it was quite possible that an appeal would be heard by the judge of first instance.[67] In addition to hearing minor criminal matters, the justices also heard civil cases and matters that would be heard by the courts Christian in England: sabbath-breaking,

---

[60] Justices were limited to imposing a sentence of no more than twenty lashes. Scott, supra. p. 44 Note 7.

[61] Certain citizens were exempt from arrest (e.g., a member of the House of Burgesses could not be arrested ten days before or after a session of the assembly other than if suspected of treason, a felony or breach of the peace. Also a witness summoned to appear at a trial held before the General Court could not be arrested during the time that they were a witness). C.f. Hening, W. W., *Statutes at large: being a Collection of all the Laws of Virginia*, Richmond, VA, Franklin Press, 1823. Vol. 3. p. 244.

[62] Constables, churchwardens, justices and all citizens could raise the hue and cry upon which all males over the age of fifteen had to make themselves available for a *posse comitatus* if required. Clergymen, the sick and the lame were exempt from posse service. C.f. Rankin, supra. p. 53.

[63] Appeals from the single court were to the General Court but limited to points of law or when expressly permitted by English statute.

[64] For a list of offense reductions see table 3. Hoffer & Scott, supra. p. xxxiv.

[65] The only cases that left the county were those of felony charges against freemen. Felonious slaves were tried locally and were subject to loss of life or limb; further evidence of the justice authorized to act as an English assize judge. Hoffer, & Scott, supra. p.xviii.

[66] County justices were the gentry of Virginia: landowners, judges, burgesses and law makers in the capital, sheriffs, tobacco inspectors and coroners.

[67] Hoffer, P.C., & Scott, W.B., *Criminal Proceedings in Colonial Virginia [Records of] Fines, Examination of Criminals, Trials of Slaves, etc., from March 1710[1711] to [1754] [Richmond County, Virginia]* Athens, GA., University of Georgia Press, 1984. p. xvii.

gambling, swearing, bastardy and fornication.[68] More serious criminal matters that could result in loss of life or limb were heard exclusively before the General Court in the state capital.[69] To ensure that spurious prosecutions were not brought before the General Court, county courts were charged with examining the evidence against any person charged with a non-clergyable felony. Felonies were sent from the county justice to a grand jury that sat in the capital. The grand jury examined the bills of indictment on "Criminal Day" and found a true bill, *billa vera*, or in favor of the defendant, *ignoramus*, resulting in immediate discharge.[70]

The mode of trial followed England and a petty jury of twelve freeholders was empaneled to hear the case. Following common law, defendants were required to enter a plea at trial. In England failure to do so resulted in being subjected to pressing, *peine forte et dure*. This practice was not adopted in Virginia and a defendant who refused to enter a plea was subject to immediate sentence of death and hanging.[71] The burden of proof lay with the prosecution other than in cases of illegitimate child infanticide and killing deer out of season. In these two instances the burden of proof shifted to the defendant.[72] During the trial, witnesses were called for the prosecution and defense;

---

[68] E.g., for fornication. McIlwaine, supra. p. 141. The 5 of March 1626.

[69] The solemnity of the English courtroom was far greater. Assembly members did not wear wigs and gowns and they sat beneath Van Dyck's portrait of Queen Anne rather than the royal coat of arms. There were very few lawyers in the early years. By 1734 the Assembly passed legislation that in capital cases all defendants were entitled to counsel. Rankin, supra. pp. 58-59.

[70] C.f. Rankin, supra. p. 57.

[71] Not surprisingly there are no records of a person standing mute before the General Court. The defendant was also permitted twenty peremptory challenges and if he exceeded this number was again subject to immediate hanging. Rankin, supra. p. 61.

[72] Infanticide is the killing of a child of less than twelve months age by the mother. A person was permitted to kill a deer out of season if the meat was needed for food. The onus of need rested with the hunter. Hening, supra. Vol. III. 516.

children under fourteen years of age,[73] wives,[74] Negroes,[75] mulattos and Indians, free or slaves, were not permitted to give evidence.[76] Convicted felons were generally not permitted to give evidence[77] but this was relaxed occasionally; for example, in the case of Patrick Gibling, a convicted felon who gave evidence against his accomplice. Gibling was found guilty and convicted, then permitted to turn king's evidence and branded in exchange for securing the gallows for his co-accused.[78] At the conclusion of the evidence the jury was instructed by the judge and retired, without "meat, drink, fire or candle,"[79] until they had reached a unanimous verdict. Once the jury had reached a verdict the defendant was either acquitted or, if found guilty, remanded into custody to await sentencing. Sentencing took place at the conclusion of the court session when all convicted prisoners were sentenced at one sitting. At the sentencing hearing the prisoners were brought to the bar and asked if they had anything to say. It was at this stage that benefit of clergy,[80] pleading the belly or a plea of clemency was entered.[81]

---

[73] Children of any age were permitted to give evidence against parents in charges of witchcraft. Rankin. supra. p. 63.

[74] In keeping with established common law wives were considered *feme covert*, under their husband's power and ineligible to give testimony against the husband and also Matthew 19, verses 5-6 and Ephesians 5. Verses 22-24.

[75] John Philips, a negro slave, was a baptized Christian and he was invited by the court to give evidence in a kidnapping case where the victim was a white female. McIlwaine, supra. p. 33. Nov. 30, 1624.

[76] Other than in the case of giving evidence against other Negroes, mulattos or Indians. Rankin, supra. p. 63. And Hening, supra. 4: 126-134 at p. 127 Law of May 1723.

[77] E.g., Thomas Binkes convicted of perjury. Twenty lashes on bare back and disability as a witness in future. York Res (MSS) Dec, 21, 1657.

[78] After 1748 convicted transported felons were permitted to give evidence against other convicts. Rankin, supra. p. 63.

[79] Rankin, supra. p. 65. If they ate or drank before reaching a verdict the entire jury was liable to pay a fine. This bizarre instruction by a judge was not unprecedented. In fact the famous Bushell's case, in England, exposed the problem of judges bullying juries and holding them without food and water, as a result of which the law changed and judges had to modify the manner in which they behaved towards juries. C.f. Jones, M. & Johnstone, P., supra. pp. 101-102.

[80] After 1732 there was a general increase in use of the claim as it was now available to women as well as men, and there was no longer any reading requirement for *clericus*. Rankin, supra. p. 66. and Hening, supra, Vol. VI. p. 326.

Successfully claiming clergy resulted in the now traditional branding of the left thumb,[82] often with a cold iron,[83] conducted at the rear of the court.[84] Following the practice in England, the members of the General Court could now also impose a custodial sentence on the convicted felon. Offenders convicted of a capital crime were treated in much the same way as in England. Death by hanging was carried out ten days after the warrant was issued. Hanging day was a public spectacle. The convicted person was taken from gaol to the gallows by cart accompanied by the ordinary. The sentence was carried out at noon, after which the body was taken down and buried or in cases of offenders committing particularly heinous crimes they might be handed over to surgeons for dissection.[85] If found guilty of high treason the offender was hanged, drawn and quartered or hanged and placed in the gibbet. Following common law Virginian felons suffered loss of life,

---

[81] A "Pardon of Grace" from the governor could be granted to any felon except murderers and traitors. The pardon could result in deportation from Virginia to the Sugar Islands or to serve in His majesty's Navy. The applicant was required to fall upon his knees before the governor in the courtroom and make his plea. Rankin, supra. p. 69.

[82] Also much like in England the iron was not always hot and the procedure was often merely symbolic. E.g., December 14, 1739. Virginia Gazette article commenting on the application of a cold iron. Cited in Rankin, supra. p. 67. Also for branding in colonial Virginia see: Rowe, L. *The Benefit of Clergy Plea*. http://research.history.org/Historical_Research/Research_Themes/ThemeReligion/Clergy.cfm#n1.

[83] Starke, R. *The Office and Authority of a Justice of the Peace Explained and Digested, under proper Titles*, Williamsburg, Alexander Purdie and John Dixon, 1774. p. 88. cited in Rankin, supra. p.67. note 62.

[84] Generally the information supplied by the courts is limited and does not detail the crime or the sentencing. E.g., in the case of manslaughter against William Reade, a fourteen-year-old boy, the court document records "Reade was guilty of Manflaughter who being asked what hee had to fay for himfelfe that he ought not to dy demaned his Clergy wherevppon hee was delivered to the ordinary." McIlwaine, supra, p.184. 24 {date of} January A 1628. Brydon, G.M. *Religious Life in Virginia in the Seventeenth Century*, Williamsburg, 1957 at p. 19 makes the comment that the governor was the Ordinary. I cannot find any other references to this that would either confirm or refute this statement.

[85] In keeping with English practice where since 1540 Henry VIII permitted four executed murderers a year to be handed over to Surgeons Hall for public dissection, Anthony Dittond (Ditton, Dissond) was hanged in Williamsburg for the murder of William Evans on the 24th of November 1738 and his remains were handed over to surgeons for dissection. *Virginia Gazette*. 11/24/1738 p.41. The Murder Act 1752 extended this provision to permit the dissection of all executed murderers.

loss of chattels, loss of estate and corruption of blood.[86] As the volume of cases coming before the General Court increased from 1710 onwards, a court of oyer and terminer[87] operated in Williamsburg in June and December each year to relieve the General Court of some of its workload. Since Virginia was subject to English law, appeals from the General Court lay with the Privy Council in London. In reality appeals to London were rare.[88]

One significant difference between the courts of England and those of Virginia is that trials against freemen felons were always heard in the capital.[89] In England most serious criminal matters, including those that attracted the death penalty, were regularly heard in the county before assize justices travelling on circuit from the King's Bench. By the end of the sixteenth century, England had developed a class of professional paid judges who were trained in the law and had served as lawyers before elevation to the bench. This was never the case in Virginia and the local justices were more closely identifiable with English magistrates albeit, confusingly, they are frequently referred to as judges. Colonial justices had extensive civil jurisdiction and an assumed ecclesiastical jurisdiction[90] but they were never authorized to decide cases involving loss of life or limb. In reality, the colonial justices had judicial authority greater than the English justice of the peace but less than that of the professional assize judge. However,

---

[86] No ancestor, heir or posterity.
[87] Oyer and terminer was initially developed in England to provide a speedy trial for felons who prior to the creation could wait months (even years) before justices arrived to hear criminal cases.
[88] Scott, supra. p. 47.
[89] After 1692 cases involving felonious slaves were heard by special oyer and terminer commission of the governor by county justices. Cases were heard without a jury and the justices were empowered to pronounce the death sentence. Scott, supra. p. 47.
[90] "The General Court hath, by our Law, universal Jurisdiction over all persons, and in all Causes, ecclesiastic and civil." Scott. Supra. p. 239. Ecclesiastic courts had become unpopular in England and they were abolished in 1640. Virginia recognized the procedures of England whereby a person was excommunicated first and then put before the civil tribunals but this method (after consultation with the governor) was never adopted in Virginia. C.f. Scott. supra. p. 254.

unlike the English counterparts, the colonial county court never heard matters on indictment and all criminal cases came before it by presentment; juries, constables, churchwardens and sworn presenters could all make presentments.[91] Presentment ordinarily resulted in conviction but could be avoided if the defendant elected for jury trial.[92] One feature common to Virginia and England was that local magistrates performed their functions without pay; whereas judges were remunerated. Throughout the colonial period, the superior criminal courts of Virginia always remained in the capital despite periodic attempts to create county courts of superior jurisdiction.[93]

In order that the courts functioned efficiently it was necessary to import a number of other officials into the framework of Virginian criminal justice. The office of sheriff, in England a one-year, renewable, royal appointment, traversed the Atlantic and appeared in Virginia as the provost marshal.[94] The functions were very similar in both countries; sheriffs had responsibility for tax collection, summoning a jury, the custody of prisoners awaiting trial and acting as court bailiffs during criminal trials. The colonists also brought constables with them, but unlike England where they were locally appointed, in Virginia they were appointed by the governor. Constables usually served in office for one year. In England where the position of constable was derided and frequently performed by paid substitutes who were often unwilling or incapable of undertaking the duty, in Virginia they were paid and had a greater sphere of responsibility than in the English model.[95] Both sheriffs and constables had authority to demand the assistance of

---

[91] Presentment resembled the English leet procedures more closely than indictment. Unlike the leet, Virginia county courts permitted jury trial.
[92] Chapin, B., *Criminal Justice in Colonial America 1606-1660*, Athens, GA, University Press of Georgia, 1983. p. 85.
[93] Hoffer & Scott, supra. p. xvii.
[94] Once counties were established the name reverted back to sheriff.
[95] Chapin, supra. p. 96.

citizens in making an arrest and failure to do so could result in a fine. All citizens were responsible for apprehending felons caught *in flagrante*. However, the normal method of arrest was by warrant following a complaint laid before a magistrate by an aggrieved citizen. Following English law it seems that habeas corpus was respected in Virginia and there are no recorded cases of unlawful detention without trial.[96]

In the fledgling colony of Virginia the community was in need of direction, leadership and legal order and it appears that the early settlers were comfortable to concede power, and a large amount of discretion, to their local justices. The administration of justice was a parochial affair; juries comprised local citizens,[97] courthouses were small and allowed the community easy visual access to the proceedings and actors. Sentences were swiftly applied, fines were often paid in tobacco and corporal punishment was conducted immediately and in public. Society was in direct contact with its legal system and the close proximity and public nature of proceedings confirmed the legitimacy of the justices' actions. In the diverse society of colonial Virginia county courts provided a form of neutrality where kinship and reputation[98]

---

[96] Scott, supra. p. 58.

[97] Sheriffs were ordered by the justice to bring twelve male freeholders, whose property must be valued at fifty pounds sterling or more. Refusal to serve was punishable with a fine of two hundred pounds of tobacco. Hoffer & Scott, supra. p. xxiii.

[98] E.g., Slander prosecutions were one way of demonstrating the enforcement of standards of behavior. C.f. Snyder, T., Legal History of the Colonial South: Assessment and Suggestions, *The William and Mary Quarterly*, Third Series, Vol. 50, No. 1. Law and Society in Early America (Jan., 1993), p. 25. Also, e.g., the case against Richard Evers for slander of captain William Epps. Gen. Court. xxjth of June 1624. McIlwaine. Supra. p. 15. Also in 1624 Richard Barnes was sentenced to have his weapons removed and his tongue bored through and then to pass a guard of forty men to be "butted" by each and then outlawed from the fort for speaking ill of the governor. Scott. Supra. p. 181-182 and at V.M.H. I. 229. Anne Gaskine alleged that the child of Anne and Richard Foster had not been born of wedlock and on April 15, 1641 Gaskine was sentenced to ten lashes for her libel. She refused to accept the punishment of the court and the sheriff was ordered to impose ten then fifteen then twenty lashes every week until she apologized for her behavior. It is not known at what point Gaskine accepted the

were as much a part of criminal proceedings as evidence and procedure. Justices were drawn from the social elite; however, this planter aristocracy held themselves accountable to the courts in the same way as every other citizen[99] so that the role and function of the

---

sentence. *Lower Norfolk County Minutes Book 1637-1648,* p. 98. For further instances of slander cases see Scott. Supra. p. 182 and note 99.

[99] E.g., the range of people brought before the courts included not only offenders but also sheriffs, churchwardens and the justices themselves who had failed to secure the presence of witnesses or defendants. A justice was removed from office for slander, Scott, supra. p. 184. Again in 1702 Mr. Justice Byrd was removed from office for publishing a scandalous report that alleged the king was about to raise taxes in the colony. In 1676 in response to the number of justices who came to court drunk a law was passed to fine justices 500 lbs of tobacco rising to 2000 lbs of tobacco and removal from office for a third offense, Scott. Supra. p. 256. Ministers and churchmen persistently drunk were to lose half a year's salary. Ibid. members of the general assembly were also fined for drunkenness. Ibid. Gregroy Glasnock was brought before the Richmond County Court in 1721 for assisting his father flee from a murder scene. The court noted his standing in the community and took no further action against him. Richmond Court Proceedings, RCP. January 1723/24. Hoffer & Scott. supra pp. 59-60. In 1727 a justice acted as surety in the case he was hearing. Justice William Downman removed himself from the bench in the case against Thomas Livack in order that he could act as surety in the bond that he had set against the defendant. Hoffer & Scott. supra. p. xxi. In February 1723 Justice John Tarpley stood down from the bench to bond himself for good behavior after he had been indicted for swearing. On the same day fellow justice Gregory Hinch bound himself over for twelve months to be of good behavior. From the same bench justices Charles Barber and Robert Tomlin bound themselves over for notorious swearing. John Metcalfe, surveyor and justice, was fined fifteen shillings at the same hearing for his failure to clear and repair a bridge as ordered to do so by fellow justice John Tarpley. The final justice to appear before his fellow justices on February 7 1722/23 was Joseph Belfeild (sic) who with John Metcalfe had failed to clear and repair a bridge as ordered to do so by the bench. Belfeild was also fined fifteen shillings. RCP February 1722/23. Hoffer & Scott. supra. pp. 47-50. In 1723 Rawleigh Chinn ran from the courthouse and was captured outside by the sheriff. Chinn was whipped immediately and the members of the public who failed to assist the sheriff were brought before the justice concerned and fined on the spot. RCP, 53-5 (1723). The justices were often liberal in how they applied the laws; for example, decriminalization of felony to misdemeanor but also reducing a crime in exchange for information against other defendants. E.g., in 1734 Anthony Dent had his charge of grand larceny reduced to petty larceny after he agreed to give evidence against a group of men suspected of stealing tobacco. Dent was given twenty-five lashes for the misdemeanor theft. RCP January 1734/35. Hoffer & Scott. supra. pp. 152-153. In 1715 a constable, Thomas Reeves, was fined 500 lbs of tobacco by Justice John Tarpley for failing to execute warrants. RCP March 1715/16 Hoffer & Scott. supra. pp. 22-23. In April 1719 a sheriff, Henry Ward, was fined twenty shillings for failing to summon a jury. RCP April, 1719. Hoffer & Scott. supra. p. 35. Daniel McCarty was fined 500 lbs of tobacco for unlawfully voting at an election. Sheriff Daniel McCarty was also fined 500 lbs of tobacco for failing to prevent the fraud. RCP. August 2, 1721. Hoffer & Scott. supra. p. 43-44. Even ministers were not

courts matured over time through use to provide much more than a means of redress for civil and minor criminal wrongs. The county courts of Virginia were a center point of social life that brought stability and obedience[100] to society as a whole.[101] Judicial discretion was a key ingredient in this mix in a frontier region where the resources of a sophisticated city were not available to the administration of justice. County justices needed to be flexible and operate with a degree of neighborly consent considerably greater than that required in London. In Virginia the courts were agents of social control for legitimate society and criminals alike.

The fate of criminals in colonial Virginia largely depended upon where they appeared for trial. If they confessed, they could put themselves upon the country and have Ch 3 a jury trial or they could elect to have the matter tried summarily before a single county justice. If suspected of a felony the defendant would appear before an examining court where the justice might: acquit, bind the matter over for indictment and trial before the General Court or reduce the charge and dispose of the matter in the county court.[102] It is these last two courses of action that most closely resemble the application and manipulation of benefit of clergy that was becoming common practice in England: offense reduction to avoid capital punishment trial or offense reduction at trial.[103]

---

immune from prosecution for morality offenses and a notoriously drunk clergyman in addition to losing a half-year's salary was forbidden from officiating at church services. Scott. Supra. p. 256.

[100] Between Feb 1622 and March 1624 40% of the cases brought before the General Court were for lack of respect for authority. Scott. supra. p. 150.

[101] C.f. Snyder, L. Legal History of the Colonial South: Assessment and Suggestions, *The William and Mary Quarterly*. Third series, Vol. 50. No. 1. Law and Society in Early America (Jan., 1993), pp.18-27.

[102] In one instance the justices adopted the ancient English method of requiring a murder suspect to touch the body of the victim, to see if it bled. Chitwood, supra. p.105.

[103] For a comprehensive list of offense disposition at examining courts see: Hoffer & Scott, supra. p. lxx.

Chapter 4. English law in Virginia: Local variances in the application of *clericus*

Clericus and non-*clericus* crimes

Common law had developed the doctrine that all felonies were clergyable for the first offense; statute law removed this provision for murder and then, during the reign of Henry VIII, to a broad array of other serious crimes. By the time that Virginia was first colonized, clergy was admitted to all men who could read. By the laws of England James I attempted to allow clergy in cases of manslaughter[1] and women were permitted to claim their cCh 4lergy by the twentieth year of his reign.[2] Virginia followed established English law from the outset[3] and incorporated *privilegium fori* into its legal system.[4]

When a felony was committed in colonial Virginia every citizen was responsible for ensuring that the matter was reported as promptly as possible to the nearest justice of the peace or a constable.[5] In the event of a suspicious death the coroner was informed immediately. The coroner was responsible for issuing a warrant to the constable to summon twenty-four freeholders to attend the scene and view the dead

---

[1] 2 Jac. I. C. 8. (1604). Manslaughter was a common law felony but came within clergy by this statute.
[2] 21 Jac. I. C. 6. (1623) Larceny of goods valued at greater than twelve pence and under ten shillings permitted women to claim clergy as men and be branded.
[3] The matter was tested in 1624 when a master was investigated but not prosecuted for the killing of a servant. He administered five hundred lashes to a maidservant and she died. The governor and council held there was no malice aforethought and therefore no murder under English law. Scott, A.S. *Criminal Law in Colonial Virginia*, Chicago, University of Chicago Press, 1930. p. 201. By 1729 a slave owner was convicted and sentenced to death (but pardoned by the governor) for the same crime. In 1739 and 1755 slave owners were actually hanged for murder of slaves in similar circumstances. Scott, supra. p. 202-203.
[4] An interesting legal challenge was to arise in 1709 as to whether legislation passed before establishment of Virginia in 1607 was binding on the colony. See Scott, supra. p. 200.
[5] Constables were responsible for detaining suspected felons, in gaol or if none were in the area they held suspects at their own homes or placed them in irons in the local stocks. C.f. Rankin, supra. p. 54.

body[6] to establish the cause of death.[7] Accidental deaths followed deodand Anglo-Saxon common law.[8] Murder in Virginia was unclergyable,[9] so too were counterfeiting[10] and arson.[11] In 1684 the Assembly made arson of a warehouse by eight or more persons an offense of high treason. Once public storage houses were erected in counties, the law extended to these also. In 1730 the Assembly passed legislation that made any arson of a warehouse, tobacco storage facility or domestic premises a felony without clergy. Grand larceny[12] was clergyable upon first conviction and following common law petty larceny of goods valued at less than twelve pence was a misdemeanor punishable with a whipping, fine or imprisonment. Burglary and burglary committed within a dwelling at night followed English law and was punishable with death without clergy. In 1730 a law was enacted in Virginia to make breaking and entering into a warehouse or stealing goods valued at greater than twenty shillings a non-clergyable

---

[6] Even if the deceased had been buried the jury had to view the body resulting in exhumation of the cadaver. Rankin, supra. p. 52. Suicide was also a suspicious death and required a jury. E.g., McIlwaine, supra. p. 53. *X Aperill, 1625.*

[7] From the original twenty-four, twelve were selected to serve as a coroner's jury. C.f. Rankin, H., Criminal Trial Proceedings in the General Court of Colonial Virginia, *The Virginia Magazine of History and Biography*, Vol. 72, No. 1, Part One (Jan., 1964), pp. 50-74. p. 50.

[8] Defined as moveable animate or inanimate objects to which the death could be attributed. A murder weapon was also a deodand. C.f. Pollock, F., and Maitland, F. W., *The History of English Law* (2nd Ed), Cambridge, Cambridge University Press, 1909. p. 473.

[9] It was also not eligible for bail. Additionally bail was not granted to blasphemers, minsters who violated marriage laws and free white men who married Negroes, mulattos or Roman Catholics. Rankin, supra. p. 55. In 1607 Capt. John Smith was charged with conspiring to murder members of the original council, usurp the government and proclaim himself king.
http://archive.org/stream/historyofcolonia00crid/historyofcolonia00crid_djvu.txt. The first known murder trial occurred in 1609 when Sir George Percy sentenced an unnamed colonial man to death by burning (unknown in English law for the offense) for the alleged murder and consumption of his wife. Percy, G. *Jamestown :1609-10 Starving Time*,
http://nationalhumanitiescenter.org/pds/amerbegin/settlement/text2/JamestownPercyRelation.pdf.

[10] English coin was of course the legal tender for Virginia.

[11] Specific laws relating to burning warehouses containing tobacco were enacted by the Council. Scott, supra. p. 236.

[12] Theft of goods valued at twelve pence or greater.

felony.[13] Robbery was non-clergyable under English statute. Virginia adopted part of this to make robbery committed in a dwelling or on the king's highway non-clergyable. Other types of robbery retained clergy in Virginia. Pick-pocketing was a non-clergyable capital crime in England from the eighth year of Elizabeth's reign;[14] this was not followed in Virginia where pick-pockets were allowed to claim their clergy. Forgery and smuggling were clergyable and frauds were considered clergyable also but most of these rarely committed crimes appear to have been heard before the General Court rather than locally.[15] Over the course of the following one hundred years Virginia enacted specific legislation relating to hog stealing,[16] horse theft, arson, theft of free person[17] and slavery.[18] Whereas in England the common law was reliant upon a mix of precedent and increasingly statute law, in early colonial Virginia the law was shaped by local use and judicial interpretation, particularly in instances where the crimes were

---

[13] The wording followed 3 W. & M. c. 19. 1691. However the English version made it a non-clergyable felony for goods valued at greater than five shillings.

[14] 8 Eliz. I. c. 4. 1565.

[15] Scott, supra. p. 236.

[16] Guild, J. P., Black laws of Virginia: A Summary of Legislative Acts of Virginia Concerning Negroes From Earliest Times to the Present, *Afro-American Historical Association*. Chapter VII. 1699. Hog stealing was subject to twenty-five lashes well laid on, upon a second conviction branded with "H," third offense, death. Hog stealing by a Negro or slave: thirty lashes for a first offense "On the back, well laid on." Second offense two hours in the pillory with "both ears nailed thereto, at the expiration of the two hours the ears are to be cut off close by the nails." Third offense, death.

[17] Guild, supra. Chapter VII. 1788. "Whoever steals a person knowing them to be free shall suffer death without benefit of clergy."

[18] Frontier life was dependent upon hogs and horses more so than England. Consequently specific legislation was enacted by the Council to prevent these crimes. In Virginia horse stealing was deemed to be a non-clergyable crime resulting in the death sentence or being outlawed. Stealing sheep or cattle was not a capital non-clergyable crime in Virginia whereas it was in England. Stealing a domestic hog was a non-clergyable capital crime (1647), this was reduced to ear-cropping and thirty-five lashes in 1705. The death penalty for a third offense was abolished in 1796. Scott. Supra. p. 226. Negro stealing was declared a felony without clergy in 1753. Prior to this they were regarded as property and not subject to larceny laws. Killing of slaves due to excessively harsh treatment was held not to be murder in 1669 and this remained the case until 1705 if malicious intent was proven against the slave owner. Scott. Supra. p. 200.

themselves unique to the colony.[19] This resulted in quick and summary justice that looked far more like justice in England during the Tudor era than the eighteenth century. As the population of the colony increased and fewer citizens knew their neighbors intimately reliance upon statutory provisions increased and the justice system began to resemble that of England more closely.[20]

Virginia avoided adopting some eighteenth-century English laws as they were not applicable to the colony.[21] Offenses against religion were subsumed into the general laws of the colony so that matters that had once been the exclusive jurisdiction of the bishop's court, those deemed de facto clergyable, were tried before the secular county courts or the General Court. The Bishop of London was represented in the colony and his commissary Rev. James Blair[22] was given instructions to attempt to reinvigorate the status of the church when he arrived in 1685.[23] Though he was a popular cleric, there was no chance that the church could establish itself as a voice in the legal system of the colony by this time and all offenses, ecclesiastic or secular, remained within the province of secular jurisdiction.[24] Attending church was required

---

[19] For a discussion about unique crimes see: Scott. Supra. pp. 221-238.

[20] For discussion see Snyder. supra. p.22. Hoffer & Scott note that most defendants were compliant and admitted guilt at first opportunity. For the first one hundred years sentences and punishments were relatively minor and yet as the population increases so too does the tendency to impose more serious punishments. Post 1700 also sees an increase in the use of statutory legislation. See Hoffer & Scott. supra. p lxxii.

[21] Inter alia, The Black Waltham Act 1762 aimed at problems of groups of poachers operating in North London.

[22] Blair also operated the one ecclesiastic court in the colony. It dealt with the immoralities of ordained clergy.

[23] The Commissary Courts of London were very active; e.g. between November 1638 and November 1640, eighteen hundred people were prosecuted. Scott, supra. p. 252.

[24] An attempt to introduce English legislation of 1699 that made denying the holy trinity a crime was not successful. Secular law to this effect was enacted in Virginia but was never prosecuted by the courts. Scott, supra. p. 240. There is no evidence that I have found of any attempts to establish ecclesiastical jurisdiction over any crimes in Virginia. C.f. Rev. Hugh Jones, *The Present State of Virginia*, New

by law and miscreants were subject to a fine. By 1623 a single absence resulted in a fine of one pound of tobacco. By 1705 the law was far less severe and non-attendees could miss one month of church services before being subject to a fine.[25] Entertaining Quakers was never well received in Virginia and this crime was subject to a fine of one hundred pounds sterling. Being a Quaker was clergyable by inference in England as royal pardons were granted. The governor of Virginia was not minded to pardon Quakers and continued membership was subject to imprisonment.[26] By 1660 the Baptists were also targeted for unclergyable crimes and parents who refused to have their children baptized were fined.[27] Gross infractions of public morals had been the preserve of the Christian courts for centuries. The church had succeeded in convincing secular law makers to enact legislation that placed unnatural[28] crimes before the spiritual courts first and upon degradation offenders were then tried and convicted before the temporal courts. This was an important piece of ownership for the Church as it clearly demonstrated that these matters were so serious the church should deal first and then having sentenced the offender to the harshest spiritual sentence possible, degradation and excommunication, the lesser courts, by inference, could now sentence you to a mortal punishment.

Life in Virginia was unsuited to an elaborate system of courts. In 1619 the Assembly[29] considered excommunicating offenders and then

---

York, Joseph Sabin 1865. Sabin's Reprint Vol. 5. Part III. Pp. 66-70. Available at: http://www.gutenberg.org/files/29055/29055-h/29055-h.htm#Page_59.

[25] Scott, supra. p.244.

[26] York Recs. (MSS), Aug. 26, 1661: W. and M. Quart., I, 92.

[27] Act of Assembly 1660. Scott, supra. p. 249.

[28] This term has seen many interpretations including buggery, bestiality and lesbian acts. C.f. Crompton, L., Homosexuals and the Death Penalty in Colonial America, *Journal of Homosexuality*, Vol. I (3), 1976. pp. 277-293. p. 278.

[29] In 1619 it was proposed by the General Assembly that, "If any person, after two warnings, does not amend his or her life in point of evident suspicion of incontinency or of the commission of any other

holding a civil trial but these did not amount to concrete action.[30] What transpired was mimicry of ecclesiastic courts sentencing without the establishment of a spiritual forum. Virginian justices imposed sentences of public humiliation, corporal punishment, public confession and fines. Drunks were placed in the stocks or pillory; sometimes they were soaked in the ducking pond.[31] Repeat offenders were barred from holding public office or giving testimony in court. Presentment of moral crime miscreants was invariably given by local churchwardens in conjunction with the local clergy.[32] Cursing and swearing followed English law[33] and was subject to a fine of one shilling or three hours in the stocks. By 1699 the offense carried a five shilling fine or ten lashes.[34] Sabbath breaking under English law was an ecclesiastic offense.[35] The offense was committed when a person participated in activities deemed inappropriate for the Sabbath, for

---

enormous sins, that then he or she be presented by the church wardens and suspended for a time from the church by the minister. In which interim, if the same person do not amend and humbly submit him or herself to the church, he is then fully to be excommunicated and soon after a writ or warrant to be sent from the Governor for the apprehending of his person and seizing all his goods. Provided always, that all the ministers do meet once a quarter, namely at the feast of St. Michael the Archangel, of the Nativity of our Saviour, of the Annunciation of the Blessed Virgin, and about mid-summer, at James City or any other place where the Governor shall reside, to determine whom it is fit to excommunicate, and that they first present their opinion to the Governor ere they proceed to the act of excommunication." Complete text is taken from H. R. McIlwaine and John P. Kennedy, eds., *Journals of the House of Burgesses of Virginia*, vol. I (Richmond, 1905), 9–14. August 2–4, 1619. http://oll.libertyfund.org/?option=com_staticxt&staticfile=show.php%3Ftitle=694&chapter=102705&layout=html&Itemid=27. In 1634 the General Court ordered that Henry Coleman be excommunicated for forty days for scornful speeches and wearing his hat in church. Minutes Gen Council and Gen Court. p.481.

[30] Scott, supra. p. 255.

[31] Sentences were often made up e.g. ordering repairs to a bridge, repairing the church roof. Chitwood, supra. p. 90-91.

[32] For responsibility of churchwardens to present offenders, and general concerns about the lack of enforcement see: Scott. Supra. p. 71-72.

[33] 3 Car. I. c.20 (1605).

[34] Scott, supra. p. 261.

[35] For example in Virginia. McIlwaine, supra. p. 123. 6 day of Nouember [sic] 1626.

example, attending fairs, dancing, drinking alcohol and singing.[36] A limited number of sporting activities were permitted but spectator sports such as bear baiting and cock-fighting were not permitted. Following English canon law the General Assembly passed legislation in 1629 that forbade working or journeying on the Sabbath. Over the next eighty years the Virginia legislature would enact five more pieces of legislation[37] that followed established canon law with regard to taking unnecessary boat, horse and foot journeys on the Sabbath, shooting, attending disorderly meetings, gaming and tippling. Sentences ranged from the imposition of fines in cash or tobacco, or public whippings.[38] In England gambling was an offense that offended canon and secular laws. It was popular in colonial Virginia and represents one of the most frequently committed offenses alongside drunkenness.[39] The first Assembly proposed laws that would impose a ten shilling fine on gamblers and forfeiture of any winnings as well as a ten shilling reward to the person reporting the crime. Gambling in taverns was considered particularly offensive and the innkeeper was liable to loss of license if he knowingly permitted gambling on the premises.[40] Punishment of gamblers generally copied established English law; cheats were fined and infamous gamblers received corporal punishment.[41] Lotteries were prohibited in England but allowed in colonial Virginia until 1769.[42] Vagrancy was not the problem

---

[36] Scott. supra. p.252. Notes that from November 1638 to November 1640 eighteen hundred persons were summoned before the commissary's court in London. Three-quarters of these were prosecuted for tippling during services, breaking the Sabbath or non-observance of saint's days. Thomas Branfbey was fined one hundredweight of tobacco by the General Court on 6th Nouember [sic] 1626 for "being absent from church." McIlwaine. Supra. p. 123.

[37] 1642, 1657, 1661, 1691 and 1705.

[38] Scott, supra. p. 265.

[39] E.g., between 1645 and 1731 in York County four hundred ninety persons were prosecuted for gambling. During the same period just seven were prosecuted for Sabbath breaking. Scott, supra. p. 266.

[40] Act of Assembly 1705.

[41] See 9 Anne. c. 14. 1710.

[42] Scott, supra. p. 271.

in Virginia that it presented to England. Early colonialists arrived with a spirit of entrepreneurship and once benefit of clergy transportation was in force the arriving convicts had no choice but to work. Idleness was not going to be tolerated. As the population grew, vagrancy emerged and by 1672 the Assembly found it necessary to enact legislation that directed justices or constables to put vagrants into houses of correction until employment for them was secured. They were also given a whipping to remind them of the attitude colonial society held towards those who were not prepared to work. If employment was not found among the local community the offender was given thirty nine lashes and released. Repeat offenders were branded with the letter R to signify rogue.[43]

Sexual offenses often also involved matters of moral turpitude. Bigamy for example was traditionally a spiritual offense resulting in excommunication followed by secular trial. English magistrates had some jurisdiction over matters of bastardy and prostitutes were commonly dealt with by inferior civil courts. Generally bigamy, fornication, adultery and incest (never a civil crime in England) were all viewed as ecclesiastic crimes justiciable by the bishop's court; *de facto* within benefit of clergy.[44] Fornication and sex crimes amounted to a total of fifteen per cent of all the business dealt with by the

---

[43] Scott, supra. p. 273.

[44] Distribution of offenses within this category is available for Richmond County 1714-1749. The data shows that regulatory and moral crimes account for 44.3% of the total number of crimes committed. During the period justices heard a total of 423 cases, 188 moral crimes, 128 minor assaults, 89 crimes against property and 18 homicides. See Hoffer & Scott. Supra. p. lvi. Table 5. Interestingly prosecutions for offenses of sexual immorality declined overall throughout the eighteenth century. This would support the view expressed previously that the justices started to rely more heavily on statute rather than local information and summary justice. As the colony's demographics changed it became less common for people to know each other's business or even to know each other and consequently the volume of promiscuity reported to the church by neighbors declined progressively. This can be seen in the Richmond County Court records, RCP where cases of adultery and bastardy decreased significantly from a high point of twenty-two case in one year to fewer than three cases towards mid-century. See Hoffer & Scott. Supra. p. xxviii. Figure I. Prosecution of Sexual Immorality in Richmond County Courts 1712-1751.

superior courts in Virginia between the years 1622 and 1629.[45] The first Assembly of Virginia assumed that crimes of incontinency would be reported to the authorities by church wardens. Offenders would then be excommunicated, arrested and punished. In keeping with common law the excommunicant would lose their goods and chattels and these would become the property belonging to the colony. By Assembly legislation of 1657 fornication was subject to whipping and a fine of five hundred pounds of tobacco.[46] By 1691 the penalty had increased to a fine of ten pounds and thirty lashes. Adultery was considered twice as serious as fornication and therefore the penalty doubled. Cases of bastardy were troubling to local communities as they bore the cost of providing for the child if the father was not identified. Consequently women were dealt with harshly under colonial law for having illegitimate children and concealment of birth, by the mother, or other, was also viewed as a serious matter and subject to tobacco fines and twenty-five lashes.[47] Unnatural crimes were not subject to individual legislation in Virginia and existing English law was applied, thus rendering them unclergyable.

Every justice system needs a mechanism to ensure defendants are brought before a tribunal and that rules and procedures are followed and sentences are served in accordance with the law. Resisting arrest, escaping from custody or prison, perjury and bribery all featured in colonial Virginia from its beginnings and as it transitioned from a royal colony to an independent state. Actively resisting arrest was punishable with a fine and occasionally imprisonment. Escape from lawful pre-trial custody was rare considering how easy it would be to escape from the enclosures referred to as gaol. At common law

---

[45] Chapin, B., *Criminal Justice in Colonial America 1606-1660*, Athens, The University of Georgia press, 1983. p. 77. Table 3.1. and also see Preyer, K. Penal measures in American Colonies: An Overview, *The American Journal of Legal History*, Vol. 26. No. 4 (Oct., 1982), pp. 326-353.

[46] By mid-eighteenth century ten pounds of tobacco was worth approximately one shilling.

[47] Scott, supra. p. 280.

escaping from prison was clergyable unless the escapee was charged with a felony in which case it became unclergyable.[48] This was followed in Virginia until 1647 when the Assembly attempted to curb prison breakouts by making any escape a non-clergyable felony.[49] Assisting a person to escape from prison or harboring an escapee was a misdemeanor punishable with a fine. Perjury is traditionally viewed as a crime that has the ability to pervert any judicial system and is consequently invariably treated as a non-clergyable felony. A conviction for perjury defines the offender as infamous and at common law renders the offender incapable of giving testimony in the future.[50] Sentences ranged from fines to ears being nailed to the pillory post. Though rarely prosecuted in Virginia there is one example from 1639 when the Council sentenced a perjurer to the pillory with loss of ears.[51] Although transportation was a common occurrence after 1619 no felons during the seventeenth century were transported as a result of a legal sentence.[52] Returning to England before the end of the servitude period[53] was punishable with death. Criminals who were sentenced to transportation from Virginia for committing a felony in the colony were most usually deported to the West Indies.[54] Returning from

---

[48] I Edw. II. c. 2. 1309.

[49] This was repealed in 1684 when colonial law reverted back to the original 1309 provisions. Scott, Supra. p.188.

[50] 5 Eliz. c.9. 1562.

[51] Scott. Supra. p. 191.

[52] Smith, A.E., The Transportation of Convicts to the American Colonies in the Seventeenth Century, *The American Historical Review,* Vol. 39, No. 2 (Jan., 1934), pp. 232-249. p.233. Prisoners were sent by royal commission and not by judicial sentence.

[53] The standard seven-year term commenced upon arrival at the port of departure in England and not from time of commission pardon. C.f. Smith. Supra. p. 240.

[54] This was not a common occurrence. I have found seven cases of transportation from Virginia to the West Indies. In October 1701 Robert Evans was sentenced to transportation for the manslaughter of his wife. Oct. 1701. Minutes of Gen. Ct. p.154. Also in 1701 John Quidley and Edward Crowther for burglary. Dalzell, supra. p. 98. Arthur Johnson was transported in 1707 for horse stealing. Va. Coun. Jour. (MSS) Oct. 31, 1707. In 1713 Andrew Maclenan was transported for manslaughter. Va. Coun. Jor. May 2, 1713. In 1731 two boys, Matt Inglish and John Fitzpatrick, were transported for burglary. Va. Coun. Jour. (MSS). June 10, 1731.

transportation carried the same sentence as in England, death. As enthusiasm for transportation increased[55] the number of men and women deported rose so that during the last half of the seventeenth century more than four thousand four hundred prisoners were pardoned for transportation.[56]

When disputes arose over applicable law they were heard first before the General Court and then, if accepted, by the Privy Council in London. In theory, the laws of England were binding on the Virginian courts; in practice they were used when it suited the particular case and modified when not. Conflicts of law were rare as local justices invariably applied the laws enacted in Virginia. Appeal to London was never assured and when permitted it was a long process; in the meantime the decision stood and the local laws were considered applicable. If and when London overturned a decision it was accepted and applied but the general view was that English law was not of binding precedence but more of persuasive value. When ordered to apply the laws of England a proficient Virginian justice could always raise the question, which? Weight was greatly added to this when in 1681 the attorney-general of England held that English statute was not binding in Virginia unless the act expressly named the colony to which it applied.[57] What this amounted to in practice was that Virginia was bound by common and statute law if applicable to the circumstances at the time. If disputed, it would be decided by reference to the king's instructions, the royal charters and subsequent specific legislation enacted in London. Locally enacted legislation would be applicable

---

[55] The colonists started to resist the export of criminals; the first attempt was legislation introduced in 1670. It was ignored by London. See McIlwaine, H.R., (ed) *Minutes of the Council and General Court of Colonial Virginia, April 20th 1670*, Richmond, 1924. "The order about Jayle [sic] birds." pp. 209-210. After 1700 there is a clear decrease in transportation numbers to Virginia with as few as eleven convicts being deported in 1705. C.f. Smith. Supra. p. 243-245.

[56] Smith, supra. p. 238. He suggests a minimum figure of 4431 based upon interpretation of the Patent Rolls and all Newgate and provincial pardons for a ten-year period.

[57] Scott. supra. p. 31.

unless it was in direct conflict with the laws of the realm and laws created by the Assembly were binding until disallowed by English law. No acts of parliament were binding on Virginia after 1607 unless the colony was specifically included in the legislation. Although somewhat crude, the emerging judicial system of Virginia bore similarities and differences to that of England. Divisions between spiritual and secular law did not feature, many aspects of the common law were subsumed into practice and procedure, if not relevant they were avoided. Punishments were similar to those inflicted in England and benefit of clergy was immediately taken up without question. It was so much a part of the fabric of common law that its continued use in the colony was given from the outset. Like most of the developments that took place in criminal justice in the colony, as soon as the existing law proved to be unworkable or redundant it was replaced. Crime control in Virginia needed to achieve peace and good order in a society that was highly stratified from the outset. Unless the criminal community was prepared to accept the system, it could not work. Benefit of clergy provided a recognized mechanism for offense reduction that resulted in sentencing leniency that was beneficial to those on the receiving end of the criminal law and to those applying it.[58] Ultimately clericus would outlive its purpose sooner in Virginia[59] than in England.[60]

---

[58] C.f. Snyder, supra. pp. 18-27.

[59] Sawyer, supra, p. 59. Proposes that between 1767 and 1776 between one-fourth and one-third of all felony convictions resulted in a claim of benefit. These figures and cases will be discussed in the following chapter.

[60] Benefit of clergy was abolished in Virginia in 1796 for free persons. It was abolished for slaves in 1848. *Journal of Negro History*, VIII at 445 cited in Kellen, W.V. Gifts to the Society: Benefit of Clergy. *Proceedings of the Massachusetts Historical Society.* Third series, Vol. 61 (Oct., 1927-Jun., 1928) pp. 153-211. p. 166. It survived in England until 1827.

Benefit of clergy in the Virginia courts: Establishing a framework for permitting the plea

From 1607 onwards benefit of clergy was available to all white males in colonial Virginia. However, it was not first tested as a mitigatory plea until 1622 and it was another decade before the courts were faced with whether or not a white woman could claim her clergy. The female defendant was unsuccessful, not because she was a woman but because the plea was traditionally only available for use once, since 1487 claimants were limited to one use of clergy,[61] and in her case she had pleaded clergy previously. For the following one hundred years benefit of clergy was available to white men and women but never slaves, mulattos or Indians. Resistance to permitting Negroes, Indians and mulattos the benefit of the plea reflected the instability of society in Virginia. Benefit of clergy was familiar to the early inhabitants and represented a practical way of ensuring compliance with legal principles without necessarily inflicting a harsh and rigid criminal law upon a fledgling colony that needed all the labor and social harmony it could harness, without depleting small village groups of their citizens. To extend this privilege to native Indians or slaves would have been considered far too liberal and felt to reflect an implied tolerance that could be misinterpreted as leniency verging towards equity. Recognition of all Christians as equal before the law would take another hundred years in the life of the colonial benefit plea and would occur in Virginia at the same time that abolition of the reading test was incorporated into domestic legislation. Once it was accepted that any person who could read was eligible to claim their clergy it followed that this would mean not only any white male but any female, Indian, Negro or mulatto as well.

---

[61] 4 Hen. 7. C. 13. (1487). Persons "lettered" (branded) but not within holy orders who have once had clergy shall not have clergy for subsequent offenses.

The first few decades of life in Virginia were harsh and the burgeoning legal institutions needed to establish appropriate parameters of behavior that would set the framework for stable communities. It was left to the early legislators to set the standards of behavior but it was the courts' responsibility to regulate how people conducted their daily lives. Locally appointed magistrates were ideal for this role as they were drawn from the communities they served. In England, ecclesiastic courts had lost all jurisdiction over criminal matters since 1576 and the magistrate quickly and effectively filled the legal lacuna this created. With the general level of distrust towards the clergy and decline in piety that had taken place in England over the fifty years prior to the establishment of Virginia,[62] the English magistrate had risen to the forefront in defining the parameters of acceptable behavior among local citizens. To mimic this success in Virginia made perfect sense and it very soon became the case that locally appointed magistrates would become the backbone of the legal system and they would deal with the vast majority of all civil and criminal disputes of a minor nature. Benefit of clergy was always a plea exclusively available to the felony defendant and consequently it was not magistrates but the justices of the Virginia General Court that would hear cases against white defendants. In the stratified society of colonial Virginia Negroes were considered property and as such when they committed a felony it was local magistrates that would hear those cases under the provision of a commission of oyer and terminer. The logic of this discriminatory model was twofold; the defendant was not of the same status as white felony defendants and could never de facto be tried by his peers, therefore local knowledge of the slave defendant and his master was crucial to determine justice. Secondly, when a Negro committed an offense that might result in loss of life or limb, his or her owner was also inadvertently punished through the forfeiture of that labor source.

---

[62] C.f. Wrightson, K., & Levine, D., *Poverty and Piety in an English Village: Terling, 1525-1700*, Oxford, Oxford University Press, 1995.

It followed that local magistrates familiar with the circumstances should determine the appropriate compensation payable to the master and penalty for the miscreant slave. Felony cases against white defendants would always be heard before the highest tribunal as it was uniquely placed to determine the appropriate criminal sanction against the most important members of colonial society; the white freemen.

For the earliest migrants to colonial Virginia a new model of social control was required. Virginia was an original experiment; a commercial enterprise that relied upon convict labor and later slaves. To prosper, Virginia needed to learn how to develop from a male dominant authoritarian regime into a colony that would accommodate all of its citizens with equity and fairness. Benefit of clergy provides a vignette of this transition as its use progressed from application to white males, women and then slaves; each era having its own micro-development that reflects greater adaption to the emerging American legal system rather than continued reliance upon established English common law. In a new land, society would be constantly witnessing change and the need for a flexible legal system that could accommodate the growth of a new country was paramount. The cases discussed in this chapter reflect the growth of the Virginian justice system. We do not know how prevalent the use of clergy was throughout Virginia. We only know of those cases that managed to get heard before the highest court for white defendants or those heard before the courts of oyer and terminer that involved Negro defendants. How many cases of larceny, burglary or assault were downgraded by local justices to ensure the matter never became a life or limb trial we shall never know because the records of the early magistrate's courts are so few and where available contain so little criminal trial information. We do know of those cases that managed to make their way to James City and then Williamsburg, but even these are incomplete. We also know of those cases of oyer and terminer heard before the Richmond justices from 1710 onwards; all cases of benefit of clergy use from this period until

1777 are included. Overall, what we have is a patchwork from which certain conclusions may be drawn. Local justices clearly applied their discretion to ensure that certain matters never proceed to clergy trial. This happened in England not only before magistrates but also juries who regularly devalued the monetary worth of property stolen to ensure defendants could claim clergy. We do know that the use of clergy was not uniform between England and Virginia. Even though Virginia was strictly speaking required to apply English common law, it most definitely applied a local version that occasionally meant clergy was not permitted when it would have been in England; a clear example is the non-clergyable criminalization of hog stealing in the colony, another is the localized application of monetary value in the case of white defendants compared with Negro defendants. In England, the monetary tariff that established whether a matter was clergyable or not was constant regardless of the ethnicity of the defendant. We also know that the application of the branding iron was as inconsistent as it was in England; for example some white defendants were permitted a cursory branding with a cold iron at the back of the courtroom whereas in other cases the defendant was branded with a hot iron. We also know that justices varied sentences and even created new sentences without any recourse to Westminster; once Negroes were permitted to claim their clergy they were subject to receive humiliating public whippings and ear cropping in addition to branding. This was rarely the case with white defendants. As we know, transportation to America was one of the main drivers of benefit of clergy. Once it is in use in Virginia we see colonial transportation where criminal defendants are transported from the colony to the West Indies as a clergy sentence. In a few instances the defendants entered into early plea bargaining arrangements where they are found not guilty in exchange for transportation. In one case, a defendant, Evan Roberts, was found unable to read. He sought permission to be transported and the court agreed to spare his life. He voluntarily left Virginia. Additionally clergy was clearly applied in a number of cases although the court record is a single line entry that does not reveal the plea yet the sentence is so similar to those where clergy is recorded that it is reasonable to assume the plea was entered.

The availability and quality of court records

Court records for the period between 1607 and 1776 are limited. Clergy cases involving white defendants were heard before the General Court and records exist as the Minutes of the Council and General Court of Colonial Virginia for the period 1622-1629 and 1670-1676 and with notes and excerpts from 1676 into 1683. Records for the period 1630-1670 are lost. Sentences against felony defendants are recorded in the Executive Journals of the Council of Colonial Virginia from 1680 forward. The details of the trial proceedings contained in these records are very limited. Negro felony cases heard before the commission of oyer and terminer for Richmond County are recorded from 1710 forward; also brief accounts of some felony trials and sentences appear in the *Virginia Gazette* from 1730 onwards. A few cases are reported in the *Virginia Magazine of History and Biography* due to the nature and reach of the findings such as the matter against female Negro slave Mary Aggie, a case that was to become the turning point in the law towards the availability of the clergy plea for Negroes in Virginia. In all cases, primary and secondary, the entries are frequently very brief and contain a minimum of detail. The case against Edward Reddish is typical,

> Edward Reddish being indicted upon Suspition for murthering of Richard Davis was by the Grand Jury found *Billa vera* and by the petitt Jury found Guilty of Manslaughter upon which he craved the

> benefitt of his Clergy and did read and by the Governors Clemency and mercy was acquitted from burneing.[63]

The cases discussed in this chapter are in four groups. The initial series of cases comprise those trials where white males were successful in pleading their clergy. The first of these is against Edward Sharpless who in 1624 was charged with a manufactured offense for the purpose of making an example of him. He was permitted to claim his clergy for what may have been a summary offense anyway. The confusion around his trial and sentence are symptomatic of the erratic application of clergy for the following one hundred fifty years. The cases in this group conclude with three manslaughter clergy pleas in 1777.

The second group of cases discussed involves the very limited number of cases of clergy against women. In the patriarchal society of colonial Virginia, women rarely appeared in felony cases. This can be explained for a number of reasons including the general attitude males held towards women in the seventeenth century, that they were inferior to men and were most suitable to serve the role of child bearers and housekeepers. Consequently, on the rare occasions a woman might commit a crime it was viewed as probably due to male influence or the effects of childrearing. Negative male influence could be construed as an example of a neighbor in some way not controlling womenfolk; brabbling women and disobedience towards one's husband were at most a matter for the local magistrate. Concealment of birth or death of an infant might result in a felony trial as could serious injury to a child, but the instances of such prosecutions are very rare. Even more unusual are cases where those deaths resulted in a successful clergy plea. Another reason for prosecuting women was based upon the belief that they were susceptible to influence from the devil and used their femininity to lure men into acts of sexual misconduct outside of wedlock. This position resulted in the madness of witch-hunts that a

---

[63] Minutes of the Gen. Council. 4/7/1671. 252. And infra.

number of Northern colonies were to become famous for. It was never the case in any American colony that witchcraft was clergyable and consequently it does not feature in the cases discussed. In terms of use of benefit of clergy in Virginia between 1607 and 1777 I have found five cases that involve female defendants.

The third group of cases discussed is those against Negroes. No slave was permitted to claim their clergy until 1732 when legislation that abolished the reading test also extended clergy to all people in Virginia. The 1732 act should not be underestimated in terms of the changes it introduced into society across the colony. The white population was fearful of the slave population generally and had treated the Negro differently than white citizens in legislation and criminal trial practices. Local justices who dealt mostly with trivial disputes and minor assaults were permitted to impose the death sentence on slaves. This extraordinary power reinforced the perception that a slave life was of little more value than a dispute over the ownership of a hog or a piece of land. On more than one occasion slaves had attempted to assert that as Christians they should be entitled to the privileges and protections of clergy. Eventually, as we shall see, the impact of more enlightened thinking prevailed and the case of a female slave, Mary Aggie, who was charged with a felony larceny, caught the attention of the Lieutenant Governor. Quite why this particular case was identified as being of such significance that the governor should involve himself personally is not clear. However, her status as a Christian was clearly important to Governor Gooch and featured in his written commentary on the matter to the Bishop of London. Perhaps also the governor sensed that it was time to generally extend the rights of Negroes as appeasement to both whites and Negroes for the better development of an increasingly independent colony. As it transpired when Mary claimed her clergy before the General Court, they were divided on the issue and the decision was remitted to the Privy Council. However, before Westminster had reached its decision, Gooch stepped in again and ordered Mary to be transported, most probably because he feared a negative decision would result in her receiving the death sentence. As is so often the case in the development of the law, an individual defendant may not be the recipient of the changes to the law but they are often the catalyst. This can certainly be said of Mary Aggie. The volume of cases involving slaves increases significantly from this point onwards. Also from this point onwards there is clear evidence of the courts of oyer and terminer as well as the highest court actively encouraging use of the plea; in some cases it is seen that the defendant, being unaware of clergy, is informed of the plea by the presiding justices, upon which it is claimed and granted.

The final group of cases to be discussed in this chapter are those where it is likely clergy was pleaded but the courts records are unclear. They are those cases where I believe clergy was introduced due to the manner of case sentence disposal. In some instances, I have drawn an inference; for example I would suggest that the banishment for seven years of Jeremiah Hooke and his two co-defendants replicates common use of clergy sentencing in England whereupon defendants successfully pleading their clergy received a seven-year transportation term. This is also seen in the case of Andrew McClenahan where he agreed to a self-imposed clergy plea of transportation from Virginia for seven years. Within this final category I have also included the few reported unsuccessful clergy pleas: Elizabeth Blair who attempted to claim her clergy a second time, contrary to established English law; defendants who could not read when the reading test was still required; and Alexander Rigsby who was convicted of manslaughter. The court record states he was burnt in the hand but there is no mention of a clergy plea. By inference I believe this is also a case of successfully claiming clergy.

The use of the clergy plea by white males

The first use of the term benefit of clergy occurred in 1624 when Edward Sharpless was prosecuted for violation of oath of office.[64] It was an unfortunate incident altogether as Sharpless was acting under lawful orders and the trial itself was a shambles. The defendant was employed as clerk to the Council when in 1624 the English crown sent a number of commissioners to the colony to work on revoking the Virginia Company charter in preparation for transition to royal colony status.[65] Prior to his death James I had expressed the view that he wished for the Virginia tobacco industry to be under royal control and he had set in motion transition from corporate status to that of royal colony for Virginia.[66] King James had appointed a group of royal commissioners to deal with the transference of status and Sharpless was required to report to them. A number of the Virginian burgesses held allegiance to the Virginia Company and were opposed to the proposed change in status as this would likely mean a decrease in revenue for the Virginia Company at the expense of royal involvement. Sharpless was caught between two factions: his immediate supervisors in Virginia and his ultimate employer, the English crown. Upon their arrival Sharpless was ordered by the crown commissioners to hand over Virginia Company records, which he did. Members of the council objected to the proposed moves by the English monarch and viewed

---

[64] C.f. Neill, E. D., *Virginia Carolorum: The Colony under the rule of Charles the First and second A.D. 1625-A*, Albany, NY, Munsell and Sons, 1886 at
http://www.archive.org/stream/virginiacaroloru00neil/virginiacaroloru00neil_djvu.txt

[65] For an overview of the events see: Minutes of the Council and General Court 1622-24 *Virginia Magazine of History and Biography*, Vol. 19. No. 2 (Apr., 1911), pp. 113-148 at pp. 118-120.

[66] C.f. Neill, E.D. *Virginia Carolorum: The Colony Under the Rule of Charles the First and second A.D. 1625-A.D. 1685,* Albany, New York, Joel Munsells, 1886. Chap I. 8-48. As of June 1624 the Virginia Company was held to be "null and void." Influence by Sir Thomas Smith of the East India Company over the newly crowned Charles I ensured that the tobacco industry would henceforth "bring the trade into one hand" and exclude that raised in foreign lands and "to fix his own price upon that raised in Virginia." Neill, supra. p. 13. It is the same Smith that obtains the initial contract for the supply of convicts to Virginia for labor to the tobacco industry.

Sharpless' actions as treason.[67] On the 10th of May 1624 Sharpless appeared before the General Court.[68] He was found guilty. He claimed his clergy and was sentenced to stand in the Jamestown pillory and there to have his ears nailed to the pillory and then cut off.[69] At the same court a number of cases of slander were heard. These cases do not state that clergy was pleaded but the manner in which sentence was applied—the use of whippings, pillory and banishment—are in keeping with other cases discussed later where clergy was entered. Given the poor quality of court reporting during this period it is hard to know whether or not a formal plea of clergy was entered or in fact the liberal use of punishments for a wide range of offending reflects a general acceptance of the application of clergy without a formal record being entered into the minutes.[70] As seen previously, by the seventeenth century it was common practice in England for benefit of clergy pleas to become de facto transportation warrants. It would appear that the

---

[67] 25 Edw.3. St.3.c.2. (1344) Treason other than that which touched the king or royal family was clergyable.

[68] Rex v Sharpless. Minutes of the General Court. 1624-1625. May 10, 1624. And at McIlwaine, H.R., *Minutes of the Council and General Court of Colonial Virginia 1622-1632, 1670-1676 With Notes and Excerpts From Original Council And General Court Records Into 1683 Now Lost*, Richmond, VA, MCMXXIV. p. 14. C.f. Nelson, W.E., *The Common Law in Colonial America: Volume I The Chesapeake and New England 1607-1660*, Oxford, Oxford University Press, 2008. p.21.

[69] Questions relating to the manner of the trial itself were the subject of discussion at the General Court in November 1624. C.f. Minutes of the General Court 1624-1625. McIlwaine, supra. pp. 21 and 61.

[70] Rex v Barnes Gen Court 1624. p. 14. Slander. Sentence tongue bored through with awl, butted by a line of forty guards and banishment. Rex v Quaille Gen Court 1624 p. 12. Defamatory language used against the Virginia Company administration. Degraded in rank (from captain) banished with an ax on his shoulder and to return to James city as a carpenter when he was pilloried and ears cropped. Rex v Nevell Gen Court 1625/26. p.85 Slander. Sentence; Stand in the pillory with a paper over his head, lose both ears and be banished for one year and forever be incapable of being a freeman of Virginia. On the same day John Henry was ordered to be whipped for making threats to kill. Ibid. On 6th February 1625 Thomas Hatch was ordered to be whipped from the court to the gallows and back and then placed in the pillory and loss of one ear. His offense was he criticized the court for the wrongful imposition of the death sentence for buggery upon Richard Williams alias Cornish. Gen Court 1625. p. 93.

fledgling courts of colonial Virginia exercised the same degree of liberal legal interpretation as their London counterparts.[71]

During the afternoon of January 1, 1628, William Reade, a boy of about 14 years of age, stabbed another boy, John Burrows. Burrows died shortly afterwards. The two boys had gotten into a dispute over a knife and the fight between them that ensued resulted in the fatal injuries. William Reade was tried for murder. His defense was that Burrows ran onto the knife and his actions were not deliberate. The incident occurred outside the home of Benjamin Jackson. At his trial John Gay, a servant to Benjamin Jackson, informed the court that about two or three in the afternoon he was mending a pot when William Reade and John Burrows (Burrowes) came out of the house and sat with him. The two soon got into a dispute about some lead Burrows had been using to repair the pot. And

> vppon a fudden William Reade faid vnto John Burrowes oh, yo theefe Wherevppon Burrrowes letting fall his knife vppon the ground faid haue I tole any thing from thee...Reade ftooping downe took vpp the knife and therew ftabbed Burrowes in the belly below the Navell, and about an hower after this, Burrowes dyed.

The court then heard testimony from Reade who reported that he was holding the knife when "Burrowes came in vppon this exaiat and ran his belly [upon] the knife." The justices then proceeded to record the details of the indictment, one knife valued at two pence, and that "Reade did make an assault and an affray upon the body of John

---

[71] As referred to in chapter 2 at note 156. In October 1701 Robert Evans was sentenced to transportation for the manslaughter of his wife. A clergyable felony in England. Oct. 1701. Minutes of Gen. Ct. p.154. Also in 1701 John Quidley and Edward Crowther for burglary. Clergyable in England unless committed at night. Dalzell, supra. p. 98. Arthur Johnson was transported in 1707 for horse stealing. Unclergyable under 37 Hen. 8. C.8. (1554). Va. Coun. Jour. (MSS) Oct. 31, 1707. In 1713 Andrew Maclenan was transported for manslaughter. Va. Coun. Jour. May 2, 1713. In 1731 two boys, Matt Inglish and John Fitzpatrick, were transported for burglary. Va. Coun. Jour. (MSS). June 10, 1731.

Burrows resulting in a mortal wound resulting in feloniously killing John Burrows." The names of the jury members were then entered into the record as well as a single entry for the verdict of manslaughter. Reade was asked what he had to say before sentence was passed and he "had to fay for himfelfe that he ought not to dy demanded his Clergy wherevppon hee was delivered to the ordinary, &c."[72]

On the 5th of March of the same year, 1628, William Bently appeared before Governor John Pott and the General Court to answer for the murder of Thomas Godby. Godby and two witnesses, Richard Peck and William Parker, were drinking claret at Parker's house in Merrypoint on February 8, 1628 when about 11pm they heard William Bently shouting for help as his boat had run aground. Apparently the three had been drinking heavily throughout the day, Godby in particular, they did not respond to Bently's appeal for assistance. Bently managed to get to shore and entered Parker's house. Soon after there was an argument between Godby and Bently about the lack of assistance he had received. Peck stated that Godby gave Bently many "provoking words" which included calling Bently a rogue and a rascal. At some point during this altercation Bently struck Godby to the face and then hit him with a chair once Godby was on the floor. Parker and Peck then helped Godby to bed where he was heard to cry out a number of times "Oh Bently thou haft killed mee." The following morning Godby was found to be dead. Parker gave testimony that supported what Peck had already stated. The indictment was read to Bently and the names of the jury members then entered into the court record. The indictment stated that William Bently had caused an "affaulte and affray" and did

---

[72] Gen Court Minutes 24th January 1628. pp. 183-184. Of note: The speed of trial. Testimony lasted a few minutes, the trial was for the felony of murder yet the jury returned a verdict of manslaughter, and the trial itself took place just 23 days after the incident. The sentence was delivered immediately after the jury returned its verdict. Dalzell, G. *Benefit of Clergy in America*, Winston-Salem, NC, Blair, 1955. p. 97 says that after claiming his clergy Reade was handed over to the rector of the parish to test his literacy. There is no evidence I can find that this ever occurred in colonial Virginia and as previously suggested in this work the governor of the state was de facto the ordinary.

feloniously kick Thomas Godby and that on the 9th day of February 1628 "feloniously did kill against the peace." The jury returned a verdict of manslaughter. "And hee being asked what hee had to fay for himfelfe that hee ought not to dye demaunded his Clergie wherevppon he was Dd to the ordinary & c."[73]

We have no General Court records for the years 1632-1670; it is therefore not possible to know how many cases were dealt with by way of clergy during this period. Records resume in 1670 and in June of that year the case of Alexander Phillis was heard. Phillis was indicted for larceny of goods from a store. The value is not specified in the indictment but the jury returned a verdict of guilty of felony "upon which his clergy was granted" and the court ordered that Phillis should be "well burnt in the hand."[74] The branding was conducted immediately at the rear of the courtroom.[75]

On 12th October 1675 the General Court sat in the morning and during the afternoon. At the afternoon session Robert Walker was acquitted of murdering Mary Vickers.[76] Walker's case was followed by the usual speedy trial of Jonathan Dowglace.[77] He had been indicted for murdering Jonathan Taylor which the petty jury found to be manslaughter. He pled[78] his clergy and was burnt in the hand. This case was then followed by the trial of Edward Washington (Wafhington) who had been indicted for the murder of William

---

[73] Minutes of Gen. Court. 1628. 190.191.192.
[74] The requirement that a defendant be "well burnt" is not unfamiliar. Ensuring the iron is hot is a stated requirement in some sentences, particularly it would seem once clergy is available to slaves. Equally there are instances of the iron being cold and this too is known to the justices. There would appear to be no particular pattern in terms of the branding procedure and ensuring the iron is hot may reflect a particular justice's dislike for the criminal or the crime.
[75] Gen. Court Minutes. 22 June 1670. 224.
[76] Gen. Court. Minutes. 12th October 1675. 428.
[77] Gen. Court. Minutes. 12th October 1675. 429.
[78] The word "plead" is recorded in early colonial court proceedings and has remained in use commonly within the American legal system. The English courts show preference for the word pleaded.

Norcott. The petty jury found the matter to be one of manslaughter and Washington pleaded his clergy and was burnt in the hand at the rear of the court.[79]

The Executive Journals of the Councils of Virginia entry for Matt Inglish and John Fitzpatrick does not specify their age, it simply records "being Very young."[80] Inglish and Fitzpatrick had been tried and convicted of burglary and felony at the Williamsburg court of oyer and terminer; breaking into the storehouse of John Washington and stealing diverse goods. Sentencing had been remitted to the executive council presumably due to their young age. Both boys claimed their clergy before the governor and were then pardoned and transported for a period of seven years indentured service. This decision was handed down on June 10th 1731. It is extremely unlikely that the defendants were less than eight years of age as custom and established common law[81] viewed children less than seven years of age as incapable of committing a crime. Regrettably children under fourteen years of age in England and Virginia were not protected by the law to any meaningful degree until the 1840's.[82] The importance of this case is that it again demonstrates the diversity of use of benefit of clergy and

---

[79] Gen. Court. Minutes. 12th October 1675. 429.
[80] *Executive Journals of the Councils of Colonial Virginia* Vol 4. Oct. 25, 1721-Oct. 28, 1739. Richmond, Virginia State Library, 1930. p. 249.
[81] C.f. Blackstone's *Commentaries on the Laws of England*. Book IV. Chapter II, "Of the persons capable of committing crimes" at:
http://ebooks.adelaide.edu.au/b/blackstone/william/comment/book4.2.html follows established law and custom to the effect that a child under seven years of age is regarded as an infant and *doli incapax* and an adult is a person aged fourteen years and older. The grey area is between seven and fourteen years and in England during the seventeenth and eighteenth centuries children as young as eight years of age were hanged (John Dean 1629 hanged for arson and William Jennings twelve years of age hanged for burglary 1716).
[82] Juvenile Justice Act 1847. C.f. King, P. and Noel, J., The origins of the problem of juvenile delinquency: the growth of juvenile prosecutions in London in the late eighteenth and early nineteenth centuries, *Criminal Justice History*, Vol. 14, (1993), pp. 17-41, and King, P., The Rise of Juvenile Delinquency in England, 1780-1840: Changing Patterns of Perception and Persecution, *Past and Present*, Vol. 160, (1998), pp. 116-166.

the flexibility of the sentencing process in colonial Virginia. As we have seen women and children were claiming their clergy regardless of whether or not the English law was settled on the issue. Courts of summary first instance were actively substituting felonies for clergyable felonies and misdemeanors and the highest court in the colony was using clergy, pardons, transportation and a variety of corporal punishments as well as non-afflictive sanctions that were either in direct response to claims of clergy or by implication an application of clergy to the individual case.

John Oldham appeared before the Richmond oyer and terminer court on Tuesday, November 6th, 1739 in answer to a charge of murder. According to witness testimony Oldham became involved in a heated dispute with John Hutchins at a horseracing meeting at Dews race ground on October 30th 1739. The argument developed into a fight between the two men and Hutchins died of the injuries he received from Oldham. Seven witnesses were called to give evidence for the crown. Oldham was remanded to the county gaol and returned to appear before the justices on December 14th for trial and sentencing. He was found guilty of manslaughter, pleaded his clergy and branded at the rear of the court. On May 18th 1751 Thomas Smith appeared before the Northumberland county court of oyer and terminer charged with the manslaughter of Robert Knowles. He returned before the justices on May 9th whereupon he pleaded his clergy and was burnt in the hand.[83] John Floy of Culpepper appeared for sentencing before the Williamsburg court of oyer and terminer on December 12th 1751. He had been found guilty of manslaughter. Floy pleaded his clergy and was burnt in the hand.[84] John Goble from Prince William County was charged with murder in October 1755. In November he was sentenced

---

[83] Vir. Gaz. 4/1/1751. 22. and Vir. Gaz. 5/9/1751. 32.
[84] Vir. Gaz. 12/12/1751. 32.

to branding having been found guilty of manslaughter and pleaded his clergy before the Williamsburg justices.[85]

The next manslaughter clergy plea recorded occurred in 1763. In November of that year John Sims from Chesterfield was brought before the Williamsburg justices for sentencing. He had been charged with murder and found guilty of manslaughter. Sims pleaded his clergy and was burnt in the hand.[86] No further clergy pleas are entered until 11th May 1769 when James Hurst from Fairfax County was burnt in the hand after praying his clergy before the Williamsburg justices. Hurst had been charged with murder and found guilty of manslaughter.[87] Also in 1769 on the 15th June the Williamsburg justices ordered Matthias Hite to be burnt in the hand for manslaughter.[88] On the 25th of October 1770 the General Court sitting at Williamsburg bound John Booth over for trial. He reappeared 13th December charged with murder. He was found guilty of manslaughter and pleaded his clergy whereupon Booth was burnt in the hand at the rear of the court.[89] The court record for Henry Collier is as brief as most entries for the period. Unusually though Collier was not only burnt in the hand but he was also sentenced to twelve months' imprisonment for manslaughter. He had been charged with murder.[90] On May 7th, 1772, John Highwood was sentenced by the Williamsburg justices. Highwood was granted his clergy for the offense of maiming. The court record does not show who he maimed or what part of the victim's body he forcibly removed. John

---

[85] Vir. Gaz. 10/24/1755. 21. and Vir. Gaz. 11/14/1755. 21.
[86] Vir. Gaz. 11/4/1763. 21.
[87] Vir. Gaz. 4/20/1769. 23.
[88] Vir. Gaz. 6/15/1769. 31.
[89] Vir. Gaz. 10/25/1770. 22. and Vir. Gaz. 12/13/1770. 22. It is noticeable that the white defendants, identifiable due to full names, are not instructed in the option of claiming their clergy whereas a number of the slave defendants had to be advised to this effect by the court.
[90] Vir. Gaz. 5/9/1771. 31 & 33. "Henry Collier, from Surrey, for murder, guilty of manslaughter burnt in hand and imprisoned for twelve months."

Highwood was branded.[91] Arthur Johnson appeared before the General Court on October 31, 1707 indicted for horse stealing.[92] He was convicted and sentenced to death. Johnson pleaded his clergy and was transported "to one of her Majesty's plantations in the West Indies, and there sold as a servant for seven years."[93] This was followed in October 1773 when Benedict Alderson and Thomas Moody were jointly charged with murder. Moody was acquitted of murder but presented to the grand jury for manslaughter. He was acquitted at trial. Alderson was found guilty of manslaughter; he prayed his clergy and was burnt in the hand.[94] In December 1773 Jesse May from Hanover County was indicted for manslaughter. He was found guilty before the Williamsburg oyer and terminer justices. May prayed his clergy and was burnt in the hand.[95] Three cases of manslaughter came before the Williamsburg court in 1774. In April Henry Bullard was convicted of manslaughter, claimed his clergy and was burnt in the hand.[96] At the same court John Conner from New Kent County appeared in answer to a charge of manslaughter. He was convicted, prayed his clergy and burnt in the hand.[97] The final recorded use of the clergy plea in 1774 occurred at the June sitting of the Williamsburg oyer and terminer court when John Lowe appeared in answer to a charge of manslaughter. He was found guilty and prayed his clergy, whereupon he was burnt in the hand.[98] Three more clergy pleas were entered in 1775; Julius Kirk from York in May,[99] Robert Clodd in June,[100] indicted for murder and found guilty of manslaughter, and James Howell in

---

[91] Vir. Gaz. 5/7/1771. 3.
[92] A non-clergyable felony per. 31 Eliz. c. 4. (1589).
[93] Scott. Supra. p. 119. Note. 232. Va. Coun. Jour. (MSS), Oct 31, 1707.
[94] Vir. Gaz. 10/21/1773. 21.
[95] Vir. Gaz. 12/16/1773. 22.
[96] Vir. Gaz. 4/21/1774. 23. & 5/5/1774.
[97] Vir. Gaz. 4/21/1774. 23. & Vir. Gaz. 5/5/1774.
[98] Vir. Gaz. 6/16/1774. 21.
[99] Vir. Gaz. 4/22/177. 31. & 4/20/1775 & 4/21/1775. 42.
[100] Vir. Gaz. 6/15/1775. 31. & 10/27/1775 at Gen. Court.

October.[101] All three defendants were burnt in the hand. The last three recorded uses of the clergy plea entered into the minute books for Williamsburg until 1782 occurred in 1777; Zachariah Jones pleaded his clergy in January,[102] Habbakkuk Pride in April[103] and David Chapel at the same hearing as Pride in April, 1777.[104]

Clergy claims by women

Court appearances for felony charges against women are rare in colonial Virginia. The few examples we have, five in total for the period, represent circumstances in which it was absolutely necessary to bring a female before the highest court. The first case, that of Margaret Hatch, is interesting because it demonstrates use of another familiar English common law plea exclusively available to women; pleading the belly. This exceptional plea did not allow the defendant to avoid the gallows; it simply delayed application of the sentence until after the child was born. In practice though a number of women were successful in having their death sentence commuted once they had given birth and therefore for those women who could not claim clergy this was a last chance diversion mechanism for them to delay or preferably avoid hanging.[105] On 24 June 1633 Margaret Hatch was indicted for the murder of her infant daughter, Pet. The jury found her guilty of manslaughter and she sought to claim clergy. Although the law of

---

[101] Vir. Gaz. 10/27/1775.13. & 10/16 at Gen. Court.
[102] Vir. Gaz. 1/24/1777. 2 & 23.
[103] Pride was charged with the murder of Richard Tryer. Found guilty of manslaughter and burnt in the hand. Vir. Gaz. 4/18/177. 11 & 12. & Minute Book 10. McIlwaine, supra.1773-1782. p. 121.
[104] David Chapel, his wife Mary Chapel and a third defendant Sarah Martin were joint charged with murdering Joel Cornish. Mary Chapel was discharged by the court of first instance. David Chapel was found guilty of manslaughter before the General Court and pleaded his clergy. Sarah Martin was acquitted. Vir. Gaz. 4/18/1777. & Minute Book. McIlwaine. supra. p.123.
[105] C.f. Emsley, C., Hitchcock, T., & Shoemaker, R., *Crime and Justice-Punishments at the Old Bailey.* www.oldbaileyonline.org

James I 1623[106] had extended clergy to women for larceny of goods valued at more than twelve pence and less than ten shillings (upon conviction they were to be branded and imprisoned for not more than twelve months), this did not of course extend to manslaughter. Hatch was denied her clergy and she then pleaded the belly. A jury of matrons were summoned but found her not to be pregnant and she was hanged.[107] On Tuesday November 6th, 1739 Dorothy Ambler appeared before the General Court sitting at Williamsburg. She was found guilty of an unspecified felony and branded.[108] There is no further information recorded about the matter. Bridget Rogers was granted clergy for grand larceny on May 7th 1772. The court record does not specify the value of the goods stolen; applicable law at the time would limit a clergy plea to a monetary value of less than twenty shillings but this was not applied with uniformity by the courts across the colony. Rogers was branded at the rear of the court.[109]

There are two further cases of clergy that involve women, Mary Aggie and Elizabeth Blair. Mary Aggie is discussed under the following section; it deals with Negroes and the use of clergy after new legislation was introduced in 1732. Elizabeth Blair is another example of the rare instances when clergy was denied to a defendant. In her case she had previously used the clergy plea and was therefore barred from entering the plea a second time. Blair's case is discussed in the final section that deals with unsuccessful pleas and cases where the plea was used but not recorded.

---

[106] 21 Jac. I. c.6. (1623). Emsley, supra, estimates 550 women used the plea throughout English history until 1848, after which all pregnant females have had death sentences remitted.
[107] Records of Accomack-Northampton 1640-1645. Minutes of Gen. Court 192. Interestingly in the same entry [75] In a Roll No 10. 479. Former Governor Dr. John Potts, who presided at the clergy trial of Bently, was indicted and found guilty of cattle stealing. A non-clergyable crime. He was not sentenced, however. The matter was respited to his King's pleasure. The final outcome is not known which suggests there was no further action taken. Hatch was the second woman to be executed in America. The first was also in Virginia, Jane Champion in 1632.
[108] Va. Gaz. Dec. 14, 1739. p. 3. And Hoffer & Scott, supra. pp. 195-197.
[109] Vir. Gaz. 5/7/1771. 3.

The 1732 act and use of clergy by Negroes

In England restricted benefit of clergy had been granted to women by Charles I in 1623 and full benefit by William and Mary in 1691.[110] The reading test was abolished for all claimants in 1706.[111] In colonial Virginia women were not included in legislation that specifically permitted them to plead clergy until 1732, this was also the case for slaves, free blacks and Indians. By implication the English law applied to the colonies and therefore clergy was available to women from 1623 onwards. This is seen in practice above when in 1633 Margaret Hatch attempted to plea her clergy but was denied as the applicable law restricted women to claiming clergy in larceny cases only.[112] The law of 1732 was still discriminatory, however, as whites could claim their clergy for manslaughter and bigamy whereas slaves, free blacks and Indians could not.[113]

Prior to the 1732 act[114] a number of events relating to slaves[115] stimulated the assembly to act as it did.[116] In 1723[117] an anonymous

---

[110] 21 Jac. I. c. 6. (1623). This was limited to goods of greater than twelve pence and less than ten shillings in value. Then 3 W. & M. c. 9. (1691) and 10 & 11 Wm. 3. C. 23. (1699).

[111] 5 Anne. c. 6. (1706).

[112] Case of Margaret Hatch, infra.

[113] 1732 Act for Settling Doubts and Differences of Opinion, in Relation to the Benefit of Clergy; for allowing the same to Women; and taking away of Reading; and to disable certain persons; therein mentioned; to be Witnesses. Laws of Virginia MAY 1732 5&6 Geo. II. 325. Henings Statutes at Large http://vagenweb.org/hening/vol04-16.htm#bottom This law was restricted also as it allowed clergy for manslaughter and bigamy for whites but not slaves, free blacks and Indians. Also the monetary value for grand larceny for whites was greater than twenty shillings. For slaves, free slaves and Indians it was set at five shillings.

[114] E.g., Governor Spotswood communicated with the Bishop of London November 11, 1711 about the church's lack of realistic policy towards Christianization of slaves and Indians. Brook, R.A., (Ed) Spotswood letters (Richmond, 1884) Vol. I. 126. And McIlwiane. Supra. 364. Cited in Jones, J. W., The Established Virginia Church and the Conversion of Negroes and Indians, 1620-1720, *The Journal of Negro History*, Vol. 46. No. 1 (Jan., 1961), pp. 12-23. P. 13. Note. 4.

[115] There had been six slave insurrections between 1687 and 1731. C.f. Jones. supra. p. 18. And p. 19. Note 29.

[116] Ingersoll. Infra. p. 779 Note 11. References numerous sources for a discussion of these events and general objections by the burgesses to Christianization and emancipation of the slaves.

letter authored by a slave(s) was sent to Edmund Gibson, Bishop of London. The contents passionately explained the plight of slaves in the colony. Titled "Releese us out of this Cruell Bondegg,"[118] the letter's author argues that emancipation is desired by all slaves but even a modified version that would permit slaves to learn to read and be instructed as Christians would be far better than their current situation. Clearly the author(s) recognized that a plea to the Bishop of London,[119] who was de facto head of the Anglican Church in the colony, about the inability of slaves to receive catechism was likely to yield some sympathy.[120] To become literate and full members of the church would place slaves on a near equal footing with the white population and for the purposes of the criminal law would ensure they were treated in exactly the same way as white men and women. The letter concludes,

> wee dare nott Subscribe any mans name to this for fear of our masters for if they knew that wee have Sent home to your honour wee should goo neare to Swing upon the gallas tree.[121]

Mary Aggie,[122] a Christian slave belonging to Anne Sullivan, a widow of Williamsburg, became the principal in a court case that would change

---

[117] It was also this year that the burgesses passed legislation, "A bill directing the trial of Slaves committing capital Crimes and for the more effectual punishing Conspiracies & Insurrections of them and for the better Government of Negroes, Mulattoes & Indians, bond or free." *Journal of the House of Burgesses.*1723-1726 (June 15, 1723). Cited in Jones. p. 20. Supra. Note 33.

[118] Anonymous to the Bishop of London August 4, 1723. Reprinted as *The Fulham Papers*, American Colonial Section, 42 Vols. Lambeth Palace Library London. vol. XVII. reproduced in Ingersoll, T.N., "Releese us out of this Cruell Bondegg": An Appeal from Virginia in 1723, *The William and Mary Quarterly*, Third series, Vol. 51. No. 4 (Oct., 1994) pp. 777-782. p. 780.

[119] Importantly the author(s) did not take the matter up with the Bishop's commissary, James Blair, as he had clearly shown his support for Governor Gooch when in May, 1731 Blair wrote to his bishop that the slave population had grown "saucy and angry" as a result of the governor stating he did not accept that baptized slaves were *ipso facto* freemen. Jones. Supra. p.18.

[120] Gibson expressed interest in the Christianization of slaves soon after assuming the see. C.f. Ingersoll. Supra. p. 778.

[121] Ingersoll. supra. p. 782.

the law of Virginia. On November 7, 1730 Mary Aggie was indicted to appear before the York County court of oyer and terminer for stealing three sheets, valued at forty shillings, from the home of Anne Sullivan. The outcome, if she were found guilty, would be the death sentence. Aggie had previously appeared before Lieutenant Governor William Gooch in 1728 in an unsuccessful attempt to sue for her freedom. Clearly Aggie had made an impression upon Gooch as he ordered an attorney to observe the trial proceedings in 1731 and to obtain benefit of clergy for her if she were found guilty. Apparently Gooch believed that Aggie would have been entitled to her clergy if she were free. It transpired that the York justices were not of a mind to allow a clergy plea. Aggie attempted her clergy but it was refused. However, Gooch managed to have the case remitted to the General Court. In April 1731 Aggies case was heard before the court[123] and Gooch sat as presiding judge. She was found guilty of theft and pleaded her clergy. The bench was divided six to six on the question of her claiming clergy. Gooch ordered the case to be referred to the attorney general and solicitor general in England for a ruling. Before receiving a reply Gooch convened an executive session of the General Court on May 6, 1731, and ordered that Aggie be transported. Aggie had been spared her life and received a form of clergy sentence. The issue of whether or not a slave could claim clergy remained unresolved however until 1st July 1732 when the new law permitting limited clergy to all Virginians was brought into effect. The letters from Governor Gooch to the Bishop of

---

[122] C.f. Mary Aggie fl.1728-1731 http://www.encyclopediavirginia.org/Aggie_Mary_fl_1728_1731. And see Synder, T. L., *Brabbling Women: Disorderedly Speech and the Law in Early Virginia*, Ithaca, Cornell University Press, 2003. pp. 113-116.

[123] We have no record of the proceedings as court records for this period have been destroyed. The record of dates and the hearings is provided by Gooch in the Fulham Manuscripts and a copy of the Aggie pardon (transportation) order is available to view at the Virginia Library, Richmond, VA. C.f. *Executive Orders of the Council of Colonial Virginia*, Vol. 4. October 25, 1721-October 28, 1739, Richmond, Virginia State library, 1930. p.243. I have not been able to locate any records of the York county oyer and terminer trial. The earliest records of this court are from 1765.

London[124] clearly demonstrate the basis for his intervention into the Aggie case was based upon his firm belief that, "as I knew her to be a Christian,"[125] all Christians should be entitled to claim their benefit. [126]

With the passing of the 1732 clergy act[127] it meant that clergyable felony cases against Negro slaves would be heard before the county courts of oyer and terminer. The first recorded case of this nature is recorded at the Richmond Court House on Wednesday the nineteenth of October 1737. The defendant was entered into the court documents as Jack a Negro Slave belonging to Dennis M'Carty. He had been indicted for a nighttime burglary that occurred on the eighteenth of September 1737 when goods and chattels to the value of thirteen pounds belonging to Simon Sallard were stolen. Jack was also charged with the theft of a jacket in June 1737 and other items of clothing in September 1737. The court record shows that Jack was brought to the bar and arraigned for burglary and felonies. He pleaded not guilty. The court heard evidence against him and returned a verdict of guilty, "within the benefit of Clergy, whereupon the said Jack pray'd the said Benefit and accordingly was burnt in the hand at the bar with a Hott Iron, and ordered that he stand in the Pillory one hour, and at the Expiration thereof; one ear to be cut off."[128] Of note from this case is that the court

---

[124] "The Virginia Clergy," Governor Gooch's Letters to the Bishop of London 1727-1749. Edited by Rev. G. McLaren Brydon. From the Fulham Manuscripts. May 28, 1731. pp. 323-325. Available at *The Virginia Magazine of History and Biography.* Vol. 32. No. 3 (July. 1924).
[125] Fulham Manuscripts. 324.
[126] Synder. *Brabbling Women*, Supra. p. 115 suggests that at least three hundred enslaved defendants successfully claimed their clergy between 1734 and 1784.
[127] June 15, 1723. supra.
[128] Hoffer, P. C. & Scott, W. B., (eds) *Criminal Proceedings in Colonial Virginia [Records of] fines, Examinations of Criminals, Trials of Slaves, etc., from March 1710 [1711] to [1754] [Richmond County, Virginia],* Washington, DC, American Historical Association, 1984. pp. 180-181. This case should be contrasted with that of Jacob who also appeared before the Richmond court of oyer and terminer on Wednesday November 9th, 1737. Jacob broke into a dwelling at nighttime (Jack broke into a store at nighttime) and was hanged for the crime. Both crimes were non-clergyable according to 10 & 11 Wm. 3, c.23. (1699). As seen in previous chapters the courts of Virginia did not consider

took a proactive role in informing the defendant of the clergy plea and that he was sentenced to not only branding but the additional punishment of pillory and ear cropping. As the first recorded instance of a slave being granted clergy it demonstrates the willingness of the court to apply the law to all people from Virginia while at the same time drawing a continuing distinction between the sentencing that was imposed on a Negro when compared with similar cases against white defendants. The sentencing disparity between white and Negro defendants continued in the case of Harry a Negro. Harry appeared before the Richmond court of oyer and terminer on Thursday the thirteenth of July 1738. He was charged with stealing four shirts, one pair of britches, one pair of trousers, three silk handkerchiefs, two worsted caps and an assortment of knives, thimbles, needles and buttons. Harry was brought to the bar and confessed his guilt. The court determined the offenses were within clergy and presumably advised Harry to this effect[129] and he prayed his clergy. Harry was then branded, ordered to stand in the pillory for one hour and then have one ear cut off.[130]

May 3rd 1742 is the next recorded instance of clergy being used by a Negro. The case was against the slave Samson belonging to James Carter. The allegation was that Samson had committed a nighttime burglary. The indictment stated that Samson entered the home of Maurice Lynn by force and stole eighty pounds of bacon valued at thirty shillings. According to the 1732 law the value at which a felony was non-clergyable for slaves was set at five shillings. Any larceny or

---

themselves bound by English laws unless they specifically stated they were applicable to the colony. This appears to be a further, clear, example of sentencing fluidity practices in the colony.

[129] Hoffer & Scott, supra. p.188 note 125 confirms that this is not clear and they note, "It is not clear whether the justices or Suggit [the owner of Harry] *my brackets*, informed harry of this fact. They were not required by law to assist a defendant pleading his clergy. The scope of clergyable offenses at this time in the colony was confused and required statutory classification in 1732." True but a somewhat unusual comment given a law to this effect had been passed the previous year.

[130] Hoffer & Scott, supra. pp. 187-188.

burglary involving the theft of property valued at greater than this amount was not clergyable. Samson pleaded not guilty before the Richmond oyer and terminer justices. He was found guilty "within benefit of clergy," whereupon Samson prayed his clergy and was sentenced to branding and twenty-five lashes at the whipping post to be applied by the sheriff.[131] On Monday, the 5th of January 1746 Grinney (Gunney), a slave belonging to Edgeworth Suggit, appeared before the Richmond justices of oyer and terminer for allegedly breaking into the home of Sarah Hill sometime during July 1745. Twenty pieces of bacon valued at twenty shillings were taken. The offense occurred during the daytime and was clergyable subject to the value of the property stolen. Grinney pleaded not guilty. He was convicted on the evidence and advised by the justices that the crime was within clergy; whereupon he claimed his clergy and was branded at the rear of the court and released.[132] Unlike many of the examples above there is no record of Grinney receiving any additional punishment. Two Negro slaves, Harry and Aron, belonging to Joseph Morton of King George County, appeared before the Richmond court of oyer and terminer on the 1st of December 1748 charged with stealing a calf. The yearling was valued at fifteen shillings. Both defendants pleaded not guilty, were convicted and then advised by the court that the offense was within clergy. The defendants then claimed their clergy and were burnt in the left hand at the rear of the court and ordered to receive thirty-nine lashes each at the common whipping post.[133] From

---

[131] Hoffer & Scott, supra. pp. 213-214. Again we see the courts moving outside of the statute and decriminalizing the value of the property stolen so that the defendant may successfully claim their clergy.

[132] Hoffer & Scott, supra. pp. 222-223.Hoffer notes p. 223 Note 147. "Under the 1732 benefit of clergy statutes, theft of goods in excess of 5s. After breaking and entering should not have been clergyable. The judges told Grinney the opposite and granted his prayer for clergy. Here was another example of the great discretion that was assumed by (not granted to) the justices." Dalzell, supra. p. 109. Cites the name of the defendant as Gunney. According to the official court records he was known as Grinney.

[133] Hoffer & Scott, supra. pp. 239-240.

the above six examples it can be seen that, other than in one case, Grinney, all Negro clergy defendants were subjected to additional punishment over and above the statutory branding. For all five this amounted to the pillory and ear cropping and/or whipping. There is no recorded explanation for the differential sentencing applied between white and negro defendants and neither do there appear to be any objections to this stratified sentencing practice.

Unsuccessful pleas and clergy by implication

This final group of cases explores those trials where clergy was apparently involved but never expressly recorded by the court. In some instances a reasonable inference can be drawn as the sentence imposed mirrors a clergy sentence exactly. In some instances the matter will remain unclear because we do not have accurate court transcripts. Overall I am of the view that when a defendant is tried for murder, found guilty of manslaughter, and then branded this is a clergy case, albeit the sparse court reporting does not disclose the plea being formally entered.

On the 1st of March 1622 Daniell Ffranke and George Clarke were brought before the General Court in James City indicted with theft of food, from the house of justice Dr. John Potts, and stealing a calf belonging to another General Court justice, Sir George Yardley. The stolen food was valued at ten shillings and the calf at three pounds. Neither crime was clergyable. The jury was sworn in on August 5th, 1623 and the trial proceeded immediately. Ffranke admitted killing the calf. Clarke admitted assisting Ffranke and according to law should have received the same punishment; nevertheless he was apparently successful in claiming his clergy and was reprieved by the governor. The verdict amounts to a three-line entry in the court report and informs the reader that Ffranke was sentenced to death and Clarke was reprieved. No further explanation is supplied. There are few plausible explanations for Clarke avoiding the death sentence other than him convincing the court that his involvement in the crime was less than Ffranke's and accordingly the court chose to consider his crime within the range of clergy. This case represents a high point in colonial judicial dexterity as it occurred at an early stage in the development of the colony and at a time when the application of English criminal law was stronger than at any time in the future. Quite how the justices felt empowered to avert established law and decriminalize the criminal conduct of a co-accused, if this is what they did, will remain a mystery. I remain of the view that Clarke entered a clergy plea and the justices were of a mind to accept it as he had played a lesser role in the criminal enterprise.[134]

The case against Richard Williams represents another example of the Virginian judicial system straining to find its own identity during the early years of the colony's existence. On an unknown day in January 1625 Richard Williams alias Cornish was hanged in James City for the crime of sodomy. Williams, captain of the ship Ambrose, had allegedly buggered the ship's cabin boy, William Couse aged nineteen years at the time, as the ship lay anchor in the James River during August 1624. Captain Williams probably maintained that the sexual act never occurred or if it did it was consensual. The latter would not negate the felony at common law but there were a number of known instances of buggery that had not resulted in hangings since the early colonization of Virginia[135] and Williams may well have believed that a benefit of

---

[134] Gen. Court Minutes. 1622/3. 3,4,5. I believe this case is erroneously entered in Scott, A.S. *Criminal Law in Colonial Virginia*, Chicago, University of Chicago Press, 1930. p. 151. As 1662/3.

[135] Smith, J., *A Map of Virginia. With a Description of the Country, the Commodities, People, Government and Religion.* Oxford; Joseph Barnes, 1612. Reprinted in Philip L. Barbour, ed., *The Jamestown Voyages under the First Charter, 1606-1609: Documents Relating to the Foundation of Jamestown and the History of the Jamestown Colony Up to the Departure of Captain John Smith, Last President of the Council in Virginia Under the First Charter, Early in October 1609*, Vol. 2, London Cambridge University Press, 1969, p. 384. Sodomy was presumably common practice as in 1610 a law

clergy application would be tacitly approved by the court. Cabin boy Couse testified on November 30, 1624 that Williams had forcibly sodomized him on board the ship and that later Williams had apologized. On January 3, 1625 the ship's boatswain, Walter Mathew, testified that he had overheard part of a conversation between Williams and Couse. Couse later told Mathew that the captain would have "bugard" him. The testimony of Couse and Mathew are the only records of the event. There was apparently no trial as such. Most surprisingly what appears to have taken place was a summary hearing before the justices of the General Court. There was no precedent for this and it is questionable as to whether or not this tribunal was lawful. Over the course of the first one hundred fifty years of operation the courts of Virginia were creative and did occasionally create new procedures or at least circumvent established procedures, particularly with regard to sentencing.[136] This particular matter is quite exceptional, however, and probably represents the abhorrence of the court for the alleged offense. As no trial records are available it is not possible to know how the matter proceeded but at some point after Mathews' testimony Williams hanged. The paucity of meaningful court records in the case leave it open to interpretation as to whether or not a

---

was passed to curb buggery in the army. *For the Colony in Virginea Britannia. Lavves Diuine, Morall and Martiall, etc.,* London, Walter Barre, 1612, page 5, §9. This law was enacted May 24, 1610. Writing on the sodomy laws of Virginia George Painter comments: "Virginia, the first of the English colonies to be founded, apparently did not recognize sodomy as a crime except for less than a decade, and then as a military regulation. Early reports from the all-male colony showed sexual activity, but there appeared to be no suppression of it. A man was hanged for sodomy in 1625, but the authority for the prosecution remains unclear. It was not until 1661 that English laws specifically were adopted in the colony. Thomas Jefferson commented that there is no proof that English laws were followed in the colony prior to that time." http://www.glapn.org/sodomylaws/sensibilities/virginia.htm#fn6 For further discussion of the Cornish case see: Murrin, J.M. Things fearful to name: Bestiality in Colonial America. Paper presented at the Shelby Cullom Davis Center for Early American Studies. Princeton University January 16, 1998 *Pennsylvania History.* Special supplement to Vol. 65 (1998) pp. 8-43 at pp. 11-12. *Rex v Cornish Minutes of the General Court 1624/25. 34, 42 47,81,85.*

[136] A number of these shall be seen throughout this chapter, e.g. accepting a plea of clergy in exchange for voluntary transportation from the colony. I am not aware of any repeat of the extraordinary summary trial proceedings conducted against Williams.

clergy plea was entered. In my view it is likely that Williams believed the matter was being dealt with as a minor issue, a morality matter that might result in time in the pillory or perhaps ear cropping. The evidence against Williams was very thin; the cabin boy alleged sodomy but the one other witness told the court the victim believed he would be buggered not that he had been, prosecutions for buggery were unknown in the colony and the trial proceeding itself suggested a summary matter not a felony. It transpires that if Williams was under the impression he was not facing the death sentence he was wrong. Perhaps not surprisingly the entire incident has subsequently been somewhat of a cause célèbre for the gay movement in America.[137]

In 1644 a husband and wife, Robert and Ellinor Wyard, were walking home early morning from a neighbor's house when they saw Nathaniel Moore, servant of one of the neighbors, buggering a calf in a field. Mr. Wyard approached Moore and remonstrated with him. Moore was subsequently charged with bestiality to appear before the General Court. The matter never went before the General Court, however, as it was downgraded by the local justices to a minor felony justiciable summarily that could be punished within the range of clergyable offenses.[138]

At the court session of April 7, 1671 Edward Reddish (Reddifh), having been indicted on suspicion of the murder of Richard Davis, was found

---

[137] C.f. Katz, J. *Gay History in America: Lesbian and Gay Men in the U.S.A.* New York, Crowell, 1976 and establishment in 1993 of the Richard Cornish Endowment Fund for Gay and Lesbian Resources by the William and Mary Gay and Lesbian Alumni. According to the *Encyclopedia of Virginia* entry, after the US Supreme Court ruling in 2003 to the effect that consensual homosexual acts in private were not illegal an anonymous note was left on the grave of Richard Cornish "In memoriam RICHARD CORNISH, American Sodomite. Rest in Peace."
http://www.encyclopediavirginia.org/Cornish_Richard_alias_Richard_Williams_d_after_January_3_1625

[138] King v Moore. Northampton County Court. 1644. Records of Accomack-Northampton, 1640-1645. 371-372, 376. Also at Nelson, W.E., *The Common Law in Colonial America. Volume I. The Chesapeake and New England, 1607-1660.* Oxford, Oxford University Press, 2008. p. 145. and Murrin, supra. pp. 12-13.

billa vera[139] by the grand jury and subsequently guilty of manslaughter by the petty jury. He pleaded his clergy. In this instance the court record shows that Reddish was required to read, which he could not do, and according to law his clergy was denied. He did not suffer the death sentence though as in lieu of successfully pleading his clergy the governor immediately acquitted him from burning. Since there is no further explanation one must assume that the normal practice of branding by burning for successful clergy pleas was being referred to in the court record and that in this instance no penalty at all was applied and Reddish was released. As we saw in the first case in this group, George Clarke was reprieved by the governor; in this case Reddish was also given an immediate accommodation by the governor. In Reddish's case he failed to read and the ensuing death sentence was averted due to the governor's direct involvement. In colonial Virginia the governor sat as the highest-ranking judge at the General Court and therefore an immediate pardon was possible. How the governor managed to interpret the failure to read into a clergy plea pardon is yet another example of extraordinary judicial sentencing dexterity more commonplace in a developing legal system than one established for several hundred years such as that being practiced in England at common law.[140]

Evan Ward appeared before the General Court on the same day as Robert Walker was acquitted of the murder of Mary Vickers,[141] the 12th of October 1675. He was indicted for the murder of Jonathan Button.[142] The court was dissatisfied with the jury verdict as the body of the deceased was not found and it decided to banish Ward rather than impose the death sentence upon him. Unusually Ward was banished for life rather than the more commonly imposed seven years. Whether

---

[139] A true bill.
[140] Gen. Court Minutes. 7th April 1671. 253.
[141] Supra. Gen. Court. Minutes. 12th October 1675. 428.
[142] Ward and Button were runaway servants together. McIlwaine, supra. 372 and 382.

a formal plea of clergy was entered is not clear from the court records and why a lifetime exile was imposed is also open to speculation.[143] On March 22nd 1676 the General Court sentenced three men to banishment for their part in a rebellious uprising. The terms of banishment are very similar to those stipulated in England when courts sentenced clergy convicts to transportation for seven years. In this case Jeremiah Hooke, Jonathan Wisedom and Thomas Warr were banished to New England, Barbados, Jamaica or any other island with the stipulation that they depart within two months.[144] Another transportation clergy was imposed on October 28, 1698 when the General Court sentenced Arthur Jarvis to leave the colony for his burglary conviction. Jarvis had also been charged with non-clergyable arson of the statehouse; however, there was insufficient evidence to secure a conviction for this offense.[145]

In October 1701 Evan Roberts was tried before the General Court for the murder of Alice Evans. He was found guilty of manslaughter and claimed his clergy. He was found unable to read[146] and sought permission from the court to be transported, which was granted.[147] There is no discernible distinction between Reddish and Roberts. Both were suspected of murder, both claimed clergy and then failed to read, yet Reddish was reprieved and Roberts transported. Possibly one of the defendants found mercy in the governor and the other failed to or that in Roberts' case he voluntarily submitted himself for transportation whereas Reddish did not. Also in 1701 three criminals were convicted

---

[143] Gen. Court. Minutes. 12th October 1675. 429.
[144] Gen. Court. Minutes. 22nd March 1676. 533.
[145] Scott. Supra. p. 119. Note. 232. Scott cites: Cal. St. Pap. Col. (1697-98) No. 946. Oct. 28, 1698. I have not been able to verify this reference.
[146] Abolition of the reading test was not introduced until 5 Anne. c. 6. (1706).
[147] McIlwaine, H.R. (ed) *Executive Journals of the Council of Colonial Virginia*, Richmond, Virginia State Library, 1927. Vol. 2. 154-155.

of manslaughter and robbery.[148] They sought to claim their clergy but admitted to the court they could not read. The court decided to permit their transportation for the manslaughter and the non-clergyable robbery.[149]

The case of Andrew McClenahan (Macclanaham) of Princess Anne County started with the murder of John Curry. According to the General Court record McClenahan was indicted to the General Court for murder in 1707. Five years later Joan Curry, wife of the murder victim, claimed that McClenahan was now threatening her life. It transpired that McClenahan never appeared before the General Court in answer to the murder indictment as his local justices failed to return the documentation necessary to secure McClenahan's appearance for trial and he remained at large for some time. At the 2nd of May 1713 hearing the General Court expressed displeasure at the lax attitude of the Princess Anne County justices and now sought to deal with McClenahan for the murder as well as the threats against the deceased's wife. McClenahan entered into what appears to be one of the first recorded plea bargains. He agreed to a self-imposed clergy plea transportation for seven years in exchange for a pardon and non-forfeiture of his estates.[150]

Alexander Rigsby was tried for murder at Williamsburg in April 1755. He was convicted of manslaughter. No clergy plea or punishment is

---

[148] Manslaughter was clergyable but robbery was not under 3 W & M. c. 9. (1691) Made perpetual by 6 & 7 Wm. 3. c. 14. Sec. I. (1695).

[149] The court day is not specified in the Two Year List. It is known the trial took place in November. Two year List of General Court trials, November, 1701. PRO CO5/1312. Va. CO1. Rec. microfilm. It is likely two of the defendants were John Quidley and Edward Crowther. Dalzell. supra. p. 98. Also mentioned in Rankin, H. F., Criminal Trial Proceedings in the General Court of Colonial Virginia, *The Virginia Magazine of History and Biography*, Vol. 72. No. 1. Part One (Jan., 1964), pp. 50-74. p. 66. Note. 59.

[150] Scott. Supra. p. 119. Note. 232. McIlwaine. supra. Executive Journals. 329.343. It was the case that since the 1679 31. Car. 2. C.2. Habeas Corpus Act any person convicted of a felony could "in open court" pray to be transported beyond the seas. C.f. Dalzell. Supra. p. 48-49.

recorded. It is most probable, given the trend of the courts, that Rigsby was burnt in the hand at the rear of the court and then released.[151] An example of the rare denial of clergy, in this instance against a woman, occurred in October 1758 when Elizabeth Blair appeared with three male defendants; John Strickland, James Tool and John Dunabe. Blair was charged with a felony, the details of which are not recorded. Although she attempted to pray her clergy it was denied because she had used the plea previously. Since 1487[152] it was the case that no felon could claim their clergy twice and branding was introduced for the very purpose of overcoming this opportunity. Consequently the number of cases where clergy is denied is very rare as most defendants having been branded were unable to deny they had previously used the plea. In those instances where a court failed to supervise the branding or there was collusion between the sheriff and the defendant it would have been possible to avoid branding. There are also a few recorded instances of symbolic branding such as in the case of John Oldham referred to above. Elizabeth Blair was presumably marked by her first clergy plea. As a recidivist she was sentenced to death and hanged.[153]

Clergy under American common law

The cases above span a period of one hundred fifty years of pervasive use of *privilegium clericus* in colonial Virginia.[154] During this period

---

[151] Vir. Gaz. 4/18/1755. 22. Given the common use of clergy and branding by the courts it is perhaps the case that the *Virginia gazette* did not think it necessary to always include the obvious sentence that would follow a finding of guilt for manslaughter.

[152] 4 Hen. 7. C.13 (1487). supra.

[153] Vir. Gaz. 4/10/1758. 3. Note that in Scott, supra. The date entered p. 105, is incorrect. The trial did not take place in 1738 as stated.

[154] The number of times clergy was prayed is difficult to calculate given the manner in which court proceedings were recorded. Also the frequency with which county court justices reduced charges from felony to misdemeanor will never be known. Scott, supra. pp. 314-323 attempts a total number but as we have seen some of the cases have been recorded inaccurately and as Scott states "the *Gazette* is

can be tracked the development and use of a plea that was sanctioned in England then adapted locally to suit domestic needs. English law prevailed in principle but in practice local judicial interpretation and a body of emerging customs drove the criminal justice system. Records of the courts are sparse during the first fifty years,[155] but we do know that clergy was available to white males from 1622 onwards. With greater use the plea became embedded into the colonial legal system so that it was not just used but encouraged as a practical measure that would ensure males, then females and finally slaves would have the opportunity to avoid harsh and repressive punishments for a wide variety of crimes. It can be seen from the forty-eight examples discussed that the most frequent use was in cases of manslaughter for white males. Then after 1732, although not sanctioned by legislation, increasingly slaves were permitted to pray their clergy in manslaughter cases also.[156] In Virginia clergy was pleaded in larceny, burglary, arson and maiming trials, even when the established English statute law did not permit the plea. Colonial Virginia society was less stratified than

---

provokingly silent as to the others." p. 320. I have identified 53 cases of confirmed clergy pleas between 1622 and 1777, details of which are supplied in this chapter. The work of Hoffer & Scott is important in this area and represents some of the most accurate information and interpretation of data pertaining to the criminal trials heard at the Richmond County Court, c.f. Hoffer & Scott, supra. Introduction. Hoffer states that elsewhere in the colony clergy spared the lives of at least thirty convicted slaves between1733-1749. p. lxxii.

[155] Minutes of the General Court 1622-1632 and then 1670-1676 and forward in the series edited by McIlwaine, supra. In 1692 county courts of oyer and terminer heard cases against slaves that included loss of life or limb but no slaves were permitted to claim clergy at this time. Post 1732 the county courts of oyer and terminer become more useful as clergy pleas are recorded. e.g., A slave named Peter. Manslaughter. Prayed his clergy. Burnt in the hand. York County Judgments and Orders 1753. 2. pp. 323-324. The proceedings are available in county minute books. In 1736 the *Virginia Gazette* commenced very brief reports on criminal cases heard before the General Court and the Williamsburg court of oyer and terminer. The busiest court outside of the capital was Richmond and its oyer and terminer proceedings were recorded from 1710 onwards and published by the American Historical Association.

[156] This legislation was restrictive and did not permit clergy for manslaughter or larceny offenses where the goods were valued at more than five shillings. It was not until 1748 that slaves were given the same rights as whites in terms of value of goods stolen and for all claimants when goods valued at less than twenty shillings was clergyable. See Hening, supra. 6:106.

England and there was a sense that everybody was responsible for preventing and reporting crime. Laws were tailored to suit local needs so that, for example, hog stealing was a more serious crime than stealing sheep, a reversal of the situation in England. The judiciary was an integral part of colonial society; they all served on a part-time basis and most were planters and landowners, not aristocracy, who lived alongside those they sat in judgment of. These men engaged in an early form of plea bargaining to ensure the law worked; but this does not mean it was applied with commonality as frequently slaves, once eligible to claim clergy, received whippings in addition to a hot iron. Even the heat of the branding tool was itself capricious. We know a white defendant John Oldham convicted of manslaughter at the racetrack was ordered to receive a cold iron at the rear of the court;[157] no such judgment was ever handed down to a Negro. The use of clergy is symptomatic of a country in transition between an established and inherited legal system and a unique application of that system. It can be said that by the time of the Revolution America's growing nationalism meant a strong commitment to American common law and a general abandoning of the English model that was brought over in 1607. Benefit of clergy was a crucial part of this transition in Virginia and also in Massachusetts where it was reluctantly applied in its own unique way.

---

[157] Va. Gaz. Dec. 14, 1739. p. 3. and Hoffer, supra. pp. 195-197.

Chapter 5. Benefit of clergy in Massachusetts

Establishing a justice system

The second colony to be formed in colonial North America established a form of government by consent that differed greatly from the regime in Virginia. The separatist group that landed on Plymouth Rock on November 11th 1620, a mistake as they had intended upon landing south of Virginia, did not arrive with a charter formed in London but rather more a strong Calvinist faith in using covenants as the basis for legal order.[1] So strong was their conviction that rules and regulations should be binding upon all citizens equally that the small group constructed the *Mayflower Compact* before setting foot on land in the New World. The compact served as the basis for the legal system in the colony until Plymouth merged with Massachusetts on October 17, 1691. The wording of the compact demonstrates attempts by the writers to create a document that could be viewed as an early constitution for the region and it sets out the parameters for behavior not just for the pilgrims but also for the gentiles who were members of the community.[2] Notwithstanding the mixed origins of the early settlers, a significant number who landed at Plymouth were former members of

---

[1] The *Mayflower Compact* was constructed and signed on board the *Mayflower* before any settlers had landed. Ten years later John Winthrop, lawyer, minister and later governor of the Massachusetts colony gave a sermon on board the Arabella before it landed at what would become Massachusetts. His sermon was titled "A Model of Christian Charity" during which he espoused the value of congeniality and a covenant between the settlers that would help them establish a "city upon a hill"; a clear reference to Thomas More's utopian vision of a society that blended together the best of theological and secular elements. C.f. Coquillette, D.R., (ed) *Law in Colonial Massachusetts 1630-1800. A Conference held 6 and 7 November 1981 by the Colonial Society of Massachusetts*, Boston, The Colonial Society of Massachusetts, 1984. Introduction. pp. xxi-lxiii.

[2] *The Mayflower Compact* 1620. "...Do by these Presents, solemnly and mutually, in the Presence of God and one another covenant and combine ourselves together into a civil Body Politick...". Hall, K., Wiecek, W.M., Finkelman, P., *American Legal History: Cases and Materials,* Oxford, Oxford University Press, 1991. p. 11.

one Calvinist congregation from Scrooby, England. They had left England for Leyden in The Netherlands and from there headed to the New World with the hope of preserving their customs, lifestyle and religion. Nonbeliever emigrants brought a dynamic into the social mix that meant church discipline would not be accepted wholesale. A degree of secularization in the legal system was anticipated to ensure a common level of compliance with the overall underlying aim of achieving a new life built upon equity and respect for all its members. Although Plymouth did not remain an independent colony, the compact made a lasting impression upon its laws and form of government, particularly with regard to establishing the process for electing officials into office rather than by appointment.[3]

Plymouth's neighbor, Massachusetts, was established by charter in 1629 and settled the following year on the 12th of June.[4] A cohort of the early settlers to Massachusetts can be regarded as Puritan aristocracy; they were of wealth and position in England and came together through a common bond of marriage, friendship and idealism.[5] Other settlers shared similar religious and political goals, beliefs that would influence and shape how the entire group would approach lawmaking. They believed that laws should benefit the whole group and that the welfare of the community was more important than the achievement of

---

[3] For information relating to the development of the colony see: www.plymouth.us/history.html. and http://mayflowerhistory.com also Stratton, E.A. *Plymouth Colony: Its History and People 1620-1691*, Salt Lake City, Ancestry Publishing, 1986.

[4] The Massachusetts Bay Company was a joint stock company to be run by a governor, deputy governor and a board of eighteen assistants elected to office annually by freemen of Massachusetts. C.f. Haskins, G.L. *Law and Authority in Early Massachusetts: A Study in Tradition and Design*, New York, Macmillan, 1960. p.9.

[5] For history of the colony of Massachusetts see: http://www.britannica.com/EBchecked/topic/368431/Massachusetts-Bay-Colony. http://www.u-s-history.com/pages/h572.html. For the post King Williams charter period see: Hutchinson, T. *History of the Province of Massachusetts Bay, From the Charter of king William and Queen Mary, in 1691, Until the year 1750*, London, Fleet, 1777 available at: http://archive.org/stream/historyofprovinc02hutc#page/n3/mode/2up.

one individual.[6] Both the Plymouth and Massachusetts colonists also held similar aspirations with regard to the rule of law and the range of offenses that should be deemed as criminal. Importantly the settlers to Plymouth and Massachusetts shared the same heritage, former heretics, traitors and criminals in the eyes of many Englishmen.[7] A number had been subjected to the infamous Court of Star Chamber in London and experienced trial by rumor first hand. Consequently, the new settlers were motivated to create a legal system that incorporated a jury system from the outset.[8] Prosecution by powerful state machinery was the hallmark of the colonists' experiences in England and the settlers were keen to ensure that the justice system adopted for the New World would encompass the best features of the common law and not the negative aspects that had criminalized many of them solely due to their religious beliefs. The idea that the region was a Puritan oligarchy is rather severe and in reality it was likely premised upon an ideology of communal social control vested in local magistrates that permeated collective early settler thinking.[9]

Many of the colonists were familiar with the role of the ecclesiastical courts in England and the dominant role they played in the moral life of its citizens. Those who emigrated to Massachusetts and Plymouth

---

[6] C.f. Haskins, supra. p. 17-18.

[7] The establishment of the Anglican Church and the attempts by the English church courts to suppress alternative religious points of view was a significant factor in the migration to New England that began in 1630 and continued until the execution of Charles I in 1649. C.f. Jones, M. & Johnstone, P., *History of Criminal Justice* (5th Edition) Waltham, Andersons, 2011. Esp. pp. 120-123.

[8] The first statute to require a jury, in all civil actions, including debt, was introduced in Plymouth, 1623. C.f. Julius Goebel, Jr. King's Law and Local Custom in Seventeenth Century New England, *Columbia Law Review*, Vol. 31. No. 3 (Mar., 1931), pp. 416-448. p. 436 and note 35. Also p. 441. Notes. 46 & 47.

[9] For example contrast Goebel, J. supra, Chapin, B. *Criminal Justice in Colonial America, 1606-1660*, Athens, University of Georgia Press, 1983, concluding chapter and Nelson, W.E., *The Common Law in Colonial America, Volume I The Chesapeake and New England, 1607-1660*, Oxford, Oxford University Press, 2008, his introduction. Also Coquillette, supra, introduction and Stoebuck W.B., Reception of English Common Law in the American Colonies, *William and Mary Quarterly Review*, Vol. 10. No. 2. (1968) pp. 393-426 available at: http://scholarship.law.wm.edu/wmlr/vol10/iss2/7.

were intent on transferring the entire jurisdiction of the courts Christian[10] to the secular forum as soon as possible. Certainty, transparency and efficacy were the desired features for the new legal order. Locally this was to be achieved through the appointment of magistrates who would undertake a huge array of judicial responsibilities, criminal, ecclesiastic and civil.[11] Felonies would be heard before a jury under the direction of, ideally, a legally trained judge. In the early years of operation the judiciary applied their discretion in determining the offense classification and guilt of the defendant. This was soon to be controlled though as it failed to achieve the levels of certainty the settlers were seeking. The solution was to create a body of laws that were written down for all users to inspect and apply. Massachusetts drafted a series of codes beginning in 1636;[12] the most important of these, the Body of Liberties, was enacted by the Massachusetts legislature in 1641.[13] This extraordinary document was substantially revised in 1648.[14] Under this code idolatry, blasphemy, witchcraft, murder, sodomy,[15] adultery, kidnapping, bearing false

---

[10] For a discussion about the move to avoid a courts Christian see: Julius Goebel, Jr. supra. Esp. p. 425 note. 16 that contains numerous further references. Also Haskins, G.L., Codification of the Law in Colonial Massachusetts: A Study in Comparative Law, *Indiana Law Journal*, Vol. 30. No. 1 (Fall, 1954), pp. 1-17.

[11] C.f. Haskins, *Law and Authority*, supra. p. 183-184.

[12] The First was titled *Moses: His Judicials*. This code never became law. The most important of all the codes was the Body of Liberties of 1648. See Appendix II.

[13] It comprised 100 laws that represented constitutional provisions more than a prescriptive code. Many issues were dealt with in a broad sense with no particular chronology. It has been viewed as a Bill of Rights more than a legal code. It did not purport to be a set of legal rules nor did it provide specific guidelines to the courts. It does, however, reflect a strong sense of biblical influence. C.f. Haskins, supra. p. 129.

[14] Hall et al, supra. pp. 15-16. Refer to the 1648 version as "extraordinary." Their comments reflect the depth and sophistication of a document that embraced community, equality, philosophical and legal theory that formed the basis for the American Constitution.

[15] As early as 1636, the Reverend John Cotton had been invited by the Massachusetts General Court to draft a body of laws. Cotton proposed to include lesbianism and place it on a par with male homosexual acts to make both capital crimes. English buggery law had been construed to mean anal sex between two men or anal sex between a man and a woman or relations by a male or a female with animals. It had never been interpreted as sexual activity between two women. This example provides further evidence of

witness, conspiracy and insurrection were all felonies punishable with death.[16] Making adultery and idolatry capital crimes represented a significant departure from English law. In keeping with the settlers' intentions to treat all of its congregation as equal, regardless of their status or domicile, the code provided that all defendants should receive the same legal protections.[17] Since many of the emigrants knew firsthand the partiality of English law, they held a profound distrust of it. This translated into a criminal law that was a fusion of the ideals enunciated in the Plymouth compact and the enactment of rules laid down in the first five books of the Old Testament. The result was a conscious move away from the English version of common law towards a new adaptation, one that would inform the development of precedent and customs pertinent to Plymouth and Massachusetts. The Puritans had no intention of replicating the common law of England; rather more they sought to develop a system of criminal justice that reflected respect for the Old Testament as well as the opportunity to create a new justice system that depended upon elected professionals who

---

the ways in which the early settlers were set upon rewriting established common law to suit local religious aspirations. C.f. Crompton, L., Homosexuals and the death Penalty in Colonial America, *Journal of Homosexuality*, Vol. I. No. 3. 1976. pp. 277-293. p. 278. Although Cotton's proposals were not taken up once the Body of Laws was adopted, it still varied from English law in a number of ways especially with regard to sodomy which, contrary to English law, was a capital crime for both of the participants. Crompton, supra. p. 279.

[16] Cursing or smiting a parent, rape, idolatry, stubbornness or rebelliousness by a son against his parents and murder by poisoning were also all capital crimes under the code. Manslaughter is not a biblical term and was not utilized by Ward and Winthrop as they drafted the code.

[17] Interestingly these were similar concepts as the reformers in England sought during the Interregnum: local courts for small causes, pleading in English, the adoption of civil marriages to end the stranglehold the Church had over marriage and intestacy issues, the right to counsel for all felony defendants, the death sentence for adultery and the abolition of benefit of clergy. C.f. Haskins, supra. p. 191. In 1650 Cromwell succeeded in passing a law, the adultery Act a.k.a Puritan Act, that made fornicators liable to three months' imprisonment on first conviction and death on the second. This law was repealed with the Restoration. May 1650: An Act for suppressing the detestable sins of Incest, Adultery and Fornication, *Acts and Ordinances of the Interregnum, 1642-1660* (1911), pp. 387-389. URL: http://www.british-history.ac.uk/report.aspx?compid=56399.

would, over time, create a body of reference material and practice specific to the needs and beliefs of the people of the two colonies.[18]

For the first twenty years, the settlers relied heavily upon locally appointed magistrates to apply the law. This system accommodated a significant degree of discretion to the justices to the point where it could be viewed as autocratic. During the late 1630's Nathaniel Ward, a lawyer trained in England and a minister, drafted a code of laws, the Body of Liberties. It was adopted in 1641. This work represents the first codification of laws in America and remains a reference point for legislation and the embodiment of what today is termed due process. The code articulates what actions are criminal and stipulates the punishment applicable to each specific crime. It also formalized the assumption of jurisdiction over marriage and divorce by the government of Massachusetts.[19] Although the code closely follows the bible it also differs. In many respects it can be seen as a re-interpretation of English common law on biblical principles; for example, the code develops early concepts such as *mens rea*, premeditation and conspiracy, issues in contemporary criminal law that did not exist in the bible.[20] One might question how it was possible for two small colonies to enact a body of laws that were clearly and deliberately different from the laws of England. Given the period of time when this occurred, England was being governed by a monarch who had disbanded Parliament and the country was moving towards civil war, it is most likely that Westminster was preoccupied with domestic issues and was either not interested or simply did not pay

---

[18] For commentary on the similarities and differences between the biblical codes and the Body of Liberties, see: Jones & Johnstone, supra. pp. 123-124.

[19] Making marriage a civil ceremony was a significant move away from established, church dominated, practice in England. Marriage had been a simple exchange of vows between the parties since 1621. The Code was a formalization of practice. The next step was assumption of jurisdiction over divorce; this too was achieved. C.f. Haskins. Supra. p. 194-195.

[20] Jones & Johnstone, supra. pp. 123.

particular attention to the moves abroad. In England this would be followed in due course by growing support for major legislative reform.

The interregnum period, 1649-1660, was a time when England sought to establish republican government. At the vanguard of this movement were the Levellers and the Fifth Monarchists, who believed that laws should be subject to reason. They also wanted legislation that conformed to Holy Scripture[21] and biblical practices. To these ends the newly written Massachusetts code looked an attractive model. In 1653 the English parliament appointed a Committee on Law Reform to consider adoption of the proposals. Bipartisanship and disputes within the Levellers movement resulted in the proposal being dropped. Although England soon returned to a monarchy, the impact of the reformists was important in terms of driving forward an agenda for fundamental human rights and the provision of a statutory basis for the prosecution and punishment of criminals. It was also successful in achieving abolition of the Courts of High Commission, the Star Chamber and revitalizing the desire for a written constitution.[22]

Egalitarianism was a key feature of the Body of Laws and consequently there is no mention of benefit of clergy in the code.[23] As we shall see, this does not mean, however, that the clergy plea did not exist, for as seen in colonial Virginia, it was possible to incorporate clergy through judicial discretion and sentencing procedures; this was especially so in the first fifty years of the two northern colonies' existence. It is also reasonable to propose that the application of clergy in England had

---

[21] A proposed statute made adultery and incest capital crimes. Jones & Johnstone, supra, p.99.
[22] C.f. Cotterell, M., Interregnum Law Reform: the Hale Commission of 1652, *English Historical Review*, Vol. 83. No. 329 (Oct., 1968), pp. 689-704., Shapiro, B., Law Reform in Seventeenth Century England, *The American Journal of Legal History*, Vol. 19. No. 4 (Oct., 1975), pp. 280-312. and Jones & Johnstone, supra. pp. 99-101. Also re John Lilburne www.british-history.ac.uk/subject.aspx?subject+6&gid=44 and www.british-history.ac.uk/subject.aspx?subject+6&gid=43.
[23] Preyer, K., Penal Measures in the American Colonies: An Overview, *The American Journal of Legal History*, Vol. 26, No. 4 (Oct., 1982), pp. 326-353. p. 333 and note. 12.

been capricious to say the least. Felons with varying degrees of literacy had escaped the criminal law for centuries. This represented a particularly strong objection for the Puritans who may well have viewed clergy as further evidence of a worn out system; one that failed to effectively treat defendants with equal rights and failed to provide certainty of punishment, a system that instead relied upon the ability of a person to read or at least pretend that they could.[24]

In an era of rapidly developing societies,[25] when communities of primitive settlements became major urban cities within a few decades,[26] legal and social growth needed to be flexible and responsive. The early settlers found much of value in the English traditions and legal system; they also resented and distrusted much due to their own personal persecution. Not surprisingly over the course of the first one hundred fifty years of existence the legal systems of Plymouth and Massachusetts would change a great deal. Elements of the English system, initially discarded, would be taken up again[27] after the early enthusiasm for experimentation gave way to a more tolerant and mature criminal justice system in the eighteenth century.

Society was stratified in Plymouth and Massachusetts[28] and the law reflected these differences; the behavior of women, children, slaves and

---

[24] This was also one of the primary objections the Levellers had to the continuation of clergy in England. Jones & Johnstone *supra.* p. 100.

[25] 44,000 in 1691 to 280,000 1765. Source: Coquillette. supra. p. xxxvii.

[26] It is noted that emigration actually decreased during the English Civil War period 1642-1651. See Coquillette. supra. p. xxxii.

[27] Giddings v Brown 1657 is an example of where the Massachusetts Court of Assistants for Essex County used established English law and made references to legal opinion written by Sir Henry Finch, Recorder of London. C.f. Hall, supra. pp. 25-26.

[28] Haskins, supra, estimates that of the group who arrived with Winthrop a tenth were above the rank of yeoman and of this tenth nobility was non-existent. He believes that the first settlers were mainly drawn from the lower and middle classes with a small percentage of the gentry. Many were of some substance in terms of wealth. Haskins refers to five social classes in Massachusetts in the early years. Haskins, supra, p. 98-99. His opinion should be contrasted with the fact that Winthrop and at least five of the Scrooby settlers were from the English gentry and they soon moved themselves into positions

freemen was regulated by laws that did not extend full political or legal capacity to many members of society. The criminal law served numerous purposes: behavioral regulation, economic order and policing of morals.[29] In effect it encompassed the full array of social controls deemed necessary by Freeman male elders to establish their view of good order upon the community, a legal order that in lieu of a police force was dependent upon private citizens taking an active part in the reporting of community members who failed to adhere to proscribed codes of conduct. The basis for the establishment of the settlers' legal system was biblical communalism, a congregation of people with ordained leaders who orchestrated a living compact between neighbors and families. One commentator is of the opinion that "notwithstanding their substantial reliance upon traditional legal ideas, the colony leaders felt free...to adopt legal rules"[30] based upon the principles upon which the colony was founded. This would inevitably change over time as economic opportunity and greater secularization within society pressurized communities to modify their original goals in light of changing conditions.[31] What had started as a homogenous group in the early years of settlement had become a highly litigious society towards the end of the seventeenth century.[32] Material possession acquisition and a decrease in piety have been

---

of authority within the colony. For further information relating to the social mix of the early Plymouth and Massachusetts settlers see: Stratton, supra and www.plymouth.us/history.html, http://mayfloweristory.com, www.britannica.com, www.ushistory.com/pages/h572.html

[29] For example it was not only criminal and moral behavior that was regulated under the 1648 Laws. The code extended to the regulation of marking casks used to transport liquor and it empowered local magistrates with authority to appoint a gauger and pay that person four pence for every tun appropriately marked. Hall, supra. pp. 49-50.

[30] Haskins, supra. p. 114.

[31] Church enrollments generally plummeted over the period 1629-1682. E.g. Salem 1682 only 17% of listed ratepayers were members of a congregation. Source: Konig, infra. p.91. and see the examples cited by Konig, D.T., *Law and Society in Puritan Massachusetts: Essex County, 1629-1692.* Chapel Hill, University of North Carolina Press, 1979. pp. 93-96 of personal liberties being protected *from* the church; 1657 Ipswich Town Meeting re Cobbet and 1661 Ipswich Court re. Longley.

[32] Konig, supra. Between 1672 and 1686 2,942 court cases were heard in Essex County from a community of just 2,000 males. This averages more than 200 cases per year. Konig. p. xi.

viewed by some commentators as the primary factors in stimulating these societal and legal changes;[33] others view the law and legal institutions as drivers of the new paradigm.[34] Perhaps it was always the case that no matter how motivated the Puritan leaders were to establish a biblical utopia, the reality was that the mix of new settlers was sufficiently diverse that the people themselves were not unanimously sympathetic towards Congregationalism. In fact it was discovered, to the dismay of leaders such as John Endecott and Samuel Skelton,[35] that only thirty of two hundred people living at the Bay in 1629 signed the covenant when presented to them. In a sense it was all forms of oppressive authority that many settlers were hoping to leave behind and the rigidity of the proposed legal order was potentially as stringent and repressive as the systems they had emigrated from. What was needed, and eventually achieved, was a compromise. Egalitarian utopias were philosophically attractive but the early leaders were pragmatic enough to recognize that rescuing fellow citizens from sinfulness was a prerequisite to a colony of goodness. In early Massachusetts, the ministers were to be the mouth of the law and magistrates the controlling hand.

Given the history of magisterial intervention in the classification and sentencing of crimes in England, it was most likely there would be significant adaptations to legal formalities and procedures in the New World. Despite the church leaders' distain for the clergy plea it seemed inevitable that it would manifest in Massachusetts. Many of the achievements in the law were at the expense of personal freedom in the sense that the settlers' lives were closely supervised and monitored and personal liberty was secondary to collective advancement.[36] The desire of the leaders that citizens live a code of moral conduct based upon

---

[33] See Konig, supra. p. xii.
[34] Konig, supra, is of this opinion. p. xiii.
[35] Konig, supra. p. 3.
[36] C.f. Haskins. supra. pp. 223-224.

scripture created an environment of frequent reporting of misbehavior; excessive consumption of alcohol was an offense,[37] possession of dice or card games too,[38] excess in apparel was viewed as immoral[39] and even smoking in public, recently fashionable in London, was liable to a fine in Plymouth.[40] Unlike Virginia, this was not a colony established on the potential for wealth; it was a base for people escaping all forms of authority, not exclusively the established church. They were a contentious and litigious people. We know the founders were mistrustful of secular power in clerical hands as experienced in England and therefore Massachusetts magistrates were empowered to hear church matters as well as secular. By 1639 the volume of congregational discipline cases reported to the secular courts was so excessive that the General Court requested legislative intervention ordering that churches, not the secular courts, should discipline their own members. Only in cases of persistent refusal to adhere to church regulation were matters to be brought before the secular courts.[41] Magistrates were local citizens who held quarter sessions of the peace much like their counterparts in England.[42] These courts had no grand juries and therefore matters were often referred to them from the superior Court of Assistants. The Massachusetts magistrates court also had no petty jury and consequently did not hear cases involving

---

[37] 1648 Body of Laws. http://www.commonlaw.com/Mass.html#HE46.

[38] 1648 Body of Laws. Records of Quarterly Essex Court May 1664 show four defendants being fined five shillings each for possession of playing cards. *Crime and Punishment in a Triangular Perspective: Assessing Theocracy and Transfer of Culture.* http://projectalbion.online.fr.

[39] With "frugality and modesty" and accept the place that God had given them in society. http://projectalbion.online.fr. Magistrates and public officials were free to dress as they thought fit. Colonial Laws of Massachusetts. Sumptuary Laws. 1651.

[40] Colonial Laws of Massachusetts. Sumptuary Laws. 1651.

[41] Mass. Rec. 1:274. See Kong, supra. p. 31. Also excommunication in Massachusetts did not bar inheritance or continuation of legacy. Anyone who did not repent and seek readmission to the church within six months was liable to a secular fine imposed by the magistrates. Mass. Rec. 1: 242.

[42] One magistrate was a quorum but the governor, John Winthrop, himself a former magistrate in England, suggested they sit as a bench of two. Winthrop Family, *The Winthrop Papers*, Vol. I, 1498-1628, Boston, 1929 1:310. Cited by Konig, supra. p. p.17. n. 52.

banishment or loss of life or limb.[43] Overlaying the magistrates courts was the superior court, the Court of Assistants. We have seen that the first governor of the colony, John Winthrop,[44] was a former English magistrate, he took the post at just eighteen years of age. He was also a member of Gray's Inn and Inner Temple. A number of other legislators and judges in the first wave of settlers had received formal legal training in England; Richard Bellingham had been Recorder of Boston, England, and Reverend Nathaniel Ward, barrister of Lincoln's Inn[45]. Assistants Isaac Johnson, Roger Ludlow, Simon Bradstreet, Herbert Pelham and Thomas Dudley[46] were also legally trained in London before emigration to Massachusetts. When compared with the members of the highest court in colonial Virginia, the Massachusetts colony had a convincing bench of professional jurists. Although this body chose to ignore benefit of clergy, or at least not formally accept the plea because it was in use by implication through sentencing, they certainly would have known of the plea having been jurists themselves in England. Additionally, Winthrop and his colleagues obtained copies of the leading English law texts and in 1647 the General Court agreed, "to the end that we may have better light for making and proceeding about laws"[47] ordered two copies of Coke on Littleton, two books of Coke on the Magna Carta, two copies of Dalton's Justice of the Peace and two of Sir Edward Coke's reports. As Dalzell has pointed out, most of these have specific references to benefit of clergy and in the case of Coke's reports there is at 11.29 a lengthy discussion of the plea. It cannot be through any degree of ignorance that the General Court did not legislate for the use of clergy at this time but rather more that the

---

[43] Order No. 281.

[44] He was also justice of the court leet at Groton Manor and an attorney to the Court of Wards and Liveries. Source. Coquillette, supra. p. xxvii.

[45] Nathaniel Ward practiced law for ten years before joining the ministry. Coquillette, supra. p. xxvii.

[46] Thomas Dudley was steward to the Earl of Groton's estate, John Winthrop's father. He and Richard Bellingham were parishioners of John Cotton in the parish of Boston, England. C.f. Haskins, G.L. *Law and Authority in Early Massachusetts: A Study in Tradition and Design*, New York, Macmillan, 1960.

[47] Dalzell, G.W. *Benefit of Clergy in America*, Winston-Salem, Blair, 1955. p. 186.

leaders were not motivated to endorse an English legal mechanism that had matured out of Catholic protectionisms that were fundamentally abhorrent to the Puritans.[48] As we shall see, branding[49] was liberally applied to criminals but it took King William's Charter to force clergy out from applied discretionary sentencing and onto the statute book.

Power in the early years in Massachusetts was vested in an intimate group of Englishmen who had worked and prayed with each other before deciding to form a new world of godliness in America. Members of the General Court, the law-making machinery, were for all practical purposes the same people who comprised the Court of Assistants, the governing body of the colony and its superior court judiciary.[50] The concentration of power to a group of around twelve men lasted until 1634 when it was decided that membership in the Court of Assistants should be made available to any elected freeman.[51] From 1636 onwards the Assistants held four courts each year at Boston. These sessions were known as Great Quarter Courts. Four inferior trial courts were also established in 1636, one each for Boston, Salem, Ipswich and Cambridge. These courts were referred to as the county courts. County courts sat with a bench of five (although three was a quorum providing one member of the bench was a magistrate).[52] Both the Court of Assistants and the four county courts employed juries. In 1639 the

---

[48] For some discussion of religious intolerance in England and the hostility that developed between the puritans and both the catholic and Anglican churches see: Coffey, J., *Persecution and Toleration in Protestant England 1558-1689*, London, Longman, 2000. and Haigh, C., Puritan Evangelism in the Reign of Elizabeth I, *The English Historical Review*, Vol. 92. No. 362 (Jan., 1977), pp. 30-58.

[49] The most common form of corporal punishment was whipping, whereas branding carried the same stigma as wearing of symbols and labels, the pillory and stocks. It was all a manifestation of naming and shaming offenders. Branding had the added advantage of permanency which prevented recidivists from leniency a second time. Corporal punishment was also immediate and cost effective. Restitution was also very popular in colonial Massachusetts. Treble restitution was applied to most property crimes, also sale into servitude was a possibility. C.f. Preyer, supra. pp. 348-329, 351. Esp. note. 60.

[50] Somewhat confusingly the justices of the Court of Assistants were appointed as "magistrates."

[51] Haskins, supra. p. 19.

[52] The other two could be laymen and frequently were. Haskins, supra. p. 33.

strangers' courts were created.[53] This court could be summoned on demand by a stranger who could not wait for the regular court session. The court consisted of the governor or deputy-governor and two magistrates. They were empowered to hear any civil matter or criminal trial that would ordinarily be heard before the county court by a jury. After the restructuring of the courts in 1634, the General Court assumed a new role as appellate court to the Court of Assistants.[54] In real terms this set the path for the General Court to become the supreme court within the colony. Until its union with Massachusetts, the Plymouth colony operated a similar system, with the quarterly General Court for serious felonies and local magistrates appointed to hear minor criminal matters. The only substantive difference between the two systems was that in Massachusetts the deputies entered the General Court four years before those in Plymouth. As early as 1639, the General Court recognized the value of precedent and it noted that recording of judgments should be recorded in a book, "to bee kept to posterity."[55]

Original charters and early laws

According to the original charters, Plymouth and Massachusetts were required to follow established English law, common and statute. The Puritan aristocracy clearly had an alternative view and sought to create

---

[53] Mass. Recs. I. 264. A "stranger" was a person not resident in the colony, sometimes referred to as a "transient."

[54] Appeal against conviction was only available in very restricted circumstances in England; therefore to introduce an appellate procedure was innovative. Appeals against a single justice at the County Court were available as a matter of right. Massachusetts was also in advance of England in terms of bail and double jeopardy where it was available in all criminal proceedings and matters of civil trespass. Haskins, supra. p. 198-199. Also the use of an oath and torture was vigorously opposed in Massachusetts. Torture was imposed upon the system with the introduction of pressing, infra.

[55] Coquillette, supra. p. xxxix. Note. 2. The first statutory compilation appeared in 1648 as the *Lawes and Libertyes*, there were no printed case reports until 1804.

their own version of laws as seen through the close resemblance to biblical scripture. There was always the risk of course that once England's internal struggles dissipated closer attention would be paid to the legal framework of the colonies; also the emigrants themselves might view the Assistants as overbearing and autocratic and express this through elections held annually for Assistant and magisterial positions. The first blush of legislative change started in 1636 with the re-writing of the *Mayflower Compact*; further revisions were made in 1658, 1671 and 1684. Unlike its larger neighbor, Plymouth recognized benefit of clergy in 1654 when Robert Latham was convicted of manslaughter and branded.[56] Legislation followed in 1684 to the effect that for serving with a hostile enemy, meaning the French, the defendant "shall suffer the pains of Death without benefit of clergy."[57]

Massachusetts utilized the clergy plea, by inference, as early as 1632[58] but did not enact binding statutory provisions until 1691.[59] Written references to clergy in England do appear in the 1646 Massachusetts "Fundamentals" paragraph 13: "simple theft and some other felonies are not punished with death, if the offender can reade in Scripture."[60] Much like Virginia, the northern colonies of Plymouth and Massachusetts took an individualistic approach towards the use of clergy. Offenses that were deemed as clergyable in England were not always followed; burglary and robbery were unclergyable under English law, both offenses were clergyable with branding on the face in Massachusetts. Arson, being a fugitive felon and assisting or harboring

---

[56] Dalzell, G.W. *Benefit of Clergy in America*, Winston-Salem, Blair, 1955. p. 170.
[57] Dalzell, supra. p. 170.
[58] The case of Richard Hopkins, infra. Mass. Court. Recs. 1632. p. 99. Hopkins was convicted of selling powder shot to Indians. He was branded in the cheek.
[59] Under legislation that incorporated the King William Charter, infra.
[60] Hutchinson, T., *A Collection of Original Papers Relating to the History of the Colony of Massachusetts-bay*, Carlisle, Applewood, 1769. p. 204. Number 13. Hutchinson is giving the reader an overview of the English common law. This is not a proposal to adopt the provision. See also: Morris, R.B., Massachusetts and the Common Law: The Declaration of 1646, *The American Historical Review*, Vol. 31. No.3 (Apr., 1926), pp. 443-453. p. 448.

a felon were non-clergyable capital crimes in England; all of these were treated as suitable for branding in Massachusetts.[61] As one commentator has observed "In short, there is considerable discrepancy between non-clergyable felonies in England and capital crimes in Massachusetts Bay."[62] In effect a large degree of local discretion was being applied in the first twenty years followed by various statutory provisions that formalized the plea towards the end of the seventeenth century.[63] This represents a very different picture than that of Virginia and reflects the growth of the region from one of intense Puritan ideals to a more English-compliant environment; Massachusetts followed English law more closely at the end of the seventeenth century than at any other time, before or afterwards.

The trend towards Anglicization[64] of Massachusetts law and procedure started during the reign of Charles II. Within England, there was a move towards paying greater attention to the status of a number of charters pertaining to English and colonial cities. The objective was most probably to force new, and more lucrative, franchises and cause a redistribution of power among the cities and away from the Whigs. Massachusetts was viewed as a valuable asset, a Whig stronghold and a colony suspected of circumventing English law.[65] The grant to its charter was annulled in 1684. This forced a situation of legal compliance with England and for the first time benefit of clergy was expressly accommodated in the colony's legislation. Soon after the events of 1684, a new governor was appointed, one who had strong allegiance to the English crown. Edmund Andros was unpopular for a

---

[61] The distinction between a felony and misdemeanor was also different than in England. In Massachusetts the distinction was set at 40 shillings. Dalzell, supra. p. 188.
[62] Morris. supra. pp. 449-450.
[63] English law was not abandoned, however, and in a number of instances the legislation was copied. E.g. Stealing from orchards and gardens was copied from 43. Eliz. I. c. 7. Also 37. Henry VIII, c.6. 5. Eliz. I. c. 21, 3. James. I. c. 13. Cited by Haskins, supra. p. 278. Note. 86.
[64] See: Coquillette. supra. p. xliv.
[65] Dalzell, supra.

number of reasons and he remained in the post for just three years, from 1686 to 1689. Under Andros, Joseph Dudley served as the chief justice. Dudley was born in Massachusetts. He was the son of one of the founding fathers, Thomas Dudley, who had come over in the first wave of Puritan aristocrats around the time of John Winthrop. Joseph Dudley attended Harvard College and moved within the circle of Massachusetts government that would ensure a lifetime of judicial and administrative appointments. To these ends he was appointed as chief justice in 1686 and presided at the first recorded case of benefit of clergy.[66]

In 1691 a new charter was issued to Massachusetts that made it a royal dominion.[67] It was also the event that merged Plymouth[68] with Massachusetts. This sequence of royal proclamations effectively ended Puritan dominance of the colony and the measures introduced by Andros and Dudley were now fixed into law. With consolidation, all Massachusetts citizens were given the same protections as a person born within the realm of England. The administration of justice was henceforth firmly within the control of those sympathetic to England and to officials who would respect and apply English law. The following year, the Supreme Judicial Court of Massachusetts was created and one of its first appointees was an Anglican clergyman.[69] The new structure incorporated two English procedures, benefit of clergy and the limited use of torture. It should be qualified that in England, unlike continental Europe, torture was never a standard procedure. Its use was largely restricted to encouraging defendants to make a plea. It was not used to

---

[66] The case involved a charge of theft against Peleg Heath, infra. A special court was summoned and presided over by Dudley. The court record states heath pleaded his clergy, was required to read from scripture and then granted clergy and his hand was burnt.

[67] See: http://avalon.law.yale.edu/17th_century/mass07.asp.

[68] As well as Maine and Nova Scotia, temporarily.

[69] Dalzell, supra. p. 182. Also for a list of the occupations of the members of the Massachusetts Superior Court 1692-1774 see: McKirdy, C. R., *Massachusetts Lawyers on the Eve of the American Revolution: The State of the Profession,* in Coquillette, supra. pp. 313-358.

secure a conviction. The approved method was pressing, *peine forte et dure*. Traditionally, defendants in English felony trials who refused to enter a plea were taken from the courtroom and weights were applied to their chests until they agreed to enter a plea or they died under the weights. A third option was that an official believed they were innocent and authorized release. After 1691, pressing was *de facto* incorporated into the law of Massachusetts along with benefit of clergy. Clergy was now used a number of times over the next seventy years. Mercifully, pressing was used just once, on April 19, 1692 when an eighty-year-old man was charged with witchcraft as part of the Salem atrocities. Giles Corey was illiterate and disliked by his local community; he was arrested for suspicion of witchcraft on what was most probably a trumped up charge brought about by neighbors whom he had fallen out with over the years. Witchcraft was unclergyable under English law and Corey would have known he faced death by burning. He would also have known that the court had the power to order him to be pressed if he refused to enter a plea. The benefit of pressing, if there was any benefit at all, was that if a defendant could resist the pain and either die or be released, they were not a convicted felon and could therefore pass on their estate to their family—as a convicted felon English law prohibited this and the goods and chattels went to the Crown. Corey was not a wealthy man so it is hard to understand what his motive may have been to resist entering a plea. According to English law he was given three opportunities to enter a plea; he refused to do so. Giles Cory died under the weight of being pressed.[70]

Once the clergy plea was openly available, it was adapted for local use. Adultery had never been a capital offense in England but was deemed so in Massachusetts as early as 1648; bigamists too were now added to

---

[70] C.f. Brown, D.C., The forfeiture at Salem, 1692. *The William and Mary Quarterly*, Law and Society in America, No. I, (Jan., 1993), pp. 85-111.

the list of unclergyable felons by legislation introduced in June 1694.[71] Contrary to English law, in 1704 Massachusetts counterfeiters were permitted their clergy;[72] this lasted until 1736 when Massachusetts followed England and made forgery and counterfeiting non-clergyable.[73] Branding in the face for robbery—a local aberration—was rescinded in 1712 and the Massachusetts courts were required to return to burning of the hand.[74] Robbery remained a non-clergyable capital crime in England until abolition of clergy. One of the most common uses of clergy throughout its history has been in cases of manslaughter. Manslaughter became clergyable in Massachusetts after the 1691 charter. It was not unanimously appreciated though; in 1765 Massachusetts Chief Justice Hutchinson[75] expressed his considerable degree of animosity towards the plea when he referred to it as the "benignity of English law." In 1767 he advised a jury that a man was entitled to stand his ground against a home invader, regardless of the intruder's intentions, and should he kill the intruder the defendant would be entitled to a charge of manslaughter and "have his clergy."[76] As we have seen, the reading test was recognized as early as 1646 and was recorded in the proceedings of the Court of Assistants in 1686; Massachusetts followed English law and abolished the reading test in 1706.[77]

Many of the New World settlers were living in small rural communities that were bound by deference to authority, strong ideologies, stable families and religious homogeneity. As a group they did not tolerate

---

[71] 1st session. Province Laws 1694-95.
http://archives.lib.state.ma.us/actsResolves/1694/1694acts0005.pdf.
[72] Act of 19th August, 1704. http://www.lib.muohio.edu/multifacet/record/mu3ugb3382745.
[73] Province Laws. 1736-37. Chapter 10.
http://archives.lib.state.ma.us/actsResolves/1736/1736acts0009.pdf.
[74] Dalzell, supra, p.188.
[75] He was the presiding judge in the trials which involved the ransacking of his home by a mob, August 26, 1765. C.f. Coquillette. Supra. p. lvi.
[76] Dalzell, supra. p. 192.
[77] 5. Anne. c. 6. 1706.

serious crime and they sought to detect and harshly punish offenders as quickly as possible; a legal system that could be easily referenced and was orderly in content and form was the requirement of Massachusetts society. Initially, it was a place sensitive to moral crimes and this was reflected in the laws. Restructuring in 1691 and a stronger English presence shifted the emphasis of life and the laws began to reflect greater English influence and secularization. Serious crimes increased, moral crimes were less frequently reported and the judiciary was encouraged to apply established legal devices in an adapted format to suit local needs.[78] The high point of legal independence had been reached, for the time being, and the laws and its operators were to move forward applying such despised practices as clergy despite any personal abhorrence for the legal fiction.

Criminal courts and the role of lawyers

The Massachusetts court system comprised three levels, inferior, superior and appellate.[79] Magistrates courts were courts of inferior jurisdiction authorized to hear minor criminal cases, misdemeanors.[80] Also a specialized stranger's court was established in 1639; this only lasted until 1672 when its functions were absorbed by the county courts. The stranger's court allowed transients to demand a case be heard if there was not a local magistrates court available to try the matter. The purpose of the court was to facilitate criminal actions that involved strangers who might otherwise not be available due to their

---

[78] C.f. Greenberg, D. Crime, Law Enforcement, and Social Control in Colonial America, *The American Journal of Legal History*, Vol. 26, No. 4 (Oct., 1982), pp. 293-325.

[79] Trial courts comprised county courts and the Court of Assistants. Magistrates courts were not trial courts but of summary jurisdiction only. These courts were also referred to as magistrates colony courts. Date of establishment was June 14, 1631. (1631-1686). Renamed Justices of the Peace courts 1687 onwards.

[80] Thefts of value less than 40 shillings, minor assaults and a broad range of moral matters that would have fallen under the jurisdiction of ecclesiastical courts in England.

mobile and impermanent status in the colony. The criminal trial courts comprised the county courts and the Court of Assistants. Four county courts were established in 1636 at Boston, Ipswich, Salem and Cambridge. The bench consisted of magistrates appointed by the General Court. County courts heard theft cases involving values of greater than 40 shillings and all other felony[81] cases other than those punishable with loss of life or limb. This court became known as the Quarter Court of General Sessions from 1692 onwards.[82] The highest criminal trial court was the Court of Assistants, also known as the Greater Quarter Court. It comprised the governor, deputy governor and twelve assistants.[83] The court met twice a year to hear cases punishable with loss of life, limb or banishment. This court also served as the governor's council. During this period England did not have an appeals system; Massachusetts implemented an appeal structure when it created its court system.[84] Appeals from the county court were heard by the Court of Assistants and appeals from decisions of the Court of Assistants lay to the General Court. After revocation of the charter in 1684, reorganization prompted a number of name changes; however, the basic three-tier structure of courts, inferior, superior and appellate, remained in force until the American Revolution.[85]

In the New England colonies of Plymouth and Massachusetts, the legislators, executives and judiciary were subject to annual elections. No governor had the power to veto legislation and the executive did not have the power to appoint judges or other officials. All judges and

---

[81] Massachusetts law never used the term felony or misdemeanor. It is employed in this work in the same way as in Virginia and England to distinguish between the severity of the criminal action and potential punishment.

[82] As part of the reorganization and Anglicization of the colonies' legal system introduced through King William's Charter. The court was disbanded in 1827.

[83] Replaced by the Superior Court of Judicature, 1687-1780.

[84] *The Laws and Liberties of Massachusetts*. Section: Courts. Part I. "And if any shal finde himself grieved with the sentence of any the said County courts he may appeal to the next court of Assistants."

[85] For a comprehensive overview see: Hindus, M. S., *A Guide to the Court Records of Early Massachusetts* in Coquillette, supra. pp. 519-540.

officials were subject to impeachment. The township was the primary unit of legislative and judicial representation and church membership was required for voting. In the colony English law was viewed as obscure, inconsistent and in need of codification;[86] these factors all contributed to a general hesitance towards creating a powerful judiciary and the demonstrably strong reliance upon accountability.

Legal professionals existed in the Bay from the time the first settlers arrived. Winthrop and many of his contemporaries had been legal practitioners in England and a number of this group achieved magisterial appointments within a short time of entry; as such they were able to exert some degree of influence upon the design and practice of the law from the outset. The most obvious influence was through the drafting of legislation that would lead to the codification of the law and the establishment of due process. As a part of this progression notaries were permitted to be engaged by clients as early as 1638. One of the first was a Londoner, Thomas Lechford. Lechford had some training in law and a limited amount of experience but was hampered in his aspirations by the rule that providing legal services for a fee was not permitted in seventeenth-century London.[87]

Legal terminology can prove challenging and the distinction between attorney, barrister, solicitor and notary can be perplexing. As far as use in colonial Massachusetts is concerned, in 1638 a practitioner of law was not restricted in meaning to contemporary American usage (i.e., an attorney or barrister). Thomas Lechford,[88] Robert Saltonstall, Edward

---

[86] It should not escape attention that it was the Massachusetts Body of laws that were used in England as the basis for proposed revision of the criminal law during the interregnum. The second edition of The Body of Laws was published in England in 1655 and was endorsed by the English reform movement. See: Warden, G.B., Law Reform in England and New England, 1620-1660. *The William and Mary Quarterly*, Third Series, Vol. 35, No. 4 (Oct., 1978), pp. 668-690. p. 675. Note. 15.

[87] The privilege of counsel for all felony cases was not a legal right in England until 1836. In England, defendants were not permitted to be represented by counsel other than in cases of treason.

[88] Lechford, the first to arrive, left England after he was committed for contempt of court in London. He no doubt felt his opportunity for a legal career was more likely in the New World than the old.

Colcord and others[89] were not legally trained at one of the Inns of Court in London nor had they been called to the bar. However, they were all familiar with the law and provided a range of legal services to clients in Massachusetts acting as solicitors—a profession considered to be of dubious stature due to the manner in which its practitioners sought to "solicit" clients to represent.[90] The tacit acceptance of defense counsel was formalized in the Body of Liberties that provided that a defendant was entitled to employ a man for assistance as long as the defendant did not reward the advisor for his work.[91] Since the Body of Liberties did not permit fee taking and there was a degree of resistance to advocacy, one way in which the Massachusetts lawyers could engage clients was through offering their skills as legal scriveners.[92]

By the early eighteenth century attorneys were practicing as criminal defense lawyers and they were receiving a fee for their services.[93] The anti-lawyer rhetoric of the early settlers had dissipated. Even the prominent Puritan minister Cotton Mather recognized the development of lawyering into a profession when he wrote that a

---

[89] Barnes, T.G., *Thomas Lechford and the Earliest Lawyering in Massachusetts, 1638-1641* in Coquillette, supra p.3. Incudes George Keyser and Robert Lord also.

[90] In England Lechford was a member of Clement's Inn (Chancery) and as such was regarded as an officer of the court. This provided the status of attorney; he could not plead or advocate at the bar but was permitted to advise clients and appear on their behalf.

[91] Clause 26. Of note is that the author of the work is Nathaniel Ward who had been called to the English bar, Lincoln's Inn. One voice against moves to include lawyers in the courtroom was the Reverend John Cotton. He was of the view that the appearance of lawyers was a negative incursion into the courtroom - one that had the potential to delay and complicate procedures. Coquillette, supra. p. 7. Even John Winthrop, himself a lawyer, had drafted a bill while still in England to parliament requesting a reduction in the number of practicing lawyers. Winthrop Papers, I, 295-310, 371-374, 418-419. Cited in Coquillette, supra. p. 41.

[92] A writer of legal pleadings.

[93] Flaherty, D. H., *Criminal Practice in Provincial Massachusetts* in Coquillette, supra. pp. 191-242. pp. 204-205. Particularly important to a comparative discussion of the work of lawyers in England is Professor John Langbein. Criminal Trials Before the Lawyers, *University of Chicago Law Review* 263 (1978) 307-313 and
http://digitalcommons.law.yale.edu/cgi/viewcontent.cgi?article=1547&context=fss_papers.

lawyer should be a "scholar and be wise" in order to do good.[94] In 1713 a new courthouse for Boston was opened at which Justice Samuel Sewell implored lawyers to remember their role: to advise the court and plead for their clients.[95] Though slow in growth, over time a limited number of men with knowledge of the law were permitted to achieve rights of audience and perform legal services that would equate with the role of an attorney.

---

[94] Cotton Mather, *Bonifacius, An Essay upon the Good*, Flaherty, D.H., in Coquillette, supra. p. 206.
[95] *Sewell Diary*, 714. Flaherty in Coquillette, supra. p. 209.

Chapter 6. Due process and clergy in the northern colony

Law as a union with God

The burgeoning justice system in Massachusetts was radical; elected officials, rights of audience, equal treatment before the law, the defendant knowing the alleged charges before trial, the right of appeal, codification, a full suite of due process. Unless the initial leaders of Massachusetts wanted to alert London to these moves, the best course of action was implied application of English law and generally keeping a low profile. To these ends benefit of clergy is not specifically mentioned for the first fifty years but, as will been seen in the following chapter, if asked by Westminster it was being applied. Benefit of clergy, first utilized in 1632, was in discreet use and application through individualized sentencing that would be familiar in England and colonial Virginia. However, unlike both of those jurisdictions, clergy was not pronounced in law or by the justices until Anglicization of the law took place towards the end of the seventeenth century. From then onwards, it was a statutory provision, applied widely and duly recorded in court documents.

By the time of the American Revolution, the Massachusetts criminal defendant could expect to have his case heard before a magistrate, if of a minor nature, or an elected judge and jury. He would be made aware of the charges against him before trial, the applicable law would be clearly stated in codes, he was entitled to legal representation and he had a right of appeal through a system of appellate courts to the governor. Although the punishment of loss of life, limb or banishment existed for a number of crimes he was unlikely to receive the death sentence and in many cases he would be subject to restorative provisions, humiliation and moral reprimand or corporal punishment including branding.[1]

The Massachusetts legislators were remarkable in their ability to produce a cogent body of codified laws—one that even represented a model for England. Although influenced by English law it was not a replica of the common law, neither was it a religious system. Rather more, it represented an autochthonous growth based upon communal needs and beliefs that represented concerns for the law of God and a secular rule of law. In Virginia the rule of law meant importation of English common law, in Massachusetts it meant elected officials empowered to administer the law through close community involvement. In Virginia the legal system was built upon the foundations of common law with adaptations relevant for a small and impoverished local labor force. In Massachusetts the early law was based upon the belief that a better world was possible in union with God. For the two colonies it was not that the fundamental purpose of the law changed, it was that the law needed to be applicable to each colony's distinctive characteristic. What remains to be discussed is how the accommodation of benefit of clergy was put into practice in Massachusetts compared with what has already been discussed in Virginia.

---

[1] Powers, E., *Crime and Punishment in Early Massachusetts 1620-1692: A Documentary History*, Boston, beacon press, 1966. pp. 404-408. Powers cites one ten-year period when the courts heard fifty-one death-eligible cases; of these the death sentence was imposed twenty-one times. He further comments that of these twenty-one the death penalty was substituted for banishment, forfeiture of land and ear cropping in a number of cases. p. 408. note to Table 5. At p. 275 he notes "Many individuals were indicted and tried for capital crimes in the bay Colony. Most of them, on conviction, were administered a 'grievous' penalty, but their lives were spared." He continues that even later in the colony's history actually dying for your crime was rare unless murder or piracy was proven. This too is questionable as we see in the first recorded case of benefit against Peleg Heath, supra, who claimed his clergy for theft, was later sentenced to death for piracy and was then reprimanded by the governor and spared his life along with five co-defendants.

Massachusetts court records

The most comprehensive compilation of Massachusetts court records are those authored by John Noble, Clerk of the Supreme Judicial Court of Massachusetts and Editor of Publications for the Colonial Society, between 1883 and 1907. Known as the *Suffolk Files*, this work comprises: minute books, record books, 1,289 file papers from the Superior Court of Judicature and miscellaneous papers from county courts, the Court of Assistants, general sessions, common pleas and admiralty. Criminal proceedings most frequently appear as "Records." Cases where benefit of clergy may be implied should appear exclusively before the Court of Assistants, *Mass Court Recs*, as these would be instances where a murder case was found to be one of manslaughter or the felony was liable to a loss of life or limb sentence. This may not be the case, however, due to the opportunity magistrates had to decriminalize offenses and retain jurisdiction or in instances where from the outset the crime was deemed to be manslaughter, not murder. In this latter case the defendant would appear before the county courts accused of manslaughter, which never attracted the death sentence in colonial Massachusetts and was therefore justiciable at the lower criminal court. Clergy plea decriminalization could occur at any level, however, if the magistrate applied his discretion and devalued property values or the seriousness of an assault. Transcriptions of the earliest county courts cases appear as the *Records and Files of the Quarterly Court of Essex County, Massachusetts, 1636-1686* and the individual county court records dating from the foundation of the first four counties in 1643. Some criminal cases are reported in the press, particularly the *Boston Gazette*. Generally, newspaper reports are shorter than written court records with very brief entries relating to the name of the defendant, the crime, verdict and sentence. When applied, benefit of clergy is reported in newspapers. As noted in the chapter dealing with clergy in colonial Virginia, we may never know the full extent of the use of the plea due to the manner in which it was adapted locally. This situation is compounded in Massachusetts where there is a specific intent to avoid replication of English law until such time as it was forced upon the colony after 1691. Noticeably from this point forward, we see clergy being entered into court records. Prior to this period it may be inferred through sentencing, references to the plea in draft legislation and the single specific application of clergy by a special court in 1686. The *Plymouth Colony Archive Project* is the source for the few clergy pleas recorded during that colony's independent status.

One observation with regard to terminology is important. The language employed in criminal pleadings can be misleading and on occasions fictitious. Massachusetts juries, conscious of the extreme penalty for some moral offenses, were known to take liberties by defining actions as tantamount to committing a capital crime but falling short of the actual capital offense. An example would be where a person is accused of adultery but found guilty not of unlawful fornication but the lesser crime of 'laying down' with a man. The implication is that unlawful sex took place between the parties but the language employed is sufficiently vague to allow juries the opportunity to find the defendants guilty of the lesser offense and avoid a death sentence.[2]

In this chapter, cases have been grouped together in a similar manner to those in Virginia. Proven cases of clergy use is the first category, followed by those cases where the sentence clearly implies clergy use, albeit the court record does not state the plea. The instances of clergy use by slaves are noticeably fewer and only involve male slaves; I have therefore kept these cases together with the first category. Examples of clergy use by women as sole defendants are rare, just two cases both in

---

[2] This example is taken from the very helpful essay on court records as sources presented by William E. Nelson Court records as Sources for Historical Writing at the Law in Colonial Massachusetts 1630-1800 Conference 6 & 7 November 1981. Proceedings published as *Law in Colonial Massachusetts 1630-1800*, Coquillette, D.R., (ed), Boston, University Press of Virginia, 1984. pp. 499-518. Esp note. 4. *King v Donham*, Plymouth General Sessions, October 1763. In David T. Konig (ed) *Plymouth Court Records, 1686-1859*, Wilmington, Delaware, 1978. p.59.

the same year; more frequently women appear as co-defendants in morality cases. I have not treated these examples as a separate category and they are included in the general clergy use illustrations. Finally there are a small number of cases where the sentence is so extraordinary that they are subject to individual commentary.

Benefit of clergy cases before the Massachusetts courts

The first example of the clergy plea being entered and accepted by the court occurred during the special court session of 1686-1687. This was the first time the special court had been formed since the appointment of the new chief justice, Dudley, and this may be interpreted as an example of an English court wanting to assert its authority over the Massachusetts justice system, particularly given the use and application of clergy. Defendant Peleg Heath and co-accused Richard Hulins, John Stickey, Thomas Waters, William Hawkins and Joseph Aramatu were being sentenced for "felonious stealings."[3] They "pleaded guilty & praying the benefit of Clergie was called to the booke & reading was burned in the left hand with letter T."[4] It transpired that Waters had already received his clergy at some point previously; in keeping with English law, prohibiting the use of clergy twice,[5] the court substituted his clergy for the death sentence.[6] Peleg Heath was

---

[3] This is most unusual as the term felony never appears in the laws of Massachusetts yet the court entry clearly states, "felonious stealings."
[4] Superior Court Records Minute Book 1686-1687. 1.12.17-20. Also Dalzell, G.W. *Benefit of Clergy in America*, Winston-Salem, Blair, 1955. p.181.
[5] 4. Hen. 7. C.13. (1487).
[6] Sir Thomas Dudley, supra, chapter four, Chief Justice, presided at the trial. "Dudley made himself the major agent in the business of replacing Puritan law with English law. As President of the Council for New England, he held his first court in May 1686. The records of his courts are the only ones surviving from the period that Massachusetts's historians long called "the Usurpation." Acting as if he held commissions of oyer and terminer and general gaol delivery on an assize in an English county, Dudley admitted Peleg Heath to his clergy and extended the Jacobean statute in favor of women to Charity Williams after convictions for grand larceny. He let Thomas Waters to his clergy after one conviction

apparently a habitual criminal; he went on to be prosecuted for piracy, a non-clergyable crime, and received the death sentence.[7]

A further example of the Anglicization of the law occurred in the same governor's special court, 1686-1687, when Dudley and the Assistants heard the only examples of clergy pleas being entered by individual female defendants. Charity Williams was accused of stealing goods, value not recorded. She pleaded guilty and "praying the benefit of the Statute of Jacobi in favour of women omitting small felonies was burned in the left hand with letter T."[8] Mercy Windsor was sentenced to branding after she had claimed her clergy for theft.[9] The court record does not specify the amount of value associated with the charges. The applicable English law permitted women their clergy in cases where the material value was less than ten shillings. These cases occurred at a time when English law was being reintroduced to the colony; therefore it may have been the case that the ten shilling value was applied, conversely given the history of disregard for English precedent the magistrates may have applied their own version of the monetary tariff. These cases also demonstrate the limited amount of information being recorded when compared with the details entered by court reporters in the following century; every eighteenth-century clergy case that I have found has greater details of the crime. This may

---

but sentenced him to death after the jury returned a guilty verdict on a second indictment." Ms. Massachusetts Superior Court of Judicature, Special Courts, 1686-1687, pp. 2-21. Chapin, B., Written Rights: Puritan and Quaker procedural guarantees, *The Pennsylvania magazine of History and Biography*, Vol. 114, No. 3 (July, 1990), pp. 321-348. p. 340.

[7] Along with John Stickerton, William Dunn, Richard Griffin, Daniel lander, William Warren, Samuel Watts, William Coward and Thomas Storey for "piracy in Massachusetts Bay three leagues from Half Way Rock." The gang appeared before the Court of Assistants in January 1690. All of the defendants received the death sentence. *Mass Court Recs*. Noble, supra. p. 62.

[8] *Superior Court Records Minute Book 1686-1687*. 1.12.17-20. And Noble, J. Notes on the Trial and Punishment of Crimes in the Court of Assistants in the time of the colony, and in the Superior Court of Judicature in the first years of the province, *The Colonial Society of Massachusetts*, 'Transactions' 1895-1897 (Feb, 1985) pp. 51-65. p. 64.

[9] Dalzell, supra. p. 181.

reflect both increased professionalization of court reporting and the frequent presence of counsel.

There is now a lull in proven clergy pleas. A number of defendants appeared before the justices charged with clergyable crimes and received branding punishments during the next thirty years but the court records do not confirm that a clergy plea was entered. Consequently, I have chosen not to follow the work of some commentators[10] and assume these are clergy pleas, instead I will discuss these cases under the section that deals with implied clergy use.

Known clergy cases reappear in February 1732 when William Wheeler Jr. appeared before Superior Court charged with murder. He was represented by William Shirley, a member of the English bar who had arrived in Boston the month before. The jury found Wheeler guilty of manslaughter and counsel directed his client to claim his clergy.[11] Immediately following this trial the General Council met to draft a proposal for removing the benefit of clergy from all criminal cases.[12] The bill proceeded to its third reading in March but then failed to progress. Apparently the efforts of Dudley back in 1684 had finally paid off; clergy was not only part of Massachusetts law but attempting to remove it failed also.

On January 29, 1732 Simon Hue, an Indian laborer, appeared before the Nantucket county court charged with murder. The court proceedings recorded that at "Sherbourn m.[murdered] Jethro

---

[10] Notably Dalzell, supra. and Preyer, K. Penal Measures in the American Colonies: An Overview, *The American Journal of Legal History*, Vol. 26. No. 4. (Oct., 1982), pp. 326-353. Esp. p. 342. Note. 36, relies upon the evidence of Dalzell. Conversely Cross, A.L. Benefit of Clergy in the American Criminal Law, *American Historical Review*, Third series, Vol. 61. (Oct., 1927-Jun., 1928), pp. 153-181. p. 159. Erroneously reports that only two cases have been recorded.
[11] Superior Court Records, Minute Book, 19.
[12] C.f. Flaherty, D.H., Criminal Practice in Provincial Massachusetts *in Law in Colonial Massachusetts 1630-1800* Coquillette, D.R. (ed) A conference held 6 and 7 November 1981 by The Colonial Society of Massachusetts, University of Virginia Press, 1984. pp. 191-242. p. 237.

Quanset (Indian) malice aforethought, kicked & beat in breast with cord wood stick. d. [died] 2/9. P. NG. fG of MANSL. Whereupon he prayed the Court, that he might have the privilege or benefit of the law of England that Englishmen have in the case of manslaughter, i.e., the Benefit of Clergy."[13] This is rather suggestive wording employed by the court reporter; it could have meant that Hue was advised by counsel of the localization of clergy, it could also have implied that the court reporter was not too familiar with the term and used the terms privilege and benefit. Conversely it could be construed as an attempt to overtly recognize the status of colonists as Englishmen with all of the rights associated with that designation; a poignant message from the colony's highest court given that abolition legislation had just failed. Hue was branded on the left thumb. At Barnstaple county court in April 1733 advocate James Otis successfully pleaded clergy for his client Jeremiah Ralph Jnr. Ralph had been charged with murder but found guilty of manslaughter.[14] In June 1736 Robert Auchmuty represented John Macdonald for the offense of counterfeiting. He succeeded in obtaining clergy for his client although the offense was non-clergyable. Macdonald was branded and sentenced to six months' imprisonment. At Barnstaple, in June 1739, David Stevens[15] was granted his clergy for manslaughter. Allegedly Stevens had killed Samuel Tomkins during a robbery. The deceased was found with bruises and a severe blow to the head; he had been robbed of his clothing. During the trial Stevens escaped from the jurisdiction of the court. He was apprehended, the trial resumed and he was found guilty of manslaughter. The justices directed that he be burnt with a "hot marking iron" in the right hand with an M. Stevens was also ordered to pay costs. It appears that no further action was taken with regard to the escape. Another case of murder was decided as manslaughter at the

---

[13] Superior Court Records, 1730-1733, 175.
[14] Superior Court Records, Minute Book. 23, 5.
[15] Superior Court Records, 1739-1740, 47. Minute Book. 35.

Bristol sessions in October 1739. The defendant Silas Holmes also escaped with a branding of the thumb.[16]

The precedent set in 1736, which allowed a clergy pleading for counterfeiting, was followed in 1739 when Joseph Parker appeared before the Salem County Court.[17] Both the 1736 and 1739 decisions are particularly noteworthy as it was in 1736 that the Massachusetts legislators decided to reverse the clergyable status of counterfeiting (first introduced in August 1704)—it would appear that Massachusetts justices were not only content with abrogating English law but domestic colonial legislation as well.[18] In addition to deciding a counterfeiting matter during the same year the justices had to consider an appeal for clergy from a Negro indicted for the rape of a child. In June 1739 George Necho was found guilty of raping a three-year-old white girl. His attorney, Matthew Livermore, entered a plea of clergy. Counsel argued that applicable English law held that rape of a child was not punishable with death.[19] Livermore was probably correct in his law; however, the justices decided to apply the law pertaining to rape of a woman rather than a child.[20] Necho was denied his clergy and sentenced to death.[21]

During the 1740's, a number of defendants successfully claimed their clergy; the first three examples relate to the crime of counterfeiting. In 1742, Eleazer Lyndsey successfully pleaded his clergy for the offense of counterfeiting.[22] Before the same court Robert Neal claimed his clergy;

---

[16] Bristol Assizes, October 1739.
[17] Superior Court Records, Minute Book. 24,51.
[18] C.f. Dalzell, supra. p. 190.
[19] At common law rape was forcible carnal knowledge of a woman without her consent; however, it did not attract the death penalty *per se* and the argument was presumably that statute law could not supersede common law unless specifically enacted. c.f. Flaherty in Coquillette, supra. p. 239.
[20] 18 Eliz. c. 7. (1576) sec. 1. Rape and burglary excluded from clergy. Section 4, states that "carnal knowledge of female under 10 declared felony without benefit of clergy."
[21] Superior Court Records, 1739-1740, 225.
[22] Superior Court Records, 1740-1742, 253-254.

in his case he had been counterfeiting Rhode Island bills. To the surprise of the convicting court, Neal produced a governor's pardon that exempted him from having his hand burnt. Governor's pardons operated in much the same way as a royal pardon and like royal mercy appear to have been applied with considerable latitude. The Body of Liberties provided that the governor had the power to reprieve but a full pardon could only be authorized by the General Court.[23] The extraordinary Neal affair was then repeated in 1745 when another counterfeiter, Gideon Rice, managed to produce another governor's reprieve before the Suffolk Assizes. He too was granted his clergy and escaped a branding for the non-clergyable crime of counterfeiting.[24] Also in 1745, Sack Cut, a Negro, was granted his clergy for manslaughter.[25] David Doughty was granted his clergy for the offense of manslaughter in 1747.[26] The final clergy case for the decade also involved a Negro. In 1747 Medad was charged with arson, a clergyable offense in Massachusetts. He was found guilty and entered his clergy plea. For a variety of unrecorded reasons, the court delayed sentencing until September 1749. When they did reconvene Medad was branded; he had also spent three years in prison on remand.[27]

In 1751,[28] we see one of the few clergy pleas entered for an ecclesiastical crime. Ezekiel Eldridge appeared charged with bigamy. He was found guilty and pleaded his clergy whereupon he was burnt in the hand in the 'face of the court'.[29] Additionally his marriage to the second wife was annulled and his first wife was granted a divorce. This case makes

---

[23] Body of Liberties. 72. See Chapin, supra. pp. 60-61. James I reserved the right to grant all pardons in Virginia. Also see Hen VIII. c.25.
[24] C.f. Flaherty In Coquillette, supra. p. 238. 2 Geo. 2. C.25. (1729) Sec. 1. Forgery made felony without benefit of clergy.
[25] Superior Court Records, Minute Book. 24,51.
[26] Superior Court Records 1743-1747,158. Minute Book 33.
[27] Superior Court Records, Minute Books, 54,59.
[28] Two cases are cited by Grinnell, infra. p. 598 for the year 1750 when George White and Patrick Freeman were granted their clergy for burglary. I have not been able to substantiate this case.
[29] Dalzell, supra. p. 191.

an interesting comparison with that of James Luxford who one hundred years previously, in 1640, was fined £100 and placed in the stocks for having two wives. Five months later Luxford appeared before the magistrates again charged with forgery, a non-clergyable crime, lying and "foule offences." He was sentenced to be whipped, have both ears cropped and was ordered to be returned to England at the first opportunity.[30]

A rare example of a Negro and a white defendant appearing together came before the Boston Superior Court of Judicature on November 17th, 1752. Alexander (a "Negro Fellow") and Thomas Chubb were jointly charged with the murder of John Crabb. The record shows that the deceased was "struck and assaulted with a club in the street." The skull was terribly fractured and "great Clodders of blood settled in his brain."[31] The defendants pleaded not guilty. They were found not guilty of murder but guilty of manslaughter whereupon they claimed their clergy and were burned in the hand at the rear of the court. This case was also reported in the *Boston Gazette*. The newspaper erroneously reports that the defendants were burnt with a T "in the face of the court."[32]

On September 24, 1754 brothers Robert and Stephen Cooke appeared before the Superior Court charged with the murder of an Indian, Wamppoungcoss. Allegedly, Robert and Stephen had stolen a horse from the victim and he had pursued them. They had responded by shooting at him and then attacking him with a hatchet. Wamppoungcos had died as a result of the injuries he received. The trial lasted unusually long; from 9am until 10pm. The following morning the jury returned a verdict of manslaughter. Robert and Stephen then entered a plea of clergy and were branded in the hand

---

[30] M.C.R. Vol. I. p. 295.
[31] Superior Court Records 1752.
[32] *Boston Gazette*, 1/9/1753 "Homicide in Massachusetts."

with the letter T, (denoting the theft, not the manslaughter). They were, however, also imprisoned for one year.[33] The following year Joshua Sachamus, an Indian, appeared before Plymouth magistrates in answer to a charge of murder. Allegedly Sachamus had killed Sarah Robins with malice "afortho't." He was remitted to the Superior Court where he was found guilty of manslaughter. Sachamus pleaded his clergy and was burnt on the hand and ordered to pay costs.[34]

In 1773 James Bell was indicted for the murder of his wife, Christian (Christine). He appeared before the Superior Court in March. The trial lasted for six hours after which the jury retired for ninety minutes before delivering its verdict of manslaughter. Bell pleaded his clergy and after "a moving Admonition given him by his Honor the Chief Justice," according to the *Boston Gazette*, he was burnt in the hand.[35]

1776 was a tumultuous year in Massachusetts. The activity of a few British troops was itself to be the cause of a major clergy trial and may well have stimulated the early repeal of the provision federally as well as within the state. Before discussing the Boston Massacre, two cases are worthy of mention: the first involves two brothers who committed counterfeiting at the height of the Revolution and they appear to have managed to escape justice due to the events of 1776, the second involved a dispute between a landlord and tenant; it is the only recorded incident of this nature in which the clergy plea appears.

On March 30th, 1776 two brothers, Joseph and Asa Butler, appeared before the justices suspected of counterfeiting two Commonwealth of Massachusetts bills of credit. The Butlers admitted their guilt and prayed the mercy of the court. Although their age is not stated, the court record shows they were both minors and also soldiers of the

---

[33] Superior Court Records 1754. Also at Suffolk Court 73333,Vol 449.
[34] Superior Court Records 1755.
[35] Superior Court Records 1773.

Continental Army. Joseph and Asa were bound over to appear back before the Superior Court in September. It is not known what happened to the defendants after this and whether or not they ever appeared again. What is of note is the leniency of the court in respect of allowing two forgers, of Massachusetts credit bills, to be given bail and for such a lengthy period of time. This could be construed as denoting a general sense of pleasure within the Commonwealth at freedom from the manacles of British rule. If so, this is an extreme example, as it must be one of the first reported offenses of forgery within the new commonwealth and, if all cases of counterfeiting and forgery of the currency were to be treated so lightly, this would very soon destabilize the currency. Alternatively, it could be that the fervor of victory combined with the youth of the defendants and that they had served in the Continental Army held sufficient sway that the court decided to allow them enough leeway that they could disappear into history without testing the clergy plea in the new nation. [36]

Andre Kinchlalius boarded at the home of Jacob Lash. On the evening of October 14, 1776 the two became engaged in a dispute which resulted in the pair leaving the house and fighting each other in the street. Kinchlalius was alleged to have possession of a knife which he used to inflict a number of wounds upon Lash. As a result of one stab wound to the chest, Lash died. At trial, the jury returned a verdict of manslaughter against the defendant and he claimed his clergy; Kinchlalius was then burnt in the hand. Additionally he had his possessions forfeited and was ordered to spend six months in prison.[37]

The last known clergy plea[38] to be entered in the Commonwealth of Massachusetts occurred in 1779. The case involved a group of sailors.

---

[36] C.f Dalzell, supra. p. 190-191.
[37] Superior Court Records 1776.
[38] Dalzell, supra, states the last plea was entered in 1770. He is referring to the Boston Massacre. See pp. 192-206.

On November 16, 1779 Anthony Barber, Joseph Gasket, John Bowen and John Figonier murdered John Reynor by stabbing him through the chest with a bayonet. At trial it was alleged that Barber and Bowen inflicted the fatal wound and Gasket and Figonier assisted. Court-appointed counsel for the defendants, John Lowell and Benjamin Fishbourne, advised their clients to enter pleas of not guilty. The jury found Barber and Bowen guilty of manslaughter. Gasket and Figonier were acquitted. The convicted defendants then prayed their clergy and were burnt in the hand.[39]

On March 11th 1785 the "Act for taking away the Benefit of Clergy in all cases whatsoever and directing adequate Punishment for the Crimes where the same used to be allowed" was passed.[40] Henceforth any person who could have claimed their clergy would spend one hour in the gallows with a rope around their neck, pay a fine not exceeding £500 and be whipped, not more than thirty-nine lashes.[41] This marked the abolition of the clergy plea in Massachusetts and the substitution of one English legal custom for an American; the humiliation of standing in the gallows with a rope around your neck.[42]

---

[39] Mass Court Recs. 1778-1780. 152-3.
[40] 1784. Chapter 56. January Session. Senate and House of Government of Massachusetts. (Chap. 23) also see Grinnell, F.W., Probation as an Orthodox Common Law Practice in Massachusetts Prior to the Statutory Regime, *Massachusetts Law Quarterly*, Vol. II. No. 2. (1916/17), pp. 591-639. p. 598.
[41] The Perpetual Laws of the Commonwealth of Massachusetts, Boston. 1801, I. 227. Also cited in Cross, A.L., Benefit of Clergy in the American Criminal Law, *Proceedings of the Massachusetts Historical Society*, Third Series, Vol. 61 (Oct., 1927-Jun., 1928) pp. 153-181. p. 165.
[42] On execution day in England the convict was permitted up to one hour to stand beneath the gallows and make a speech and it was practice to leave the body for one hour to ensure the convict was dead. I have found no English cases where the sentence was to stand in the gallows. In colonial America standing in the gallows with a rope around your neck had been used prior to the 1785 act e.g. Elizabeth Smith was sentenced to stand in the gallows for one hour for her second theft conviction. She was also whipped twenty times. John Ennet received the remarkably lenient sentence of standing in the gallows for one hour and thirty-nine lashes for his conviction for bestiality in May 1772. Both Smith and Sennet were sentenced on the same day before the Massachusetts Superior Court. *Boston Gazette*, March 16, 1772. p. 3. See also the case against Huldah Dudley for allegedly committing incest. Hafner, D.L., "To be set upon the gallows for the space of one hour" A Tale of crime and Punishment in

Cases of implied use of clergy

It should be noted from the outset that Dalzell cites a number of the following cases as proven use of clergy. I believe that he was bold in doing so and I prefer a more reserved interpretation. Certainly the range of cases and the pattern of sentencing follows a trend seen in colonial Virginia; an adaptation of clergy to suit the local environment. In the case of Massachusetts there is potentially an additional layer which is the strong dislike of English criminal law and English ecclesiastical courts which combined may have added to the desire to obscure recorded use of clergy but continue its application in practice. Certainly the number of cases involved strongly suggests that clergy was applied from the beginning and with uniformity until its abolition.

In 1631 Phillip Ratcliff appeared before the Court of Assistants in Boston charged with "scandalous invectives against our churches and government." Ratcliff was a resident of Salem and appeared to struggle with maintaining good relations with his neighbors. In the spirit of neighborly watchfulness Ratcliff was charged with blasphemy and given an extremely severe sentence; he was ordered to have both ears cropped, pay a fine of £40 and then to be banished. Interestingly Ratcliff returned to England for his banishment.[43] As seen in this work, ear cropping and banishment were used extensively as clergy punishments, sometime in lieu of, sometimes in addition to, branding. Ratcliff stood little chance of a sentence remission; the presiding judge was the governor John Winthrop. The sole basis for the sentence appears to be the interpretation of scripture placed upon the offense by

---

Colonial Lincoln, Massachusetts at: https://www2.bc.edu/donald-hafner/To%20Be%20Set%20Upon%20the%20Gallows.pdf. among numerous other examples defendants Cook and Pellat were sentenced by Boston justices to stand in the gallows for one hour for the offense of dueling in 1753. *Halifax Gazette*, 14 April 1753.

[43] Powers, E., *Crime and Punishment in Early Massachusetts 1620-1692*, Boston, Beacon Press, 1966. esp. p. 182-183. For further discussion of the extraordinary Ratcliff case see: Adams, C.F., Sir Christopher Gardiner, *Massachusetts Historical Society*, Vol. 20 (Jan., 1883) pp. 61-88. esp. p. 74.

the governor, his deputy and the Court of Assistants.[44] The following year on September 4th Richard Hopkins was branded on the cheek and whipped for his crime, selling guns, gunpowder and shot to Indians.[45] Of note is that this offense carried the death sentence, which was not applied, and that immediately after the trial the court held that henceforth the offense should not attract the death sentence. One month later, Nicholas Frost appeared charged with theft, drunkenness and fornication. He was fined and ordered to be severely whipped, branded with a hot iron in the hand and then banished. The court warned Frost that should he return he would be put to death.[46] Rofite Scarlett appeared before the Assistants as a "knowen theife." Charged with "divers felonies," he was ordered to be severely whipped and branded in the forehead with a T and then handed to his master to be sent out of the jurisdiction.[47] Scarlett did not leave and one year later the justices noted that "on hope of amendment, hee is admitted to stay."[48] Presumably, since the magistrates noted he was a known thief, they allowed Scarlett to plea clergy twice, contrary to English law but not unusual given the degree of local ad hoc law making and sentencing taking place during trials. William Brumfield was an indentured servant who appeared before the Court of Assistants in 1637 charged with plotting to run away from his master, stealing, lying, drunkenness and idleness. He was ordered to make double restitution to his master, to be branded and then whipped.[49] The court record does not specify where Brumfield was to be branded or what letter was to be burnt into him. In the same year we see three adulterers, John

---

[44] Noble, J., Notes on the Trial and Punishment of Crimes, *Colonial Society of Massachusetts*, Transactions 1895-1897. (Feb., 1895). pp. 51-65. pp. 53-54.
[45] Mass. Court. Recs. pp. 99-100. (1632). The court held that hereafter the crime should not be punishable with death.
[46] M.C.R. 1632. p. 100. Apparently, Frost was in breach of sentence at some point as there is a court entry 3. Nov. 1635 "Imprisoned till trial for breach." The disposition of the case is not entered.
[47] M.C.R. 1635. p. 163.
[48] M.C.R. 1636. 28 October. p. 183.
[49] M.C.R. 1637. 19 Sept. p. 203.

Hathaway, Robert Allen and Margaret Seale receiving the sentence of whipping and banishment "never to return upon pain of death."[50] It was another six years before the Massachusetts courts imposed literal, rather than social, execution upon two adulterers.[51]

In 1638 Edward Shaw appeared before the Plymouth court indicted for stealing fifteen shillings, a clergyable offense in England. He was found guilty and ordered to be burnt in the shoulder with a hot iron then severely whipped.[52] This unusual sentence of shoulder burning is the only example found anywhere, in Massachusetts or Plymouth, during the entire colonial period. By contrast, twenty years later Thomas West was found guilty of burglary and theft on the Sabbath; he received the proportionately lenient sentence of one ear cropped and was branded with B on his forehead.[53] Burglary was still a non-clergyable crime in England at this time. Two further examples from Plymouth colony follow. The first involved the beating to death of a fourteen-year-old servant boy, John Walker, by his master and master's wife, Robert and Susanna Latham. John Walker died in January 1655 as a result of sustained beatings to his body and head. Robert Latham was indicted for murder, Susanna was deemed culpable by the court but she was not prosecuted. In March 1655 Robert Latham was found guilty of manslaughter. He pleaded his clergy and was burnt in the hand and released.[54] Three years after this, Robert Trayes was indicted for the murder of Daniell Standlake. Apparently Standlake had died from gunshot wounds received during a dispute with the defendant. It was alleged that the gun went off accidently. The jury agreed and Trayes

---

[50] M.C.R. 1637-38. 12 March.
[51] James Brittane and Mary Lathame, infra.
[52] P.C.R. vol. I. p.183.
[53] Essex County Court. Vol. 2. p. 48. (1657).
[54] C.f. Goodwin, J., *The Pilgrim Republic: An Historical Review of the Colony of New Plymouth*, New York, Klaus, 1970. p. 401.

was found guilty of death by misadventure. He was ordered to be whipped and pay a fine.[55]

During the 1660's and 70's there was a flurry of adultery cases where the defendants received a variety of clergy-style sentences. These cases will be discussed subsequently. The last implied clergy plea of the 1660's occurred in 1668 when John Woolcott was branded in the forehead and ordered to pay triple restitution for burglary and theft.[56] Branding on the forehead for burglars had been enacted in Massachusetts in 1647. Of course the crime was not clergyable under English law either in 1647 or 1668. Two years after Woolcott another recidivist, William Barnes, was branded in the forehead for burglary.[57] Recidivists were denied clergy for all offenses under the English statute 18 Car. 2, c.3. (1666). Also in 1668 runaway servant Nicolas Vauden, with previous convictions for theft of money, stole £7 and nine shillings from his master. He was sentenced to pay £40 compensation and to be branded in the forehead with the letter R, denoting runaway.[58] In 1672 the Court of Assistants heard the case against Philip Keyn and John Smith. Keyn was charged with burglary of an occupied home and stealing thirty-five shillings from within. He was sentenced to be branded with the letter B on his forehead and pay treble the value of the theft in restitution. John Smith was also convicted of non-clergyable house burglary. He too was sentenced to be branded on the forehead; however, unlike Keyn, he was not ordered to pay restitution.[59] Another burglar, George Major, was convicted of house-breaking and theft of pork and beef in 1677. He was sentenced to branding on the forehead and bound over to keep good behavior.[60] By

---

[55] P.C.R. 6. p141. and see: http://www.histarch.illinois.edu/plymouth/inquest.htm#N_4_.
[56] Dalzell, supra. p. 189.
[57] Dalzell. Supra. p. 189.
[58] Essex County Court. Vol. 4. P. 234. (1670).
[59] Suffolk County Court. p. 235. (1672).
[60] Essex County Court. Vol. 6. P. 253. (1677).

39 Eliz. c.9 (1597), clergy was denied to all house-breakers, regardless of the value of the property stolen.

This period also experienced a number of adulterers being prosecuted and it is interesting to compare the sentences for serious felonies such as house burglary with adultery. In 1675 Maurice Brett was found guilty of adultery. He was sentenced to stand in the pillory with a rope around his neck, to be whipped at the cart's tail and then banished. He had his ears cropped as he was removed from the pillory. Co-defendant Mary Gibbs received the same punishment except she was spared banishment.[61] Thomas Davis and his un-named co-defendant were found not guilty of adultery in 1675. However, the court found him guilty of "very suspicious acts" leading to adultery. Both defendants were whipped at the cart's tail after they had stood in the gallows with a rope around their necks.[62] Peter Cole and Sarah Buckman and Darby Bryan and Abigail Johnson all received similar sentences for their criminal immorality.[63] By comparison one year later John Flynt was fined £40 for manslaughter. He was not branded and left the court after making payment; £20 costs and £20 restitution to the family of the victim.[64] Also in 1676 Samuel Hunting was found guilty of manslaughter. He was ordered to pay £20 to the widow of his victim and £5 costs. John Dyer paid £6 compensation, payable over five years, to the family of an Indian he killed.[65] Why clergy was not pleaded in either of these manslaughter cases is not recorded. What seems clear, however, is that in the mind of the sentencing magistrates, morality had a higher price than life and the death sentence of banishment was more frequently applied to fornicators than burglars and killers.

---

[61] Noble, supra. p. 59.
[62] Noble, supra. p. 59.
[63] Noble, supra. p. 59.
[64] M.C.R. 1676.
[65] M.C.R. 1676 and 1680.

By the 1680's, sentencing in burglary cases was following a distinct pattern, branding, occasional banishment and never the death sentence, regardless of whether or not the offender was a recidivist. This was a flagrant disregard for English law and, as discussed above, was soon to change. The early part of the decade experienced a number of clergy burglary trials; Thomas Davies and John Eggington were an exception. They managed to get themselves transported out of the colony to "any of the English plantations" only after they had escaped from prison and committed further thefts. The pair was finally deemed to be "incorrigible thieves and robbers."[66] In 1681 a recidivist burglar, George Fairfax, was branded then whipped and after sentence sold to a new master. One can surmise that his burglary was perpetrated against his master and this was the cause of the sentence that he be sold. It does not, however, negate the continuing disregard sentencing justices had for established English law that forbade clergy to burglars and to recidivists. Henry Spencer committed house burglary and horse theft;[67] he was branded on the forehead with a B. Zacheus Perkins received the same sentence for his burglaries,[68] and in 1685 Uriah Clements was branded on the forehead and had one ear cropped for a second burglary conviction.[69] There were few prosecutions for manslaughter; one recorded was against Leonard Pomeroy in 1683.[70] It is worth reflecting that during this time of sentencing liberalism to which thieves were the beneficiaries, adulterers and women who concealed the birth of bastards were liable to severe whippings and banishment. In one instance Elizabeth Payne received the almost unheard sentence of eighty lashes for her fornication[71] and Frenchman Peter Lorphelin had *both* ears removed

---

[66] M.C.R. 1680.
[67] Unclergyable. 37 Hen. 8. C.8 (1545) and Edw. 6. C.12., 2&3 Edw. 6. C. 33., 31 Eliz. c.12.
[68] Dalzell, supra. p. 189.
[69] M.C.R. 1681, 1683, 1685.
[70] M.C.R. 1683.
[71] M.C.R. 1683.

for making insulting speeches against the government of Massachusetts.[72] The last possible implied clergy plea appears to have taken place in 1693 when Samuel White was branded in the forehead with the letter B. Curiously the crime was robbery but the court ordered a B. White was also ordered to pay treble damages to his victims.[73] There are no cases of implied clergy after reversion back to English control in the mid-1680's. From 1691 forward clergy becomes available to all defendants in accordance with the applicable English law.

Special cases

Before discussing the most celebrated clergy case to be decided in Massachusetts, the Boston Massacre, there are a couple of unusual cases from the colony that warrant mention. They are interesting in particular because they highlight the capricious and arbitrary manner in which justice was applied and the wide variety of sentences that were being imposed with a truly surprising degree of disregard for the law or sentencing precedent, either of English common law or developing colonial law.

In 1641 adultery was declared a capital crime under the Body of Lawes. On March 5th 1643 James Brittane and Mary Latham appeared before the Assistants' Court charged with criminal adultery. They were found guilty and sentenced to death. Brittane and Latham were executed sixteen days later. Mary Latham was eighteen years of age at the time of her punishment. Only two years before this extreme sentence, Thomas Owen was ordered to sit upon the gallows with a rope around his neck for his adultery[74] and Thomas Scott and his wife, for

---

[72] M.C.R. 1679.
[73] M.C.R. 1693.
[74] M.C.R. 1641.

committing fornication before marriage, were required to sit in the marketplace with letters F on their heads.[75] Conversely in 1637 adulterers John Hathaway, Robert Allen and Margaret Steale were banished from the colony with the threat of death should they return.[76]

Further evidence of sentencing disparity can be seen throughout the century. Maurice Bretts was found not guilty of murder in 1675. He was tried for adultery the same year and acquitted, but the court viewed him as "not legally guilty but of very filthy carriage" and duly sentenced him to have both ears cropped, be whipped and banished.[77] He appealed to the court for mercy and they remitted the ear cropping. In 1683 William King was convicted of blasphemy and, despite his apparent madness, he was still given twenty lashes.[78] Shortly after this, Peleg Heath and his gang of pirates were granted clergy for the non-clergyable crime of piracy. The same year Elizabeth Payne was sentenced to eighty lashes for fornication. Two years before this, in 1681, a Negro, Marja, was found guilty of arson and sentenced to be burnt to death.[79] One of the rare cases of bestiality recorded occurred in 1673. Benjamen Goad was given a special verdict, "If the prisoner's confession against himself upon his first apprehantion [sic] and before his trial together with one evidence be sufficient for legal conviction, then we find him guilty according to the Indictment; otherwise not guilty of the fact but of a most horrid attempt." He was found guilty and hung. Clearly a case of damned if you do and damned if you do not. Goad was going to be an example to the community regardless of the

---

[75] M.C.R. 1641
[76] M.C.R. 1637-38.
[77] M.C.R. 1675.
[78] M.C.R. 1683.
[79] M.C.R. 1681. There are two examples in 1770 where the recorded verdicts are manslaughter and the sentence is branding but the court record does not state that clergy was pleaded. The case of John Daily found guilty of the manslaughter of Benjamen Gustalow. March 1778. Mass SCJ Records. 1775-8. 212-213 and Thomas Lot for the murder of Timothy Blish. Verdict manslaughter. Sentence burned in the hand, forfeiture of goods and chattels. June 1778. Mass. SCJ Records 1778-80. 124-5.

law.[80] It was around this time that Thomas Davis was found guilty of "very suspicious acts"; the court meant adultery.[81] If it was anticipated that the imposition of English law would immediately stabilize sentencing disparity, that was not the case. In 1694 Hannah Newall and Lambert Despar were convicted of adultery. She received fifteen lashes and Despar twenty-five. Just three years beforehand, Martin Williams, a stranger, was convicted of the non-clergyable crime of counterfeiting. He was sentenced to stand in the Boston market square with a paper around his neck signifying his crime.[82] Seven years prior to this sentence Joseph Gatchell was sentenced to have his tongue pierced with a hot iron. His conviction was for blasphemy.[83]

The Boston Massacre clergy case

The tragedy of 1770 that led to the death of five Bostonians on King Street is a familiar event in the history of the American Revolution. What is not so well known is the irony of the situation that caused British soldiers to be represented by American lawyers during which the Americans would successfully plead clergy for their clients. This was an event that could not have happened in England as lawyers had no right of audience other than in treason trials. Compounding this unique scenario is that some of the lawyers would go forward in history as the founders of America and in the defense team was a future president and a number of signatories to the Declaration of Independence.

---

[80] M.C.R. 1673.
[81] M.C.R. 1675.
[82] M.C.R. 1691. Compare with James Luxford case, supra, who in 1640 had both ears cut off and was then banished back to England for the crime of forgery.
[83] M.C.R. 1684.

British troops were stationed in Boston due to a request from the governor to England for assistance. The killings of March 5th started as a result of an incident involving a British officer, Captain John Goldfinch, and a local youth, Edward Garrick, when Garrick verbally taunted Goldfinch to the effect that he had not discharged a lawful debt owed to a Boston wigmaker. The situation deteriorated and a crowd gathered, during which a British sentry entered the crowd and struck Garrick with his musket. At the same time as this incident a number of other small disturbances were taking place across Boston all directed at the British troops. At some point one of the crowd announced its intention to move towards the British barracks at King Street; Captain John Preston, accompanied by seven sentries, was on duty at the main entrance. On arrival, one of the crowd, a mulatto named Cripsus Attucks, moved towards the soldiers and knocked one of them to the ground. The soldiers responded with gunfire and within a few minutes five civilians, including Attucks, lay dead. Just after midnight Captain Preston was arrested on suspicion of murder. One week later a further eight soldiers were arrested and charged. Boston attorney John Adams was assigned as defense counsel.

Captain Preston was tried first. Samuel Quincy, solicitor general, represented the prosecution. John Adams was assisted by Robert Paine and Josiah Quincy in the defense. After six days of hearing Preston was acquitted of all charges. The trial against the remaining defendants took place eight weeks later. Adams, Paine and Quincy represented all eight soldiers. The jury retired for less than three hours before returning a verdict of not guilty against six of the defendants and manslaughter against Hugh Montgomery and Matthew Kilroy. On December 14, 1770, in accordance with applicable English law, Montgomery and Kilroy pleaded their clergy and were branded in court. Adams went on to become president of the United States. In later life he reflected upon the Boston trial as one of the best pieces of service he ever rendered his country. "Judgment of death against those soldiers would have been as foul a stain upon this country as the executions of Quakers or witches, anciently. As the evidence was, the verdict of the jury was exactly right."[84] The clergy plea was entered seven more times[85] before Massachusetts abolished it in 1784.

---

[84] John Adams Diary 19, 16 December 1772-18 December 1773. [electronic edition]. Adams Family Papers: An Electronic Archive. Massachusetts Historical Society. p.16.
[85] James Bell pleaded his clergy for manslaughter in 1773. Source: *Massachusetts Law Quarterly*, supra. p.598. Also Barber et al, supra, 1779. Thomas Lot, 1779. John Daly, 1777, Andrew Kinchlalius, 1776 and James Bell, 1773, supra.

Chapter 7. Abolition of benefit of clergy in America

Shrugging off the veneer of ecclesiasticism

Massachusetts was the first colony to abolish benefit of clergy;[1] Virginia was to follow with abolition for free persons in 1796 but not until 1848 for slaves.[2] Throughout its one hundred seventy years of use in these two colonies, clergy was applied as capriciously and individually as ever could be imagined. What had once been a tool for use by a Tudor dynasty to lure Englishmen into believing the Crown intended to treat citizens as equals when it abjectly did not, clergy was accommodated by use to become as much an American legal fiction as it ever was in England. Regrettably the adaptation of clergy in Virginia and Massachusetts was as cruel as in England because the chance of escaping punishment was itself a gamble. In Virginia, the application of clergy was more closely aligned with established practices in England. In Massachusetts, magistrates and judges introduced personal bias and blatant indifference towards any corpus of established law other than a modified version of scripture with "elevated penalties"[3] for sexual miscreants. The result was a piecemeal use of clergy that fluctuated between tolerating the plea and sentencing within understood recognizable parameters akin to English law—to a most bizarre rendering of sentencing that had no benchmark whatsoever, albeit the clergy plea may have been accepted during the trial proceedings. Benefit of clergy existed in Virginia because it helped the fledgling legal system gain momentum and direction; it came as part of the baggage the colonists brought with them and was never the source of ideological

---

[1] It was abolished by U.S. Congress April 30, 1790.
[2] Cross, A.L. Benefit of Clergy in the American Criminal Law, *American Historical Review*, Third Series, Vol. 61. (Oct., 1927-Jun., 1928), pp. 153-181. p. 166.
[3] Chapin, B., *Criminal Justice in Colonial America*, 1606-1660, Athens, University of Georgia Press, 1983. p. 147.

rejection that it was to the northern settlers. From 1732 onwards, the judiciary of Virginia were themselves actively promoting use of clergy by informing defendants of the right. For the first seventy years of operation in Massachusetts it existed at the whim of Puritan aristocrats who applied their own view of justice modified according to local exigency. Once this judicial freedom was reined in, through the enforced reception of English law,[4] clergy started to gather some assemblage of recognition and provide a reliable mechanism for defendants to avoid the death sentence.[5] Despite the aspirations of the founding Bay settlers, what clergy never achieved, during the first seventy years, was certainty.

Virginia was more inclined towards use of the English law from its beginnings. Some commentators have referred to this as a "reception."[6] I feel this can be misleading, as what really occurred was a passage of the English law into America, in different ways, in different locations. Virginia was established for a number of unique reasons that made it susceptible to using the common law with greater entirety than would be the case further north. That is not to say that biblical legal models were ignored in Virginia; on one occasion a man was burnt to death for the murder of his wife, a direct application of Leviticus, but generally the emphases of criminal sanctions were property offenses and civil order. Theft of Virginia Company property and theft of the mainstays of life, such as hogs, attracted the death sentence. Therefore, the issue for the Virginian colonists was not one of which law to apply but more which sentence.

Many offenses attracted the death penalty in England and in Virginia but a rigid application of bloody punishments would severely deplete a

---

[4] Preyer, infra, discusses the increase in both categories of crime and trials in both colonies at p. 339-340.

[5] I found no instances of a Massachusetts court advising a defendant of their right to clergy.

[6] E.g. Nelson, W.E. *The Common Law in Colonial America, Volume I The Chesapeake and New England, 1607-1660*, Oxford, Oxford University Press, 2008, himself and citing others. p. 3.

meager workforce. The initial response was overwhelming; Dale's laws had the appearance of being vindictive and arbitrary. In reality the severity was rarely put into practice and the death sentence was frequently substituted for amercements and corporal punishments. The renewed attention Virginia received from the English crown after Dale's era meant the common law would continue to be featured, albeit with increasing localization. The Church had never assumed a judicial role in the criminal law of Virginia and this was not about to change. Much like the newest northern colony of Plymouth, ecclesiastic and secular law were merged from the outset and always part of the civil process.

Benefit of clergy was familiar to the earliest Virginians and provided them with a practical tool; apply the known law and then generously allow mitigation in a fashion modeled to suit local needs. This is seen in operation almost immediately with a range of strange and dubious trials that allow clergy pleas for crimes that were not clergyable according to English law. Offense, venue and sentencing disparity with England remained a feature of colonial legal systems for most of the seventeenth century. It was not until the end of the seventeenth century that the colonies experienced an enforced enthusiasm for the application of English law and Virginia gradually moved towards harsher sentencing that appeared more in keeping with London; by the first quarter of the eighteenth century, one-third of all Virginian felony convictions resulted in dismemberment.[7]

Just as clergy was modified across England by juries, judges and the crown, so too it was adjusted in Virginia in order that the resentment expressed towards enforced reception of criminals to the colony was counterbalanced with Virginia itself transporting criminals out of the

---

[7] C.f. Preyer, K., Penal Measures in the American Colonies: An Overview, *The American Journal of Legal History*, Vol. 26. No. 4 (Oct., 1982) pp. 326-353.

colony to other British dominions. Appeals against Virginian clergy transportation were possible: to the governor and then in principle to London. The fact that Virginia had established an appellate system appears not to have caused England too much concern, which is noteworthy given that England had no appellate procedure in place during the same period. Alongside clergy the Virginians also picked off the pleas they felt useful; pleading the belly was adopted but the horrors of *peine forte et dure* were not. Virginia followed English law with regard to felons being deprived of their chattels and estates upon conviction. Numerous offenses that were non-clergyable in England were granted clergy in Virginia; robbery (unless committed within a dwelling or on the king's highway), burglary was clergyable, pickpocketing and after 1707, horse theft. Counterfeiting was always non-clergyable in Virginia; as we have seen in the previous chapter, this was not the case in Massachusetts. Massachusetts also permitted the families of convicted felons to inherit. Unnatural crimes followed English law in Virginia, whereas the law relating to these offenses mimicked Mosaic law further north. Bigamy, a church crime in England, was dealt with by the secular courts in Virginia and Massachusetts; it was clergyable in England and Virginia and not in Massachusetts. By the latter part of the eighteenth century both colonies experienced fewer prosecutions for morality offenses and an increase in property crime trials; clergy had finally shrugged off its veneer of ecclesiasticism and was fully employed protecting the rising class of consumer criminals.

The availability of the clergy plea for slaves varied greatly between different states. In Virginia slaves were treated as property until 1732. Before this time they were subject to the whims of individual magistrates who had the power to impose the death sentence or highly variable corporal punishments. The landmark decision of 1732 involving Mary Aggie[8] and the legislation that followed this decision permitted all men and women of the colony to plead their clergy. This is not to say that vast differences between the laws and sentences between whites and Negroes did not continue to exist for years; they did. But the principle of allowing clergy to Negroes was significant and forced the Virginian courts to face the status of Negroes as Christian before the law. Massachusetts had permitted its variation of clergy applicable to Negroes and slaves from the first implied use of the plea. Post 1732 and to their credit, there is evidence of the Virginian criminal courts advising Negro defendants of the clergy plea in instances where it was apparent that the defendant was ignorant of the life-sparing opportunity. I found no instances of the Massachusetts courts advising any defendants of their clergy either before Anglicization of the plea or after. Women in Virginia had been reluctantly permitted the clergy plea in a very limited number of cases. No legislation addressing women and the clergy plea was enacted until the 1732 changes occurred.

Pardons as clergy sentences were utilized in England and Virginia. In England they became the basis for transportation. Virginia followed this model in fewer instances and with extraordinary outcomes: juveniles pardoned and then transported for burglary, adult male defendants bartering for transportation in exchange for entering a clergy plea and Robert Evans, who could not read, suffering perpetual banishment as a clergy sentence. Equally strange, though largely uninvestigated to date,[9] is the evidence of gubernatorial clergy pardons. This work has reflected upon a few of the more unusual examples, Reddish and Clarke in Virginia and counterfeiters in Massachusetts, a further example of transgressory judicial behavior. Counterfeiting was never clergyable in England. It can be said that

---

[8] Of note is that throughout the period of study none of the colonial superior courts published their opinions. Recognition of the importance of the Aggie case appears to be evidenced in the reports produced by lay authors and the subsequent changes to the law.

[9] See: Preyer, supra.

neither Virginia nor Massachusetts felt obliged to follow the English legal maxim, *judicandum est legibus non exemplis*.[10]

The end of the legal anomaly

The utilization of the clergy plea in Virginia and Massachusetts reflected absorption of a much-used legal anomaly that had applied in England for at least the previous six hundred years. To understand why the clergy plea so varied in application it is necessary to recognize that the common law was not itself codified; it was, and would remain, *lex non scripta*. As such there was no cogent body of rules that articulated how and when clergy should be applied; codification had never appealed to common lawyers. If this is combined with the unique factors that caused the development of the two colonies, their differing cultural, religious and motivating heritage, then perhaps it becomes possible to start to appreciate why it is that clergy existed in colonial America at all; it was a fundamentally necessary part of an effective legal system and as codification of the laws expanded the need for clergy decreased. Legislation was always more important to the colonists than English common lawyers and in part this explains the continuation of clergy in England long after its abolition in America.

For the early Virginians carrying clergy across the Atlantic was never repugnant, it just needed adaptation. For the Puritans it was morally and ideologically objectionable; it was familiar but distasteful.[11] The early leaders were well versed in the common law[12] as well as the bible; fusion rather than outright rejection was needed. Their challenge was

---

[10] Execution must be according to the judgment.
[11] C.f. Goebel, J., King's Law and Local Custom in Seventeenth Century New England, *Columbia Law Review*, Vol. 31. No. 3 (Mar., 1931), pp. 416-448.
[12] Chapin, B. *Criminal Justice in Colonial America, 1606-1660*, Athens, University of Georgia Press, 1983. At p. 146 comments: "No man who came out to America in a position of leadership could have been unaware of the agitation for law reform in England."

to merge religious objectives with practical secular legal experience; actual employment of the term clericus appears to have been unacceptable, it was never used until imposed by the British. Whether implicitly applied or by common law, Massachusetts used the clergy plea with all of the vagaries apparent in Virginia and England and with all of their sentencing absurdities. It might have been the case that, had the first wave of colonists all subscribed to a biblical code, clergy would have perished at Plymouth Rock. This was not the case, and the presence of non-conformists clearly influenced the incorporation of clergy into the fabric of the early justice system.[13]

Justice Wendell Holmes once noted that the law will only become entirely consistent once it has stopped growing.[14] If that is the case, then it would be reasonable to think that a mitigatory defense that grew for more than one thousand years might be recognized for the important role it has played in shaping the common law, American and English, now that the plea has stopped. This does not appear to be the case; consistency has never been a feature of *privilegium fori*, nor has clergy attracted any significant degree of legal importance—just two books have been produced on the subject and perhaps thirty articles. In America benefit of clergy was a quiet force. It contributed to fundamental constitutional guarantees: right to a fair trial, right to counsel, double jeopardy, the distinction between a felony and a misdemeanor, the right to know what offense is charged and, eventually, the right to certainty before the law. Of these much has been written; of the route to these achievements there is still much to be said. The great Leviathan English common law could have consumed the American colonies; it did not. In part this is due to the

---

[13] For a discussion of the different religious entities in colonial America see: Pyle, R.E. &Davidson, J.D. The origins of Religious Stratification in Colonial America, *Journal for the Scientific Study of Religion*, Vol. 42. No. 1 (Mar., 2003), pp. 57-76. Of note also is that the basis for the justice system was equity before God and to these ends treating all "sinners" equally before god made a great deal of sense. c.f. Preyer, supra.

[14] Dalzell, G.W. *Benefit of Clergy in America*, Winston-Salem, Blair, 1955. p. 270.

employment of the clergy plea, a use that resulted in a curious mixture of criminal justice which would itself become its own, incongruous, American common law.[15]

---

[15] Chapin, supra. p. 147 comments: "Neither English attempts at standardization after 1690 nor the amalgamation of jurisdictions into a nation in 1789 could create a common American criminal law. Where once there were seven, now there are fifty." Contrast with Nelson, W.E. *The Common Law in Colonial America, Volume I The Chesapeake and new England, 1607-1660,* Oxford, Oxford University Press, 2008 at p. 7, "Only after 1660, when the crown launched a long-term effort to fashion England's colonies into a coherent empire, did these legal orders begin to converge in the direction of a single common-law system."

Appendix One

For The Colony in Virginea Britannia.
Lawes Divine, Morall and Martiall, &c.

Alget qui non Ardet.
Res nostrae subinde non sunt, quales quis optaret, sed quales esse possunt.

Printed at London for Walter Burre. 1612.

To the Right Honorable, the Lords of the Councell of Virginea.
Noblest of men, though tis the fashion now
Noblest to mix with basest, for their gaine:
Yet doth it fare farre otherwise with you,
That scorne to turn to Chaos so againe,
And follow your supreme distinction still,
Till of most noble, you become divine
And imitate your maker in his will,
To have his truth in blackest nations shine.
What had you beene, had not your Ancestors
Begunne to you, that make their nobles good?
And where white Christians turn in maners Mores
You wash Mores white with sacred Christan bloud
This wonder ye, that others nothing make
Forth then (great L.L.) for your Lords Saviours sake.

By him, all whose duty is tributary to your Lordships, and unto so excellent a cause.

William Strachey.

To the constant, mighty, and worthie friends, the Committies, Assistants
unto his Majesties Councell for the Colonie in Virginea-Britannia.

When I went forth upon this voyage, (Right worthy Gentlemen) true it is, I held it a service of dutie, (during the time of my unprofitable service, and purpose of stay in the Colonie, for which way else might I adde unto the least hight of so Heoricke and pious a building) to propose unto myself to be (though an unable) Remembrancer of all accidents, occurrences, and undertakings therunto, adventitiall: In most of which since the time our right famous sole Governour then, now Lieutenant Generall Sir Thomas Gates Knight, after the ensealing of his Commission hasted to our fleete in the West, there staying for him, I have both in the Bermudas, and since in Virginea beene a sufferer and an eie witnesse, and the full storie of both in due time shall consecrate unto your viewes, as unto whom by right it appertaineth, being vowed patrones of a worke, and enterprise so great, then which no object nor action (the best of bests) in these time, may carry with it the like fame, honour, or goodnesse.

Howbet since many impediments, as yet must detaine such my observations in the shadow of darknesse, untill I shall be able to deliver them perfect unto your judgements why I shall provoke and challenge, I do in the meane time present a transcript of the Toparchia or State of those duties, by which their Colonie stands regulated and commaunded, that such may receive due checke, who malitiously and desperately heretofore have censured of it, and by examining of which they may be right sorie so to have defaulked from us as if we lived there lawlesse, without obedience to our Countrey, or observance of Religion to God.

Nor let it afflict the patience of such full and well instructed judgments, unto whom many of these constitutions and Lawes Divine or Marshall may seeme auncient and common, since these grounds are the same constant, Asterismes, and starres, which must guide all that travell in these perplexed wayes, and paths of publique affairs; & whosoever shall wander from them, shall but decline a hazardous and by-course to bring their purposes to good effect.

Nor let another kind quarrell or traduce the Printing of them to be delivered in particular to officers and private Souldiers for their better instruction, especially unto a Company for the grievous, unsettled and unfurnished, since we know well how short our memories are oftentimes, and unwilling to give stoage to the better things, and such things as limit and bound mankind in their necessariest duties.

For which it transcends not the reach of his understanding, who is conversant, if but as for a festivall exercise, (every privy Moone) in reading of a booke, that records and edicts for manners or civill duties, have usually beene fixed upon ingraven Tables, for the Commons daily to over-looke: a custome more especially cherished by those not many yeeres since in Magnuza who have restored (as I may say) after so great a floud and rage of abused goodnesse, all Lawes, literature and Vertue againe, which had well night perished, had not the force of piety and sacred reason remaining in the bosomes of some few, opposed itselfe against the fury of so great a calamity, of whom it is an undenyable truth, that the meanes and way whereby they reduced the generall defection, was by printing thereby so houlding uppe those involved principles, and Instructions wherein (as in a mirror, the blind and wandering judgement might survaye, what those knowledges were, which taught both how to governe, and how to obey, (the end indeed of sociable mankinds Creation) since without order and government, (the onely hendges, whereupon, not onely the safety, but the being of all states doe turne and depend) what society may possible subsist, or commutative goodnesse be practised. And thus lawes being published, every common eye may take survey of their duties, and carrying away the tenour of the same, meditate, & bethinke how safe, quiet, and comely it is to be honest, just, and civill.

And indeed all the sacred powers of knowledge and wisedome are strengthened by thse two waies, either by a kind of divine nature, which his happy creation hath blessed him with, the vertue whereof comprehendeth, foreseeth and understandeth the truth and clearenesse of all things: or by instruction and tradition from others, which must improve his wants, and by experience render him perfect, awaking him in all seasons a vigilant observer of civill cautions and ordinances, an excellent reason in forcing no lesse unto the knowledge of him that will shine a starre in the firmament, where good men move, and that is, that no man doth more ill them hee that is ignorant.

For the avoiding of which, and to take away the plea of I did not know in him that shall exorbitate or goe aside with any delinquencie which may be dangerous in example or execution, albeit true it is how hee is indeede the good and honest man that will be good, and to that needeth fewe other precepts. It hath appeared most necessary unto our present Ethnarches Deputy Governor Sir Thomas Dale knight Marshall, not onely to exemplifie the old Lawes of the Colony, by Sir Thomas Gates published & put in execution by our Lord Generall Laware during his time one whole yeere of being there, but by vertue of his office, to prescribe and draw new, with their due penaltyes, according unto which wee might live in the Colony justly one with another, and performe the generall service for which we first came thither, and with so great charges & expences, are now setled & maintained there.

For my paines, and gathering of them, as I know they will be right welcom to such young souldiers in the Colony who are desirous to learne and performe their duties, so I assure me, that by you I shall bee encouraged to go on in the discharge of greater offices by examining and favouring my good intention in this, and in what else my poore knowledge or faithfulnesse may enable me to be a servant in so beloved and sacred a businesse. And even so committing to your still most abstract, grave and unsatisfied carefulnesse, both it and myselfe, I wish returne of seven fold into such his well inspired bosome, who hath lent his helping hand unto this new Sion.

From my lodging in the Black Friers,

At you best pleasures, either to returne unto the Colony, or to pray for the successe of it heere.

William Strachey.

Articles, Lawes, and Orders, Divine, Politique, and Martiall

for the Colony in Virginea:

first established by

Sir Thomas Gates Knight, Lieutenant Generall,
the 24. of May 1610.

exemplified and approved by
the Right Honourable Sir Thomas West Knight, Lord Lawair, Lord
Governour
and Captaine Generall
the 12. of June 1610.

Againe exemplified and enlarged by
Sir Thomas Dale Knight, Marshall, and Deputie Governour,
the 22. of June. 1611.

    Whereas his Majesty like himselfe a most zealous Prince hath in his owne Realmes a principall care of true Religion, and reverence to God, and hath alwaies strictly commaunded his Generals and Governours, with all his forces wheresoever, to let their waies be like his ends, for the glorie of God.

    And forasmuch as no good service can be performed, or warre well managed, where militarie discipline is not observed, and militarie discipline cannot be kept, where the rules or chiefe parts thereof, be not certainly set downe, and generally knowne, I have (with the advise and counsell of Sir Thomas Gates Knight, Lieutenant Generall) adhered unto the lawes divine, and orders politique, and martiall of his Lordship (the same exemplified) an addition of such others, as I have found either the necessitie of the present State of the Colonie to require, or the infancie, and weaknesse of the body thereof, as yet able to digest, and doe now publish them to all persons in the Colonie, that they may as well take knowledge of the Lawes themselves, as of the penaltie and punishment, which without partialitie shall be inflicted upon the breakers of the same.

Article 1

1.1 First since we owe our highest and supreme duty, our greatest, and all our allegeance to him, from whom all power and authoritie is derived, and flowes as from the first, and onely fountaine, and being especiall souldiers emprest in this sacred cause, we must alone expect our successe from him, who is onely the blesser of all good attempts, the King of kings, the commaunder of commaunders, and Lord of Hosts, I do strictly commaund and charge all Captaines and Officers, of what qualitie or nature soever, whether commanders in the field, or in the towne, or townes, forts or fortresses, to have a care that the Almightie God bee duly and daily served, and that thy call upon their people to heare Sermons, as that also they diligently frequent Morning and Evening praier themselves by their owne exemplar and daily life, and dutie herein, encouraging others thereunto, and that such, who shall often and wilfully absent themselves, be duly punished according to the martiall law in that case provided.

1.2 That no man speake impiously or maliciously, against the holy and blessed Trinitie, or any of the three persons, that is to say, against God the Father, God the Son, and God the holy Ghost, or against the knowne Articles of the Christian faith, upon paine of death.

1.3 That no man blaspheme Gods holy name upon paine of death, or use unlawful oathes, taking the name of God in vaine, curse, or banne, upon paine of severe punishment for the first offence so committed, and for the second, to have a bodkin thrust through his tongue, and if he continue the blaspheming of Gods holy name, for the third time so offending, he shall be brought to a martiall court, and there receive censure of death for his offence.

1.4 No man shall use any traiterous words against his Majesties Person, or royall authority upon paine of death.

1.5 No man shall speake any word, or do any act, which may tend to the derision, or despight of Gods holy word upon paine of death: Nor shall any man unworthily demeane himselfe unto any Preacher, or Minister of the same, but generally hold them in all reverent regard, and dutiful intreatie, otherwise he the offender shall openly be whipt three times, and ask publike forgivenesse in the assembly of the congregation three several Saboth daies.

1.6 Everie man and woman duly twice a day upon the first Towling of the Bell shall upon the working daies repaire unto the Church, to hear divine Service upon pain of losing his or her dayes allowance for the first omission, for the second to be whipt, and for the third to be condemned to the Gallies for six Moneths. Likewise no man or woman shall dare to violate or breake the Sabboth by any gaming, publique, or private abroad, or at home, but duly sanctifie and observe the same, both himselfe and his familie, by preparing themselves at home with private prayer, that they may be the better fitted for the publique, according to the commandements of God, and the orders of our Church, as also every man and woman shall repaire in the morning to the divine service, and Sermons preached upon the Saboth day, and in the afternoon to divine service, and Catechising, upon paine for the first fault to lose their provision, and allowance for the whole weeke following, for the second to lose the said allowance, and also to be whipt, and for the third to suffer death.

1.7 All Preachers or Ministers within this our Colonie, or Colonies, shall in the Forts, where they are resident, after divine Service, duly preach every Sabbath day in the forenoone, and Catechise in the afternoone, and weekely say the divine service, twice every day, and preach every Wednesday, likewise every Minister where his is resident, within the same Fort, or Fortresse, Townes or Towne, shall chuse unto him, foure of the most religious and better disposed as well to informe of the abuses and neglects of the people in their duties, and service to God, as also to the due reparation, and keeping of the Church handsome, and fitted with all reverent observances thereunto belonging: likewise every Minister shall keepe a faithful and true Record, or Church Booke, of all Christenings, Marriages, and deaths of such our people, as shall happen within their Fort, or Fortresses, Townes or Towne at any time, upon the burthen of a neglectfull conscience, and upon paine of losing their Entertainement.

1.8 He that upon pretended malice, shall murther or take away the life of any man, shall bee punished with death.

1.9 No man shal commit the horrible, and detestable sins of Sodomie upon pain of death; & he or she that can be lawfully convict of Adultery shall be punished with death. No man shall ravish or force any woman, maid or Indian, or other, upon pain of death, and know ye that he or shee, that shall commit fornication, and evident proofe made thereof, for their first fault shall be whipt, for their second they shall be whipt, and for their third shall be whipt three times a weeke for one month, and aske publique forgivenesse in the Assembly of the Congregation.

1.10 No man shall bee found guilty of Sacriledge, which is a Trespasse as well committed in violating and abusing any sacred ministry, duty or office of the Church, irreverently, or prophanely, as by beeing a Church robber, to filch, steale or carry away any thing out of the Church appertaining thereunto, or unto any holy, and consecrated place, to the divine Service of God, which no man should doe upon paine of death: likewise he that shall rob the store of any commodities therein, of what quality soever, whether provisions of victuals, or of Arms, Trucking stuffe, Apparrell, Linnen, or Wollen, Hose or Shooes, Hats or Caps, Instruments or Tooles of Steeles, Iron, &c. or shall rob from his fellow souldier, or neighbour, any thing that is his, victuals, apparell, household stuffe, toole, or what necessary else soever, by water or land, out of boate, house, or knapsack, shall bee punished with death.

1.11 Hee that shall take an oath untruly, or beare false witnesse in any cause, or against any man whatsoever, shall be punished with death.

1.12 No manner of person whatsoever, shall dare to detract, slaunder, calumniate, or utter unseemely, and unfitting speeches, either against his Majesties Honourable Councell for this Colony, resident in England, or against the Committies, Assistants unto the said Councell, or against the zealous indeavors, & intentions of the whole body of Adventurers for this pious and Christian Plantation, or against any publique booke, or bookes, which by their mature advise, and grave wisedomes, shall be thought fit, to be set foorth and publisht, for the advancement of the good of this Colony, and the felicity thereof, upon paine for the first time so offending, to bee whipt three severall times, and upon his knees to acknowledge his offence and to aske forgivenesse upon the Saboth day in the assembly of the congregation, and for the second time so offending to be condemned to the Galley for three yeares, and for the third time so offending to be punished with death.

1.13 No manner of Person whatsoever, contrarie to the word of God (which tyes every particular and private man, for conscience sake to obedience, and duty of the Magistrate, and such as shall be placed in authoritie over them) shall detract, slaunder, calumniate, murmur, mutenie, resist, disobey, or neglect the commaundments, either of the Lord Governour, and Captaine Generall, the Lieutenant Generall, the Martiall, the Councell, or any authorised Captaine, Commaunder or publike Officer, upon paine for the first time so offending to be whipt three severall times, and upon his knees to acknowledge his offence, with asking forgivenesse upon the Saboth day in the assembly of the congregation, and for the second time so offending to be condemned to the Gally for three yeares: and for the third time so offending to be punished with death.

1.14 No man shall give any disgracefull words, or commit any act to the disgrace of any person in this Colonie, or any part thereof, upon paine of being tied head and feete together, upon the guard everie night for the space of one moneth, besides to bee publikely disgraced himselfe, and be made uncapable ever after to possesse any place, or execute any office in this imployment.

1.15 No man of what condition soever shall barter, trucke, or trade with the Indians, except he be thereunto appointed by lawful authority, upon paine of death.

1.16 No man shall rifle or dispoile, by force or violence, take away any thing from any Indian comming to trade, or otherwise, upon paine of death.

1.17 No Cape Marchant, or Provant Master, or Munition Master, or Truck Master, or keeper of any store, shall at any time imbezzell, sell, or give away any thing under his Charge to any Favorite, or his, more then unto any other, whome necessity shall require in that case to have extraordinary allowance of Provisions, nor shall they give a false accompt unto the Lord Governour, and Captaine Generall, unto the Lieuetenant Generall, unto the Marshall, or any deputed Governor, at any time having the commaund of the Colony, with intent to defraud the said Colony, upon paine of death.

1.18 No man shall imbezzel or take away the goods of any man that dyeth, or is imployed from the town or Fort where he dwelleth in any other occasioned remote service, for the time, upon pain of whipping three severall times, and restitution of the said goods againe, and in danger of incurring the penalty of the tenth Article, if so it may come under the construction of theft. And if any man die and make a will, his goods shall bee accordingly disposed; if he die intestate, his goods shall bee put into the store, and being valued by two sufficient praisers, his next of kinne (according to the common Lawes of England) shall from the Company, Committies, or adventurers, receive due satisfaction in monyes, according as they were praised, by which meanes the Colonie shall be the better furnished; and the goods more carefully preserved, for the right heire, and the right heire receive content for the same in England.

1.19 There shall no Capttain, Master, Marriner, saylor, or any else of what quality or condition soever, belonging to any Ship or Ships, at this time remaining, or which shall hereafter arrive within this our River, bargaine, buy, truck, or trade with any one member in this Colony, man, woman, or child, for any toole or instrument of iron, steel or what else, whether appertaining to Smith Carpenter, Joyner, Shipwright, or any manuall occupation, or handicraft man whatsoever, resident within our Colonie, nor shall they buy or bargaine, for any apparell, linnen, or wollen, householdstuffe, bedde, bedding, sheete towels, napkins, brasse, pewter, or such like, eyther for ready money, or provisions, nor shall they exchange their provisions, of what quality soever, whether Butter, Cheese, Bisket, meal, Oatmele, Aquavite, oyle, Bacon, any kind of Spice, or such like, for any such aforesaid instruments, or tooles, Apparell, or householdstuffe, at any time, or so long as they shall here remain, from the date of these presents upon paine of losse of their wages in England, confiscation and forfeiture of such their monies and provisions, and upon peril beside of such corporall punishment as shall be inflicted upon them by verdict and censure of a martiall Court: Nor shall any officer, souldier, or Trades man, or any else of what sort soever, members of this Colony, dare to sell any such Toole, or instruments, necessary and usefull, for the businesse of the Colonie, or trucke, sell, exchange, or give away his apparell, or household stuffe of what sort soever, unto any such Seaman, either for money, or any such foresaid provisions, upon paine of 3 times severall whipping, for the one offender, and the other upon perill of incurring censure, whether of disgrace, or addition of such punishment, as shall bee thought fit by a Court martiall.

1.20 Whereas sometimes heeretofore the covetous and wide affections of some greedy and ill disposed Seamen, Saylers, and Marriners, laying hold upon the advantage of the present necessity, under which the Colony sometimes suffered, have sold unto our people, provisions of Meale, Oatmeale, Bisket, Butter, Cheese &c, at unreasonable rates, and prises unconscionable: for avoiding the like to bee now put in practise, there shall no Captain, Master, Marriner, or Saylor, or what Officer else belonging to any ship, or shippes, now within our river, or heereafter which shall arrive, shall dare to bargaine, exchange, barter, truck, trade, or sell, upon paine of death, unto any one Landman member of this present Colony, any provisions of what kind soever, above the determined valuations, and prises, set downe and proclaimed, and sent therefore unto each of your severall ships, to bee fixed uppon your Maine mast, to the intent that want of due notice, and ignorance in this case, be no excuse, or plea, for any one offender herein.

1.21 Sithence we are not to bee a little carefull, and our young Cattell, & Breeders may be cherished, that by the preservation, and increase of them, the Colony heere may receive in due time assured and great benefite, and the adventurers at home may be eased of so great a burthen, by sending unto us yeerely supplies of this kinde, which now heere for a while, carefully attended, may turne their supplies unto us into provisions of other qualities, when of these wee shall be able to subsist our selves, and which wee may in short time, be powerful enough to doe, if we wil according to our owne knowledge of what is good for our selves, forbeare to work into our owne wants, againe, by over hasty destroying, and devouring the stocks, apu authors of so profitable succeeding a Commodity, as increase of Cattel, Kine, Hogges, Goates, Poultrie &c. must of necessity bee granted, in every common mans judgement, to render unto us: Now know yee therefore, these promises carefully considered, that it is our will and pleasure, that every one, of what quality or condition soever hee bee, in this present Colony, to take due notice of this our Edict, whereby wee do strictly charge and command, that no man shall dare to kill, or destroy any Bull, Cow, Calfe, Mare, Horse, Colt, Goate, Swine, Cocke, Henne, Chicken, Dogge, Turkie, or any tame Cattel, or Poultry, of what condition soever; whether his owne, or appertaining to another man, without leave from the Generall, upon paine of death in the Principall, and in the accessary, burning in the Hand, and losse of his eares, and unto the concealer of the same foure and twenty houres whipping, with addition of further punishment, as shall be thought fitte by the censure, and verdict of a Martiall Court.

1.22 Ther shall no man or woman, Launderer or Launderesse, dare to wash any uncleane Linnen, drive bucks, or throw out the water or suds of fowle cloathes, in the open streete, within the Pallizadoes, or within forty foote of the same, nor rench, and make cleane, any kettle, pot, or pan, or such like vessell within twenty foote of the olde well, or new Pumpe: nor shall any one aforesaid, within lesse than a quarter of one mile from the Pallizadoes, dare to doe the necessities of nature, since by thse unmanly, slothfull, and loathsome immodesties, the whole Fort may bee choaked, and poisoned with ill aires, and so corrupt (as in all reason cannot but much infect the same) and this shall they take notice of, and avoide, upon paine of whipping and further punishment, as shall be thought meete, by the censure of a martiall Court.

1.23 No man shall imbezzell, lose, or willingly breake, or fraudulently make away, either Spade, Shovell, Hatchet, Axe, Mattocke, or other toole or instrument uppon paine of whipping.

1.24 Any man that hath any edge toole, either of his owne, or which hath heeretofore beene belonging to the store, see that he bring it instantly to the storehouse, where he shall receive it againe by a particular note, both of the toole, and of his name taken, that such a toole unto him appertaineth, at whose hands, upon any necessary occasion, the said toole may be required, and this shall he do, upon paine of severe punishment.

1.25 Every man shall have an especiall and due care, to keepe his house sweete and cleane, as also so much of the streete, as lieth before his door, and especially he shall so provide, and set his bedstead whereon he lieth, that it may stand three foote at least from the ground, as he will answere the contrarie at a martiall Court.

1.26 Every tradsman in their severall occupation, trade and function, shall duly and daily attend his worke upon his said trade or occupation, upon perill for his first fault, and negligence therin, to have his entertainment checkt for one moneth, for his second fault three moneth, for his third one yeare, and if he continue still unfaithfull and negligent therein, to be condemned to the Gally for three yeare.

1.27 All overseers of workemen, shall be carefull in seeing that performed, which is given them in charge, upon paine of such punishment as shall be inflicted upon him by a martiall Court.

1.28 No souldier or tradesman, but shall be readie, both in the morning, & in the afternoone, upon the beating of the Drum, to goe out unto his worke, nor shall hee return home, or from his worke, before the Drum beate againe, and the officer appointed for that businesse, bring him of, upon perill for the first fault to lie upon the Guard head and heeles together all night, for the second time so faulting to be whipt, and for the third time so offending to be condemned to the Gallies for a yeare.

1.29 No man or woman, (upon paine of death) shall runne away from the Colonie, to Powhathan, or any savage Weroance else whatsoever.

1.30 He that shall conspire any thing against the person of the Lord Governour, and Captaine Generall, against the Lieutenant Generall, or against the Marshall, or against any publike service commaunded by them, for the dignitie, and advancement of the good of the Colony, shall be punished with death: and he that shall have knowledge of any such pretended act of disloyalty of treason, and shall not reveale the same unto his Captaine, or unto the Governour of that fort or towne wherein he is, within the space of one houre, shall for the concealing of the same after that time, be not onely held an accessory, but alike culpalbe as the principall traitor or conspirer, and for the same likewise he shall suffer death.

1.31 What man or woman soever, shall rob any garden, publike or private, being set to weed the same, or wilfully pluck up therin any roote, herbe, or flower, to spoile and wast or steale the same, or robbe any vineyard, or gather up the grapes, or steale any eares of the corne growing, whether in the ground belonging to the same fort or towne where he dwelleth, or in any other, shall be punished with death.

1.32 Whosoever Seaman, or Landman of what qualitie, or in what place of commaund soever, shall be imployed upon any discovery, trade, or fishing voiage into any of the rivers within the precincts of our Colonie, shall for the safety of those men who are committed to his commaund, stand upon good and carefull guard, for the prevention of any treachery in the Indian, and if they touch upon any shore, they shal be no lesse circumspect, and warie, with good and carefull guard day and night, putting forth good Centinell, and observing the orders and discipline of watch and ward, and when they have finished the discovery, trade, or fishing, they shall make hast with all speed, with such Barke or Barkes, Pinisse, Gallie, Ship. &c. as they shall have the commaund of, for the same purpose, to James towne againe, not presuming to goe beyond their commission, or to carry any such Barke or Barkes, Gally, Pinnice, Ship. &c. for England or any other countrey in the actuall possession of any Christian Prince, upon perill to be held an enemie to this plantation, and traitor thereunto, and accordingly to lie liable unto such censure of punishment (if they arrive in England) as shall be thought fit by the Right Honourable Lords, his Majesties Councell for this Colonie, and if it shall so happen, that he or they shall be prevented, and brought backe hither againe into the Colonie, their trecherous flight to be punished with death.

1.33 There is not one man nor woman in this Colonie now present, or hereafter to arrive, but shall give up an account of his and their faith, and religion, and repaire unto the Minister, that by his conference with them, hee may understand, and gather, whether heretofore they have beene sufficiently instructed, and catechised in the principles and grounds of Religion, whose weakenesse and ignorance herein, the Minister finding, and advising them in all love and charitie, to repair often unto him, to receive therin a greater measure of knowledge, if they shal refuse so to repaire unto him, and he the Minister give notice thereof unto the Governour, or that chiefe officer of that towne or fort, wherein he or she, the parties so offending shall remaine, the Governour shall cause the offender for his first time of refusall to be whipt, for the second time to be whipt twice, and to acknowledge his fault upon the Saboth day, in the assembly of the congregation, and for the third time to be whipt every day until he hath made the same acknowledgement, and asked forgivenesse for the same, and shall repaire unto the Minster, to be further instructed as aforesaid: and upon the Saboth when the Minister shall catechise, and of him demaund any question concerning his faith and knowledge, he shall not refuse to make answere upon the same perill.

1.34 What man or woman soever, Laundrer or Laundresse appointed to wash the foule linnen of any one labourer or souldier, or any one else as it is their duties so to doe, performing little, or no other service for their allowance out of the store, and daily provisions, and supply of other necessaries, unto the Colonie, and shall from the said labourer or souldier, or any one else, of what qualitie whatsoever, either take any thing for washing, or withhold or steale from him any such linnen committed to her charge to wash, or change the same willingly and wittingly, with purpose to give him worse, old and torne linnen for his good, and proofe shall be made thereof, she shall be whipped for the same, and lie in prision till she make restitution of such linnen, withheld or changed.

1.35 No Captaine, Master, or Mariner, of what condition soever, shall depart or carry out of our river, any Ship, Barke, Gally, Pinnace &c. Roaders belonging to the Colonie, either now therein, or hither arriving, without leave and commission from the Generall or chiefe Commaunder of the Colonie upon paine of death.

1.36 No man or woman whatsoever, members of this Colonie shall sell or give unto any Captaine, Marriner, Master, or Sailer, &c. any commoditie of this countrey, of what quality soever, to be transported out of the Colonie, for his or their owne private uses, upon paine of death.

1.37 If any souldier indebted, shall refuse to pay his debts unto his creditor, his creditor shall informe his Captaine, if the Captaine cannot agree the same, the creditor shall informe the Marshals civill & principall officer, who shall preferre for the creditor a bill of complaint at the Marshals Court, where the creditor shal have Justice.

All such Bakers as are appointed to bake bread, or what else, either for the store to be given out in generall, or for any one in particular, shall not steale nor imbezzell, loose, or defraud any man of his due and proper weight and measure, nor use any dishonest and deceitfull tricke to make the bread weigh heavier, or make it coarser upon purpose to keepe backe any part or measure of the flower or meale committed unto him, nor aske, take, or detaine any one loafe more or lesse for his hire or paines for so baking, since whilst he who delivered unto him such meale or flower, being to attend the businesse of the Colonie, such baker or bakers are imposed upon no other service or duties, but onely so to bake for such as do worke, and this shall hee take notice of, upon paine for the first time offending herein of losing his eares, and for the second time to be condemned a yeare to the Gallies, and for the third time offending, to be condemned to the Gallies for three yeares.

All such cookes as are appointed to seeth, bake or dresse any manner of way, flesh, fish, or what else, of what kind soever, either for the generall company, or for any private man, shall not make lesse, or cut away any part or parcel of such flesh, fish, &c. Nor detaine or demaund any part or parcell, as allowance or hire for his so dressing the same, since as aforesaid of the baker, hee or they such Cooke or Cookes, exempted from other publike works abroad, are to attend such seething and dressing of such publike flesh, fish, or other provisions of what kinde soever, as their service and duties expected from them by the Colony, and this shall they take notice of, upon paine for the first time offending herein, of losing his eares, and for the second time to be condemned a yeare to the Gallies: and for the third time offending to be condemned to the Gallies for three yeares.

All fishermen, dressers of Sturgeon or such like appointed to fish, or to cure the said Sturgeon for the use of the Colonie, shall give a just and true account of all such fish as they shall take by day or night, of what kinde soever, the same to bring unto the Governour: As also of all such kegges of Sturgeon or Caviare as they shall prepare and cure upon perill for the first time offending heerein, of loosing his eares, and for the second time to be condemned a yeare to the Gallies, and for the third time offending, to be condemned to the Gallies for three yeares. Every Minister or Preacher shall every Sabboth day before Catechising, read all these lawes and ordinances, publikely in the assembly of the congregation upon paine of his entertainment checkt for that weeke.

The Summarie of the Marshall Lawes.

Yee are now further to understand, that all these prohibited, and forefended trespasses & misdemenors, with the injoyned observance of all these thus repeated, Civill and Politique Lawes, provided, and declared against what Crimes soever, whether against the divine Majesty of God, or our soveraigne, and Liege Lord, King James, the detestable crime of Sodomie, Incest, Blasphemie, Treason against the person of the principall Generals, and Commaunders of this Colonie, and their designs, against detracting, murmuring, calumniating, or slaundering of the Right Honourable the Councell resident in England, and the Committies there, the general Councell, and chiefe Commaunders heere, as also against intemperate raylings, and base unmanly speeches, uttered in the disgrace one of another by the worser sort, by the most impudent, ignorant, and prophane, such as have neither touch of humanitie, nor of conscience amongst our selves, against Adultery, Fornication, Rape, Murther, Theft, false witnessing in any cause, and other the rest of the Civill, and Politique Lawes and Orders, necessarily appertaining, & properly belonging to the Government of the State and Condition of the present Colony, as it now subsisteth: I say ye are to know, that all these thus joyned, with their due punishments, and perils heere declared, and published, are no lesse subject to the Martiall law, then unto the Civill Magistrate, and where the Alarum, Tumult, and practise of arms, are not exercised, and where these now following Lawes, appertaining only to Martiall discipline, are diligently to be observed, and shall be severely executed.

Article 2

2.1 No man shall willingly absent himselfe, when hee is summoned to take the oath of Supremacy, upon paine of death.

2.2 Every Souldier comming into this Colonie, shall willingly take his oath to serve the King and the Colonie, and to bee faithfull, and obedient to such Officers, and Commaunders, as shall be appointed over him, during the time of his aboad therein, according to the tenor of the oath in that case provided, upon paine of being committed to the Gallies.

2.3 If any Souldier, or what maner of man else soever, of what quality or condition soever he be, shal tacitely compact, with any Sea-man, Captain, Master, or Marriner, to convay himselfe a Board any shippe, with intent to depart from, and abandon the Colony, without a lawful Passe from the Generall, or chiefe commander of the Colonie, at that time, and shall happen to bee prevented, and taken therwith, before the shippe shall depart out of our Bay, that Captaine, Maister or mariner, that shall so receive him, shall lose his wages, and be condemned to the Gallies for three yeeres, and he the sworne servant of the Colony, Souldier, or what else, shall bee put to death with the Armes which he carrieth.

2.4 When any select, and appointed Forces, for the execution and performance of any intended service, shall bee drawne into the field, and shall dislodge from one place unto another, that Souldier that shall quit, or forsake his Colors, shall be punished with death.

2.5 That Souldier that shall march upon any service, shall keepe his Ranke, and marching, the Drum beating, and the Ensigne displayed, shall not dare to absent himselfe, or stray and straggle from his ranke, without leave granted from the cheefe Officer, upon paine of death.

2.6 All Captaines shall command all Gentlemen, and Common Souldiers in their Companies, to obey their Sergeants, and Corporals, in their offices, without resisting, or injuring the said Officers, upon paine, if the injurie be by words, he the offender shal aske his Officer pardon in the place of Arms, in the mead of the troopes. If by Act, he the offender shall passe the pikes.

2.7 That Souldier that in quarrel with an other shall call upon any of his companions, or Countrimen to assist, and abette him, shall bee put to death with such Armes as he carrieth.

2.8 Hee that shall begin a mutiny, shall bee put to death with such Armes as he carrieth.

2.9 Where a quarrell shall happen betweene two or more, no man shall betake him unto any other Arms then his sword, except he be a Captaine or Officer, upon paine of being put to death with such Armes as he shall so take.

2.10 If a Captaine or Officer of a Companie shall come where two or more are fighting with their drawne swords, so soone as hee shall cry Hold, and charge them to forbeare, those that have their swords in their hands so drawne, shall not dare to strike or thrust once after upon paine of passing the Pikes.

2.11 That Souldier that having a quarrell with an other shall gather other of his acquaintance, and Associates, to make parties, to bandie, brave second, and assist him therin, he and those braves, seconds, and assistants shall passe the Pikes.

2.12 He that shall way-lay any man by advantage taken, thereby cowardly to wound, or murther him shall passe the Pikes.

2.13 If any discontentment shall happen betweene Officers, or Souldiers, so as the one shall give words of offence, unto the other, to moove quarrell, the Officer or Souldier shall give notice thereof, to his Corporall, or superior officer, and the Corporall, or superior officer, shall commit the offender, and if it happen between Commanders, the officer offended shall give notice to the Generall, or Marshal, that he may be committed, who for the first offence shall suffer three daies imprisionment, and make the officer wronged, satisfaction before his squadron to repair him, and satisfie him, without base submission, which may unworthy him to carry Armes. And the officer, or Souldier so offended, having satisfaction offered, shall with all willingness receive it, for which both producing it to his Officer, and accepting of satisfaction, hee shall bee reputed an officer, or souldier well governed in himselfe, and so much the fitter to be advanced in Commaund over others, and if any shall upbraid him, for not having sought a savage headlong revenge against his fellow, the officer or souldier so upbraiding, shall bee punished and make satisfaction as the first offender, and if any shal so offend the second time he shall suffer ten nights lying head and heeles together, with Irons upon the guard, and have his entertainment checkt for one month, and make satisfaction to the officer or souldier, as before remembered, and for the third offence, hee shall bee committed to the Gallies three yeeres. And if upon the first offence given by any officer or souldier, unto any other, in words as aforesaid, and the other returne injurious words againe, they shall both be taken as like offenders, and suffer like punishment, saving that he who gave the first offence, shall offer first repaire unto the offended, which he the offended shall accept, and then shal hee proceed to returne the like satisfaction unto the other, and if any shall bee obstinate in this point of repaire, and satisfaction, hee shall suffer sharpe and severe punishment, until hee shall consent unto it, the words or manner of satisfaction, to be given unto the Party, or parties offended, shall be appointed by the chiefe officer of the Company, under whom the officer, or souldier shall happen to bee, with the knowledge of the provost Marshall, provided, that if the Officer or souldier shall desire it, hee may appeale unto the cheife officer of the Garrison, or unto the Marshall, if hee shall be present to Judge of the equity of the satisfaction. And if any Lanceprizado, Corporall, or other officer, shall happen to bee present, or shall take knowledge of any such offence offered of one partie, or Quarrell sought and accepted of more parties, he shall presently cause the partie, or parties so offending to bee committed to prison, that due execution may follow, as is formerly provided. And if any Lanceprizado, Corporall, or superior officer shall neglect his or their duty, or duties heerein appointed, by not bringing the offender, and their offences, to the knowledge of the superior office, that satisfaction as aforesaid, upon the fault committed, may orderly follow, the officer so offending, shal for his first omission, negligence, and contempt, suffer ten daies Imprisonment, for the second twenty, and for the third losse of his place, and to bee put to the duty of a Centinell: And if any officer or Souldier shall be present when two or more shall draw weapons, with intent to fight, or shall fight, they shall presently doe their best to part them, and if he be an officer he shall commit them, or put them under safe guard to bee committed, and if hee bee a private souldier, hee shal give notice to the provost, marshall, or unto the first officer that he shal meet with, of the parties offending, who shall presently take order, that they may be apprehended, and committed to the Provost Martialcy, and if any officer or souldier, shall happen to see any officer or souldier so fighting, and shall not doe his best to part them, without favouring one part or other, hee shall bee punished at the discretion of the officer in chiefe, and the punishment shall extend to the taking away of life, if the cause shal so require, and if any officer, or souldier shall know of any purpose in any to fight, and shall not stay them, or discover them to such officers, as are competent to stay them, but that they goe to fight, and doe accordingly fight, that officer, or souldier shall bee taken, and shall bee punished cleerely and in the same sort, as the offence deserveth punishment betweene them fighting.

2.14 That officer, or Souldier that shall challenge another to fight, and hee that shall carry any Challenge, knowing it to be a Challenge, and hee that accepteth any such Challenge with a purpose and returne of answere, to meete the saide Challenger to fight with him, in this case they shall all three be held alike culpable, and lie subject to the Censure of a Martiall Court.

2.15 That officer who shal command the guard and let such Challengers and Challenged, passe the ports, upon his to fight, shall be casseird, and if the officer be under the degree of a Captaine, hee shall bee put to doe the duty of a Centinell.

2.16 No officer shall strike any souldier, for any thing, not concerning the order, and duty of service, and the publique worke of the Colony, and if any officer shall so doe, hee shall bee punished as a private man in that case, and bee held unworthy to command, so perverting the power of his place and authority.

2.17 No man shall be Captaine of the watch at any time, under the degree of an Ensigne.

2.18 He that shall take the name of God in vain or shall play at Cards or dice, upon the Court of guard, for the first time so offending, he shall bee committed to prison, there to lie in Irons for three daies, for the second time so offending, hee shall bee whipt, and for the third time so offending hee shall bee condemned to the Gallies for one yeere.

2.19 Hee that shall absent himselfe from the Court of Guard, uppon his watch above one houre without leave of his Corporall or superior officer, shall for his first time so offending, at the relieving of the watch bee committed to prison, and there to lye in Irons for 3. dayes, for the second time he shall be committed to prison and there lye in irons for one weeke, and have his entertainement checkt for one weeke, and for the third time, hee shall be committed to the Gallies for six moneths.

2.20 He that shall swagger, and give injurious words upon the court of guard, for the first offence, hee shall aske forgivenesse upon his knees, of the officers, and rest of the Guard, before the Captain of the watch at that time: for his second time so offending, he shall bee committed to the Gallies for one yeere.

2.21 He that draweth his sword upon the Court of Guard, shall suffer death by the Armes which he weareth.

2.22 Hee that should draw his sword in a towne of Garrison, or in a Campe shall lose his right hand.

2.23 That souldier that shall goe out of the Fort, Towne or Campe, other then by the ordinary guards, issues, waies, or ports, shall suffer death by the Armes which he carrieth.

2.24 He that shall abuse and injure the Serjant Major, the provost Marshall, either by word, or deede, if hee bee a Captaine, hee shall be casseird, if a Souldier he shall passe the pikes.

2.25 When the Officer or Souldier shall have committed any Crime, or have made breach of the publique Lawes, his Captaine shall commit him unto the serjeant Major, who having taken his examination, shall send him to the Provost Marshall, committed unto prison, that he may bee brought to be censured by a court Marshall.

2.26 No Souldier shall withstand or hinder the Provost Marshall, or his men in the execution of his office, upon paine of death.

2.27 All Captaines, Lieutenants, Serjeants, and Corporals, shall be diligent at convenient times, to traine and exercise their Companies, & shall have a care of their Armes, as they tender their entertainment, and upon paine of casseiring, and other corporall punishment, as shall be inflicted by vertue of a Marshall court.

2.28 No man shall goe twelve score from the quarter, his colours, towne or fort, without leave of his Captaine, upon paine for the first time of whipping, for the second offence to be committed to the Gallies for one yeare, and for the third offence to suffer death.

2.29 No man shall sell, give, imbezzell, or play away his Armes, or any part thereof, upon paine of death.

2.30 No common Souldier shall sell, or make away any of his apparell, which is delivered unto him by the Colonie, or out of the store, upon paine of whipping.

2.31 No man shall depart from his guard without leave of his officer, upon paine of punishment: and who so shall be set Centinell, shall not depart from it, untill he be relieved, nor sleepe therof upon paine of death.

2.32 No man shall offer any violence, or contemptuously resist or disobey his Commaunder, or doe any act, or speake any words which may tend to the breeding of any disorder or mutinie in the towne or field, or disobey any principall Officers directions upon paine of death.

2.33 He that shall not appeare upon the guard, or not repaire unto his colours, when the Drum upon any occasion shall beate either upon an Alarum, or to attend the businesse which shall be then commaunded, shall for his first offence lie in Irons upon the court of guard all one night, and for his second be whipt, and for the third be condemned to the Gallies for one yeare.

2.34 That Souldier who fighting with an enemie, shall lose his Armes, or runne away cowardly, or yeeld himselfe but upon apparant and great constraints or without having performned, first the part of a good souldier, and an honest man, shall suffer death with the armes which he carrieth.

2.35 That Souldier that shall let go any caution delivered upon a treatie, or any prisoner of warre by his negligence, shall be punished with death.

2.36 No Souldier shall let goe any prisoner of war, which he hath taken without consent of his Captaine, who shall advertise the chiefe Commaunder, upon paine of being committed to the Gallies for one yeare.

2.37 That Souldier which upon an assault, or taking of any towne, that shall not follow his colours, and the victory, but shall fall to pillage for his private profit, after the place taken, shall suffer death with the armes which he weareth.

2.38 No Souldier may speake or have any private conference with any of the salvages, without leave of his Captaine, nor his Captaine without leave of his chiefe Officer, upon paine of death.

2.39 When the Marshall or Governour of a towne, shall demaund a Souldier that hath made breach of these lawes, that Captaine or any other that shall conceale him, or assist him to flie away, shall bee punished with the punishment which the fact of the said fugitive deserved.

2.40 That Captaine that shall ipso facto, find any Souldier breaking these fore declared lawes and ordinances, of whatsoever company he shall be, he shall commit him to the Provost Marshall to be punished according as the offence committed commeth under the construction of the Martiall law in that case provided.

2.41 No Souldier shall unprofitably waste his pouder, shot, or match, by shooting it idly away, or at birds, beasts, or fowle, but shall give an account unto his Corporall of the same, who shall certifie his Captain upon peril for his first fault so committed, to be committed to prison, there to lie in Irons head & heeles togither eight & forty hours, for the second to the condemned six moneths to the Gallies, and for the third offence to be condemned two yeares to the Gallies.

2.42 All Captaines, Officers, and common Souldiers, or others of what condition soever, members of the Colonie, shall doe their endeavours to detect, apprehend, and bring to punishment all offenders, and shall assist the officer of that place for that purpose, as they will answere the contrary at our Marshall court.

2.43 All other faults, disorders, and offences that are not mentioned in these Lawes, Articles, and Orders shall be & are supplied in the instructions which I have set downe, and now shall be delivered unto every Captain, and other Officer, so farre forth as the infancie, and as yet weake condition of this our present Colony will suffer, and which shall be punished according to the generall custome, and therfore I commaund all men to looke to their charges, and him that hath no charge to looke to his owne carriage, and to keepe himselfe within the bounds of dutie, for the discipline shall be strictly kept, and the offenders against the lawes thereof severely punished.

2.44 Whosoever shall give offence to the Indians in that nature, which truly examined, shall found to have beene cause of breach of their league, and friendship, which with so great travaile, desire, and circumspection, we have or shall at any time obtaine from them without commission so to doe, from him that hath authoritie for the same, shall be punished with death.

2.45 Whosoever shall wilfully, or negligently set fire on any Indian dwelling house, or Quioquisock house or temple, or upon any storehouse, or garner of graine, or provision of what quality soever, or disvaledge, ransacke, or ill intreat the people of the countrey, where any warre, or where through any march shall be made except it be proclaimed, or without commandement of the chiefe officers shall be punished with death.

2.46 Whosoever shall not do his endeavour and best to regaine & recover his colours, if by hap it fall into the Indians hands shall lie subject to the censure of a Marshall court.

2.47 Whosoever shall faine himself sick, upon the point of fight, or when any worke is to be done or slip away from the service of either, shall be punished by death.

2.48 Whosoever shall raise any question, brabble or braule in the watch, or Amboscado, or in Scout, or Sentinel in any other effect, or make any noise or rumor where silence, secrecie, and covert is to be required, shall be punished with death.

2.49 Whosoever shall not retreat when the drum or trumpet soundeth the same, whether it be upon any sallies, made out of any town or fortres, or in skirmish, or in any incounter, shall be punished with death.

2.50 It now resteth, that all Captaines and supreme officers, whether governor in towne, fort or fortes, or Captaine of companies shall be advised to do their indevors joyntly, and to agree in one accord, that the true and never failing Justice, may be executed with all integrity of all these foredeclared lawes, according to the dignitie, power, and censure of the Martiall court, that by the exemplar lives, and honourable practises of all that is good & vertuous, all things may be governed in good order, as no doubt, our Right Honorable Lord Generall doth assure himselfe, that all good and upright men that have the feare of God, and his service, and their owne honour in regard, will demean themselves no lesse, then according to the dignity of their place, and charge of their command, the united powers of his Lordships knowledge, being so full of approved noblenesse, and the well knowne, and long time exercised grounds of Piety, as without question he cannot but desire rather a little number of good men, obedient & tractable, submitting to good order & discipline, then a great armie, composed of vitious prophane, quarrellous, disobedient, and ignoble persons, wherefore in his Lordships behalfe, I must intreat all Governors, Captains, Officers, and Soldiers, and neverthelesse do injoyne, ordaine and command them to carry themselves in their severall duties and charges, according to the intention of his Lordship, declared by these present Ordinances.

2.51 Every Captaine shall cause to be read all these lawes which concerne martiall discipline, every weeke upon his guard day, unto his company upon paine of censure of a Martiall court.

Instructions of the Marshall
for better inhabling of the Colonell or Governour,
to the executing of his or their charges in this present Colony
the 22. of June. 1611.

  Albeit the zeale which I beare unto this businesse that we have all now in hand touching the subsistance of this plantation, might justly take up all my spirits, and would require a large and passionate explanation of mine owne thoughts and promptnesse to gaine & possesse the hearts of all understanding, noble and religious spirits therunto, yet I must crave pardon (considering at this time many present impediments) if I wrap up any impatient desires & good affection hereunto, to all such unto whom these necessarie effects of my dutie and office shall appertaine, and must be declared in few words and advises, appertinent yet (if not essentiall, as heat to bloud, to the advancement hereof) my desire then by these is chiefly to let all the worthier & better sort to understand, how well it shall become their Honors, birthes, breedings, reputations & faithes, to do their bests, and emulously to actuate in this worke, the upmost of their cleerest powers of body and mind, where the travaile of both is so deerely valued, and highly interpreted by al good and wise men, who knowing the grounds of all goodnes, cannot but know this, how this hazardous voyage (as yet in her earely daies, reflecting onely the comfort of faire hopes) is undertaken by you, more to honour God, your country, & to profit your knowledges, then for any other ends of profit, which speakes for you (in despight of envie and calumnie) that you have mindes much in love with vertue, & are right noble and worthy instruments, to be imployed in so sacred and heroicke a cause, if it were well knowne heere, the care that is had of this plantation in England, and the travel that is taken therein, and the fire that doth not only burne in the generall body of our deare countrymen, to the encouragemet & joy one of another amongst themselves, but flames out (even to the view of strange nations, as well our neighbours, as far remote) for the furtherance & advancement of this honorable enterprise, there is no man here would thinke that this my induction, had either fashion or purpose of a complement. If the wisest man that ever spake or writ (except him that was both God & man) summed up all the reckonings of worldly felicities in these two words Laetari & benefacere, imploying a cheereful mirth with well doing (from which it cannot be severed) who hath more cause to be cheerfull, and inlie glad then you that have the comfort of so great weldoing, to which no other may be compared? for what weldoing can be greater then to be stocks & authors of a people that shall serve and glorifie God, which is the end of all our Creation, & to redeeme them from ignorance and infidelity, to the true knowledge and worship of God, whereby you are made partakers of this promise, that they which lead others into Righteousnesse, shal shine like the starres in the firmament, wherein be right well assured, that your happinesse is envied by many a right knowing, and excellent vertuous man in England, who cannot happly by reason of their imployments and callings, bee partakers of that Comfort heere, as they are by their Endeavors there at home. I shall not need to advise any Colonel, or Governor here for the present how to carry himself, for each mans owne experience here hath made him out go al use of my admonition, which my affection wold willingly else afford if there were cause. Only to discharge my service to god whose souldier I doe now professe my selfe imprest, in this so glorious and great a cause of his, my duty to my Soveraigne Liege Lord and King, & to his Highnesse my Royall Prince and Master, to my Country and the expectation of many Honorable select, painful, and Religious adventurers, Patrones of this businesse, I have conceived no whit impertinent to deliver and publish to every imminent officer in this Colony heere present, and for the direction and guiding of such who may heereafter arrive heere such and so many few in structions as may the better inable them to execute their charges, no whit doubting, but every Colonell, Governour Captaine, and other Officer may sufficiently understand his and their duties, as they are Souldiers, but happily not yet as they are, or may be Coloni, members of a Colony, which compriseth and involveth here, as well as all the industrious knowledges & practises of the husbandman & of his spade, as of the Souldier, and of his Sword, since as Monie is the paiment & wages of the one, so of the other are the fruits of the earth the tillage and manuring of the Land, and in very truth of more necessity & use shall we heere be of the latter then of the other, whether of you be comprehended the souldier himselfe or his Salarie, since more easie it is to make a Husbandman a Souldier, then a Souldier a husbandman. And indeed the necessity of our subsisting, and the very daunger which our enemies of this Country can any way put us unto (our Companies and people well commaunded) requiring the choise rather of the one then the other. These being then the ends and intents of this work, and so understood, by every supreme and chiefe commander, I refer him to these following instructions.

 All Governors of Town or Towns, Fort or Forts, shall be ready (when so be it they shall be summoned thereunto) to take their Oaths of Allegeance unto his Majestie & of faithfulnes unto such his majesties Lieftenant, or to his Deputy or Deputies (authorised by Commission to command over and within the precincts of this whole Colony, or Colonies, by the Tenor of which Oathes they shall solemnly attest to perform all Integrity, uprightnesse, Justice and sincere administration of the discipline and Lawes in all causes and cases, for the good of the Colony or Colonies, provided and declared, and shal indevor the best they may, with all carefulnesse to advance the dignity, and subsistance of the same, as well by giving often in charge, and taking no lesse in to their owne care, both the particular preservation of all such helpes of what condition soever (especially of cattell, and all kinde of such breeders) which mayest soones redound unto the utility, and profit of the same, as by rendring the provisions of the store, and the well husbanding of the same, be they of what severall quality soever. Nor is he meanely to be watchfull, and jealous over his own waies and carriage in all particulars, makeing profession, and practise of all vertue and goodnes for examples unto others to imitate, it being true that examples at all times prevaile farre above precepts, men beeing readier to bee led by their eies, then their eare, for seeing a lively pattern of industry, order and comlinesse, wee are all of us rather swayed unto the same by a visible object, then by hearing much more in wel instructed Arguments.

 Every such Governor therefore shall make it his first duty to resort dayly and usually to the divine Service, next to put in execution the Lawes duly against offenders, and withall cherish and reward the well deserving, and lastly with all worthines & circumspection, abeare himselfe unto and towards his Garrison, intreating all men as well strangers as others, with al Grace, humanity, and sweetnes of a noble nature, & manlinesse, unto all which I hartily advise, and withall injoyne every such Governor of Town or Townes, to be most indulgent, and carefull to performe, as hee will answer the contrary (beside with the losse of his own Honor with such other penalties, as the neglect of so behoofefull and necessary businesse in him, may draw upon the Colony.

Further he ought to be most vigilant, circumspect, and provident for the conservation, defending, & keeping the Town or Fort, for & unto his Majesty, wherin he is placed cheefe commander, & therfore ought the more duely to strengthen his Judgement, and remember his reputation, that he fall into neither of those extreames, which the needy and prodigall are most what culpable of, the one wasting the stocks, commodities and provisions of the store, by which he must subsist, and the other by being ravenous and corrupt in himselfe become likewise enforced to tolerate the same in his inferior captaines, and so leave the poore Souldier and Labourer, miserably pilled, oppressed, and starved.

Further he ought to provide that the companies be trained, and that they may bee made ready for the publique service, and for that the condition of this country doth require rather shot then other Armes, either for offence or defence, and time being pretious with us in respect of our dayly labours and works abroad belonging to our subsisting, in so much, as a small portion therof may bee affoorded and allowed unto such exercising and training, therefore it is appointed by the Marshall, that the Captains that shall have the Guard, during their time of Guard (their people as then being exempted from their dayly labour and work abroad) and their Officers shall teach every Souldier to handle his peece, first to present it comely, and souldier like, and then to give fire, by false firing, and so to fall his Piece to the right side with the nose up, & when their souldiers are hardy and expert in this, they shall set up a convenient mark fast by the court of Guard, at which every Souldier shall twice discharge his peece, at the releeving of the watch, morning and evening, and he that shall shoot neerest the Governor shall do wel to allow some addition of victuals, or pay, or some prize of incouragement, that every one may therby emulously contend to do best: Concerning the training, and cleanely exercising of their Armes, & their postures, the captains shall have order and directions for the same under the Marshals hand which they shall put in Execution during the time of their Guard.

It is also required that the Governor never lie out of his Towne or Fort whereby hee may the better keepe good espiall upon all officers, that they perform their several duties each one in his place especially in good observation of the watch & Guard, for the more confident securing the charge committed to him:

Hee shall not suffer in his Garrison any Souldier to enter into Guard, or to bee drawne out into the field without being armed according to the Marshals order, which is, that every shot shall either be furnished with a quilted coate of Canvas, a headpeece, and a sword, or else with a light Armor, and Bases quilted, with which hee shall be furnished: and every Targiteer with his Bases to the small of his legge, and his headpeece, sword and pistoll, or Scuppet provided for that end. And likewise every Officer armed as before, with a firelocke, or Snaphaunse, headpeece, and a Target, onely the Serjeant in Garrison shall use his Halbert, and in field his Snaphaunse and Target.

The Governour shal have a Principall care, that he use his Garrison to the dayly wearing of these Armors, least in the field, the souldier do finde them the more uncouth strange and troublesome.

Lastly the Governor shall have a singular care to put in execution all such Orders and Instructions as shall bee delivered unto him from the Generall, or his deputie or deputies, concerning the imployments of his Garrison upon such manuall works and duties, as shall be thought necessary and convenient for the better subsisting both of the Laborer, and the Garrison committed unto him: In which is not to bee forgotten the chary conservation of powder, and munition, which will the better inhable him for the defence of his Charge.

The Governor shall be better instructed by taking notice of the Lawes published, that these following abuses are provided for, impious and malicious speaking against the holy and blessed Trinity, Blasphemy, and taking Gods holy name in vain, traiterous words against his majesties person, or Royall Authority, unreverent Demeanor towards the Ministers and preachers of the same, the detestable crime of Sodomie, incest, theft, murther, false witnessing, treason against the person of the Generall, and principall Commaunders of this Colony, and their designes, against Detraction, Murmuring or slaundering of the Right Honourable, the Councell resident in England, and the Committies there, the Generall Councel and Subalternate Commanders, heere, as also against intemperate raylings & base unmanly speeches uttered in the disgrace one of another, all which the Marshall Law, as well as the Civil Magistrate is to punish, but these which concerne in particular the military Discipline, to inable your judgement for your sentence to be required, that it may with greater cleerenes, and understanding, called to censure offences in the Marshal court be delivered, I have abstracted, as followeth

Article 3

3.1 Conference with the enemy, without leave or warrent, from the Lord Generall, Lieutenant Generall, Marshal, or chief & principal command for the present.

3.2 The designes, enterprises, and estate of the Colony, revealed to what enemy soever, by privy messengers, or missives, or otherwise in what sort soever.

3.3 The not present advertising, & giving notice unto a cheefe Commaunder, of such things as any man knoweth intended any way, or by any body, for the domage, mischiefe, or ill of the Colony, or the concealement in any one of any matter of importance, and moment for the good of the Colony.

3.4 Running unto the enemy, or intending, and plotting to runne albeit prevented.

3.5 Of any one taken prisoner by the enemy, having meanes to escape, & not returning to the Colony againe, unlesse hee have given faith.

3.6 Of attempting commotion, giving occasion of sedition, or Muteny in the Colony, or seducing any labourer or souldier from their duty, divine, civill, or martiall, or from their appointed works and labours.

3.7 Of disclosing or giving the word unto the enemy, or unto any other, where it ought not to be given.

3.8 Of receiving, or protecting any Indian, stranger, or suspected spie, or supposed enemy, into house, or any covert, without making it knowne to the General, or chiefe officer, and without leave from him so to do.

3.9 Suspitious and privily entring into the Campe Town, or Fort, or going out by any other waies and issues, then those which are accustomed, as over the Ramparts, Pallizadoes, Trenches, &c.

3.10 Of doing any act, or contriving any practise, which may prejudice the service of his Majesty commanded for the good of the Colony, by the Generall, or chiefe Officer.

3.11 Of breaking the Truce, or peace at any time concluded with the Indian, without leave & warrent expresly given, by him who hath power so to doe.

3.12 Of pillaging, or violently forcing from any Indian to friend, without leave.

3.13 Of ransacking, ransoming, or violently outraging, and dispoiling the Country people, or making war upon them, be it in body or goods, unles they be declared enemies, & warrant given to make prise of.

3.14 Of laying violent hands on his Captaine or other superiour officer, and generally uppon any one whatsoever, to whom duty & obedience is due, especially if it be in the executing of his Office.

3.15 Of him who shall see his superior, or chiefe officer in danger, and shall not doe his indeavour to rescue and relieve him with all his force, and power.

3.16 Of him who shall violently or hardly intreate, or kill his souldier, without good, & lawfull occasion, or that he have deserved to be so intreated, not to satisfie his owne pleasure and appetite, to punish in colour, and revenge, thereby thinking to make himselfe more redoubted, a brave man, & to be feared, remembring well, the life of a souldier, or a laborer, belongs to none to take away, but to the Lord Generall, Lieftenent General, Marshal, or their deputy or deputies.

3.17 Of killing any one, except it be in his own defence.

3.18 Of striking or fighting with an other man, having a quarell unto him, and not holding his or their hands when an officer or third party comes between and cries, Holah.

3.19 Of making debate, raising question, or laying his hand on his sword, and drawing it in the Court of Guard, in Ambush, or other place, where he ought to be modest, peaceable, silent, & keep himself in covert.

3.20 Of assaying or indevouring by bravery, & chiefly by trechery, to outrage or injury any one without a cause, in deed or in words, privately behind his backe like a slie coward, or openly to his face, like an arrogant ruffian, since words are the parents of blowes, & from quarrels infinite disorders, and mischiefes gather head whether in Campe, Towne, or Fort.

3.21 Of revenging a new wrong, or old injury, by any course, contrary to the peace of the camp or Colony.

3.22 Of running where any quarrell is a foote, and companies gathered together, furnished with other Armes then his sword.

3.23 Of taking away any money in bravery, wonne from another, or gotten by play otherwise without the will and consent of him, from whom he wonne it, or cheating or cosenage in play.

3.24 Of not repairing to the place of Armes, or Colors at the publique beating of the Drum.

3.25 Of wilfully firing any place, without order from the superior officer.

3.26 Of sacriledge or taking any goods out of Churches, or Temples, be they sacred or prophane, without license from the chiefe commander.

3.27 Of a souldier enrowling himself in two companies at one time.

3.28 Of going out of one company into another, without leave of his Captaine.

3.29 Of absenting himselfe from the Campe, towne, or fort, without permission of a superior officer.

3.30 Of him that shall receive his pay, and shall go away without speaking a word, it is a case capital, and worthy of death.

3.31 Of suborning souldiers the one from the other, which is an evill example, and which doth draw many inconveniences with it.

3.32 Of quarrels, debates, and revenge.

3.33 Of failing to go, or refusing to follow, where his ensigne shall march, or else where that he shall be commaunded by those who have authoritie so to commaund without enquiring the cause.

3.34 Of abandoning his ensigne without leave or going from the place assigned him, be it in fight, in the court of guard, Centinels, or other part, not brought of by those who placed him there, or others having the same authority.

3.35 Of a Souldier not doing his endevour to recover his ensigne, if the enemie have taken it.

3.36 Of being wanting at his watch, upon his time appointed, or of going of the Guard without leave, albeit under a colour of espie.

3.37 Of being found sleeping in Centinell, or of him who placed upon some Guard or watch by his negligence hath given meanes to the enemie, to do some spoile in the campe, towne, or fort, and to surprise them at unawares.

3.38 Of running away from the battell, conflict, or assault, &c. and of him that marcheth too slowly, or maketh delaies in any other sort.

3.39 Of a Souldier faining himselfe sicke, when any service is to be performed.

3.40 Of yeelding unto the enemy, a place which he hath in gard, without doing first his duty to the uttermost, & be not constraind unto it, according to the quality of the same, & the state whereunto he shall be drawn.

3.41 Of being appointed to defend a breach, trench, or passage, comitted unto his charge, & do forsake it altogether, without being forced thereunto by the enemy.

3.42 Of entring into any place taken by force, & pillaging the same, not following his colors, or forsaking the same, without a publike proclamation, made by the chiefe commander, that it shal be lawful so to pillage.

3.43 Of a souldier being found unfurnished of his armes, and of such furniture, as he is appointed to weare and ought to have, by losing them in play, or in cowardly runing away, or otherwise by his default or negligence.

3.44 Of a souldiers going from his quarter, town, or fort, without he have leave from a superior officer.

3.45 Of a souldier advancing himselfe, to go before the troopes, be it to come first to his lodging, of for any other occasion, or wandring heere and there, and stragling when he should march.

3.46 Of not retiring so soone as the drum or trumpet shall sound retreat, whether it be comming out of any towne, or skirmish, or any other fight.

3.47 Of speaking loud, or making a noise in the battel or any other place, where silence is to be used, except those who have power to command.

Instructions of the Marshall
for the better inhabling of the Captaine of the watch, to the executing of his charge in this present Colony. the 22. of June. 1611.

Sithence, as in every living creature, there be many and sundry members, & those distinct in place and office, and all yet under the regiment of the soule, and heart, so in every army, commonwealth, or Colonie (all bodies a like compounded) it cannot be otherwise for the establishment of the same in perfect order and vertue, but that there should be many differing parts, which directed by the chiefe, should helpe to governe and administer Justice under him. And if it be thus in this civill Audit, & courts of a well setled State, much more sure as it required, to be in their beginnings, and no lesse shall we read, how that first & great commander over the Colony of the children of Israel, conducting them from Ægypt to make their plantation in the land of Promise, appointed Captains over Tribes and hundreds for the wars, and Elders to sit upon the bench (whilest unto himselfe all great causes were brought, whether martial, or civil to direct and determine it otherwise being impossible, so many and infinite occasions both being to be thought upon, and requiring judiciall audience, should ever come by one man (of how indefatigable a spirit soever) to be decided or determined. Out of this example commended unto us by the holy writ, it may wel be, that many Officers are still continued in all united societites, religious and wel governed: having then thus religion, beside prescription and reason, (which mine owne breeding hath taught me how to make the best use of) to be my guids in this new settlement, and in this strange and heathenous (contending with all the strength and powers of my mind and body, I confesse to make it like our native country, I am not a little careful to adhere & take unto mine owne endevours, as many furtherances, as may helpe to worke out with me the ends of this great imployment, which hath now possessed and furnished all states of Christendom with discourse and expectation what may be the issue thereof, & to what perfection so great, & frequent levies of monies, & annuall transportations for these foure yeares of men, and provisions, may bring this English plantation unto. And as I have constituted subalterne officers according both to the ancient & moderne order of the wars, and well approved the government & magistracy, resembling and maintaining the lawes of England, so I have taken paines to present so many & such instructions to such speciall officers (whom our necessity teacheth to establish amongst us) as may most neerest concerne them for the present, (leaving our yet I confesse many appertinent ones) which the time & our earely daies here of settlement may not yet admit of. Let me advise therfore every officer now established, to hold it a service of duty faithfully to execute such orders and instructions, as I have made it my mindes labour to expresse and draw out for him: and amongst the rest (our no little safety consisting in our watch & guard as wel by day as night, we being set down in a stranger land, savage, and trecherous, and therfore many sodaine and barbarous accidents to be feared, I have as followeth extracted the duty of the captaine of the wrath an office not meanly appertaining and necessary unto this Colony, and whose ignorance, and supine negligence may much indanger the safetie thereof.

That Captaine who is Captaine of the watch, must have a speciall care of the safeguard and preservation of the Towne or Fort committed to his charge, and of the lives and goods of the soldiers, and Inhabitants, that through his defect, negligence, or Ignorance in his charge, he gives not the opportunity to the enemie to execute any of his deseignes, for the indamaging of the place or the Inhabitants: Now for the more faithfull executing of his charge, he shall doe well to take notice, that being the chiefe commander of the watch, he is to answere for all Disorders, Misrules, Riots, Tumults and what unquietnesse soever, shall happen in the Towne or Fort, and that if any of these shall fall out to be, he is to commit the parties so offending, to the Provost Marshall, making the Governour there-with acquainted, that the offender may receive such punishment, as his fault shall deserve, of what quality soever he be.

At the setting of the watch, he is to repayre to the place of Arms, with his Gorget about his neck, if his company have not the Guard, there to be present with the Sargeant Major, at the drawing of the Billets for the Guards, that he may the better know the strength of his watch, and how the companies are disposed upon their Guards.

He is to remaine from the setting of the watch upon the main court of Guard, or Guard appointed for him & his Rounders, that if any occassion present it selfe wherin his endeavour is to be used, hee may be the readier found to receive the chiefe Officers direction, or to reforme any abuses that shall come to his knowledge, by the misdemeanors of any to bee found in the campe, towne or fort.

The Ports being shut, and the word delivered out from the Governor, he is to see that al his Gentlemen, appointed for his assistants, doe come upon their guard, where he is so to order it that by drawing of Billets according to their lots, they may execute their rounds, whither first, second; third, &c. and after the Corporalls have set our their centinells, hee is to passe from his court of guard, with three or foure of his assistants, and so to make the round about the campe, towne, or fort, from guard to guard, receiving from every

Corporall the word of the guet, that their be no error, or abuse, by variety of word: after which he is to goe into the court of guard, to see that such officers, rounders, and soldiers, apoynted for that guard, bee there present upon their guard, then hee shall search the peices whither they be charged with Bullet, and that the soldiers bee furnished with poulder and match for the better defence of the guard, committed to his charge, so commanding and injoyning every officer, and soldier to execute his duty, for ther better security of the campe, towne, or fort: hee shall depart to the next guard there to doe the like, and so from guard to guard, until he hath visited all the guards and centinells of his watch, giving in charge to the officers of each guard to send forth their rounders, according to their order and directions. Further hee shall command all disordered people untimely (sitting up late in usuall assemblies, whither in privat meetings, publike taphouses or such like places) unto their rests, for which he shall cause all fire and candles to bee put out and raked up in the towne, and such night-walkers, or unruly persons whome hee shall meete in the streets, he shall either send to their lodgings, or to the Provost Marshall, according as their misdemeanour shall require.

Hee being returned to his owne court of guard shall see his rounders set forth every one according to his order of Billet, from houre to houre, and he shall informe himselfe from these rounders which walke their rounds, two howers before day breake, whither the Captaines and their guards, and their companies bee in armes according to their duties: if they bee not hee shall walke a round towards the morning unto those Guards, and cause them to be put in armes, and shall informe the governour of those Officers neglects, that they may receive punishment: after this at the discharge of the watch, hee is with his guard to attend the Serjeant Major for the safe opening of the Ports.

At the opening of the Ports, hee shall cause the people to stay that are to goe out of the Towne, a pretty distance from his guard, that they may give no incombrance to his guard, untill such time, as he hath sent out certaine Serjeants to discover forth right, and upon each side, as farre as the limmits of that fort are prescribed: At the returne of the

Serjeant, hee shall cause those of the Towne to goe out leisurely and without thronging or confusion, and those without to come in, in like manner, warning the Gards to stand in armes one houre after.

From thence hee shall returne to the maine Guard or place of armes to assist the Serjeant Major for the disposing of such men as are appoynted unto their severall busines and workes of the Colony for the whole day following: and likewise to see that those Captaines, who have the Guard, do put in execution the commandements of the Marshall for the trayning and disciplining of their men for the better inabling them to the service of the Colony.

After which he shall do well to present himselfe before the Governour, or chiefe Officer, to understand his further commaunds.

It shall bee his duty the time beeing come, when the general morning worke is to be left off, to cause the Drum to beate, and with his Guard of Rounders to assist the Captaines or Capt. to bring the laborers into the Church to heare divine service, which beeing ended hee is to returne to the maine Court of Guard, there to be present for the ordering of all matters whatsoever to happen, during his time of being Captaine of the watch, and when it shall so fall out that the Indians do at any time come in way of trade or visitation unto the Camp, towne or fort, he shal leave order with the Guards that they suffer not them to enter before such time as they have made him acquainted first of their beeing there, who shall informe the Governor to know his pleasure, which beeing understood hee shal so accomplish, at al times, appointing Guards uppon such Indians, that they do not steale any of our Tooles, Axes, Howes, Swords, Peeces or what thing else; and that none of our people talke publickely or privately with them, or that they truck or trade with them, or doe any other unorderly Act, without leave granted for the same from the Governour, or chiefe Officer, the omission of which duty, will be required at his hands.

Hee must likewise take notice of all such breaches of the publique Lawes and Articles, as shall bee committed in the time of his Guard, and accordingly command such persons to the Provost

Marshall, as shall bee found trespassers and breakers of the said Lawes and Articles.

 At the time or houres appoynted for the afternoone worke of the Colony, every labourer to his worke, and every crafts man to his occupation, Smiths, Joyners, Carpenters, Brick makers &. He shall cause the drumme to beate againe, to draw and call forth the people unto their labour, when againe the worke on all hands towards night being to bee left off, hee is to cause the drumme likewise then to beate, and as before assist the Capt: with the whole company to bring them to evening prayer.

 If it shall so bee that hee bee Capt. of the watch upon Sonday, it shall be his duety to see that the Saboath be no waies prophaned, by any disorders, gaming, drunkennes, intemperate meeting, or such like, in publike or private, in the streetes or within the houses.

 It shall be his duty halfe an hour before the divine service, morning & evening, to shut the Ports and place Centinels, and the Bell having tolled the last time, he shal search all the houses of the towne, to command every one, of what quality soever (the sick and hurt excepted) to repair to Church, after which he shall accompany all the guards with their armes, (himselfe being last) into the Church, and lay the keyes before the Governor. If at any time any alarme be taken, he is to strengthen himselfe from the maine court of gard, taking a compenent proportion of that guard, for the securing of his person, and so to repaire to the place where the alarme was given, to enforme himselfe by what means the alarum came, causing his rounders to command all guards to be in armes for the readier execution and resistance of any perill, and conservation of their charge, and if he find the alarum to be truly given, and that the enemy approch the Fort, towne, or campe, he is to send to advertise the Governor or chiefe officers to know his directions for the assembling of guards, and ordering and drawing a force for the better prevention of the enemies designes.

Lastly, when the guard is set, and another Captaine hath the watch, hee shall present himselfe before the Governor or chiefe Commander, to give account unto him of all such accidents, trespasses and neglects, as have been committed during the time of his watch. Thus to conclude, though his office amongst many others be a chief and principall office, and there be many weighty and frequent duties required in this great duty of the Captaine of the watch, yet these are the most essentiall and necessariest which I can yet advise, the neerest to concerne us.

Instructions of the Marshall,
for the better inabling of a Captaine,
to the executing of his charge in this present Colonie.
June the 22. 1611

      The Captaine that will honestly and religiously discharge himselfe, and the duty entrusted to him, shall doe well to conceive of himselfe, as the maister of a family, who is at all times so to governe himselfe, as knowing assuredly that all the crimes and trespasses of his people under him shall bee exacted at his hands, not onely by his superior officer and Judge here, but by the great Judge of Judges, who leaves not unpunished the sinnes of the people, upon the Magistrates, in whose hands the power and sword of Justice and authority is committed, to restraine them from all delinquences, misdeeds and trespasses. And moreover since the Captaine is to know, that not onely the command of their civill duties is at his directions, for which he is to answer, but likewise al their actions and practises which shall breake forth in them, contrary to the divine prescriptions of Piety and Religion: their perjuries, blasphemies, prophanenesse, ryots, and what disorders soever, and generally all their breaches of both the sacred Tables, divine, and morrall, to GOD and man, and in this place most especially, where the worke assumed, hath no other ends but such as may punctually advance the glory, and propagation of the heavenly goodnesse, for which so many religious lawes and ordinances are established, and declared, all tending to the subsisting of a Colony, the first seed-plot and settlement of such a new temporary kingdom and state, as may reduce, and bring poore misbeleeving miscreants, to the knowledge of the eternall kingdom of God (therefore by him first shut up in misbeliefe, that in due time, when it should so please him, hee might againe on them shew mercy) It is carefully therefore by each Captaine to be considered, how pretious the life of a poore souldier is, but how much more pretious his soule, and that he make conscience how he expose the first to apparant ruine and mischiefe, or suffer the other to run on into headlong destruction: for the first let his wisedom, knowledge, and circumspection be ever awake, and ready how to imploy, and when and with what assurances, regards and cautions, either left to his owne power, or prescribed him by vertue of these from the Marshall, and for the other, let him first be mindfull to give witnesses in his one life, how carefull hee is to please God, who must blesse all that he undertakes, and walke himselfe in a noble example of Justice and truth; which doth not onely enforce a reputation and respect from other men, but an imitation and following of the like by other men: And unto this may the diverse and frequent changes and strictnesse of the place where we are, and the hardnesse of the many with whom he shal have to do, with other changes & difficulties be motives sufficient to perswade him, in which yet let him remember this, that it is in vaine in such place as heere, to pretend onely to bee vertuous and religious, except a man bee vertuous and religious indeed, and that vertue extend it selfe to example. But since I assure my selfe that of this advice no Capt. voluntarily imploying himselfe in such a busines as this is, and onely for the businesse sake, hath any need, I commend him to the following instructions.

 Every Captaine shall (if conveniently hee may) present himselfe before his Colonel or Governor, once a day, to understand his commands, the which hee must bee carefull, neither to exceed at any time, nor bee defective in their full accomplishment, albeit he shall have a shew and presentment at any time of a better advantage, since concerning his imployment hee may bee ignorant of the chiefe commaunders ends.

 Hee shall doe well to have a speciall eye and regard over his company, that they as well breake not the publique lawes, and Orders prescribed them, but also performe all dueties and services unto which they shall bee for the present commaunded, the which that hee may with the better aptnesse and conveniency draw them unto, it shal be his duty to have knowledg, and take notice of every one of his under Officers, offices and duties; that he may the readier reforme faults committed, eyther by negligence, or ignorance, and at the time of watch he shall send his Serjeant to the Serjeant major for the word, and if he have the watch himselfe, hee shall after the word given out, call upon his court of guard, all his company (unlesse his Centinels) and assembled together, humbly present themselves on their knees, and by faithful and zealous prayer unto almighty God commend themselves and their indeavours to his mercifull protection.

After prayer, either the Captaine himselfe, or some one of his under officers, shall accompany the Centinell to the place of Guet, after which he shall search all the pieces upon the court of guard, that they be charged with bullet against the Captaine of the watch or Serjeant Major shall come to visit them, and also that they be furnished with Poulder and Match, for the discharge of their duties, during the time of their watch and ward: and it is his duty, after that the Serjeant Major or Captaine of the watch have made their round some time after midnight to walke his round, to see that his Centinels do hold good watch in their guet, & that all things be quiet and peaceable, and no disorders in the towne, and that if alarum be given, he give order to his Centinels to take it with al secrecy, without any tumult or noise made, for the exact performace whereof, he must have especiall care that he weaken not his guard, by giving leave unto any of them to be absent from the guard, but upon just and lawfull cause, & reason to be allegded: likewise he is to appoint certaine gentlemen for rounders in his company, the which are to make their said rounds from houre to houre, according to the directions of the Captaine of the watch.

Further, about two houres before day, the Captaine shall put on his armes, and cause all his company to arme themselves, and so to stand in armes until one houre after the discharge of the watch in the morning, which time expired, he shall returne with his company unto the court of guard, and there, with publike praier, give unto almighty God humble thankes and praises, for his mercifull and safe protection that night, and commend himselfe and his, to his no lesse mercifull protection and safegard for the day following.

And because that, during the watch, that time is appointed for the exercising of his men, and fashioning them to their armes, he shall set up a convenient marke by his court of guard, where hee shall teach his men the exercise of their armes, both for the comely and needful use thereof, as the offensive practise against their enemies, at which marke his men shall discharge their pieces twice, both morning and evening, at the discharge of the watch, having procured from the Governor some prize of incouragement due unto him that shall shoot neerest, then he shall file and ranke, & exercise his men in such military actions, actions, according unto such forme and exercise, as he shall receive from the Marshall, not forgetting by the way, that all the Courts of guard, and all the members of the watch and ward, are under the command of the Capt. of the watch.

 Further, the Captaine is to make it his especial duty to have religious and manly care over the poore sick soldiers or labourers under his command, for which cause he shall visite such as are sick, and provide so that they bee attended, their lodgings kept sweet, and their beds standing the same height from the ground which is provided for in the publique Injunctions, as likewise hee shall call for such things for them out of the store, or from the Phisitions or Surgeons chest, as the necessitie of their sicknesse shall require.

 Further he is to know, because we are not onely to exercise the duty of a Souldier, but of the husbandman, and that in time of the vacancie of our watch and ward wee are not to live idely, therfore the Captaine sending his Serjeant to the Serjeant Major for the word, shall likewise give in charge unto his Serjeant to make demand of the Serjeant Major, what service, worke, and businesse he hath in charge, from the Governor, to command him and his men to goe uppon him the next morning, after notice whereof, he shall so provide, that he and his men be ready at the relieving of the morning watch, the Drum summoning him there-unto to effect the same, for which he shall bring his men unto the place of Armes, by the maine Court of guard, where the Serjeant Major, or the Captaine of the watch, shall conduct them to the place of the subsisting businesse, providing them such labouring and needfull Instruments or tooles, as the worke for the present shall require, in which worke the Captaine himselfe shall do exceeding worthily to take paines and labour, that his souldiers seeing his industry and carefulnesse, may with more cheerfulnesse love him, and bee incouraged to the performance of the like in that businesse whereupon they are imploied, contrariwise himselfe taking his ease, and injoying them to toile and worke, may breed both a weariness of the businesse in the imployed, and give a way unto much hatred, and contempt unto himselfe.

Now concerning the tooles and instruments, and the furnishing his soldiers therewith, the Captaine shall send his Serjeant to the store to make demand thereof, and leaving a note under his hand for the receipt of the same, thereby charging him-selfe to the redeliverie of them againe at the finishing of the worke. The companies thus furnished, and being assembled in the place of armes, the Serjeant Major or Captaine of the watch, upon their knees shall make their publike and faithfull prayers unto almighty God for his blessing and protection to attend them in this their business the whole day after succeeding, which being done, the Serjeant Major or Captaine of the watch shal extract out of the companies howsoever devided, and deliver unto every Maister of the worke appointed, his propper and severall Ging, to take their wayes thereunto, where the said Maisters and overseers of such workes shal be present with them to labour, and hold to labour such his Ginge untill 9. or ten of the clock, according unto the coldnesse or heat of the day, at which time he shall not suffer any of his company to be negligent, and idle, or depart from his worke, untill the Serjeant Major, of Capt. of the watch causing the drum to beat shall fetch them in unto the Church to heare divine service, which beeing effected, every man shall repaire to his lodging, to provide himselfe of his dinner, and to ease and rest himselfe untill two or three of the clocke in the after-noone, acording to the heat and coldnesse of the day, at which time the drumme beating, the Capt: shall againe draw forth his company unto the place of Armes aforesaid, to bee disposed of as before uppon their worke until five or six of the clocke, at which time the drumme beating as before, at the command of the Sarjeant major or Capt: of the watch, they shalbe by one of them brought in againe unto the Church to Evening prayer, which beeing ended they shall dismisse the company; those that are to set the watch, with charge to prepare their Armes, the others unto their rests and lodgings.

All these duties the Captaine must not be ignorant nor negligent to put in execution, as being duties which will be exactly required at his hands by the Marshall, as also so to behave himselfe that he may be as well beloved as obeyed of his souldiers, that thereby they may as well know, how to obey, as he to command, and that he endevour by all meanes to conserve his men, as annoy his enemy, & painefully to execute with al diligence such matters as he is injoyned by his superiors, and to have no apprehension of feare, but of shame and infamie.

Instructions of the Marshall
for the better enabling of a Lieftenant
to the executing of his charge in this present Colonie
June the 22. 1611.

When the Captaine is present he is to be assisting to his Captaine, in providing that all directions that are commanded by the Superior Officer, as well his Captain as other, be put in execution, that the company be well and orderly governed, and such duties duly and dayly performed as are injoyned by the Governor or chiefe officer: and likewise that the duties of the inferiour officers or Soldiers be no lesse diligently and sedulously discharged, for he being, as is said, a helpe, and aide unto his Captaine, is therefore accountant to and with his Captain for such omissions, disorders and neglects, as the company shall be found faulty in.

He ought faithfully to informe his Capt: of all abuses, disorders, neglects, and contempts that shall happen in the company, of what nature or condition soever they bee. If his Captain shal at any time demand his opinion in any matter of consequence, he shall faithfully and sincerely deliver it, but not presume to advise his Capt: undemanded, unles it be upon extraordinary occasion of present and imminent perill.

It shalbe his duty in all quarrels, braules, debates, and discontentments of his soldiers to accord and agree them without partiallity, and with the least troubling of his Cap. with the same, & if he cannot with his curtesies, and gentle interposition worke them into peaceable agreement, hee shall them acquaint his Captaine, and afterwards faithfully put in execution his Captaines directions. He ought to traine & exercise the company that they may be expert in the use of their armes when they shall be commanded to publike service. He ought likewise to see that the inferiour officers be duly obei'd the one by the other without singularity or contradiction, & the soldiers obey them all in generall, each one according to his place.

By his care every Squadron shal have his armes serviceable and cleane, and at the setting of the watch that they be provided of pouder, match, and bullet, for the defence of the guard, and if the company be unfurnished to advertise his Captaine, or send his Serjeant to the munition Maister, that order may bee presently taken for the supplie thereof.

Hee shall doe well, if conveniently he may, morning and evening (or at least once a day) to present him-selfe before his Captaine, to know his commands, and to informe his Captaine of the state of his Companie.

It shalbe his duty to have care that the company bee ready (as is exprest in the Captaines duty) to go forth and attend the daily businesse, and publike labour appertayning to the Colonie, which shalbe commaunded by the chiefe officer, In which hee shall have a hand in executing, and an eye in over-seeing, that every one take his due paines, and not loyter, and idlely mispend the time appoynted unto the dispatch of such businesse.

Hee is to have a hearty and religious care that the souldiers doe not make breach of the lawes, and duties, divine, civill, or martiall, injoyned them to observe upon so necessary reasons and strict penalties, but that he informe, correct and punish to the utmost of his authority limited, the trespassers of the same, or the omission of any duty whatsoever, with the approbation of his Captaine.

Hee is not to make it his least care to over-see and take charge of the lodging and bedding of all in generall in his company, that according to publike edict the preservation of their healths be provided for, and that one point of slothfullnesse in the common soldier prevented, and met with, of lying upon or to neere the ground, which neglect in the officer hath bin the losse of many a man. For his order of command and march in the field, and quartering he shal be appoynted the manner thereof by the Marshall, when occasion of service shall so require, like-wise the order of trayning and exercising his Captaines company he shall have under the marshalls hand.

Hee is amongst other his duties most carefully, like a charitable and wel instructed Christian, mercifull and compassionate, make often and daily survey of such of his company as shalbe visited with sicknesse, or wounded by any casualty of warre, gunpoulder, or otherwise, in which hee shall take such order that the lodgings or such as shalbe so sicke or hurt, be sweet and cleanely kept, them-selves attended and drest, and to the uttermost of his power to procure either from the store, or Phisition and Surgeons chest, such comforts, healps, and remedies, as may be administred and applied unto them, and to have care that they be not defrauded of those meanes and remedies which are for them delivered out of the said store or chests.

And for that this officer is in the abscence of his Captaine to be called unto the Marshall Court as his deputie, for the better inhabling or his judgement, when his opinion is to be required in the censure of offences and crimes of what quality soever, which shalbe brought thither to be sentenced, I refer him to the abstract of the lawes in breefe anexed unto the duty of his Capt.

Instructions of the Marshall
for the better enabling of an Ensigne
to the executing of his charge in this present Colonie,
June the 22. 1611.

It is requisite for every soldier to stand upon his credit and reputation, proposing unto himselfe that there can be no lesse equall, or to be compared with dishonour, & sure in matters of armes and their execution, what dishonour can bee greater then the losse of the ensigne, for which it ought to be committed to the charge of a right valiant, and well governed soldier, who may not leave nor loose it, but where the losse of his life shall quit him of that duty.

So farre as toucheth his command, or government in the company, he is to know that he hath no command where his Captaine or Lieftenant are present, but in their absence I referre him to the duty of the Capt: which he is to execute as religiously, painfully, and circumspectly as the Captaine: he beeing answerable unto his Captaine for all defects, neglects, disorders, and contempts of duties, in his company whatsoever.

In the government of his company he is to be asistant unto his superiour officers, in teaching and inabling all his inferiours, every one his perticular duty, with faire perswasion and all gentlenes, and sweetnes of command, and if any thing shall happen, either disorders or neglects of duties, it shall be fit for him to advertise his superior officers that redresse may be had, for he hath no power of himselfe in their presence to punish, correct, or do any act of executions upon his companions.

When the time of exercise and training shalbe of the companie, he shall be there ready and assistant unto his superiour officer (if so be it his colours be not drawne forth) for the better furtherance of him in the so training, and disciplining of the men.

Hee shall see all commands of his superior Officers put in execution, and not stand ignorantly in defence (as some have) and it is the property of the ignorant so to do, that he is tyed to no other duties, but to the carrying of his colours. For no inferior officers duty, whether Sargeant or corporalls, but he is to performe and execute (if they shall be by any disaster, defeate, or visitation of sicknesse disabled personally to discharge it themselves) being so commanded by his Superior officers, during the time of guard, yea the duty of the Centinell he is to undergoe, and from which neither the Captaine nor Lieftenant are exempted upon urgent occasion.

In the hapning of any dispute, quarrell, or debate amongst the soldiers, the same being brought to his knowledge, he shall do his best to end and compound, whose authority & perswasions, if they shal not be powerfull enough to reconcile & set at one, he shal then informe his Lieftenant, or Captaine: that order with the most speed & convenience, may be taken therein.

He shall hold it his duty to visit the sick or hurt in his company, and to his power of them take the same care, and make the same charitable provision for, as is injoyned both the Captaine and Lieftenant.

It is his duty to command the Corporalls to bring their squadrons to his lodging, who shal conduct them to his Lieftenant, and they both conduct them to their Captaine, at the beating of the Drum, whither for any manuall labour and worke, for the Colony, or whither to bee lead unto the Church at any time to heare divine service.

He is to visit the armes of the Company, and at the setting of the watch to take care, and so at all time, that they be not unserviceable, and if any want bee then of match, poulder, or bullet, or what else defect, hee is to advertise his Superior Officers, that they may then and at all other times bee supplied and amended.

To bee breefe hee is an assistant to the Lieftenant in the same nature that the Lieftenant is to the Captaine, and may not by any meanes intrude into the command of the one or other, they being present.

In the absence of he Captaine, and Lieftenant (when hee is then to bee Captaine of the watch) I referre him to the duty of the sayd Captayne of the watch.

For his Order of march, and flying of his collours, and his carriage in the field, and upon service, he shal bee ordred and instructed by word of mouth from the Marshall, when occasion shalbe offered.

Thus mutch is needfull for him to know touching his command, and his carriage to his officers and company, so far forth as hee and they are soldiers, and as the necessity of this present state and condition which we are in doth require. But concerning the publike and dayly manuall businesse which appertaine to our setling there as Planters of a Colonie, he is to make it his duty, to be a diligent not onely over-seer, but labourer, himselfe accompanying therein, and seconding the example of his Captaine, and industrious Lieutenant, that the necessary and daily taskes of such workes and husbandry (without which we cannot here keepe footing, nor possibly subsist) may be in due time accomplisht and brought to passe.

Instructions of the Marshall
for the better enabling of a Serjeant
to the executing of his charge in this present Colonie,
June the 22. 1611

That Captaine who shall dispose of a Halbert, by vertue whereof a Serjeant is knowne, ought to make choise of a man well approved, that hath passed the inferior grades of a resolute spirit, quick apprehension, and active body, for it is a place of great paines and promptitude, and that Serjeant who will be able to execute his duty in sinceritie and uprightnesse, must not be slack to punish where it is deserved, nor over rash to abuse his authority, unbefitting an officer of such moment.

This officer hath in the absence of his superior officers the command of the company, to see them doe their duties, and observe lawes and orders in all things, and punishment of them by his Halbert, or otherwise in his discretion, for defect or negligence in any part of order.

This officer is to attend upon the Serjeant Major for the word upon the shutting in of the Ports, at the Governors lodging or place of armes, according as the Serjeant Major shall appoint, then he is to give the word to his Captaine, Lieftenant, and Ensigne, and unto his corporall or corporalls having the guard.

Hee must see the Soldiers of his company furnished and provided with munition, as shotte, poulder, and match, at the setting of the watch.

Hee is to call, or cause to bee called the Corporalls roule, to see who are absent or negligent in the discharge of their duties.

Hee is to see each souldiers armes cleanly kept, and serviceable, and if default be, he is to reproove the corporall for his negligence in the over-sight of that dutie, and to punish the souldier.

Hee must see the souldiers practise their armes, and therefore it is requisite that he kwow the use of all sorts of armes himselfe.

If the watch be set by squadrons, he shall leade that squadron, that is to watch to the Parado, and there draw Billets for his guard, and from thence lead them to the guard.

He shall see the setting out of the Centinels, and after shall have care that silence and good order be kept upon the guard, and that no man depart from the guard without the leave of him, or his corporall, and that no man be absent above one halfe houre, having a special regard that hee weaken not his guard, by giving leave unto above two at a time to be absent, least he disable himselfe in the performance of that duty of trust and charge which is committed unto him of the guard.

Hee shall see that his corporall or corporals, do put his or their squadrons into armes, two houres before the relieving of the watch, who shall so abide in armes, at least one whole houre after.

If the watch be set by whole companies, it is his duty to place every souldier in his order, and to see them march in ranke and file, and himselfe being eldest Serjeant to march upon the right point in the vaunt-guard: if he be the yongest he is to march upon the left point in the rere-ward, each taking care of halfe of the company, unlesse when more companies march together, they be appointed any other place by a superior officer.

When the Serjeant is appointed to lead out any shot, he shall goe upon the side of the utmost ranke, and see that they take their levell, & give fier, and do all things with comlinesse and leisure, & so likewise in the retrait.

A Serjeant of each company, presently after the discharge of the watch shall bee in the place of armes, or market place, to attend the Captaine of the watch to the opening of the Ports, that they may be imploied by him, for the discovery without the forts, or any ambushes or attempts of the enemy, with such guard as hee shall appoint them, the Captaine of the watch having caused all those of the towne, about, to go forth, to forbeare and stay untill the said Serjeants returne, which Serjeants are to command those that are comming in, to stay untill those in the towne are comming forth, & and then they shal discover right forth before the Port, and to both sides of the Port, so farre until the discoverers of the other forts meete where they end; the discoverers being returned, those of the towne shall be suffered to passe out leisurely, & after those being without shal come in as leisurely, without throng or crowd, that they be the better discerned by the guard what they are. The Ports beeing open, the Serjeants shall returne to their guards, where they shall instruct their souldiers in the practise of their armes, and shall shew them the ready use of them, and do their indeavours by their best meanes, to incourage the towardly, and instruct the ignorant.

If upon his guard, in the absence of his superior officer, any soldier of his guard shall offend, hee shall eyther punish him by his Halbert, or if the qualitie of the offence so deserve, he shall disarme him, and keepe him prisoner upon the guard, untill the watch bee relieved, and then hee shall bring him to his superior officers, that he may receive condigne punishment according to the condition of his offense.

The Serjeant ought to know every souldier, and to take notice of their particular lodgings, and to make it a point of his duty to see that they keepe their lodgings cleane, and that their beds doe stand a yard above the ground, to have an eye into their diet, their thriftinesse and conversation, to advise them to the best, whereof he is to make report unto the Captaine or chiefe officer, that they may receive estimation for good, and punishment for evill behaviour.

He is to informe himselfe of the sick, or hurt, in the company, and to visit them once a day, and to inquire whether they bee not defrauded by the Phisitons and Surgeons, of such necessary helps as are delivered unto them, for their preservations and recoveries, and to informe his Captaine of the negligence and abuse of such, who should in that case deale unjustly with them that their dishonesty may receive due punishment.

He is likewise to addresse himselfe unto the Serjeant Major and Store- maister, for the supplying of his company with munition, and victuals, upon any occasion: and concerning the munition, he is to have a principall care, that the souldier doe not spend it away in vaine, but onely at such times as they are appointed for exercising and training.

He is likewise to take notice of all defects and abuses in his company, and to enforme his superiour officers, that they may be redressed, and justice take place.

He shall with great diligence attend the commands of his Captaine, and of the Serjeant Major, and at all times put them in present execution, rebuking such as do amisse, shewing them their faults, and teaching them by a good example in himselfe, to tread in the way of all civilitie and goodnesse. If any debate shall happen betweene souldier and souldier, hee having knowledge thereof, shall doe his indeavor to agree, and reconcile them, that it come not to his superior officers, and if through obstinacie hee cannot agree them, hee shall commit them, or informe his superior officers, who may take order therein.

He is to provide that none of the company be absent when the Drum shall call them forth to worke, in which workes he is to be a president himselfe, both by labouring in the same, and calling upon others to doe the like.

He is to goe to the Store, to take out such Tooles, as are required for the workes in hand, and there to under-write unto the booke of the store- Maister, or unto a note to be filed, thereby charging himselfe to be accountable for the said tooles, when the worke shall be performed, over which he is to have a regard, that they be not neglectfully layed up, spoyled nor broken without examining by what meanes they came so broken, that the wilfull breaker thereof may receive punishment, and the said toole or tooles so broken, withall the pieces, he shall bring unto the store, to shew the same for his better discharge.

Instructions of the Marshall
for the better enabling of a Corporall unto the discharge of his duty in this present Colonie, June the 22. 1611

    The Corporall is in grade and dignity above the private soldier, and therefore care ought to bee had in the choosing of this officer, for that it is an office of good account, and by neglect of this duty, many inconveniences may come upon a camp, towne, or fort, therefore it is fit that hee surmount and excell his inferiors in valour, diligence and judgement, and likewise in the practise and use of all sorts of armes, whereby he may the better bee enabled to instruct and teach this squadron committed to his charge.

    The Corporall ought (having the third part of the company given him in command) to sort and assist them in their quartering or lodgings, to have a care that they be cleane and sweet, and that their beds in the same bee laide three foote from the ground, hee is to carry a hand over their dyet, thriftinesse, and conversation, and to advise and instruct them at all times to demeane themselves as good Christians ought to do, and to make report thereof unto his Captaine or chiefe officer, that from them they may receive credit and estimation for good behaviour, and punishment and disgrace for their misdemeanours.

    Hee is to have a speciall care of their Armes to see them duly furnished and kept in order, and when the Drum beateth to bee in a readinesse at the Colonies, and if any bee absent, hee shall make it knowne to his Serjeant or superior officer.

    When he marcheth, hee is to lead a file, hee ought to bee daily conversant with his little company committed unto his charge, and the company beeing in the field, to lodge with them, and provide to his power for their wants, and to instruct and teach them how to use and handle the weapon they carry: Likewise, to remember well how each one is armed and appointed when hee receiveth him into charge, then to see no part of his furniture or armes bee broken or spoiled, but to have care that they bee preserved cleane and service-able.

Hee ought to have a vigilant eye upon the good behaviour of his company, not suffering them to use any unlawfull and prohibited games, nor that they give them selves to excesse of drinking, surfitting and ryot, but that they bee conformable to all the Martiall lawes: that they likewise make spare of their pay and victuals, the better to furnish themselves in comely and decent manner, with apparell and other necessities fitte and requisite for them, wherein the Corporall ought to use his utmost endeavour.

In presence of his Captaine, or superior officer, he is to take uppon him no more then the condition of his office doth require, but diligently to attend and execute what they shall command, that his example may serve for a President to the rest of his squadron.

At the setting of the watch hee is to see that they be furnished with poulder, Bullet and match, and that their armes be service-able and soldier-like.

If the company watch by squadrons, he and his squadron shall be brought by the Serjeant unto the place of watch, and from him receive the word and directions, in what maner, and where he shall place his Centinels, whether by day or night, which hee is to see performed.

When the Corporall with his squadron shall bee brought to the place where he and they shall watch, he and they must provide eftsoones for wood and fyring upon the guard, that beside for their owne comfort, they may have fire ready alwayes upon the guarde to light their match upon any proffered occasion.

Hee is to cause silence to bee kept uppon the court of guard, and to guarde, and to governe the watch, so that the labour bee equally divided of his squadron, either in watch, worke, or service, and to take care in all respects, that they performe the duties of good and honest soldiers.

His Centinels being placed, hee is to let none passe without the word, unlesse it bee the Captaine of the watch, or Serjeant Major, unto whom (after hee shall have perfect knowledge of them,) hee is to deliver the word at their first round, but before the delivery of the word, hee shall take the Captaine of the watch and Serjeant Major alone within his guard, the corporall beeing accompanied with halfe a dozen of shot with Match in Cock, to have an eye over the rest of the rounders that accompany the Captaine of the watch or Sarjeant Major, and not to suffer the rounders to come within the centinell, & if at any time of the night after their first round, the Serjeant Major or Captaine of the watch shall goe their round, as it is their duties, then they are to give the word to the Corporal, unlesse they mistrust and doubt the memory of any Corporall: the Corporall is not to goe out single to take the word of any round but to take two, or three, or more of his guard with him, and if it shalbe a round of more then two, then hee shall draw out all his men in his guard in their armes, the Corporall shall at no time (to receive the word) passe beyond the Centinell, but make him that hath the word to come forward within the Centinell, and shall cause the rest to stand without the Centinell, and those that are out by the Corporall for his guard shall keepe their eies and armes in a readinesse over him that is to give or take the word of the Corporall, untill such time as the Corporall be satisfied of him.

He must make good his guard untill he bee releived the which hee shall the better doe if hee keepe his men together upon the guard; he must visite the Centinels sometimes unawares to them, and must be ready to go to them at the first call.

He shall put his men in armes two houres before the discharge of the watch, so to remayne one houre after.

Hee shall warne his Centinells to make no alarum but upon just cause, and then with as much silence as may be, and in like silence hee must advertise the Captaine of the watch, and the next guards unto him, and so without notice or signe of confusion from one guard unto another.

If upon his guard any of his soldiers shal misdemeane himselfe, or offend in any of the publique lawes, divine, civill, or martiall, he shall bring him to his superior officer, then upon the guard, that he may receive punishment.

His duty is to provide that none of his Squadron, be absent, when the drumme shall call to any labour, or worke, or at what time soever they shall be commanded thereunto for the service of the Colonie, in the performance of which said workes he is to be an example of the rest of his Squadron by his owne labouring therein, and by encouraging and calling upon others at any time negligent, idle and slothfull, that thereby giving encoraging to his superior officers he may be held by them worthy of a higher place.

Hee must likewise receive such instruments and tooles, as spades, shovels, axes, &c. imployed in the worke, from his Sarjeant to dispose, and to deliver the same unto the labourers with all the care he may, to his utmost, that none of them be broken, lost, or wilfully spoiled, without drawing the parties so breaking, loosing and wilfully spoyling the same into punishment; and after the worke done he shall gather the said tooles in againe and re-deliver them up unto his Sargeant, all, and the same, who is to be accountable unto the maister of the store unto whose booke he hath underwritten for the receipt of them.

And by reason he is well knowing of every man in his Squadron, and thereby cannot but misse the pretence of any man from any duty whatsoever, sooner then haply the superior officers may, his care shall bee to attend his squadron to the usuall workes and day- labours, and unto frequent prayers, and the devine service at all times, and uppon all the dayes in the weeke, giving due notice unto his superior officer, of the neglect of eyther duties in their kinde, that reformation may follow.

He shall not suffer any gaming, heare any prophane lewd speeches, swearing, brawling, &c. or see any disorder whatsoever uppon his court of guard, or else-where, without present information given thereof unto his superior officer, that the offenders may be duly punished.

Hee shall take notice of all bands and proclamations published by the Generall, procuring a copie of the same from the Provost Marshall, the same duly to bee read unto his squadron, that they may be made the perfecter in the knowledge of them, and thereby learne the better to forbeare the trespassing in forbidden things, remembring the penaltie of the same, and execute things commanded, considering the reward thereof, whether in Campe, Towne, or Forte, Field or garrison.

Hee shall read, or cause to bee read, the Souldiers dutye, every time of his guarde in some convenient time and place, during the same, thereby to remember them the better of their generall duties.

Instructions of the Marshall
for the better enabling of a privat soldier, to the executing of his duty in this present Colonie.
June 22. 1611

It is requisite that he who will enter into this function of a soldier, that he dedicate himselfe wholly for the planting and establishing of true religion, the honour of his Prince, the safety of his country, and to learne the art which he professeth, which is in this place to hold warre, and the service requisite to the subsisting of a colonie: There be may men of meane descent, who have this way attained to great dignity, credity, and honor. Having thus dedicated himselfe with a constant resolution, he ought to be diligent, carefull, vigilant and obedient, and principaly to have the feare of God, and his honor in greatest esteeme.

In making choyse of his familiar acquaintance, let him have care that they be of religious and honest conditions, not factious nor mutenous murmurers, nor evill languaged and worse disposed persons: his choyse beeing made he is to carry him selfe discreete, temperate, quiet and friendly, withholding himselfe from being to lavish of speech, for such as take liberty unto themselves to talke licentiously, to slander, raile, and backbite others, do usually make bankrout of their friends, of estimation, and of their own peace and quiet of conscience.

He must be carefull to serve God privately and publiquely; for all profession are thereunto tied, that carry hope with them to prosper, and none more highly then the souldier, for hee is ever in the mouth of death, and certainly hee that is thus religiously armed, fighteth more confidently and with greater courage, and is thereby protected through manifold dangers, and otherwise unpreventable events.

He must bee no blasphemer nor swearer, for such an one is contemptible to God and the world, and shall be assured to be found out and punished by the divine Justice: whereof we have instant examples.

He must refraine from dicing, carding, and Idle gaming: for common gamsters, although they may have many good parts in them, yet commonly they are not esteemed according to their better qualities, but censured according to their worst, procuring enemies, questions, brawles, and a thousand following inconveniences.

He must not set his minde over-greedily upon his belly, and continuall feeding, but rest himselfe contented with such provisions as may be conveniently provided, his owne labour purchase, or his meanes reach unto: above all things he must eschew that detestable vice of drunkennesse; for then a man is not apt nor good for any thing, and by that beastly disorder, many great armies have miscarried, and much disquiet and tumults raised in campe, and civill townes, whereupon doth fall the sword of Justice upon their necks, which in that case they have compelled to be drawne.

Chastitie is a vertue much commended in a souldier, when uncleannesse doth defile both body and soule, and makes a man stinke in the nostrils of God & man, and laith him open to the malice & sword of his enemy, for commonly it makes a man effeminate, cowardly, lasie, and full of diseases, & surely such who have unlawful women stil trudging about with them, or in whom custome hath taken away the sence of offending in that kind, commonly come to dishonorable ends.
 He is tyed in his entring or inrowling into any company, to take his oath of faithfulnesse, and sincere service to his Prince, Generall and Captaine: to be conformable to the lawes provided for the advancement for the intended businesse, and for the cherishing of the good therein, and punishment of the evill.

He must be true-hearted to his Capt. and obey him and the rest of the officers of the Campe, Towne, or Fort, with great respect, for by the very oath which he taketh hee doth binde himselfe and promise to serve his Prince, and obey his officers: for the true order of warre is fitly resembled to true religion ordeined of God, which bindeth the souldier to observe justice, loyaltie, faith, constancie, patience, silence, and above all, obedience, through the which is easily obteined the perfection in armes, and is as a meanes to atchieve great enterprises, through never so difficult: certainly, who wanteth the vertue of obedience and patience, though never so valient otherwise, yet is he unworthy of the same name.

A souldier must patiently suffer the adversities and travailes which do fall out in the courses and chances of warre: he must not be over-greedy, nor hasty of his pay, albeit he may stand in some want thereof, but must with a chearfull alacrity shew his constancy, avoyding by al possible meanes, rebellions and mutenies, which most upon such pettish occasiones are runne into: by no meanes must hee bee a pertaker with such mutiners, for the end of such is sharpe and shamefull death.

If in Skirmishes Incounters, or surprise of towne the enimies be vanquished, let him set all his care and diligence in execution of the victorie with his Armes, & not in rifling and spoiling for trash, for so he shal be accounted an unruly free booter, beside innumerable are the disorders and mischefes which do happen by ravenous Pillagers, many times to the dishonor of the action, and to the losse of their lives, therfore he shall pursue the victorie until the enimy be wholy ended & and the place fully caried and possessed, the Guards placed, and liberty granted from the chiefe Commander to sack & spoile, wherein by any meanes let him avoid murther and crueltie, and violation of women, for those are odious to God and man, rather in such cases let him shew himselfe pittiful and mercifull unto the vanquished, rather defending the sillie women and Children then procuring their hurt and damage, for in so doing it will be right acceptable to God and his Commanders.

Such Armes as he is apointed to serve with, whither Musket, Caliver or Target, let him be very dilligent to use all his industrie to excell in the use of them, for therby he may conserve his owne life and his fellows, for the which purpose he shall call upon his Serjeant and his Corporall to instruct him therein, untill hee come unto perfection. He must learne the severall sounds of the Drumme, whereby hee may obey that which he is commanded; for the Drum often-times is the voice of the Commander, hee shall carefully note and marke the signes made by the Captaine and officers, without talking or pratling unto his next companions: for that is unbefitting a Souldier, and makes him uncapable to heare what is given in command.

    In skirmishes and incounters he shal be resolute and valiant, for that souldier which is timorous and fearfull can never bring his heart to any hearty enterprise, nor dareth to attempt any hotte, bold, or audacious charge or service, by reason of his cowardly spirit and feare.

    Hee must bee carefull to bee alwayes vigilant and ready, beeing placed for a Centinell, or in the Court of guard, where he shall not put of his armes, untill hee have leave from the Captaine: for therein consisteth the security of the Campe, Towne, or Fort. Hee shall doe well to keepe his fidelity unspotted to his Prince and Generall, although his sufferings may bee intolerable and infinite, and shall not flye unto the enemy: for to bee branded with infamie of a traytor is a fowle and odious offence, and rigorously punished among all nations, and never yet traitor came to good end; of which we have examples infinite.

    Hee must not bee shifting from company to company, but serve in the company where hee first began, and if at any time hee shall depart for his preferment, let him demand the good liking of his Captaine, who if hee shall denie it him in such a case, it shall bee imputed no offense in him to appeale unto the Generall or chiefe officer.

    At the sound of the Drumme, for the setting of the watch with his armes being fix and serviceable he shall repaire to his colours, and it shall be commendable in him by the way to call upon his Corporall, so that all the Squadron meeting together at the Corporals lodging may attend the Corporall unto the colours, and if he be unprovided of munition he shall acquaint his Corporall therewith, who shall see him furnished.

    When the company or squadron march to the guard he shall hold that order in which he was placed by his Serjeant, marching in a comely and gracefull manner, and being armed at the place of guard he shall pose his armes according unto the Corporalls direction, and behave himselfe in all his actions as befitting a religious Soldier in that holy place of guard, without doing any act of prophanenesse, disorder, or ought els, tending to the pollution of the same either in word or deed.

When his Corporall shall appoint him forth for Centinell, he shall souldier his peice, both ends of his match being alight, and his peice charged, and prined, and bullets in his mouth, there to stand with a carefull and waking eye, untill such time as his Corporall shall relieve him, and to let no man passe nor come up to him, but to force him to stand, and then to call his Corporall.

He must harken diligently and looke well about him from his place of Centinell for the approch of any about the Camp, Towne, or Fort, or the dich thereof, or if he heare any noyse, to call his Corporall to advertise him of the same.

He must have a speciall care that he sleepe not upon his Centinell, nor set his armes out of his hands: for therein he maketh himselfe subject for any passenger by to take away his life, beside the generall inconvenience that may come upon the Camp, Towne, or Fort.

His Corporall having releived him and brought him to the guard, he shall do well to read the Lawes and ordinances for the government of the Camp, Towne, or Fort, constituted and prescribed by the Marshall, the better to enable him memory for the exact observance of those lawes whereby he shall not only avoyd the trespassing against the same, but also get the reputation of a well ordered and governed soldier.

Such gentlemen or others, as are appointed by their Captaine for rounders, and approoved by the Serjeant Major or Captaine of the watch, amongst them those rounders that are appointed to attend the Captaine of the watch on his guard are to receive their directions from him, as Likewise those of the companies upon the guards for their order of rounding, according to the time of the night in what hower they shal make their Rounds.

The Rounders from the guard, from the Captaine of the watch, are to visit the Centinells, and Courts of guards, making their rounds upon the rampart, harkning and listening and looking over into the ditches, if they can heare or see, or discover any troopes, or men neere the town, taking care besides that there be good watch kept both by the Centinells, and upon the court of guard, and if any noyse or tumult be neere the rampart, they may step downe and informe themselves of it, and bring the trespassers to the next guard, committing them there untill after the round made they have acquainted the Capt. of the watch of such disorders.

The rounds from the Ports are to round the streets to take in charge that no disorders, breaking up, or fiering of houses of ye store, or roberies, magazin, riots or tumult in Taphouses, or in the streetes, or in privat houses at houres untimely be committed, and the offenders to bring the next guard, and to informe the Captaine of the watch; All rounders are to be subject and obedient unto the Captaine of the watch and his commands during his time of watch.

Two houres before day he must be ready in armes with his peice charged & provided, & a match alight at both ends and bullets in mouth, there to attend the command of the Corporall untill further directions be given, and at the time appoynted for the exercise of his armes, he shall be tractable and obedient to his officers executing such commands as they shall impose upon him, that he may be the better trained and inhabled to offend his enemy, and to defend himselfe.

He shal be carefull to observe al words of command, postures and actions, according to the order of training published by the marshall.

The exercise being ended and the prise won and lost he shall pose his armes at the court of Guard, and ther give diligent attendance that he be at no time absent from his Guard, above one houre, without leave from his Officer, and that not without leave of his Officer.

    The watch being relieved and he free from the guard he is to dispose of the rest of the time for his owne perticular use untill next morning at the discharge of the watch: when at the call of the drumme, he shall attend at his corporalls lodging ther to receive such instrument, or toole as the busines of that day shall require, from whence he shall march to the place of armes or maine court of guard; there to be disposed of by the captaine of the watch for that day service of the Colonies, in which he shall doe his best indeavour like a painfull and industrious servant of the Colonies to discharge his duty for the furtherance of his worke, and incouragment of such who shall be the more stirred up by his example of goodnes, to the imitation of the like: and thus doing, he shall give cause unto the Generall, unto his Captaine, and chiefe officers, to take notice of his painfulnesse, who may according to his desert in time give him advancement for the same.

    He shall continue at his worke untill the drumme beate, and that his Captaine, his officers or overseers of the worke, give order unto a cessation for the time, and for the same purpose attendeth to lead him in, whom he shall orderly and comely follow into the Camp, Towne or Fort, by his said Captaine, officer or overseer him meeting, to be conducted unto the church to heare divine service, after which he may repayre to his house or lodging to prepare for his dinner, and to repose him untill the drumme shall call him forth againe in the afternoone, when so (as before) he shall acompany his chiefe officer unto the field, or where els the work lieth, and there to follow his easie taske untill againe the drumme beat to returne home: at which time according as in the forenoone, he shall follow his chiefe officer unto the church to heare divine service and after dispose of himselfe as he shall best please, and as his owne businesse shall require; with this caution carefully to preserve the toole or Instrument with which he wrought to serve his turne againe the next day as he will answere the contrary upon the perill prescribed.

Concerning his order of march and carriage in the field when occasion shall present it selfe, he will easily acquire and learne the same by experience, provided that he be carefull to march, ranke, and file, and not straggle, or be disobedient unto proclamation of the General for therein consisteth the principall part of his duty, untill when I leave him with this caveat, that he diligently marke, consider and remember the orders, which the higher officers do observe, in ordering their files and rankes, and surveying their squadrons of footmen, and to the placing of the great Artillery in the march and setled campe, and the plot of the quartering, according to the disposition of the ground where the campe shall then be, with the manner of entrenching, placing of Ordinances & Guards for the defense of the same, that in the knowledge and execution of these duties, the Generall having understanding of his promptitude and diligence may conferre upon him, and call him unto place of preferment and commaund.

That there be no neglect found in him, in his marching to the Guard or Field, and that in the same he doe not forget or leave behinde him any peece or parcell of his Armes appointed him by the Marshall for his owne defence, or offence of the enemie.

A Praier
**duly said Morning and Evening upon the Court of Guard,
either by the Captaine of the watch himselfe,
or by some one of his principall officers.**

Merciful Father, and Lord of heaven and earth, we come before thy presence to worship thee in calling upon thy name, and giving thankes unto thee, and though our duties and our verie necessities call us heereunto: Yet we confesse our hearts to be so dull and untoward, that unlesse thou be mercifull to us to teach us how to pray, we shall not please thee, nor profit our selves in these duties.

Wee therefore most humbly beseech thee to raise up our hearts with thy good spirit, and so to dispose us to praier, that with true fervencie of heart, feeling of our wants, humblenesse of minde, and faith in thy gracious promises, we may present our suites acceptably unto thee by our Lord and Saviour Jesus Christ.

And thou our Father of al mercies, that hast called us unto thee, heare us and pitie thy poore servants, we have indeed sinned wonderously against thee through our blindnesse of mind, prophanesse of spirit, hardnesse of heart, selfe love, worldlinesse, carnall lusts, hypocrisie, pride, vanitie, unthankfulnesse, infidelitie, and other our native corruptions, which being bred in us, and with us, have defiled us even from the wombe, and unto this day, and have broken out as plague sores into unnumberable transgressions of all thy holy lawes, (the good waies whereof we have wilfully declined,) & have many times displeased thee, and our owne consciences in chusing those things which thou hast most justly & severely forbidden us. And besides all this wee have outstood the gracious time and meanes of our conversion, or at least not stooped and humbled our selves before thee, as wee ought, although we have wanted none of those helpes, which thou vouchsafest unto thy wandering children to fetch them home withall, for we have had together with thy glorious workes, thy word calling upon us without, and thy spirit within, and have been solicited by promises, by threatenings, by blessings, by chastisings, & by examples, on all hands: And yet our corrupted spirits cannot become wise before thee, to humble themselves, and to take heede as we ought, and wish to do.

Wherefore O Lord God, we do acknowledge thy patience to have beene infinite and incomparable, in that thou hast been able to hold thy hands from revenging thy selfe upon us thus long, & yet pleasest to hold open the dore of grace, that we might come in unto thee and be saved.

And now O blessed Lord God, we are desirous to come unto thee, how wretched soever in our selves, yea our very wretchednesse sends us unto thee: unto thee with whom the fatherlesse, and he that hath no helper findeth mercy, we come to thee in thy Sons name not daring to come in our owne: In his name that came for us, we come to thee, in his mediation whom thou hast sent: In him O Father, in whom thou hast professed thy selfe to be well pleased, we come unto thee, and doe most humbly beseech thee to pittie us, & to save us for thy mercies sake in him.

O Lord our God our sins have not outbidden that bloud of thy holy Son which speakes for our pardon, nor can they be so infinite, as thou art in thy mercies, & our hearts (O God thou seest them,) our hearts are desirous to have peace with thee, and war with our lusts, and wish that they could melt before thee, and be dissolved into godly mourning for all that filth that hath gone through them, and defiled them. And our desires are now to serve and please thee, and our purposes to endeavour it more faithfully, we pray thee therefore for the Lord Jesus sake seale up on our consciences thy gracious pardon of all our sinnes past, and give us to feele the consolation of this grace shed abroad in our hearts for our eternall comfort and salvation: and that we may know this perswasion to be of thy spirit, and not of carnall presumption, (blessed God) let those graces of thy spirit, which doe accompanie salvation, be powred out more plentifully upon us, encrease in us all godly knowledge, faith, patience, temperance, meekenesse, wisedome, godlinesse, love to thy Saints and service, zeale of thy glory, judgement to discerne the difference of good & ill, and things present which are temporary, and things to come which are eternall.

    Make us yet at the last wise-hearted to lay up our treasure in heaven, and to set our affections more upon things that are above, where Christ sits at thy right hand: And let all the vaine and transitory inticements of this poore life, appeare unto us as they are, that our hearts may no more be intangled and bewitched with the love of them.

    O Lord, O God, our God, thou hast dearely bought us for thine owne selfe, give us so honest hearts as may be glad to yeeld the possession of thine owne. And be thou so gracious, as yet to take them up, though we have desperately held thee out of them in times past, and dwell in us, and raigne in us by thy spirit, that we may be sure to raigne with thee in thy glorious kingdome, according to thy promise through him that hath purchased that inheritance for all that trust in him.

    And seeing thou doest so promise these graces to us, as that thou requirest our industrie and diligence in the use of such meanes as serve thereto (good Lord) let us not so crosse our praiers for grace, as not to seeke that by diligence, which we make shew to seeke by prayer, least our owne waies condemne us of hypocrisie. Stirre us up therefore (O Lord) to the frequent use of prayer, to reading, hearing, and meditating of thy holy word, teach us to profit by the conversation of thy people, and to be profitable in our owne, make us wise to apprehend all oportunites of doing or receiving spiritual good, strengethen us with grace to observe our hearts and waies, to containe them in good order, or to reduce them quickly, let us never thinke any company so good as thine, nor any time so well spent, as that which is in thy service, and beautifying of thine Image in our selves or others.

    Particularly we pray thee open our eies to see our naturall infirmities, and to discover the advantages which Satan gets thereby. And give us care to strive most, where we are most assaulted and damaged.

And thou O God, that hast promised to blesse thine owne ordinances, blesse all things unto us, that we may grow in grace & in knowledge, and so may shine as light in this darke world, giving good example to all men, and may in our time lie downe in peace of a good conscience, enbaulmed with a good report, and may leave thy blessings entailed unto ours after us for an inheritance. These O Father, are our speciall suits, wherein wee beseech thee to set forth the wonderful riches of thy grace towards us, as for this life, and the things thereof, we crave them of thee so farre as may be for our good, and thy glory, beseeching thee to provide for us as unto this day in mercy. And when thou wilt humble or exalt us, governe us so long, and so farre in all conditions and changes, as we may cleave fast unto thee our God unchangeably, esteeming thee our portion & sufficient inheritance for evermore. Now what graces we crave for our selves, which are here before thy presence, we humbly begge for all those that belong unto us, and that by dutie or promise wee owne our praiers unto, beseeching thee to be as gracious unto them, as unto our own souls, and specially to such of them, as in respect of any present affliction or temptation may be in speciall neede of some more speedie helpe or comfort from thy mighty hand.

Yea our Lord God we humbly desire to blesse with our praiers the whole Church more specially our nation, and therein the kings Majestie our Soveraigne, his Queene and royall seede, with all that be in authoritie under him, beseeching thee to follow him and them with those blessings of thy protection and direction, which may preserve them safe from the malice of the world, and of Satan, and may yeeld them in their great places faithfull to thee for the good of thy people, and their owne eternall happinesse and honour.

We beseech thee to furnish the Churches with faithfull and fruitfull ministers, and to blesse their lives and labours for those mercifull uses, to which thou hast ordained them, sanctifie thy people O God, and let them not deceive themselves with a formalitie of religion in steed of the power thereof, give them grace to profit both by those favours, and by those chasticements which thou hast sent successively or mixedly amongst them. And Lord represse that rage of sinne, and prophanesse in all Christian states which breeds so much Apostacy and defection, threatning the taking away of this light from them: Confound thou O God all the counsel and practices of Satan and his ministers, which are or shall be taken up against thee, and the kingdome of thy deare sonne. And call in the Jewes together with the fulnesse of the gentiles, that thy name may be glorious in al the world, the dayes of iniquity may come to an end, and we with all thine elect people may come to see thy face in glorie, and be filled with the light thereof for evermore.

And now O Lord of mercie, O Father of the spirits of all flesh, looke in mercie upon the Gentiles, who yet know thee not, O gracious God be mercifull to us, and bless us, and not us alone, but let thy waies be knowne upon earth, & thy saving health amongst all nations: we praise thee, and we blesse thee: But let the people praise thee O God, yea let all the people praise thee, and let these ends of the world remember themsleves and turne to thee the God of their salvation. And seeing thou hast honoured us to choose us out to beare thy name unto the Gentiles: we therefore beseech thee to bless us, and this our plantation. which we and our nation have begun in thy feare, & and for thy glory. We know O Lord, we have the divel and all the gates of hel against us, but if thou O Lord be on our side, we care not who be against us. O therfore vouchsafe to be our God, & let us be a part and portion of thy people, confirme thy covenant of grace & mercy with us, which thou hast made to thy Church in Christ Jesus. And seeing Lord the highest end of our plantation here, is to set up the standard, & display the banner of Jesus Christ, even here where satans throne is Lord, let our labor be blessed in laboring the conversion of the heathen. And because thou usest not to work such mighty works by unholy means, Lord sanctifie our spirits, & give us holy harts, that so we may be thy instruments in this most glorious work: lord inspire our souls with thy grace, kindle in us zeal of thy glory: fill our harts with thy feare, & our tongues with thy praise, furnish us all from the highest to the lowest with all gifts & graces needful not onely for our salvation, but for the discharge of our duties in our severall places, adorne us with the garments of Justice, mercy, love, pitie, faithfulnesse, humility, & all vertues, & teach us to abhor al vice, that our lights may so shine before these heathen, that they may see our good works, & so be brought to glorifie thee our heavenly Father. And seeing Lord we professe our selves thy servants, & are about thy worke, Lord blesse us, arme us against difficulties, strength us against all base thoughts & temptations, that may make us looke backe againe. And seeing by thy motion & work in our harts, we have left our warme nests at home, & put our lives into our hands principally to honour thy name, & advance the kingdome of thy son, Lord give us leave to commit our lives into thy hands: let thy Angels be about us, & let us be as Angels of God sent to this people, And so blesse us Lord, & so prosper all our proceedings, that the heathen may never say unto us, where is now your God: Their Idols are not so good as silver & gold, but lead & copper, & the works of their own hands. But thou Jehovah art our God, & we are ye works of thy hands: O then let Dagon fall before thy Arke, let Satan be confounded at thy presence, & let the heathen see it & be ashamed, that they may seeke thy face, for their God is not our God, themselves being Judges. Arise therfore O Lord, & let thine enemies be scattered, & let them that hate thee flie before thee: As the smoke vanisheth, so let Satan & his delusions come to nought & as wax melteth before the fire, so let wickednes, superstition, ignorance & idolatry perish at ye presence of thee our God. And wheras we have by undertaking this plantation undergone the reproofs of the base world, insomuch as many of our owne brethren laugh us to scorne, O Lord we pray thee fortifie us against this temptation: let Sanballat, & Tobias, Papists & players, & such other Amonists & Horonits the scum & dregs of the earth, let them mocke such as helpe to build up the wals of Jerusalem, and they that be filthy, let them be filthy still, & let such swine still wallow in their mire, but let not ye rod of the wicked fal upon the lot of the righteous, let not them put forth their hands to such vanity, but let them that feare thee, rejoyce & be glad in thee, & let them know, that it is thou O Lord, that raignest in England, & unto the ends of the world. And seeing this work must needs expose us to many miseries, & dangers of soule & bodie, by land & sea, O Lord we earnestly beseech thee to receive us into thy favour & protection, defend us from the delusion of the divel, the malice of the heathen, the invasions of our enemies, & mutinies & dissentions of our own people, knit our hearts altogether in faith & feare of thee, & love one to another, give us patience, wisedome & constancy to goe on through all difficulties & temptations, til this blessed work be accomplished, for the honour of thy name, & glory of the Gospel of Jesus Christ: That when the heathen do know thee to be their God, and Jesus Christ to be their salvation, they may say, blessed by the King & Prince of England, & blessed be the English nation, and blessed for ever be the most high God, possessor of heaven & earth, that sent them amongst us: And heere O Lord we do upon the knees of our harts offer thee the sacrifice of praise & thanksgiving, for that thou hast moved our harts to undertake the performance of this blessed work, with the hazard of our person, and the hearts of so may hundreds of our nation to assist it with meanes & provision, and with their holy praiers, Lord looke mercifully upon them all, and for that portion of their substance which they willingly offer for thy honour & service in this action, recompence it to them and theirs, and reward it seven fold into their bosomes with better blessings: Lord blesse England our sweet native countrey, save it from Popery, this land from heathenisme, & both from Atheisme. And Lord heare their praiers for us, and us for them, and Christ Jesus our glorious Mediator for us all.

Amen.

Appendix Two

The Massachusetts Body of Liberties

December 1641

The Massachusetts Body of Liberties

December 1641

A Coppie of the Liberties of the

Massachusets Collonie in New England

The free fruition of such liberties Immunities and priveledges as humanitie, Civilitie, and Christianitie chall for as due to every man in his place and proportion; without impeachment and Infringement hath ever bene and ever will be the tranquillitie and Stabilitie of Churches and Commonwealths. And the deniall or deprivall thereof, the disturbances if not the ruine of both.

We hould it therefore our dutie and safetie whilst we are about the further establishing of this Government to collect and expresse all such freedomes as for present we foresee may concerne us, and our posteritie after us, And to ratify them with our sollemne consent.

Wee doe therefore this day religiously and unanimously decree and confirme these following Rites, liberties, and priveledges concerning our Churches, and Civill State to be respectively impartiallie and inviolably enjoyed and observed throughout our Jurisdiction for ever.

I. No mans life shall be taken away, no mans honour or good name shall be stayned, no mans person shall be arested, restrayned, banished, dismembered, nor any wayes punished, no man shall be deprived of his wife or children, no mans goods or estaite shall be taken away from him, nor any way indammaged under Coulor of law, or Countenance of Authoritie, unlesse it be by vertue or equitite of some expresse law of the Country warranting the same, established by a generall Court and sufficiently published, or in case of the defect of a law in any partecular case by the word of god. And in Capitall cases, or in cases concerning dismembering or banishment, according to that word to be judged by the Generall Court.

2. Every person within Jurisdiction, whether Inhabitant or forreiner shall enjoy the same justice and law, that is generall for the plantation, which we constitute and execute one towards another, without partialitie or delay.

3. No man shall be urged to take any oath or subscribe any articles, covenants or remonstrance, of a publique and Civill nature, but such as the Generall Court hath considered, allowed, and required.

4. No man shall be punished for not appearing at or before any Civill Assembly, Court, Councell, Magistrate, or officer, nor for the omission of any office or service, if he shall be necessarily hindered, by any apparent Act of providence of god, which he could neither foresee nor avoid. Provided that this law shall not prejudice any person of his just cost or damage in any civill action.

5. No man shall be compelled to any publique worke or service unlesse the presse be grounded upon some act of the generall Cour, and have reasonable allowance therefore.

6. No man shall be pressed in person to any office, worke, warres, or other publique service, that is necessarily and suffitiently exempted by any naturall or personall impediment, as by want of years, greatnes of age, defect of minde, fayling of sences, or impotencie of Lymbes.

7. No man shall be compelled to goe out of the limits of this plantation upon any offensive warres which this Commonwealth or any of our friends or confederates shall voluntarily undertake. But onely upon such vindictive and defensive warres in our owne behalfe, or the behalfe of our friends, and confederates as shall be enterprized by the

Counsell and consent of a Court generall, or by Authority derived from the same.

8. No mans Cattell or goods of what kinde soever shall be pressed or taken for any publique use or service, unless it be by warrant grounded upon some act of the general Court, nor without such reasonable prices and hire as the ordinarie rates of Countrie do afford. And if his cattle or goods shall perish or suffer damage in such service, the owner shall be suffitiently recompenced.

9. No monopolies shall be granted or allowed amongst us, but of such new Inventions that are profitable to the Countrie, and that for a short time.

10. All our lands and heritages shall be free from all finds and licences upon Alienations, and from all hariotts, wardships, Liveries, Primerseisens, yeare day and wast, Escheates, and forfeitures, upon the deaths of parents, or Ancestors, be they naturall, casuall, or Juditiall.

11. All persons which are of the age of 21 yeares, and of right understanding and meamories, whether excommunicate or condemned shall have full power and libertie to make theire wills and testaments, and other lawfull alienations of theire lands and estates.

12. Every man whether Inhabitant or fforreiner, free or not free shall have libertie to come to any publique Court, Councell, or Towne meeting, and either by speech or writeing to move nay lawful, seasonable, and materiall question, or to present any necessary motion, complaint, petition, Bill or information, whereof that meeting hath proper cognizance, so it be done in convenient time, due order, and respective manner.

[13.] No man shall be rated here for any estaite or revenue he hath in England, or in any forreine parties till it be transported hither.

[14.] Any conveyance or Alienation of land or other estaite what so ever, made by any woman that is married, any childe under age, Ideott, or distracted person, shall be good, if it be passed and ratified by the consent of a generall Court.

15. All Covenous or fraudulent Alienations or Conveyances of lands, tenements, or any hereditaments, shall be of no validitie to defeate any man from due debts or legacies, or from any just title, clame or possession, of that which is so fraudulently conveyed.

16. Every Inhabitant that is an howse holder shall have free fishing and fowling in any great ponds and Bayes, Coves and Rivers, so farre as the sea ebbes and flowes within the precincts of the towne where they dwell, unless the freemen of the same Towne or the Generall Court have otherwise appropriated them, provided that this shall not be extended to give leave to any man to come upon other proprietie without there leave.

17. Every man of or within this Jurisdiction shall have free libertie, not with standing any Civill power to remove both himselfe, and his familie at their pleasure out of the same, provided there be no legall impediment to the contrarie.

18. No mans person shall be restrained or imprisoned by any Authority what so ever, before the law hath sentenced him thereto, If he can put in sufficient securitie, bayle, or maniprise, for his appearance, and good behavior in the meane time, unless it be in Crimes Capitall, and Contempts in open Court, and in such cases where some expresse act of Court doth allow it.

19. If in a generall Court any miscarriage shall be amongst the Assistants when they are by themselves that may deserve an Admonition or fine under 20 sh, it shall be examined and sentenced amongst themselves, If amongst the Deputies when they are by themselves, It shall be examined and sentenced amongst themselves, If it be when the whole Court is togeather, it shall be judged by the whole Court, and not severallie as before.

20. If any which are to sit as Judges in any other Court shall demeane themselves offensively in the Court, the rest of the Judges present shall have power to censure him for it, if the cause be of a high nature it shall be presented to and censured at the next superior Court.

21. In all cases where the first summons are not served six dayes before the Court, and the cause briefly specified the warrant, where appearance is to be made by the partie summoned, it shall be at his libertie whether he will appear or not, except all cases that are to be handled in Courts suddainly called upon extraordinary occasions, In all cases where there appears present and urgent cause Any Assistant or officer appointed shal have power to make out Attaichments for the first summons.

22. No man in any suit or action against an other shall falsely pretend great debts or damages to vex his Adversary, if it shall appear any doth so, The Court shall have power to set a reasonable fine on his head.

23. No man shall be adjudged to pay for detaining any Debt from any Crediter above eight pounds in the hundred for one yeare, And not above that rate proportionable for all somes what so ever, neither shall this be a coulour or countenance to allow any usurie amongst us contrarie to the law of god.

24. In all Trespasses or damages done to any man or men, If it can be proved to be done by the mere default of him or them to whome the tresspasse is done, It shall be judged no trespasse, nor any damage given for it.

25. No Summons pleading Judgement, or any kinde of proceeding in Court or course of Justice shall be abated, arested, or reversed, upon any kinde of cercumstantiall errors or mistakes, If the person and cause be rightly understood and intended by the Court.

26. Every man that findeth himself unfit to plead his owne cause in any Court, shall have Libertie to imploy any man against whom the Court

doth not except, to helpe him, Provided he give him noe fee, or reward for his paines. This shall not exempt the partie him selfe from Answering such Questions in person as the Court shall thinke meete to demand of him.

27. If any plaintife shall give into any Court a declaration of his cause in writeing, The defendant shall also have libertie and time to give in his answer in writing, And so in all further proceedings between partie and partie, So it doth not further hinder the dispatch of Justice then the Court shall be willing unto.

28. The plaintife in all Actions brought in any Court shall have libertie to withdraw his Action, or to be nonsuited before the Jurie hath given in their verdict, in which case he shall alwaies pay full cost and chardges to the defendant, and may afterwards renew his suite at an other Court if he please.

29. In all Actions at law it shall be the libertie of the plaintife and defendant by mutual consent to choose whether they will be tried by the Bench or by a Jurie, unless it be where the law upon just reason hath otherwise determined. The like libertie shall be granted to all persons in Criminall cases.

30. It shall be in the libertie of both plaintife and defendant, and likewise every delinquent (to be judged by a Jurie) to challenge any of the Jurors. And if his challenge be found just and reasonable by the Bench, or the rest of the Jurie, as the challenger shall choose it shall be allowed him, and tales de cercumstantibus impaneled in their room.

31. In all cases where evidence is so obscure or defective that the Jurie cannot clearely and safely give a positive verdict, whether it be a grand or petit Jurie, It shall have libertie to give a non Liquit, or a spetiall verdict, in which last, that is in a spetiall verdict, the Judgement of the cause shall be left to the Court, and all Jurors shall have libertie in matters of fact if they cannot finde the maine issue, yet to finde and present in their verdict so much as they can, if the Bench and Jurors shall so differ at any time about their verdict that either of them can

not proceed with peace of conscience the case shall be referred to the Generall Court, who shall take the question from both and determine it.

32. Every man shall have libertie to replevy his Cattell or goods impounded, distreined, seised, or extended, unless it be upon execution after Judgement, and in payment of fines. Provided he puts in good securitie to prosecute his replevin, And to satisfie such demands as his Adversary shall recover against him in Law.

33. No mans person shall be Arrested, or imprisoned upon execution or judgment for any debt or fine, if the law can finde competent meanes of satisfaction otherwise from his estaite, And if not his person may be arrested and imprisoned where he shall be kept at his owne charge, not the plaintife's till satisfaction be made: unless the Court that had cognizance of the cause or some superior Court that had cognizance of the cause or some superior Court shall otherwise provide.

34. If any man shall be proved and Judged a common Barrator vexing others with unjust frequent and endless suites, It shall be in the power of Courts both to deny him the benefit of the law, and to punish him for his Barratry.

35. No mans Corne nor hay that is in the field or upon the Cart, nor his garden stuffe, nor any thing subject to present decay, shall be taken in any distresse, unles he that takes it doth presently bestow it where it may not be imbesled nor suffer spoile or decay, or give securitie to satisfie the worth thereof if it comes to any harme.

36. It shall be in the libertie of every man cast condemned or sentenced in any cause in any Inferior Court, to make their Appeale to the Court of Assistants, provided they tender their appeale and put in securitie to prosecute it before the Court be ended wherein they were condemned, And within six dayes next ensuing put in good securitie before some Assistant to satisfie what his Adversarie shall recover against him; And if the cause be of a Criminall nature, for his good behaviour and appearance, And everie man shall have libertie to complaine to the

Generall Court of any Injustice done him in any Court of Assistants or other.

37. In all cases where it appears to the Court that the plaintife hath willingly and wittingly done wronge to the defendant in commencing and prosecuting any action or complaint against him. They shall have power to impose upon him a proportionable fine to the use of the defendant, or accused person, for his false complaint or clamor.

38. Everie man shall have libertie to Record in the publique Rolles of any Court any Testimony give[n] upon oath in the same Court, or before two Assistants, or any Deede or evidence; legally confirmed there to remaine in perpetuam rei memoriam, that is for perpetuall memoriall or evidence upon occasion.

39. In all Actions both reall and personall betweene partie and partie, the Court shall have power to respite execution for a convenient time, when in their prudence they see just cause so to doe.

40. No Conveyance, Deede, or promise what so ever shall be of validitie, If it be gotten by Illegal violence, imprisonment, threatenings, or any kinde of forcible compulsion called Dures.

41. Everie man that is to Answere for any Criminall cause, whether he be in prison or under bayle, his cause shall be heard and determined at the next Court that hath proper Cognizance therof, And may be done without prejudice of Justice.

42. No man shall be twise sentenced by Civill Justice for one and the same Crime, offence, orTrespasse.

43. No man shall be beaten with above 40 stripes, nor shall any true gentleman, nor any man equall to a gentleman be punished with whipping, unless his crime be very shamefull, and his course of life vitious and profligate.

44. No man condemned to dye shall be put to death within fower dayes next after his condemnation, unles the Court see spetiall cause to the contrary, or in case of martiall law, nor shall the body of any man so put to death be unburied 12 howers, unlesse it be in case of Anatomie.

45. No man shall be forced by Torture to confesse any Crime against himselfe nor any other unlesse it be in some Capitall case where he is first fullie convicted by cleare and suffitient evidence to be guilty, After which if the cause be of that nature, That it is very apparent there be other conspiratours, or confederates with him, Then he may be tortured, yet not with such Tortures as be Barbarous and inhumane.

46. For bodilie punishments we allow amongst us none that are inhumane Barbarous or cruell.

47. No man shall be put to death without the testimony of two or three witnesses, or that which is equivalent there unto.

48. Every Inhabitant of the Countrie shall have free libertie to search and veewe any Rooles, Records, or Regesters of any Court or office except the Councell, And to have a transcript or exemplification thereof written examined, and signed by the hand of the officer of the office paying the appointed fees therefore.

49. No free man shall be compelled to serve upon Juries above two Courts in a yeare, except grand Jurie men, who shall hould two Courts together at the least.

50. All Jurors shall be chose continuallie by the freemen of the Townes where they dwell.

51. All Associates selected at any time to Assist the Assistants in Inferior Courts, shall be nominated by the Townes belonging to that Court, by orderly agreement amonge themselves.

52. Children, Idiots, Distracted persons, and all that are strangers, or new commers to our plantation, shall have such allowances and

dispensations in any cause whether Criminall or other as religion and reason require.

53. The age of discretion of passing away of lands or such kinde of herediments, or for giving of votes, verdicts or Sentence in any Civill Courts or causes, shall be one and twentie years.

54. When so ever anything is to be upt to vote, any sentence to be pronounced, or any other matter to be proposed, or read in any Court or Assembly, If the president or moderator thereof shall refuse to performe it, the Major parte of the members of that Court or Assembly shall have power to appoint any other meete man of them to do it, And if there be just cause to punish him that should and would not.

55. In all suites or Actions in any Court, the plainntife shall have libertie to make all the titles and claims to that he sues for he can. And the Defendant shall have libertie to plead all the pleas he can in answere to them, and the Court shall judge according to the intire evidence of all.

56. If any man shall behave himselfe offensively at any Towne meeting, the rest of the freemen then present, shall have power to sentence him for his offence, So be it the mulct or penaltie exceed not twentie shilings.

57. When so ever any person shall come to any very suddaine untimely and unnaturall death, Some Assistant, or the Constables of that Towne shall forthwith summon a Jury of twelve free men to inquire of the cause and manner of their death, and shall present a true verdict thereof to some neere Assistant, or the next Court to be helde for that Towne upon their oath.

LIBERTIES MORE PECULIARLIE CONCERNING THE FREE MEN.

58. Civill Authoritie hath power and libertie to see the peace, ordinances and Rules of Christ observed in every church according to his word, so it be done in a Civill and not in an Ecclesiastical way.

59. Civill Authoritie hath power and libertie to deale with any Church member in a way of Civille Justice, notwithstanding any Church relation, office, or interest.

60. No church censure shall degrade or depose any man from any Civill dignitie, office, or Authoritie he shall have in the Commonwealth.

61. No Magestrate, Juror, Officer, or other man shall be bound to informe present or reveale any private crim or offence, wherein there is no peril or danger to this plantation or any member thereof, when any necessarietye of conscience binds him to secresie grounded upon the word of god, unless it be in case of testimony lawfully required.

62. Any Shire or Towne shall have libertie to choose their Deputies whom and where they please for the General Court, So be it they be free men, and have taken there oath of fealtie, and Inhabiting in this Jurisdiction.

63. No Governor, Deputie Governor, Assistant, Associate, or grand Jury man at any Court, nor any Deputie for the Generall Court, shall at any time beare his owne chardges at any Court, but their necessary expences shall be defrayed either by the Towne, or Shire on whose service they are, or by the Country in generall.

64. Everie Action between partie and partie, and proceedings against delinquents in Criminall causes shall be briefly and distinctly entered in the Rolles of every Court by the Recorder thereof. That such actions be not afterwards brought againe to the vexation of any man.

65. No custome or prescription shall ever prevaile amongst us in any morall cause, our meaning is maintaine anything that can be proved to bee morrallie sinfull by the word of god.

66. The Freemen of everie Towneship shall have power to make such by laws and constitutions as may concerne the welfare of their Towne, provided they be not of a Criminall, but onely of a prudentiall nature. And that their penalties exceed not 20 sh. For one offensce. And that they be not repugnant to the publique laws and orders of the Countrie. And if any Inhabitant shall neglect or refuse to observe them, they shall have power to levy the appointed penalties by distresse.

67. It is the constant libertie of the freemen of this plantation to choose yearly at the Court of Elections out of the freemen all the Generall officers of this Jurisdiction. If they please to dischardge them at the day of Election by way of vote. They may do it without shewing cause. But if at any other generall Court, we hould it due justice, that the reasons thereof be alleadged and proved. By Generall officers we meane, our Governor, Deputie Governor, Assistants, Treasurer, Generall of our warres. And our Admiral at Sea, and such as are or hereafter may be of the like generall nature.

68. It is the libertie of the freemen to choose such deputies for the Generall Court out of themselves, either in their owne Townes or elsewhere as they judge fittest, And because we cannot foresee what varietie and weight of occasions may fall into future consideration, And what counsels we may stand in need of, we dedcree. That the Deputies (to attend the Generall Court in the behalf of the Countrie) shall not any time be stated or inacted, but from Court to Court, or at the most but for one yeare. that the Countrie may have an Annuall libertie to do in that case what is most behoofefull for the best welfare thereof.

69. No Generall Court shall be desolved or adjourned without the consent of the Major parte thereof.

70. All Freemen called to give any advise, vote, verdict, or sentence in any Court, Counsell, or Civill Assembly, shall have full freedome to doe

it according to their true Judgments and Consciences, So it be done orderly and inoffensively for the manner.

71. The Governor shall have a casting voice whensoever an Equi vote shall fall out of the Court of Assistants, or generall assembly, So shall the presendent or moderator have in all Civill courts or Assemblies.

72. The Governor and Deputie Governor Joyntly consenting or any three Assistant concurring in consent shall have power out of Court to reprive a condemned malefactour, till the next quarter or generall Court. The generall Court onely shall have power to pardon a condemned malefactor.

73. The Generall Court hath libertie and Authoritie to send out any member of the Commanwealth of what qualitie, condition or office whatsoever into forreine parts about any publique message or Negotiation. Provided the partie sent be acquainted with the affaire he goeth about, and be willing to undertake the service.

74. The freemen of every Towne or Towneship, shall have full power to choose yearly or for lesse time out of themselves a convenient number of fitt men to order the planting or prudential occasions of that Towne, according to Instructions given them in writeing, Provided nothing be done by them contrary to the publique laws and orders of the countrie, provided also the number of such select persons be not above nine.

75. It is and shall be the libertie of any member or members of any Court, Councell or Civill Assembly in cases of making or executing any order or law, that properlie concerne religion, or any cause capitall or warres, or Subscription to any publique Articles or Remonstrance, in case they cannot in Judgement and conscience consent to that way the Major vote or suffrage goes, to make their contra Remonstrance or protestation in speech or writing, and upon request to have their dissent recorded in the Rolles of that Court. So it be done Christianlie and respectively for the manner. And their dissent onely be entered without the reasons thereof, for the avoiding of tediousness.

76. When so ever any Jurie of trialls or Jurours are not cleare in their Judgments or consciences conserneing any cause wherein they are to give their verdict, They shall have libertie in open Court to advise with any man they thinke fitt to resolve or direct them, before they give in their verdict.

77. In all cases wherein any freeman is to give his vote, be it in point of Election, making constitutions and orders, or passing sentence in any case of Judicature or the like, if he cannot see reason to give it positively one way or an other, he shall have libertie to be silent, and not pressed to a determined vote.

78. The Generall or publique Treasure or any parte thereof shall never be exspended but by the appointmen of a Generall Court, nor any Shire Treasure, but by the appointment of the freemen thereof, nor any Towne Treasurie but by freemen of that Towneship.

LIBERTIES OF WOMEN

79. If any man at his death shall not leave his wife a competent portion of his estaite, upon just complaint made to the Generall Court she shall be relieved.

80. Everie marryed woeman shall be free from bodilie correction or stripes by her husband, unless it be in his owne defence upon her assault. If there be any just cause of correction complaint shall be made to Authoritie assembled in some Court, from which onely she shall receive it.

LIBERTIES OF CHILDREN

81. When Parents dye intestate, the Elder sonne shall have a doble portion of his whole estate reall and personall, unlesse the Generall Court upon just cause alleadged shall Judge otherwise.

82. When parents dye intestate, haveing noe heirs males of their bodies their Daughters shall inherit as Copartners, unles the Generall Court upon just reason shall judge otherwise.

83. If any parents shall wilfullie and unreasonably deny any childe timely or convenient marriage, or shall exercise any unnatural severitie towards them, Such children shall have free libertie to complain to Authoritie for redresse.

84. No Orphan dureing their minoritie which was not committed to tuition or service by the parents in their life time, shall afterwards be absolutely disposed of by any kindred, friend, Executor, Towneship, or Church, nor by themselves without the consent of some Court, wherein two Assistants at least shall be present.

LIBERTIES OF SERVANTS

85. If any servants shall flee from the Tiranny and crueltie of their masters to the howse of any freeman of the same Towne, they shall be there protected and susteyned till due order be taken for their relife. Provided due notice thereof by speedily given to their masters from whom they fled. And the next aSsistant or Constable where the partie flying is harboured.

86. No servant shall be put of for above a yeare to any other neither in the life of their master nor after their death by their Executors or Administrators unless it be by consent of Authoritie assembled in some Court, or two Assistants.

87. If any man smite out the eye or tooth of his man servant, or maid servant, or otherwise mayme or much disfigure him, unless it be by mere casualtie, he shall let them goe free from his service. And shall have such further recompense as the Court shall allow him.

88. Servants that have served diligentlie and faithfully to the benefitt of their maisters seaven yeares, shall not be sent awayt emptie. And if any have bene unfaithfull, negligent or unprofitable in their service,

notwithstanding the good usage of their maisters, they shall not be dismissed till they have made satisfaction according to the Judgement of Authoritie.

LIBERTIES OF FORREINERS AND STRANGERS

89. If any people of other Nations professing the true Christian Religion shall flee to us from the Tiranny or oppression of their persecutors, or from famine, warres, or the like necessary and compulsarie cause, They shall be entertained and succoured amongst us, according to that power and prudence god shall give us.

90. If any ships or other vessels, be it friend or enemy, shall suffer shipwrack upon our Coast, there shall be no violence or wrong offered to their persons or goods, But their persons shall be harboured, and relieved, and their goods preserved in safety till Authoritie may be certified thereof, and shall take further order therein.

91. There shall never be any bond slaverie villinage or Captivitie amongst us, unles it be lawfull Captives taken in just warres, and such strangers as willingly belie themselves or are sold to us. And these shall have all the liberties and Christian usages which the law of god established in Israell concerning such persons doeth morally require. This exempts none from servitude who shall be Judged thereto by Authoritie.

OFF THE BRUITE CREATURE

92. No man shall exercise any Tirranny or Crueltie towards any bruite Creature which are usuallie kept for mans use.

93. IF any man shall have occasion to leade or drive Cattel from place to place that is far of, So that they be weary, or hungry, or fall sick, or lambe, It shall be lawful to rest or refresh them, for a competent time, in any open place that is not Corne, meadow, or inclosed for some peculiar use.

94.

1. If any man after legall conviction shall have or worship any other god, but the lord god, he shall be put to death. DUT. 13.6.10, DUT. 17.2.6, EX. 22.20

2. If any man or woeman be a witch, (that is hath or consulteth with a familiar spirit,) They shall be put to death. EX. 22.18, LEV. 20.27, DUT. 18.10

3. If any person shall Blaspheme the name of God, the father, Sonne, or Holie ghost, with direct expresse, presumptuous or high handed blasphemie, or shall curse god in the like manner, he shall be put to death. LEV. 24.15.16

4. If any person commit any wilfull murther, which is manslaughter, committed upon premeditated mallice, hatred, or Crueltie, not in a mans mecessarie and just defence, nor by meere casualtie against his will, he shall be put to death. EX. 21.12, NUMB. 35.13.14, 30.31

5. If any person slayeth on other suddainely in his anger or crueltie of passion, he shall be put to death. NUMB. 25.20.21, LEV. 24.17

6. If any person shall slay an other through guile, either by poisoning or other such divelish practice, he shall be put to death. EX. 21.14

7. If any man or woman shall lye with any beast or brute creature by Carnall Copulation, They shall surely be put to death. And the beast shall be slaine and buried and not eaten. LEV. 19.23

8. If any man layeth with mankinde as he lyeth with a woman, both of them have committed abhomination, they both shall surely be put to death. LEV. 19.22

9. If any person commetteth Adultery with a married or espoused wife, the Adulterer and the Adulteresse shall surely be put to death. EX. 20.14

10. If any man stealeth a man or mankinde, he shall surely be put to death. EX. 21.16

11. If any man rise up by false witnes, wittingly and of purpose to take away any man's life, he shall be put to death. DUT. 19.16, 18.19

12. If any man shall conspire and attempt any invasion, insurrection, or publique rebellion against our commonwealth, or shall indeavour to surprise any Towne or Townes, fort or forts therin, or shall treacherously and perfediouslie attempt the alteration and subversion of our frame of politie or Government fundamentalie, he shall be put to death.

95. A declaration of the Liberties the Lord Jesus hath given to the Churches.

1. All the people of god within this Jurisdiction who are not in a church way, and be orthodox in Judgement, and not scandalous in life, shall have full libertie to gather themselves into a church Estaite. Provided they doe it in a Christian way, with due observation of the rules of Christ revealed in his word.

2. Every Church hath full libertie to exercise all the ordinances of god, according to the rules of Scripture.

3. Every Church hath free libertie of Election and ordination of all their officers from time to time, provided they be able and pious and orthodox.

4. Every Church hath free liberties of Admission, Recommendation, Dismission, and Expulsion, or deposall of their officers, and members, upon due cause, with free exercise of the Discipline and Censures of Christ according to the rules of his word.

5. No Injuctions are to be put upon any Church, Church Officers or member in point of Doctrine, worship or Discipline, whether for substance or cercumstance besides the Institutions of the lord.

6. Every Church of Christ hath freedome to celebrate dayes of fasting and prayer, and of thanksgiveing according to the word of god.

7. The Elders of Churches have free libertie to meet monthly, Quarterly, or otherwise, in convenient numbers and places, for conferences, and consultations about Christian and Church questions and occasions.

8. All Churches have libertie to deale with any of their members in a church way that are in the hand of Justice. So it be not to retard or hinder the course thereof.

9. Every Church hath libertie to deal with any magistrate, Deputie of Court or other officer what soe ever that is a member in a church way in case of apparent an djust offence given in their places. so it be done with due observance and respect.

10. Wee allowe private meetings for edification in religion amongst Christians of all sortes of people. So it be without just offence both for number, time, place and other cercumstances.

11. For the preventing and removeing of errour and offence that may grow and spread in any of the Churches in this Jurisdiction. And for the preserveing of trueith and peace in the several churches within them selves, and for the maintenance and exercise of brotherly communion, amongst all the churches in the Countrie, It is allowed and ratified, by the Authoritie of this Generall Court as a lawfull libertie of the Churches of Christ. That once in every month of the yeare (when the season will beare it) It shall be lawfull for the ministers and Elders, of the Churches neede adjoyneing together, with any other of the breetheren with the consent of the churches to assemble by course in each severall Church one after an other. To the intent after the preaching of the word by such a minister as shall be requested thereto by the Elders of the church where the Assembly is held, The rest of the day may be spent in publique Christian Conference about the discussing and resolveing of any such doubts and cases of conscience concerning matter of doctrine or worship or government of the church as shall be propounded by any of the Breetheren of that church, with

leave also to any other Brother to propound his objections or answers for further satisfaction according to the word of god. Provided that the whole action be guided and moderated by the Elders of the Church where the Assemblie is helde, or by such others as they shall appoint. And that no thing be concluded and imposed by way of Authoritie from one or more Churches upon an other, but onely by way of Brotherly conference and consultations. That the trueth may be searched out to the satisfying of every man's Conscience in the sight of god according to his worde. And because such an Assembly and the worke their of can not be duely attended to if other lectures be held in the same weeke. It is therefore agreed with the consent of the Churches. That in that weeke when such an Assembly is held. All the lectures in all the neighbouring Chuches for the weeke shall be forbone. That so the publique service of Christ in this more solemne Assembly may be transacted with greater diligence and attention.

96. How so ever these above specified rites, freedomes, Immunities, Authorities and priveledges, both Civill and Ecclesiasticall are expressed onely under the name and title of Liberties, and not in the exact forme of Laws, or Statutes, yet we do with one consent fullie Authorise, and earnestly intreate all that are and shall be in Authoritie to consider them as laws, and not to faile to inflict condigne and proportionable punishments upon every man impartiallie, that shall infringe or violate any of them.

97. Wee likewise give full power and libertie to any person that shall at any time be denyed or deprived of any of them, to commence and prosecute their suite, Complaint, or action against any man that shall so doe, in any Court that hath proper Cognizance or judicature thereof.

98. lastly because our dutie and desire is to do nothing suddainlie which fundamentally concerne us, we decree that these rites and liberties, shall be Audably read and deliberately weighed at ever Generall Court that shall be held, within three yeares next insueing, And such of them as shall not be altered or repealed they shall stand so ratified, That no man shall infringe them without due punishment.

And if any General Court within these next thre yeares shall faile or forget to reade and consider them as abovesaid. The Governor and Deputie Governor for the time being, and ever Assistant present at such Courts shall forfeite 20 sh. A man, and everie Deputie 10 sh. A man for each neglect, which shall be paid out of their proper estate, and not by the Country or the Townes which should choose them. And when so ever there shall arise any question in any Court among the Assistants and Associates thereof about the explanation of these Rites and liberties, The Generall Court onely shall have power to interprett them.

Appendix Three

The Laws and Liberties of Massachusetts

1647
The Laws and Liberties of Massachusetts

1647

The Book of the General Lawes and Libertyes Concerning the Inhabitants of the Massachusets Collected Out of the Records of the Genereal Court for the Several Years Wherein They Were Made and Established,

And now revised by the same Court and desposed into an Alphabetical order and published by the same Authoritie in the General Court held at Boston the fourteenth of the first month Anno 1647.

TO OUR BELOVED BRETHREN AND NEIGHBOURS

The Inhabitants of the Massachusets, the Governour, Assistants and Deputies assembled in the Generall Court of that Jurisdiction with grace and peace in our Lord Jesus Christ. So soon as God had set up Politicall Government among his people Israel hee gave them a body of lawes of judgement both in civil and criminal causes. These were brief and fundamental principles, yet withall so full and comprehensive as out of them clear deductions were to be drawne to all particular cases in future times. For a Common-wealth without lawes is like a Ship without a rigging and steeradge. Nor is it sufficient to have principles or fundamentalls, but these are to be drawn out into so many of their deductions as the time and condition of that people may have use of. And it is very unsafe & injurious to the body of the people to put them to learn their duty and libertie from generall rules, nor is it enough to have lawes except they do also just. Therefore among other priviledges which the Lord bestowed upon his peculiar people, these he calls them specially to consider of, that God was nearer to them and their lawes were more righteous then other nations. God was sayd to be amongst them or neer to them because of his Ordnances established by himselfe, and their lawes righteous because himselfe was their Law-giver: yet in the comparison are implied two things, first that other nations had something of Gods presence amongst them. Secondly that there was also somwhat of equitie in their lawes, for it pleased the Father (upon the Covenant of Redemption with his Son) to restore so much of his Image to lost man as whereby all nations are disposed to worship God, and to advance righteousness: Which appears in that of the Apostle Rom. I. 21. They knew God &c: and in the 2.14. They did by nature the things conteined in the law of God. But the nations corrupting his ordinances (both of Religion, and Justice) God withdrew his presence from them proportionably whereby they were given up to abominable lusts Rom. 2. 21. Wheras if they had walked according to that light & law of nature might have been preserved from such moral evils and might have injoyed a common blessing in all their natural and civil Ordinances: now, if it might have been so with the nations who were so much strangers to the Covenant, and may injoye the special presence of God in the pruitie and native simplicitie of all his Ordinances by which he is so neer to his owne people. This hath been no small priviledge, and advantage to us in New-England that our Churches, and civil State have been planted, and growne up (like two twines) together like that of Israel in the wilderness by which wee were put in minde (and had opportunitie put into our hands) not only to gather our Churches, and set up the Ordinances of Christ Jesus in them according to the Apostolick patterne by such a light as the Lord graciously afforded us: but also withall to frame our civil Politie, and lawes according to the rules of his most holy word whereby each do help and strengthen other (the Churches the civil Authoritie, and the civil Authoritie the Churches) and so both prosper the better without such emulation, and contention for priviledges or priority as have proved the misery (if not ruine) of both in some other places.

For this end about nine years wee used the help of some of the Elders of our Churches to compose a modell of the Judiciall lawes of Moses with such other cases as might be referred to them, with intent to make sure of them in composing our lawes, but not to have them published as the lawes of this Jurisdiction: nor were they voted in Court. For that book intitled The Liberties &c: published about seven years since (which conteines also many lawes and orders both for civil & criminal causes, and is commonly [though without ground] reported to be our Fundamentalls that wee owne as established by Authoritie of this Court, and that after three years experience &

generall approbation: and accordingly we have inserted them into this volume under the severall heads to which they belong yet not as fundamentalls, for divers of them have since been repealed, or altered, and more may justly be (at least) amended hereafter s further experienced shall discover defects or inconveniences for Nihil simul natum et perfectum. The same must we lay of this present Volume, we have not published it as a perfect body of laws sufficient to carry on the Government established for future times, nor could it be expected that we should promise such a thing. For if it be no disparagement to the wisedome of that High Court of Parliament in England that in four hundred years they could not so compile their lawes, and regulate proceedings in Courts of justice &c: but they had still new work to do of the same kinde almost every Parliament: there can be no just cause to blame a poor Colonie (being unfurnished of Lawyers and Statemen) that in eighteen years hath produced no more, nor better rules for a good, and settled Government then this Book holds forth: nor have you (our Brethren and Neighbours) any cause, whether you look back upon our Native Country, or take your observation by other States, & Commonwealths in Europe) to complaine of such as you have imployed in this service; for the time which hath been spent in makeing laws, and repealing and altering them so often, nor of the charge which the Country hath been put to for those occasions, the Civilian gives you a satisfactorie reason of such continuall alterations additions &c: *Crescit in Orbe dolus*.

These Lawes which were made successively in divers former years, we have reduced under severall heads in an alphabetical method, that so they might the more readily ye be found, & that the divers lawes concerning one matter being placed together the scope and intent of the whole and of every of them might the more easily be apprehended: we must confesse we have not been so exact in placing every law under its most proper title as we might, and would have been: the reason was our hasty indeavour to satisfie your longing expectation, and frequent complaints for want of such a volume to be published in print: wherin (upon every occasion) you might readily see the rule which you ought to walke by. And in this (we hope) you will finde satisfaction, by the help of the references under the several heads, and the Table which we have added in the end. For such lawes and orders as are not of generall concernment we have not put them into this booke, but they remain still in force, and are to be seen in the booke, but they remain still in force, and are to be seen in the booke of the Records of the Court, but all gernerall laws not heer inserted nor mentioned to be still of force are to be accounted repealed.

You have called us from amongst the rest of our Bretheren and given us power to make these laws: we must now call upon you to see them executed: remembering that old & true proverb, The execution of the law is the life of the law. If one sort of you viz: non-Freemen should object that you had no hand in calling us to this worke, and therefore think yourselvs not bound to obedience &c. Wee answer that a subsequent, or implicit consent is of like force in this case, as an express precedent power: for in putting your persons and estates into the protection and way of subsistence held forth and exercised within this jurisdiction, you doe tacitly submit to this Government and to all the wholesome lawes thereof, and so is the common repute in all nations and that upon this Maxim.

If any of you meet with some law that seems not to tend to your particular benefit, you must consider that lawes are made with respect to the whole people, and not to each particular person: and obedience to them must be yielded with respect to the common welfare, not to thy private advantage, and as thou yeildest obedience to the law for comon good, but to thy disadvantage: so another must observe some other law for them good, though to his own damage; thus must we be content to bear one anothers burden and so fulfill the Law of Christ.

That distinction which is put between the Lawes of God and the laws of men, becomes a smare to many as it is mis-applyed in the ordering of their obedience to civil Authoritie; for when the Authoritie is of God and that in way of an Ordinance Rom. 13. I. and when the administration of it is according to deductions, and rules gathered from the word of God, and the clear light of nature in civil nations, surely there is no humane law that tendeth to common good (according to those principles) but the same is mediately a law of God, and that in way of an Ordinance which all are to submit unto and that for conscience sake. Rom 13. 5.

By order of the General Court.
INCREASE NOWEL, SECR.

The book of the General Lauues and Libertyes Concerning &c: FORASMUCH as the free fruition of such Liberties, Immunities, priviledges as humanitie, civilitie & christianity call for s due to everie man in his place, & proportion, without impeachment & infringement hath ever been, & ever will be the tranquility & stability of Churches & Comon-wealths; & the deniall of deprivall thereof the disturbance, if not ruine of both:

It is therefore ordered by this Court, & Authority thereof, That no mans life shall be taken away; no mans honour or good name shall be stayned; no mans person shall be arrested, restrained, banished, dismembred nor any wayes punished; no man shall be deprived of his wife or children; no mans goods or estate shall be taken away from him; nor any wayes indamaged under colour of law or counternance of Authoritie unles it be by the vertue or equity of some expresse law of the Country warranting the same established by a General Court & sufficiently published; or in case of the defect of a law in any particular case by the word of God. And in capital cases, or in cases concerning dismembring or banishment according to that word to be judged by the General Court [1641]

ABILITIE.

All persons of the age of twenty one years, and of right understanding & memorie whether excommunicate, condemned or other, shall have full power and libertie to make their Wills & Testaments & other lawful Alientations of their lands and estates. [1641]

All Action of debt, accounts, slaunders, and Actions of the case concerning debts and accounts shall henceforth be tryed where the Plantiffe pleaseth; so it be in the jurisdiction of that Court where the Plantiffe, or Defendant dwelleth: unles by the consent under both their hands it appeare they would have the case tryed in any other Court. All other Actions shal be tried within that jurisdiction where the cause of Action doth arise. [1642]

2. It is ordered by this Court & Authoritie thereof, That every person impleading another in any court of Assistants, of County court shal pay the sum of ten shillings before his case be entred, unless the court fee cause to admit any to sue in [1642]

3. It is ordered by the Authority aforesayd, That where the debt or damage recovered shall amount to ten pounds in every such case to pay five shillings more, and where it shall amount to twenty pounds or upward there to pay ten shillings more then the first ten shillings, which sayd additions shall be put to the Judgement and Execution to be levied by the Marshall and accounted for to the Treasurer. [1647]

4. In all actions brought to any court the Plantiffe shall have liberty to withdraw his action or to be non-suted before the Jurie have given in their verdict; in which case he shall always pay full cost and charges to the Defendant, and may afterward renew his sute at another Court. [1641]

AGE.

It is ordered by this Court & the Authoritie thereof, that the age for passing away of lands, or such kinde of hereditaments, or for giving of votes, verdicts or sentences in any civil courts or causes, shall be twenty and one years: but in case of chusing of Guardions, fourteen years [1641 1647]

ANA-BAPTISTS.

Forasmuch as experience hath plentifully & often proved that since the first arising of the Ana-baptists about a hundred years apart they have been the Incendiaries of Common-Wealths & the Infectors of persons in main matters of Religion, & the Troublers of Churches in most places where they have been, & that they who have held the baptizing of Infants unlawful, have usually held other errors or heresies together therwith (though as hereticks used to doe they have concealed the same untill they espied a fit advantaged and opportunity to vent them by way of question or scruple) and wheras divers of this kinde have since our coming into New-England appeared amongst our selvs, some whereof as others before them have denied the Ordinance of Magistracy, and the lawfulnes of making warre, others the lawfulnes of

Magistrates, and their Inspection into any breach of the first Table: which opinions is conived at by us are like to be increased among us & so necessarily bring guilt up us, infection, & trouble to the Churches & hazard to the whole Common-wealth:

It is therefore ordered by this Court & Authoritie therof, that if any person or persons within this Jurisdiction shall either openly condemn or oppose the baptizing of Infants, or goe about secretly to reduce others from the approbation of use thereof, or shall purposely depart the Congregation at the administration of that Ordinance; or shall deny the Ordinance of Magistracy, or their lawfull right or authoritie to make war, or to punish the outward breaches of the first Table, and shall appear to the Court willfully and obstinately to continue therin, after due means of conviction, everie such person or persons shall be sentenced to Banishment. [1644]...

ARRESTS.

I is ordered and decreed by this Court & Authoritie thereof, That no mans person shall be arrested or imprisoned for any debt of fine if the law can finde any competent meanes of satisfaction otherwise from his estate. And if not this person may be arrested and imprisoned, where he shall be kept at his own charge, not the Plaintiffs, till satisfaction be made; unless the Court that had cognisance of the cause or some superior Court shall otherwise determine: provided neverthelesse that no mans person shall be kept in prison for debt but when there appears some estate which he will not produce, to which end any Court or Commissioners authorized by the General Court may administer an oath to the partie or any others suspected to be privie in concealing his estate, but shall satisfie by service if the Creditor require it but shall not be solde to any but of the English nation. [1641: 1647]...

BOND-SLAVERY.

It is ordered by this Court and authoritie thereof, that there shall never be any bond-slavery, villenage or captivitie amongst us; unless it be lawfull captives, taken in just wars, and such strangers as willingly sell themselves, or are solde to us: and such shall have the libertyes and christian usages which the law of

God established in Israell concerning such persons doth morally require, provided, this exempts none from servitude who shall be judged thereto by Authoritie. [1641]...

CAPITAL LAWES.

If any man after legal conviction shall HAVE OR WORSHIP any other God, but the LORD GOD: he shall be put to death. Exod. 22. 20. Deut. 13.6. & 10. Deut. 17. 2. 6.

2. If any man or woman be a WITCH, that is, hath or consulteth with a familiar spirit, they shall be put to death. Exod. 22. 18. Levit. 20. 27. Deut. 18. 10. 11.

3. If any person within this Jurisdiction whether Christian or Pagan shall wittingly presume to BLASPHEME the holy Name of God, Father, Son or Holy-Ghost, with direct, expresse, presumptuous, or highhanded blasphemy, either by wilfull or obstinate denying the true God, or his Creation, or Government of the world: or shall curse God in like manner, or reproach the holy religion of God s if it were but a politick device to keep ignorant men in awe; or shal utter any other kinde Blasphemy of the like nature & degree they shall be put to death. Levit. 24. 15. 16.

4. If any person shall commit any wilfull MURTHER, which is Man slaughter, committed upon premeditate malice, hatred, or crueltie not in a mans necessary and just defence, nor by meer casualty against his will, he shall be put to death. Exod. 21. 12. 13. Numb. 35. 31.

5. If any person slayeth another suddenly in his ANGER, or CRUELTY of passion, he shall be put to death. Levit. 24. 17. Numb. 35. 20. 21.

6. If any person shall slay another through guile, either by POYSONING, or other such devilish practice, he shall be put to death. Exod. 21. 14.

7. If any man or woman shall LYE WITH ANY BEAST, or bruit creature, by carnall copulation; they shall surely be put to death: and the beast shall be slain, & buried, and not eaten. Lev. 20. 15. 16.

8. If any man LYETH WITH A MAN-KINDE as he lieth with a woman, both of them have committed abomination, they both shal surely be put to death: unles the one partie was forced (or be under fourteen years of age in which case he shall be severely punished) Levit. 20. 13.

9. If any person commit ADULTERIE with a married or espoused wife; the Adulterer & Adulteresse shall surely be put to death. Lev. 20. 19. & 18. 20 Deu. 22. 23. 27.

10. If any man STEALETH A MAN, or Man-kinde, he surely be put to death Exodus 21. 16.

11. If any man rise up by FALSE-WITNES wittingly and of purpose to take away any mans life: he shal be put to death. Deut. 19. 16. 18. 16.

12. If any man shall CONSPIRE, and attempt any Invasion, Insurrection, or publick Rebellion against our Common-Wealth: or shall indeavour to surprize any Town, or Townes, Fort therin; or shall treacherously, & perfidiously attempt the Alteration and Subversion of our frame of Politie, or Government fundamentally he shall be put to death. Numb. 16. 2 Sam. 3. 2 Sam. 18. 2 Sam. 20.

13. If any child, or children, above sixteen years old, and of sufficient understanding, shall CURSE, or SMITE their natural FATHER, or MOTHER; he or they shall be put to death: unless it can be sufficiently testified that the Parents have been very unchristianly negligent in the education of such children; or so provoked them by extream, and cruel correction: that they have been forced therunto to preserve themselves from death or maiming. Exod. 21. 17. Lev. 20. 9. Exod 21. 15.

14. If a man have a stubborn or REBELLIOUS SON, of sufficient years & understanding (viz) sixteen years of age, which will not obey the voice of his Father, or the voice of his Mother, and when they have chastened him will not harken unto them: then shal his Father & Mother being his natural parents, lay hold on him, & bring him to the Magistrates assembled in Court & testifie unto them, that their Son is stubborn & rebellious & will not obey their voice

and chastisement, but lives in sundry notorious crimes, such a son shal be put to death. Deut. 21. 20. 21.

15. If any man shal RAVISH any maid or single woman, comitting carnal copulation with her by force, against her own will; that is above the age of ten years he shal be punished either with death, or with some other grievous punishment according to circumstances as the Judges, or General court shal determin. [1641]...

CHARGES PUBLICK

And it is further ordered that the Comissioners for the severall towns in everie Shire shall yearly upon the first fourth day of the week in the seventh month, assemble at their shire Town: & bring with them fairly written the just number of males listed as foresaid, and the assessments of estates made in their several towns according to the rules & directions in this present order expressed, and the said Comissioners being so assembled shall duly and carefully examin all the said lists and assessments of the severall towns in that Shire, and shall correct & perfect the same according to the true intent of this order, as they or the major part of them shall determine, & the same so perfected they shal speedily transmit to the Treasurer under their hands or the hands of the major part of them and therupon the Treasurer shal give warrants to the Constables to collect & levie the same; so as the whole assessment both for persons & estates may be payd in unto the Treasurer before the twentith day of the ninth month, yearly, & everie one shal pay their rate to he Constable in the same town where it shal be assessed. Nor shall any land or estate be rated in any other town but where the same shal lye, is, or was improved to the owners, reputed owners or other proprietors use or behoof if it be within this Jurisdiction. And if the Treasurer canot dispose of it there, the Constable shall send it to such place in Boston, or elsewhere as the Treasurer shall appoint at the charge of the Countrie to be allowed the Constable upon his accout with the Treasurer. And for all peculiars viz: such places as are not yet layd within the bounds of any town the same lands with the persons an estates therupon shall be assessed by the rates of the town next unto it, the measure or estimation shall be by the distance of the Meeting houses...

CHILDREN.

For as much as the good education of children is of singular behoof and benefit to any Common-wealth; and wher as many parents & masters are too indulgent and negligent of their duty in that kinde. It is therefore ordered that the Selectmen of every town, in the severall precincts and quarters where they dwell, shall have a vigilant eye over their brethren & neighbours, to see, first that none of them shall suffer so much barbarism in any of their families as not to indeavour to teach by themselves or others, their children & apprentices so much learning as may inable them perfectly to read the English tongue, & knowledge of the Capital laws: upon penalize of twentie shillings for each neglect therin. Also that all masters of families doe once a week (at the least) catechize their children and servants in the grounds & principles of Religion, & if any be unable to doe so much: that then at the least they procure such children or apprentices to learn some short orthodox catechism without book, that they may be able to answer unto the questions that shall be propounded to them out of such catechism by their parents of masters of any of the Selectmen when they shall call them to a tryall of what they have learned in this kinde. And further that all parents and masters do breed & bring up their children & apprentices in some honest lawful calling, labour or imploymet, either in husbandry, or some other trade profitable for themselves, and the Common-wealth if they will not or cannot train them up in learning to fit them for higher imployments. And if any of the Selectmen after admonition by them given such masters of families shal finde them sill negligent of their dutie in the particulars aforementioned, wherby children and servants become rude, stubborn, & unruly; the said Selectmen with the help of two Magistrates, of the next County court for that Shire, shall take such children or apprentices from them & place them with some masters for years (boyes till they come to twenty-one, and girls eighteen years of age compleat) which will more strictly look unto, and force them to submit unto government according to the rules of this order, if by fair means and former instructions they will not be drawn unto it. [1642]

2. Wheras sundry gentlemen of qulitie, and others oft times send over their children into this country unto some freinds heer, hoping at the least therby to prevent their extravagant and riotous courses, who not with standing by

means of some unadvised and ill-affected persons, which give them credit, in expectation their friends, either in favour to them or prevention of blemish to themselves, will discharge what ever is done that way, they are no lesse lavish & profuse heer to the great greif of their freinds, dishonor of God & reproach of the Countrie.

It is therefore ordered by this Court & authoritie thereof; That if any person after publication hereof shall any way give credit to any such youth, or other person under twentie one years of age, without order from such their freinds, heer, or elsewhere, under their hands in writing they shall lose their debt whatever it be. And further if such youth or other person incur any penalty by such means and have not wherwith to pay, such person, or persons, as are occasions therof shall pay it as delinquents in the like case should doe. [1647]

3. If any parents shall willfully, and unreasonably deny any childe timely or convenient marriage, or shall exercise any unnaturall severeitie towards them such children shal have libertie to complain to Authoritie for redresse in such cases. [1641]

4. No Orphan during their minority which was not committed to tuition, or service by their parents in their life time, shall afterward ne absolutely disposed of by any without the consent of some Court wherin two Assistants (at least) shall be present, except in case of marriage, in which the approbation of the major part of the Selectmen, in that town or any one of the next Assistants shall be sufficient. And the minoritie of women in case of marriage shall be till sixteen years. [1646]...

COUNCILL.

This Court considering how the weighty affairs of this Jurisdiction whether they concern this peculiarly or have reference to the rest of our confederated Colonies may be duly and speedily transacted in the vacancy of the Generall Court for the satisfaction of the Comissioners, in respect of the weighty and sodain occasions which may be then in hand, doth heerby expresse and declare, That the General Court ought to be called by the Governour, when the importancy of the busines doth require it, and that time and opportunitie will safely admit the same, and that all other necessary matters are to be ordered and dispatched by the major part of the Council of the Commonwealth, & therfore to that end letters significantly, breifly, the busines and the time and place of meeting for consultation ought to be sent unto the Assistants. Also it is heerby declared, that seven of the said Assistants meeting, the Governour of Deputy Governour being one is a sufficient Assembly to act, by impressing of soldiers or otherwise as need shall be. And in case of extream and urgent necessitie, when indeavours are reasonably used to call together the Assastants and the busines will not admit delay, then the acts of so many as do assemble are to be accounted, and are accounted valid, & sufficient. Also it is intended that the generall words aforementioned contein in them power to impresse & send forth soldiers, and all manner of victuails, vessels at sea, carriages and all other necessaries, and to send warrants to the Treasurer to pay for them. [1645]

COURTS.

For the better administration of justice and easing the Countrie of unnecessary charge and travels: it is ordered by this Court and Authoritie thereof;

That there shal be four Quarter Courts of Assistants yearly kept by the Governour, or Deputy Gover: and the rest of the Magistrates, the first of them on the first third day of the seventh month: the third on the first third day of the tenth month: the fourth on the third day of the first month called March. Also there be four County Courts held at Boston, by such of the Magistrates as shall reside in, or neer the same, viz: by any five, four or three of them, who shall have power to assemble together upo the last fift day of the eight, eleventh, second & fift months everie year, and there to hear & determin all civil causes & criminal, not extending to life, member or banishment according to the course of the court of Assistants, & to summon Juries out of the neighbour towns, & the Marshall & other Officers shall give attendance there as at other Courts. And it is further ordered that there shall be four Quarter Courts kept yearly by the Magistrates of Essex, with such other persons of worth as shall fro time to time be appointed by the General Court; at the nomination of the towns in that Shire by orderly agreement among themselves, to be joyned in Commission with them so that with the

Magistrates they be five in all and so that no Court be kept without one Magistrate at the least: and so any three of three of the Commissioners aforesaid may keep Court in the absence of the rest: yet none of all the Magistrates are excluded from any of these Courts who can, and please to attend the same. And the General Court to appoint from time to time, which of the said Magistrates shall specially belong to everie of the said Courts. Two of these Quarter Courts shall be kept at Salem, the other at Ipswitch. The first, the last third day of the week in the seventh month at Ipswitch. The second at Salem the last third day of the tenth month. The third at Ipswitch the last third day of the first month. The fourth the last third day of the fourth month at Salem. All and every which Courts shall be holden by the Magistrates of Salem and Ipswitch with the rest of that County or so many of them shall sttend the same; but no Jurie men shal be warned from Ipswitch to Salem nor from Salem to Ipswitch. Also there shall be a Grand Jurie at either place, once a year. Which Courts shall have the same power in civil and criminal causes as the courts of Assistants have (at Boston) except tryalls for life, limb or banishment, which are wholly reserved unto the courts of Assistants. The like liberitie for County courts and tryall of causes is graunted to the Shire town of Cambridge for the County of Midlesex, as Essex hath, to be holden on the last third day of the eight month, and another on the last third day of the second month from year to year. And the like libertie for County Courts and tryall of causes is graunted to the County of Norfolk to be holden at Salisburie on the last third day of the second month; and another at Hampton on such day as the General Court shall appoint to be kept in each place from time to time. And if any shal finde himself greived with the sentence of any the said County courts he may appeal to the next court of Assistants. Provided he put in sufficient caution according to law. Lastly, it is ordered by the Authoritie aforesaid that all causes brought to the courts of Assistants by way of appeal, and other causes specially belonging to the said courts, shall be first determined from time to time: & that causes of divorce shall be tryed only in the said court of Assistants. [1635 1636 1639 1641 1642]

2. For the more speedy dispatch of all causes which shall concern Strangers, who cannot stay to attend the ordinary Courts of justice, It is ordered by this Court and Authoritie therof;

That the Governour or Deputy Governour with any two other Magistrates, or when the Governour or Deputy Governour cannot attend it, that any three Magistrates shall have power to hear and determin by a Jurie of twelve men, or otherwise as is used in other Courts, all causes civil and criminal triable in County Courts, which shall arise between such Strangers, or wherin any such Stranger shall be a partie. And all records of such proceedings shall be transmitted to the Records of the Court of Assistants, to be entered as tryalls in other Courts, all which shall be at the charge of the parties, as the Court shall determin, so as the Country be no wayes charged by such courts. [1639]

3. For the electing of our Governour, Deputy Governour, Assistants and other general Officers upon the day or days appointed by our Pattent to hold our yearly Court being the last fourth day of the week (viz: Wednesday) of every Easter Term; it is solemly and unanimously decreed and established,

That henceforth the Freemen of this Jurisdiction shal either is person or by proxie without any Summons attend & consummate the Elections, at which time also they shal send their Deputies with full power to consult of and determin such matters as concern the welfare of this Common-wealth; from which General Court no Magistrates or Deputy shall depart or be discharged without the consent of the major part both of Magistrates and Deputies, during the first dayes of the first Session therof; under the penaltie of one hundred pounds for everie such default on either part. And for the after Sessions, if any be, the Deputies for Dover are at liberitie whether to attend or not. [1643]

4. Forasmuch as after long experience wee finde divers inconveniences in tht manner of our proceeding in Courts by Magistrates and Deputies sitting together, andn account it wisedome to follow the laudable practice of other States, who have layd ground works for government and order for issuing busines of greatest and highest consequence: it is therfore by this Court and Authoritie therof,

That henceforth the Magistrates may sit and act busines by themselves, by drawing up Bills and Orders which they shall see good in their wisdom, which having agreed upon, they may present them to the Deputies to be considered of, how good and wholesome such orders are for the Countrie & accordingly to give their assent or dissent. The Deputies in like manner sitting apart by themselves and consulting about such orders and laws as they in their discretion and experience shall finde meet for the common good: which agreed upon by them they may present to the Magisrates who having seriously considered of them may manifest their consent of dissent thereto. And when any Orders have passed the approbation of both Magistrates and Deputies, then to be ingrossed: which in the last day of this Court or Sessions shal be deliberately read over. Provided also that all manners of Judicature which this Court shall take cognisance of, shall be issued in like manner (unles the Court upon some particular occasion or busines agree otherwise). [1644]...

DEPUTIES FOR THE GENERAL COURT.

For easing the body of Freemen now increasing, and better dispatching the business of General Courts, It is ordered and by this Court declared;

That henceforth it shall be lawfull for the Freemen of everie Plantation to choose their Deputies before every Generall Court, to confer of, and prepare such publick busines as by them shall be thought fit to consider of at the next General court. And that such persons as shall be hereafter so deputed by the Freeme of the several Plantations to deal on their behalf in the publick affairs of the Common-wealth, shall have the full power and voices of all the said Freemen derived to them for the making and establishing of Laws, graunting of lands, and to deal in all other affairs of the Comon-wealth wherin the Freemen have to doe: the matter of election of Magistrates and other officers only excepted wherin every Freemen is to give his own voice. [1634]

2. Forasmuch as through the blessing of God the number of towns are much increased, It is therfore ordered and by this Court enacted;

That henceforth no town shall send more then two Deputies to the General Court; though the number of Freemen in any town be more then twenty. And that all towns which have not to the number of twenty Freemen shall send but one Deputy, & such towns as have not ten Freemen shall send none, but such Freemen shall vote with the next town in the choice of their Deputie of Deputies til this Court take further order. [1636 1638]

3. It is ordered by this Court and Authoritie therof, That when the Deputyes for severall towns are met together before, or at any General court, it shall be lawfull for them or the major part of them to hear and determin any difference that may arise about the election of any of their members, and to order things amongst themselves that may concern the well ordering of their body. And that hereafter the Deputies for the General court shall be elected by papers as the Governour is chosen. [1634 1635]

4. It is ordered by this Court and Authoritie therof; That the Freemen of any Shire or town have liberty to choose such Deputies for the General court either in their own Shire, Town, or elsewhere, as they judge fittest, so be it they be Freemen and inhabiting within this Jurisdiction. And because wee cannot foresee what variety and weight of occasions may fall into future consideration, & what counsells we may stand in need of: wee decree that the Deputies to attend the General court in behalf of the Country shall not at any time be stated and enacted but from court to court, or at the most but from one year, that the Countrie may have an annual liberty to doe in what case what is most behoofefull for the best welfare therof. [1641]...

ECCLESIASTICALL:

1. All the people of God within this Jurisdiction who are not in a Church way and be orthodox in judgement and not scandalous in life shall have full libertie to gather themselves into a Church estate, provided they doe it in a christian way with due observation of the rules of Christ revealed in his word. Provided also that the General Court doth not, nor will hereafter approve of any such companies of men as shall joyne in any pretended way of Church fellowship unles they shall acquaint the Magistrates and the Elders of the neighbour Churches where they intend to joyn, & have their approbation therin.

2. And it is farther ordered, that no person being a member of any Church which shal be gathered without the approbation of the Magistrates and the said Churches shal be admitted to the Freedom of this Common-wealth.

3. Everie Church hath free liberty to exercise all the Ordinances of God according to the rules of the Scripture.

4. Everie Church hath free libertie of election and ordination of all her Officers from time to time. Provided they be able, pious and orthodox.

5. Everie Church hath also free liberitie of admission, recommendation, dismission & expulsion or deposall of their Officers and members upon due cause, with free exercise of the discipline and censures of Christ according to the rules of his word.

6. No injunction shall be put upon any Church, church Officer of member in point of doctrine, worship or discipline, whether for substance of circumstance besides the institutions of the Lord.

7. Everie Church of Christ hath freedom to celebrate dayes of Fasting and prayer and of Thanksgiving according to the word of God.

8. The Elders of Churches also have libertie to meet monthly, quarterly or otherwise in convenient numbers and places, for conference and consultations about christian and church questions and occasions.

9. All Churches also have liberite to deal with any their members in a church way that are in the hands of justice, so it be not to retard and hinder the course therof.

10. Everie Church hath liberitie to deal with any Magistrate, Deputy of court, or other Officer whatsoever that is a member of theirs, in a church way in case of apparent and just offence, given in their places, so it be done with due observance and respect.

11. Wee also allow private meetings for edification in Religion amongst christians of all sorts of people so it be without just offence, both for number, time, place and other circumstances.

12. For the preventing and removing of effour and offence that may grow and spread in any of the Churches I this jurisdiction, and for the preserving of truth & peace in the severall Churches within themselves, and for the maintainance and exercise of brotherly comunion amongst all the Churches in the country.

It is allowed and ratified by the authoritie of this Court, as a lawfull libertie of the Churches of Christ, that once in every month of the year (when the season will bear it) it shall be lawfull for the Ministers and Elders of the Churches neer adjoyning, together with any other of the Brethren, with the consent of the Churches, to assemble by course in everie several church one after another, to the intent, that after the preaching of the word, by such a Minister as shal be requested therto, by the Elders of the Church where the Assemby is held, the rest of the day may be spent in public christian conference, about the discussing and resolving of any such doubts & cases of consciences concerning matter of doctrine, or worship, or government of the Church as shall be propounded by any of the Brethren of that Church; with leave also to any other Brother to propound his objections, or answers, for further satisfaction according to the word of God. Provided that the whole action be guided and moderated by the Elders of the Church where the Assembly is held, or by such others as they shall appoint. And that nothing be concluded and imposed by way of Authoritie from one, or more Churches, upon another, but only by way of brotherly conference & consultations, that the truth may be searched out to the satisfying of every mans conscience in the sight of God according to his word. And because such an Assemblie and the work therof cannot be duly attended if other lectures be held the same week, it is therfore agreed with the consent of the Churches, that in what week such an Assembly is held all the Lectures in all the neighbouring Churches for the week dayes shall be forborne, that so the publick service of Christ in this Assembly may be transacted with greater diligence & attention. [1641]

13. Forasmuch as the open contempt of Gods word and Messengers therof is the desolating sinne of civil States and Churches and that the preaching of the word by those whom God doth send, is the chief ordinary means ordained of God for the converting, edifying and saving the souls of the Elect through the presence and power of the Holy-Ghost, therunto promised: and that the ministry of the word, is set up by God in his Churches, for those holy ends: and according to the respect or contempt of the same and of those whom God hath set apart for his own work & imployment, the weal or woe of all Christian States is much furthered and promoted; it is therefore ordered and decreed,

That if any christian (so called) within this Jurisdiction shall contemptuously behave himselfe toward the Word preached or the Messengers therof called to dispense the same in any Congregation; when he doth faithfully execute his Service and Office therin, according to the will and word of God, either by interrupting him in his preaching, or by charging him falsely with any errour which he hath not taught in the open face of the Church: or like a son of Korah cast upon his true doctrine or himselfe any reproach, to the dishonour of the Lord Jesus who hath sent him and to the disparagement of that his holy Ordinance, and making Gods wayes contemptible and ridiculous: that everie such person or persons (whatsoever censure the Church may passe) shall for the first scandall be convented and reproved openly by the Magistrate at some lecture, and bound to their good behaviour. And if a second time they break forth into the like contemptuous carriages, they shall either pay five pounds to the publick Treasurie; or stand two hours openly upon a block or stool, four foot high on a lecture day with a paper fixed on his breast, written in Capital letters [AN OPEN AND OBSTINATE CONTEMNER OF GODS HOLY ORDINANCES] that others may fear and be ashamed of breaking out into the like wickednes. [1646]

14. It is ordered and decreed by this Court and Authoritie thereof; That wheresoever the ministry of the word is established according to the order of the Gospell throughout this Jurisdiction every person shall duly resort and attend therunto respectively upon the Lords days & upon such publick Fast dayes & dayes of Thanksgiving as are to be generally kept by the appointmet of Authoritie: & if any person within this Jurisdiction shal without just and necessarie cause withdraw himselfe from hearing the publick ministry of the word after due meanes of conviction used, he shall forfeit for his absence from everie such publick meeting five shillings. All such offences to be heard and determined by any one Magistrate or more from time to time. [1646]

15. Forasmuch as the peace and prosperity of Churches and members therof as well as civil Rights & Liberties are carefully to be maintained, it is ordered by this Court & decreed, That the civil Authoritie heer established hath power and liberty to see the peace, ordinances and rules of Christ be observed in everie Church according to his word. As also to deal with any church-member in a way of civil justice notwithstanding any church relation, office, or

interest; so it be done in a civil and not in an ecclesiastical way. Nor shall any church censure degrade or depose any man from any civil dignity, office or authoritie he shall have in the Commonwealth. [1641]

16. Forasmuch as there are many Inhabitants in divers towns, who leave their several habitations and therby draw much of the in-come of their estates into other towns wherby the ministry is much neglected, it is therfore ordered by this Court and the authoritie therof; That from henceforth all lands, cattle and other estates of any kinde whatsoever, shall be lyable to be rated to all common charges whatsoever, either for the Church, Town or Comon-wealth in the same place where the estate is from time to time. And to the end there may be a convenient habitation for the use of the ministry in everie town in this Jurisdiction to remain to posterity. It is decreed by the authoritie of this Court that where the major part of the Inhabitants (according to the order of regulating valid town acts) shall graunt, build, or purchase such habitation it shall be good in law, and the particular sum upon each person assessed by just rate, shal be duly paid according as in other cases of town rates. Provided always that such graunt, deed of purchase and the deed of gift therupon to the use of a present preaching Elder and his next successour and so from time to time to his successors: be entred in the town book and acknowledged before a Magistrate, and recorded in the Shire court. [1647]

ELECTIONS.

It is ordered by this Court and Authoritie therof: That for the yearly choosing of Assistants for the time to come instead of papers the Freemen shall use indian corn and beans. The indian corn to manifest election, the beans for blanks. And that if any Freeman shall put in more then one indian corn or bean for the choise or refusal of any publick Officer, he shall forfeit for everie such offence ten pounds. And that any man that is not free or otherwise hath not libertie of voting, putting in any vote shal forfeit the like sum of ten pounds. [1643]

2. For the preventing of many inconveniences that otherwise may arise upon the yearly day of Election, and that the work of that day may be the more orderly, easily and speedily issued, it is ordered by this Court and the authoritie thereof.

That the Freemen in the several towns and villages within this Jurisdiction, shall this next year from time to time either in person or by proxie sealed up, make all their elections, by papers, indian corn and beans as heerafter is expressed, to be taken, sealed up & sent to the court of Election as this order appoints, the Governour, Deputie Governour, Major Generall, Treasurer, Secretary and Comissioners for the united Colonies to be chosen by writing, open or once folded, not twisted or rolled up, that so they may be the sooner and surer perused: and all the Assistants to be chosen by indian corn and beans, the indian corn to manifest election as in Sect: I; and for such small villages as come not in person and that send no Deputies to the Court, the Constable of the said village, together with two or three of the chiefe Freemen shall receive the votes of the rest of their Freemen, and deliver them together with their own sealed up to the Deputie or Deputies for the next town, who shall carefully convey the same unto the said Court of Election. [1647]

3. For asmuch as the choice of Assistants in case of supply is of great concernment, and with all care and circumspection to be attended; It is therfore ordered by this Court and Authoritie therof,

That when any Assistants are to be supplyed, the Deputies for the General Court shall give notice to their Constables or Selectmen to call together their freemen in their severall towns: to give in their votes unto the number of seven persons, or as the General Court shall direct, who shall then and there appoint one to carrie them sealed up unto their Shire towns upon the last fourth day of the week in the first month from time to time; which persons for each town so assembled shall appoint one for each Shire to carrie them unto Boston the second third day of the second month there to be opened before two Magistrates. And those seven or other number agreed upon as aforesaid, that have most votes shall be the men which shall be nominated at the court of Election for Assistants as aforesaid. Which persons the Agents for each Shire shall forthwith signifie to the Constables of all their several towns in writing under their hands with the number of votes for each person: all which the said Constables shall forthwith signifie to their Freemen. And as any hath more votes then other so shall they be put to vote. [1647]

4. It is decreed and by this Court declared That it is the constant libertie of the Freemen of this Jurisdiction to choose yearly at the court of Election out of the Freemen, all the general Officers of this Jurisdiction, and if they please to discharge them at the court of Election by way of vote they may doe it without shewing cause. But if at any other General Court, we hold it due justice that the reason therof be alledged and proved. By general Officers we mean our Governour, Deputy Governour, Assistants, Treasurer, General of our wars, our Admirall at sea, Commissioners for the united-Colonies and such others as are, or heerafter may be of the like general nature. [1641]

FORNICATION.

It is ordered by this Court and Authoritie therof, That if any man shall commit Fornication with any single woman, they shall be punished either by enjoyning to Marriage, or Fine, or corporall punishment, or all or any of these as the Judges in the courts of Assistants shall appoint most agreeble to the word of God. And this Order to continue till the Court take further order. [1642]

FREEMEN, NON-FREEMEN.

WHERAS there are within this jurisdiction many members of churches who to exempt themselves from all publick service in the Common-wealth will not come in, to be made Freemen, it is therfore ordered by this Court and the Authoritie therof,

That all such members of Churches in the severall towns within this Jurisdiction shall not be exempted from such publick service as they are from time to time chosen to by the Freemen of the severall towns: as Constables, Jurors, Select-men and Surveyors of highwayes. And if any such person shall refuse to serve in, or take upon him any such Office being legally chosen therunto, he shall pay for every such refusall such Fine as the town shall impose, not exceeding twenty shilings as Freemen are lyable to in such cases. [1647]

FUGITIVES, STRANGERS.

It is ordered by this Court and Authoritie therof, That if any people of other nations prosessing the true Christian Religion shall flee to us from the tyranie or oppression of their persecutors, or from Famine, Wars, or the like necessarie and compulsarie cause, they shall be entertained and succoured amongst us according to that power and prudence God shall give us. [1641]

GAMING.

UPON Complaint of great disorder by the use of the game called Shuffle-board, in houses of common entertainment, wherby much pretious time is spent unfruitfully and much wast of wine and beer occasioned; it is therfore ordered and enacted by the Authoritie of this Court;

That no person shall henceforth use the said game of Shuffle-board in any such house, nor in any other house used as common for such purpose, upon payn for every Keeper of such house to forfeit for everie such offence five shillings: Nor shall any person at any time play or game for any monie, or mony-worth upon penalty of forefeiting treble the value therof: one half to the partie informing, the other half to the Treasurie. And any Magistrate may hear and determin any offence against this Law. [1646 1647]

GENERAL COURT.

It is ordered, and by this Court declared that the Governour and Deputie Governour joyntly consenting, or any three Assistants concurring in consent shall have power out of Court to reprieve a condemned malefactor till the next Court of Assistants: or General Court. And that the General Court only shall have power to pardon a condemned malefactor.

Also it is declared that the General Court hath libertie and Authoritie to send forth any member of this Common-wealth, of what qualitie and condition or office whatsoever into forrein parts, about any publick Message or negociation: notwithstanding any office or relation whatsoever. Provided the partie so sent be acquainted with the affairs he goeth about, and be willing to undertake the service.

Nor shall any General Court be dissolved or adjourned without the consent of the major part therof. [1641]

GOVERNOUR.

It is ordered, and by this Court declared that the Governour shall have a casting vote whensoever an equivote shall fall out in the Court of Assistants, or general Assemblie: so shall the President or Moderatour have in all civil Courts or Assemblies [1641]

HERESIE.

ALTHOUGH no humane power be Lord over the Faith & Consciences of men, and therfore may not constrein them to beleive or professe against their Consciences: yet because such as bring in damnable heresies, tending to the subversion of the Christian Faith, and destruction of the soules of men, ought duly to be restreined from such notorious impiety, it is therfore ordered and decreed by this Court;

That if any Christian within this Jurisdiction shall go about to subvert and destroy the christian Faith and Religion, by broaching or mainteining any damnable heresie; as denying the immortalitie of the Soul, or the resurrection of the body, or any sin to be repented of in the Regenerate, or any evil done by the outward man to be accounted sin: or denying that Christ gave himself a Ransom for our sins, or shal affirm that wee are not justified by his Death and Righteousnes, but by the perfection of our own works; or shall deny the moralitie of the fourth commandement, or shall indeavour to seduce others to any the herisies aforementioned, everie such person continuing obstinate therin after due means of conviction shall be sentenced to Banishment. [1646] &133;

IDLENES.

It is ordered by this Court and Authoritie therof, that no person, Housholder or other shall spend his time idlely or unproffitably under pain of such punishment as the Court of Assistants or County Court shall think meet to inflict. And for this end it is ordered that the Constable of everie place shall use speciall care and diligence to take knowledge of offenders in this kinde, especially of common coasters, unproffitable fowlers and tobacco takers, and present the same unto the two next Assistants, who shall have power to hear and determin the cause, or transfer it to the next Court. [1633]

JESUITS.

THIS court taking into consideration the great wars, combustions and divisions which are this day in Europe: and that the same are observed to be raysed and fomented chiefly by the secret underminings, and solicitations of those of the Jesuiticall Order, men brought up and devoted to the religion and court of Rome; which hath occasioned divers States to expell them their territories; for prevention wherof among our selves, It is ordered and enacted by Authoritie of this Court,

That no Jesuit, or spiritual or ecclesiastical person [as they are termed] ordained by the authoritie of the Pope, or Sea of Rome shall henceforth at any time repair to, or come within this Jurisdiction: And if any person shal give just cause of suspicion that he is one of such Societie or Order he shall be brought before some of the Magistrates, and if he cannot free himselfe of such suspicion he shall be committed to prison, or bound over to the next Court of Assistants, to be tryed and proceeded with by Banishment or otherwise as the Court shall see cause: and if any person so banished shall be taken the second time within this Jurisdiction upon lawfull tryall and conviction he shall be put to death. Provided this Law shall not extend to any such Jesuit, spiritual or ecclesiasticall person as shall be cast upon our shoars, by ship-wrack or other accident, so as he continue no longer then till he may have opportunitie of passage for his departure; nor to any such as shall come in company with any Messenger hither upon publick occasions, or any Merchant or Master of any ship, belonging to any place not in emnitie with the State of England, or our selves, so as they depart again with the same Messenger, Master or Merchant, and behave themselves inoffensively during their abode heer. [1647] &133;

IMPRESSES.

It is ordered, and by this Court declared, that no man shall be compelled to any publick work, or service, unlesse the Presse be grounded upon some act of the General Court; and have reasonable allowance therfore: nor shall any man be compelled in person to any office, work, wars, or other publick service that is necessarily and sufficiently exempted, by any natural or personal impediment; as by want of years, greatnes of age, defect of minde, failing of senses, or impotencye of lims. Nor shall any man be compelled to go out of this Jurisdiction upon any offensive wars, which this Common-wealth, or any of our freinds or confoederates shall voluntarily undertake; but only upon such vindictive and defensive wars, in our own behalf, or the behalf of our freinds and confoederates; as shall be enterprized by the counsell, and consent of a General Court, or by Authoritie derived from the same. Nor shall any mans cattle or goods of what kinde soever be pressed, or taken for any publick use or service; unles it be by Warrant grounded upon some act of the General Court: nor without such reasonable prizes and hire as the ordinarie rates of the Countrie doe afford. And if his cattle or goods shall perish, or suffer damage in such service, the Owner shall be sufficiently recompenced. [1641]

IMPRISONMENT.

It is ordered, and by this Court declared; that no mans person shall be restreined or imprisoned by any authoritie whatsoever before the Law hath sentenced him therto: if he can put in sufficient securitie, Bayle or Mainprize for his appearance, and good behaviour in the mean time: unles it be in crimes Capital, and contempt in open Court, and in such cases where some expresse Act of Court doth allow it. [1641]

INDIANS.

It is ordered by Authoritie of this Court; that no person whatsoever shall henceforth buy land of any Indian, without license first had & obtained of the General Court: and if any shall offend heerin, such land so bought shall be forfeited to the Countrie.

Nor shall any man within this Jurisidiction directly or indirectly amend, repair, or cause to be amended or repaired any gun, small or great, belonging to any Indian, nor shall indeavour the same. Nor shall sell or give to any Indian, directly or indirectly any such gun, or any gun-powder, shot or lead, or shotmould, or any militarie weapons or armour: upon payn of ten pounds fine, at the least for everie such offence: and that the court of Assistants shall have power to increase the Fine; or to impose corporall punishment (where a Fine cannot be had) at their discretion.

It is ordered by the Authoritie aforesaid that everie town shall have power to restrein all Indians from profaning the Lords day. [1633 1637 1641]

2. Wheras it appeareth to this Court that notwithstanding the former Laws, made against selling of guns, powder and Ammunition to the Indians, they are yet supplyed by indirect means, it is thefore ordered by this Court and Authoritie therof;

That if any person after publication heerof, shall sell, give or barter any gun or guns, powder, bullets, shot or lead to any Indian whatsoever, or unto any person inhabiting out of this Jurisdiction without license of this Court, or the court of Assistants, or some two Magistrates, he shall forfeith for everie gun so sold, given or bartered ten pounds: and for everie pound of powder five pounds: and for everie pound of bullets, shot or lead fourty shillings: and so proportionably for any greater or lesser quantitie. [1642]

3. It is ordered by this Court and Authoritie therof, that in all places, the English and such others as co-inhabit within our Jurisidiction shall keep their cattle from destroying the Indians corn, in any ground where they have right to plant; and if any of their corn be destroyed for want of fencing, or herding; the town shall make satisfaction, and shall have power among themselves to lay the charge where the occasion of the damage did arise. Provided that the Indians shall make proof that the cattle of such a town, farm, or person did the damage. And for encouragement of the Indians toward the fencing in their corn fields, such towns, farms or persons, whose cattle may annoy them that way, shall direct, assist and help them in felling of trees, ryving, and sharpening of rayls, & holing of posts: allowing one English-man to three or more Indians. And shall also draw the fencing into place for them, and allow one man a day or two toward the setting up the same, and either lend or sell them tools to finish it. Provided that such Indians, to whom the Countrie, or any town hath given, or shall give ground to plant upon, or that shall purchase ground of the English shall fence such their corn fields or ground at

their own charge as the English doe or should doe; and if any Indians refuse to fence their corn ground (being tendred help as aforesaid) in the presence and hearing of any Magistrate or selected Townsmen being met together they shall keep off all cattle or lose one half of their damages.

And it is also ordered that if any harm be done at any time by the Indians unto the English in their cattle; the Governour or Deputie Governour with two of the Assistants or any three Magistrates or any County Court may order satisfaction according to law and justice. [1640 1648]

4. Considering that one end in planting these parts was to propagate the true Religion unto the Indians: and that divers of them are become subjects to the English and have ingaged themselves to be willing and ready to understand the Law of God, it is therfore ordered and decreed,

That such necessary and wholsom Laws, which are in force, and may be made from time to time, to reduce them to civilitie of life shall be once in the year (if the times be safe) made known to them, by such fit persons as the General Court shall nominate, having the help of some able Interpreter with them.

Considering also that interpretation of tongues is appointed of God for propagating the Truth: and may therfore have a blessed successe in the hearts of others in due season, it is therfore farther ordered and decreed,

That two Ministers shall be chosen by the Elders of the Churches everie year at the Court of Election, and so be sent with the consent of their Churches (with whomsoever will freely offer themselves to accompany them in that service) to make known the heavenly counsell of God among the Indians in most familiar manner, by the help of some able Interpreter; as may be most available to bring them unto the knowledge of the truth, and their conversation to the Rules of Jesus Christ. And for that end that something be allowed them by the General Court, to give away freely unto those Indians whom they shall perceive most willing & ready to be instructed by them.

And it is farther ordered and decreed by this Court; that no Indian shall at any time powaw, or performe outward worship to their false gods: or to the devil in any part of our Jurisdiction; whether they be such as shall dwell heer, or shall come hither: and if any shall transgresse this Law, the Powawer shall pay five pounds; the Procurer five pounds; and every other countenancing by his presence or otherwise being of age of discretion twenty shillings. [1646]

INDITEMENTS.

If any person shall be indicted of any capital crime (who is not then in durance) & shall refuse to render his person to some Magistrates within one month after three Proclaimations publickly made in the town where he usually abides, there being a month betwixt Proclaimation and Proclaimation, his lands and goods shall be seized to the use of the common Treasurie, till he make his lawfull appearance. And such withdrawing of himselfe shall stand in stead of one wittnes to prove his crime, unles he can make it appear to the Court that he was necessarily hindred. [1646]

IN-KEEPERS, TRIPPLING, DRUNKENES.

FORASMUCH as there is a necessary use of houses of common entertainment in every Common-wealth, and of such as retail wine, beer and victuals; yet because there are so many abuses of that lawfull libertie, both by persons entertaining and persons entertained, there is also need of strict Laws and rules to regulate such an employment: It is therfore ordered by this Court and Authoritie therof;

That no person or persons shall at any time under any pretence or colour whasoever undertake to be a common Victuailer, Keeper of a Cooks shop, or house for common entertainment, Taverner, or publick seller of wine, ale, beer or strong-water (by re-tale), nor shall any sell wine privately in his house or out of doors by a lesse quantitie, or under a quarter cask: without approbation of the selected Townsmen and Licence of the Shire Court where they dwell: upon pain of forfeiture of five pounds for everie such offence, or imprisonment at pleasure of the Court, where satisfaction cannot be had.

And every person so licenced for common entertainment shall have some inoffensive Signe obvious for strangers direction, and such as have no such Signe after three months so licensed from time to time shall lose their license: and others allowed in their stead. Any licensed person that selleth beer shall not sell any above two-pence the ale-quart: upon penaltie of three shillings four pence for everie such offence. And it is permiteed to any that will to sell beer out of doors at a pennie the ale-quart and under.

Neither shall any such licenced person aforesaid suffer any to be drunken, or drink excessively viz: above half a pinte of wine for one person at one time; or to continue tippling above the space of half an hour, or at unreasonable times, or after nine of the clock at night in, or about any of their houses on penaltie of five shillings for everie such offence.

And everie person found drunken viz: so that he be therby bereaved or disabled in the use of his understanding, appearing in his speech or gesture in any the said houses or elsewhere shall forfeith ten shillings. And for excessive drinking three shillings four pence. And for continuing above half an hour tippling two shillings six pence. And for tippling at unreasonable times, or after nine a clock at night five shillings: for everie offence in these particulars being lawfully convict therof. And for want of payment such shall be imprisoned untill they pay: or be set in the Stocks one hour or more [in some open place] as the weather will permit not exceeding three hours at one time &133;

JURIES, JURORS.

It is ordered by this Court and Authoritie therof, that the Constable of everie town upon Proces from the Recorder of each Court, shall give timely notice to the Freemen of their town, to choos so many able discreet men as the Proces shal direct which men so chosen he shall warn to attend the Court wherto they are appointed, and shall make return of the Proces unto the Recorder aforesaid: which men so chosen shall be impannelled and sworn truly to try betwixt partie and partie, who shall finde the matter of fact with the damages and costs according to their evidence, and the Judges shall declare the Sentence (or direct the Jurie to finde) according to the law. And if there be any matter of apparent equitie as upon the forfeiture of an Obligation, breach of covenant without damage, or the like, the Bench shall determin such matter of equitie.

2. Nor shall any tryall passe upon any for life or bannishment but by a special Jurie so summoned for that purpose, or by the General Court.

3. It is also ordered by the Authoritie aforesaid that there shall be Grand-Juries summoned everie year unto the several Courts, in each Jurisdiction; to inform the Court of any misdemeanours that they shall know or hear to be committed by any person or persons whatsoever within this Jurisdiction. And to doe any other service of the Common-wealth, that according to law they shall be injoyned to by the said Court; and in all cases wherin evidence is so obscure or defective that the Jurie cannot clearly and safely give a positive verdict, whether it be Grand, or Petty Jurie, it shall have libertie to give a [verdict] or a special verdict, in which last, that is, a special verdict the judgement of the Cause shall be left unto the Bench. And all jurors shall have libertie in matters of fact if they cannot finde the main issue yet to finde and present in their verdict so much as they can.

4. And if the Bench and Jurors shall so differ at any time about their verdict that either of them cannot proceed with peace of conscience, the Case shall be referred to the General Court who shall take the question from both and determin it.

5. And it is farther ordered that whensoever any Jurie of tryalls, or Jurors are not clear in their judgements or consciences, concerning any Case wherin they are to give their verdict, they shall have libertie, in open court to advise with any man they shall think fit to resolve or direct them, before they give in their verdict. And no Freeman shall be compelled to serve upon Juries above one ordinary Court in a year: except Grand-jurie men, who shall hold two Courts together at the least, and such others as shall be summoned to serve in case of life and death or bannishment. [1634 1641 1642]

JUSTICE.

It is ordered, and by this Court declared; that every person within this Jurisdiction, whether Inhabitant or other shall enjoy the same justice and law that is general for this Jurisdiction which wee constitute and execute one towards another, in all cases proper to our cognisance without partialitie or delay. [1641] &133;

LIBERTIES COMMON.

It is ordered by this Court, decreed and declared; that everie man whether Inhabitant or Forreiner, Free or not Free shall have libertie to come to any publick Court, Counsell, or Town-meeting; and either by speech or writing, to move any lawfull, reasonable, or material question; or to present any necessarie motion, complaint, petition, bill or information wherof that Meeting hath proper cognisance, so it be done in convenient time, due order and respective manner. [1641]

2. Everie Inhabitant who is an hous-holder shall have free fishing and fowling, in any great Ponds, Bayes, Coves and Rivers so far as the Sea ebs and flows, within the precincts of the town where they dwell, unles the Freemen of the same town, or the General Court have otherwise appropriated them. Provided that no town shall appropriate to any particular person or persons, any great Pond conteining more then ten acres of land: and that no man shall come upon anothers proprietie without their leave otherwise then as heerafter expressed; the which clearly to determin, it is declared that in all creeks, coves and other places, about and upon salt water where the Sea ebs and flows, the Proprietor of the land adjoyning shall have proprietie to the low water mark where the Sea doth not ebb above a hundred rods, and not more wheresoever it ebs farther. Provided that such Proprietor shall not by this libertie have power to stop or hinder the passage of boats or other vessels in, or through any sea creeks, or coves to other mens houses or lands. And for great Ponds lying in common though within the bounds of some town, it shall be free for any man to fish and fowl there, and may passe and repasse on foot through any mans proprietie for that end, so they trespasse not upon any mans corn or meadow. [1641 1647]

3. Every man of, or within this Jurisdiction shall have free libertie, (notwithstanding any civil power) to remove both himself and his familie at their pleasure out of the same. Provided there be no legal impediment to the contrary. [1641]

LYING.

WHERAS truth in words as well as in actions is required of all men, especially of Christians who are the professed Servants of the God of Truth; and wheras all lying is contrary to truth, and some sorts of lyes are not only sinfull (as all lyes are) but also pernicious to the Publick-weal, and injurious to particular persons; it is therfore ordered by this Court and Authoritie therof,

That everie person of the age of discretion [which is accounted fourteen years] who shall wittingly and willingly make, or publish any Lye which may be pernicious to the publick weal, or tending to the damage or injurie of any particular person, or with intent to deceive and abouse the people with false news or reports: and the same duly proved in any Court or before any one Magistrate (who hath heerby power graunted to hear, and determin all offences against this Law) such person shall be fined for the first offence ten shillings, or if the partie be unable to pay the same then to be set in the stocks so long as the said Court of Magistrate shall appoint, in some open place, not exceeding two hours. For the second offence in that kinde wherof any shall be legally convicted the sum of twenty shillings, or be whipped upon the naked body not exceeding ten stripes. And for the third offence that way fourty shillings, or if the partie be unable to pay, then to be whipped with more stripes, not exceeding fifteen. And if yet any shall offend in the like kinde, and be legally convicted therof, such person, male or female, shall be fined ten shillings a time more then formerly: or if the partie so offending be unable to pay, then to be whipped with five, or six more stripes then formerly not exceeding fourty at any time.

The aforesaid fines shall be levied, or stripes inflicted either by the Marshal of that Jurisdiction, or Constable of the Town where the offence is committed according as the Court or Magistrate shall direct. And such fines so levied shall be paid to the Treasurie of that Shire where the Cause is tried.

And if any person shall finde himselfe greived with the sentence of any such Magistrate out of Court, he may appeal to the next Court of the same Shire, giving sufficient securitie to prosecute his appeal and abide the Order of the Court. And if the said Court shall judge his appeal causlesse, he shall be double fined and pay the charges of the Court during his Action, or corrected by whipping as aforesaid not exceeding fourtie stripes; and pay the costs of Court and partie complaining or informing, and of Wittnesses in Case.

And for all such as being under age of discretion that shall offend in lying contrary to this Order their Parents or Masters shall give them due correction, and that in the presence of some Officer if any Magistrate shall so appoint. Provided also that no person shall be barred of his just Action of Slaunder, or otherwise by an proceeding upon this Order. [1645]

MAGISTRATES.

THIS court being sensible of the great disorder growing in this Commonwealth through the contempts cast upon the civil Authoritie, which willing to prevent, doe order and decree;

That whosoever shall henceforth openly or willingly defame any Court of justice, or the Sentences or proceedings of the same, or any of the Magistrates or other Judges of any such Court in respect of any Act or Sentence therin passed, and being therof lawfully convict in any General Court or Court of Assistants shall be punished for the same by Fine, Imprisonment, Disfranchisement or Bannishment as the qualitie and measure of the offence shall deserve.

And if any Magistrate or other member of any court shall use any reproachfull, or un-beseeming speeches, or behaviour towards any Magistrate, Judge, or member of the Court in the face of the said Court he shall be sharply reproved, by the Governour, or other principal Judge of the same Court for the time being. And if the qualitie of the offence be such as shall deserve a farther censure, or if the person so reproved shall reply again without leave, the same Court may proceed to punish any such offender by Fine, or Imprisonment, or it shall be presented to, and censured at the next superiour Court.

2. If in a General Court any miscarriage shall be amongst the Magistrates when they are by themselves, it shall be examined, and sentenced amongst themselves. If amongst the Deputies when they are by themselves, it shall be examined, and sentenced amongst themselves. If it be when the whole Court

is together, it shall be judged by the whole Court, and not severall as before. [1637 1641]

3. And it is ordered by the Authoritie of this Court that the Governour, Deputie Governour, or greater part of the Assistants may upon urgent occasion call a General Court at any time. [1647]

4. And wheras there may arise some difference of judgement in doubtfull cases, it is therfore farther ordered;

That no Law, Order, or Sentence shall passe as an Act of the Court without the consent of the greater part of the Magistrates on the one partie, and the greater number of the Deputies on the other part.

5. And for preventing all occasions of partial and undue proceeding in Courts of justice, and avoyding of jealousies which may be taken up against Judges in that kinde, it is farther ordered,

That in everie Case of civil nature between partie and partie where there shall fall out so neer relation between any Judge and any of the parties as between Father and Son, either by nature or marriage, Brother and Brother; in like kinde Uncle and Nephew, Land-lord and Tenent in matter of considerable value, such Judge though he may have libertie to be present in the Court at the time of the tryall, and give reasonable advice in the Case, yet shall have no power to vote or give sentence therin, neither shall Sit as Judge, but beneath the Bench when he shall so plead or give advice in the Case. [1635]

MONOPOLIES.

It is ordered, decreed and by this Court declared; that there shall be no Monopolies graunted or allowed amongst us, but of such new inventions that are profitable for the Countrie, and that for a short time. [1641]

OATHS, SUBSCRIPTION.

It is ordered and decreed, and by this Court declared; that no man shall be urged to take any oath, or subscribe any Articles, Covenants, or remonstrance of publick and civil nature but such as the General Court hath considered, allowed and required. And that no oath of Magistrate, counceller or any other Officer shall binde him any farther, or longer then he is resident, or reputed an Inhabitant of this Jurisdiction [1641]

OPPRESSION.

For avoyding such mischeifs as may follow by such illdisposed persons as may take libertie to oppresse and wrong their neighbours, by taking excessive wages for work, or unreasonable prizes for such necessarie merchandizes or other commodities as shall passe from man to man, it is ordered, That if any man shall offend in any of the said cases he shall be punished by Fine, or Imprisonment according to the qualitie of the offence, as the Court to which he is presented upon lawfull tryall & conviction shall adjudge. [1635] &133;

PROFANE SWEARING.

It is ordered, and by this Court decreed, that if any person within this Jurisdiction shall swear rashly and vainly either by the holy Name of God, or any other oath, he shall forfeit to the common Treasurie for everie such severall offence ten shillings. And it shall be in the power of any Magistrate by Warrant to the Constable to call such person before him, and upon sufficient proof to passe sentence, and levie the said penaltie according to the usuall order of Justice. And if such person be not able, or shall utterly refuse to pay the aforesaid Fine, he shall be committed to the Stocks there to continue, not exceeding three hours, and not lesse then one hour. [1646] &133;

PUNISHMENT.

It is ordered, decreed, and by this Court declared; that no man shall be twice sentenced by civil Justice for one and the same Crime, offence or Trespasse. And for bodily punishments, wee allow amongst us none that are in-humane, barbarous or cruel. [1641]

SCHOOLS.

It being one chief project of that old deluder, Satan, to keep men from the knowledge of the Scriptures, as in former times keeping them in an unknown tongue, so in these later times by perswading from the use of Tongues, that so at least the true sense and meaning of the Original might be clowded with false glosses of Saint-seeming-deceivers; and that Learning may not be buried in the graves of our fore-fathers in Church and Commonwealth, the Lord assisting our indeavours: it is therfore ordered by this Court and Authoritie therof;

That everie Township in this Jurisdiction, after the Lord hath increased them to the number of fifty Householders shall then forthwith appoint one within their Town to teach all such children as shall resort to him to write and read, whose wages shall be paid either by the Parents or Masters of such children, or by the Inhabitants in general by way of supply, as the major part of those that order the prudentials of the Town shall appoint. Provided that those which send their children be not oppressed by paying much more then they can have them taught for in other Towns.

2. And it is farther ordered, that where any Town shall increase to the number of one hundred Families or Householders they shall set upon a Grammar-School, the Masters therof being able to instruct youth so far as they may be fitted for the Universitie. And if any Town neglect the performance heerof above one year then everie such town shall pay five pounds per annum to the next such School, till they shall perform this Order. [1647] &133;

STRANGERS.

It is ordered by this Court and the Authoritie therof; that no Town or person shal receive any stranger resorting hither with intent to reside in this Jurisdiction, nor shall allow any Lot or Habitation to any, or entertain any such above three weeks, except such person shall have allowance under the hand of some one Magistrate, upon pain of everie Town that shall give, or sell any Lot or Habitation to any not so licenced such Fine to the Countrie as the County Court shall impose, not exceeding fifty pounds, nor lesse then ten pounds. And of everie person receiving any such for longer time then is heer expressed or allowed, in some special cases as before, or in case of entertainment of friends resorting from other parts of this Country in amitie with us, shall forfeit as aforesaid, not exceeding twenty pounds, nor lesse then four pounds: and for everie month after so offending, shal forfeit, as aforesaid not exceeding ten pounds, nor lesse then fourty shillings. Also, that all

Constables shall inform the Courts of new commers which they know to be admitted without licence, from time to time. [1637 1638 1647]

SUMMONS.

It is ordered, and by this Court declared; that no Summons, Pleading, Judgement or any kinde of proceeding in Court or course of justice shall be abated, arested or reversed upon any kinde of circumstantial errors or mistakes, if the person and the Cause be rightly understood and intended by the Court.

2. And that in all cases where the first Summons are not served six dayes before the Court, and the Case briefly specified in the Warrant where appearance is to be made by the partie summoned; it shall be at his libertie whether he will appear, or not, except all Cases that are to be handled in Courts suddenly called upon extraordinarie occasions. And that in all cases where there appears present and urgent cause any Assistant or Officer appointed shall have power to make out Attachments for the first Summons. Also, it is declared that the day of Summons or Attachment served, and the day of appearance shall be taken inclusively as part of the six dayes. [1641 1647]

SUITS, VEXATIOUS SUITS.

It is ordered and decreed, and by this Court declared; that in all Cases where it appears to the Court that the Plaintiffe hath willingly & wittingly done wrong to the Defendant in commencing and prosecuting any Action, Suit, Complaint or Indictment in his own name or in the name of others, he shall pay treble damages to the partie greived, and be fined fourty shillings to the Common Treasurie. [1641 1646] &133;

TOBACCO.

This Court finding that since the repealing of the former Laws against Tobacco, the same is more abused then before doth therfore order,

That no man shall take any tobacco within twenty poles of any house, or so neer as may indanger the same, or neer any Barn, corn, or hay-cock as may occasion the fyring therof, upon pain of ten shillings for everie such offence, besides full recompence of all damages done by means therof. Nor shall any take tobacco in any Inne or common Victualing-house, except in a private room there, so as neither the Master of the said house nor any other Guests there shall take offence therat, which if any doe, then such person shall forthwith forbear, upon pain of two shillings sixpence for everie such offence. And for all Fines incurred by this Law, one half part shall be to the Informer the other to the poor of the town where the offence is done. [1638 1647]

TORTURE.

It is ordered, decreed, and by this Court declared; that no man shall be forced by torture to confesse any crime against himselfe or any other, unles it be in some Capital where he is first fully convicted by clear and sufficient evidence to be guilty. After which, if the Case be of that nature that it is very apparent there be other Conspirators or Confoederates with him; then he may be tortured, yet not with such tortures as be barbarous and inhumane.

2. And that no man shal be beaten with above fourty stripes for one Fact at one time. Nor shall any man be punished with whipping, except he have not otherwise to answer the Law, unles his crime be very shamefull, and his course of life vitious and profligate. [1641]

TOWNSHIPS.

It is ordered, decreed, and by this Court declared, that if any man shall behave himselfe offensively at any Town-meeting, the rest then present shall have power to sentence him for such offence, so be it the mulct or penalty exceed not twenty shillings.

2. and that the Freemen of everie Township, and others authorized by law, shall have power to make such Laws and Constitutions as may concern the welfare of their Town. Provided they be not repugnant to the publick Laws and Orders of the Countrie. And if any Inhabitant shall neglect or refuse to observe them, they shall have power to levie the appointed penalties by distresse.

3. Also that the Freemen of everie town or Township, with such other the Inhabitats as have taken the Oath of fidelitie shall have full power to choos yearly, or for lesse time, within each Township a convenient number of fit men to order the planting and prudential occasions of that Town, according to instructions given them in writing.

Provided, nothing be done by them contrary to the publick Laws and Orders of the Countrie. Provided also that the number of such Select persons be not aboue nine.

4. Farther, it is ordered by the Authoritie aforesayd, that all Towns shall take care from time to time to order and dispose of all single persons, and Inmates within their Towns to service, or otherwise. And if any be greived at such order or dispose, they have libertie to appeal to the next County Court.

5. This Court taking into considerattion the usefull Parts and abilities of divers Inhabitants amongst us, which are not Freemen, which if improved to publick use, the affairs of this Common-wealth may be the easier caried an end in the severall Towns of this Jurisdiction doth order, and heerby declare;

That henceforth it shall may be lawfull for the Freemen within any of the said Towns, to make choice of such Inhabitants (though non-Freemen) who have taken, or shall take the Oath of fidelitie to this Government to be Jurie-men, and to have their Vote in the choice of the Select-men for the town Affairs, Assessements of Rates, and other Prudentials proper to the Select-men of the several Towns. Provided still that the major part of all companyes of Select-men be Free-men from time to time that shall make any valid Act. As also, where no Select-men are, to have their Vote in ordering of Schools, hearing of cattle, laying out of High-wayes and distributing of Lands; any Law, Use or Custom to the contrary notwithstanding. Provided also that no non-Freeman shall have his Vote, untill he have attained the age of twenty one years. [1636 1641 1647]

TRYALLS.

Wheras this Court is often taken up in hearing and deciding particular Cases, between partie and partie, which more properly belong to other inferiour

Court. And that if the partie against whom the Judgment shall have any new evidence, or other new matter to plead, he may desire a new Tryall in the same Court upon a Bill or review. And if justice shall not be done him upon that Tryall he may then come to this Court for releif. [1642]

2. it is ordered, and by this Court declared, that in all Actions of Law it shall be the libertie of the Plaintiffe and Defendant by mutuall consent to choos whether they will be tryed by the Bench or a Jurie, unles it be where the Law upon just reason hath otherwise determined. The like libertie shall be graunted to all persons in any criminal Cases.

3. Also it shall be in the libertie both of Plaintiffe and Defendant, & likewise everie delinquent to be judged by a Jurie, to challenge any of the Jurors, & if the challenge be found just and reasonable, by the Bench or the rest of the Jurie as the Challenger shall choos, it shall be allowed him, & impannelled in their room.

4. Also, children, Ideots, distracted persons and all that are strangers or new comers to our Plantation shall have such allowances, and dispensations in any Case, whether criminal or others, as Religion and reason require. [1641]

VOTES.

It is ordered, decreed and by this Court declared; that all, and everie Freeman, and others authorized by Law, called to give any Advice, Vote, Verdict or Sentence in any Court, Council or civil Assemblie, shall have full freedom to doe it according to their true judgements and consciences, so it be done orderly and inoffensively, for the manner. And that in all cases wherin any Freeman or other is to give his Vote be it in point of Election, making Constitutions and Orders or passing Sentence in any case of Judicature or the like, if he cannot see light or reason to give it positively, one way or other, he shall have libertie to be silent, and not pressed to a determinate vote. And farther that whensoever any thing is to be put to vote, and Sentence to be pronounced or any other matter to be proposed, or read in any Court or Assemblie, if the President or Moderator shall refuse to perform it, the major part of the members of that Court or Assemblie shall have power to appoint any other meet man of them to doe it. And if there be just cause, to punish him that should, and would not. [1641]

USERIE.

It is ordered, decreed & by this Court declared, that no man shall be adjudged for the meer forbearance of any debt, above eight pounds in the hundred for one year, and not above that rate proportionably for all sums whatsoever, Bills of Exchange excepted, neither shall this be a colour or countenance to allow any usurie amongst us contrary to the Law of God. [1641 1643] &133;

WITNESSES.

It is ordered, decreed, and by this Court declared, that no man shall be put to death without the testimonie of two or three witnesses, or that which is equivalent therunto. [1641]

2. And it is ordered by this Court and the Authoritie therof, that any one Magistrate, or Commissioner authorized therunto by the General Court may take the Testimonie of any person of fourteen years of age, or above, of sound understanding and reputation, in any Case civil or criminal; and shall keep the same in his own hands till the Court, or deliver it to the Recorder, publick Notarie or Clerk of the writs to be recorded, that so nothing may be altered in it. Provided, that where any such witnesse shall have his abode within ten miles of the Court, and there living and not disabled by sicknes, or other infirmitie, the said Testimonie so taken out of court shall not be received, or made use of in the Court, except the witnes be also present to be farther examined about it. Provided also, that in all capital cases all witnesses shall be present wheresoever they dwell.

3. And it is farther ordered by the Authoritie aforesaid, that any person summoned to appear as a witnes in any civil Court between partie and partie, shall not be compellable to travell to any Court or place where he is to give his Testimonie, except he who shall so summon him shall lay down or give him satisfaction for his travell and expences, out-ward and home-ward; and for such time as he shall spend in attendance in such case when he is at such Court or place, the Court shall award due recompence. And it is ordered that

two shillings a day shall be accounted due satisfaction to any Witnes for travell and expences: and that when the Witnes dwelleth within three miles, and is not at charge to passe over any other Ferrie than betwixt Charlstown and Boston then one shilling six pence per diem shall be accounted sufficient. And if any Witnes after such payment or satisfaction shall fail to appear to give his Testimonie he shall be lyable to pay the parties damages upon an action of the Case. And all Witnesses in criminal cases shall have suitable satisfaction, payd by the Treasurer upon Warrant from the Court or Judge before whom the case is tryed. And for a general rule to be observed in all criminal causes, both where the Fines are put in certain, and also where they are otherwise, it is farther ordered by the Authoritie aforesayd, that the charges of Witnesses in all such cases shall be borne by the parties delinquent, and shall be added to the Fines imposed; that so the Treasurer having upon Warrant from the Court or other Judge satisfied such Witnesses, it may be repayd him with the Fine: that so the Witness may be timely satisfied, and the countrie not damnified. [1647] &133;

SUITS, VEXATIOUS SUITS.

It is ordered and decreed, and by this Court declared; that in all Cases where it appears to the Court that the Plaintiffe hath willingly & wittingly done wrong to the Defendant in commencing and prosecuting any Action, Suit, Complaint or Indictment in his own name or in the name of others, he shall pay treble damages to the partie greived, and be fined fourty shillings to the Common Treasurie. [1641 1646] &133;

TOBACCO.

This Court finding that since the repealing of the former Laws against Tobacco, the same is more abused then before doth therfore order,

That no man shall take any tobacco within twenty poles of any house, or so neer as may indanger the same, or neer any Barn, corn, or hay-cock as may occasion the fyring therof, upon pain of ten shillings for everie such offence, besides full recompence of all damages done by means therof. Nor shall any take tobacco in any Inne or common Victualing-house, except in a private room there, so as neither the Master of the said house nor any other Guests there shall take offence therat, which if any doe, then such person shall forthwith forbear, upon pain of two shillings sixpence for everie such offence. And for all Fines incurred by this Law, one half part shall be to the Informer the other to the poor of the town where the offence is done. [1638 1647]

TORTURE.

It is ordered, decreed, and by this Court declared; that no man shall be forced by torture to confesse any crime against himselfe or any other, unles it be in some Capital where he is first fully convicted by clear and sufficient evidence to be guilty. After which, if the Case be of that nature that it is very apparent there be other Conspirators or Confoederates with him; then he may be tortured, yet not with such tortures as be barbarous and inhumane.

2. And that no man shal be beaten with above fourty stripes for one Fact at one time. Nor shall any man be punished with whipping, except he have not otherwise to answer the Law, unles his crime be very shamefull, and his course of life vitious and profligate. [1641]

TOWNSHIPS.

It is ordered, decreed, and by this Court declared, that if any man shall behave himselfe offensively at any Town-meeting, the rest then present shall have power to sentence him for such offence, so be it the mulct or penalty exceed not twenty shillings.

2. and that the Freemen of everie Township, and others authorized by law, shall have power to make such Laws and Constitutions as may concern the welfare of their Town. Provided they be not repugnant to the publick Laws and Orders of the Countrie. And if any Inhabitant shall neglect or refuse to observe them, they shall have power to levie the appointed penalties by distresse.

3. Also that the Freemen of everie town or Township, with such other the Inhabitats as have taken the Oath of fidelitie shall have full power to choos yearly, or for lesse time, within each Township a convenient number of fit

men to order the planting and prudential occasions of that Town, according to instructions given them in writing.

Provided, nothing be done by them contrary to the publick Laws and Orders of the Countrie. Provided also that the number of such Select persons be not aboue nine.

4. Farther, it is ordered by the Authoritie aforesayd, that all Towns shall take care from time to time to order and dispose of all single persons, and Inmates within their Towns to service, or otherwise. And if any be greived at such order or dispose, they have libertie to appeal to the next County Court.

5. This Court taking into considerattion the usefull Parts and abilities of divers Inhabitants amongst us, which are not Freemen, which if improved to publick use, the affairs of this Common-wealth may be the easier caried an end in the severall Towns of this Jurisdiction doth order, and heerby declare;

That henceforth it shall may be lawfull for the Freemen within any of the said Towns, to make choice of such Inhabitants (though non-Freemen) who have taken, or shall take the Oath of fidelitie to this Government to be Jurie-men, and to have their Vote in the choice of the Select-men for the town Affairs, Assessements of Rates, and other Prudentials proper to the Select-men of the several Towns. Provided still that the major part of all companyes of Select-men be Free-men from time to time that shall make any valid Act. As also, where no Select-men are, to have their Vote in ordering of Schools, hearing of cattle, laying out of High-wayes and distributing of Lands; any Law, Use or Custom to the contrary notwithstanding. Provided also that no non-Freeman shall have his Vote, untill he have attained the age of twenty one years. [1636 1641 1647]

TRYALLS.

Wheras this Court is often taken up in hearing and deciding particular Cases, between partie and partie, which more properly belong to other inferiour Court. And that if the partie against whom the Judgment shall have any new evidence, or other new matter to plead, he may desire a new Tryall in the same Court upon a Bill or review. And if justice shall not be done him upon that Tryall he may then come to this Court for releif. [1642]

2. it is ordered, and by this Court declared, that in all Actions of Law it shall be the libertie of the Plaintiffe and Defendant by mutuall consent to choos whether they will be tryed by the Bench or a Jurie, unles it be where the Law upon just reason hath otherwise determined. The like libertie shall be graunted to all persons in any criminal Cases.

3. Also it shall be in the libertie both of Plaintiffe and Defendant, & likewise everie delinquent to be judged by a Jurie, to challenge any of the Jurors, & if the challenge be found just and reasonable, by the Bench or the rest of the Jurie as the Challenger shall choos, it shall be allowed him, & impannelled in their room.

4. Also, children, Ideots, distracted persons and all that are strangers or new comers to our Plantation shall have such allowances, and dispensations in any Case, whether criminal or others, as Religion and reason require. [1641]

VOTES.

It is ordered, decreed and by this Court declared; that all, and everie Freeman, and others authorized by Law, called to give any Advice, Vote, Verdict or Sentence in any Court, Council or civil Assemblie, shall have full freedom to doe it according to their true judgements and consciences, so it be done orderly and inoffensively, for the manner. And that in all cases wherin any Freeman or other is to give his Vote be it in point of Election, making Constitutions and Orders or passing Sentence in any case of Judicature or the like, if he cannot see light or reason to give it positively, one way or other, he shall have libertie to be silent, and not pressed to a determinate vote. And farther that whensoever any thing is to be put to vote, and Sentence to be pronounced or any other matter to be proposed, or read in any Court or Assemblie, if the President or Moderator shall refuse to perform it, the major part of the members of that Court or Assemblie shall have power to appoint any other meet man of them to doe it. And if there be just cause, to punish him that should, and would not. [1641]

USERIE.

It is ordered, decreed & by this Court declared, that no man shall be adjudged for the meer forbearance of any debt, above eight pounds in the hundred for one year, and not above that rate proportionably for all sums whatsoever, Bills of Exchange excepted, neither shall this be a colour or countenance to allow any usurie amongst us contrary to the Law of God. [1641 1643] &133;

WITNESSES.

It is ordered, decreed, and by this Court declared, that no man shall be put to death without the testimonie of two or three witnesses, or that which is equivalent therunto. [1641]

2. And it is ordered by this Court and the Authoritie therof, that any one Magistrate, or Commissioner authorized therunto by the General Court may take the Testimonie of any person of fourteen years of age, or above, of sound understanding and reputation, in any Case civil or criminal; and shall keep the same in his own hands till the Court, or deliver it to the Recorder, publick Notarie or Clerk of the writs to be recorded, that so nothing may be altered in it. Provided, that where any such witnesse shall have his abode within ten miles of the Court, and there living and not disabled by sicknes, or other infirmitie, the said Testimonie so taken out of court shall not be received, or made use of in the Court, except the witnes be also present to be farther examined about it. Provided also, that in all capital cases all witnesses shall be present wheresoever they dwell.

3. And it is farther ordered by the Authoritie aforesaid, that any person summoned to appear as a witnes in any civil Court between partie and partie, shall not be compellable to travell to any Court or place where he is to give his Testimonie, except he who shall so summon him shall lay down or give him satisfaction for his travell and expences, out-ward and home-ward; and for such time as he shall spend in attendance in such case when he is at such Court or place, the Court shall award due recompence. And it is ordered that two shillings a day shall be accounted due satisfaction to any Witnes for travell and expences: and that when the Witnes dwelleth within three miles, and is not at charge to passe over any other Ferrie than betwixt Charlstown

and Boston then one shilling six pence per diem shall be accounted sufficient. And if any Witnes after such payment or satisfaction shall fail to appear to give his Testimonie he shall be lyable to pay the parties damages upon an action of the Case. And all Witnesses in criminal cases shall have suitable satisfaction, payd by the Treasurer upon Warrant from the Court or Judge before whom the case is tryed. And for a general rule to be observed in all criminal causes, both where the Fines are put in certain, and also where they are otherwise, it is farther ordered by the Authoritie aforesayd, that the charges of Witnesses in all such cases shall be borne by the parties delinquent, and shall be added to the Fines imposed; that so the Treasurer having upon Warrant from the Court or other Judge satisfied such Witnesses, it may be repayd him with the Fine: that so the Witness may be timely satisfied, and the countrie not damnified. [1647] &133;

Index

A

Act for Settling Doubts and Differences of Opinion (1732), 90n113, 93, 94–95
Act of Repeals, 26, 28
"Act that Abjurers in certain cases shall not have Clergy, An," 24n33
Adams, John, 154–155
ad regimen animarum, 10
adultery
    death penalty for, in Virginia, 42
    in Massachusetts, 111, 124–125, 149, 151–152
African Americans. *see* slaves
Aggie, Mary, 77–78, 89, 91–93, 161
Alderson, Benedict, 87
Alexander ("Negro Fellow"), 141
Alfred, (King of England), 9
Allen, Robert, 147, 152
Ambler, Dorothy, 89
Andros, Edmund, 122–123
animals
    bestiality cases, 152
    theft of, in Virginia, 61
appeals
    in Massachusetts, 120n54, 127
    in Virginia, 41, 54, 69–70
Aramatu, Joseph, 135
Aron (slave), 95–96
arrest, resisting, 67–69
arson, in Virginia, 60
Assize of Clarendon, 15
Attucks, Crispus, 154–155
Auchmuty, Robert, 138

B

bail, in Virginia, 60n9
Baptists, in Virginia, 63

Barber, Anthony, 144
Beckett, Thomas (Archbishop), 6n20, 14–16
Bell, Christian, 142
Bell, James, 142
Bellamy, J., 23n31
Bellingham, Richard, 118
benefit of clergy
    abolition of, in America, 157–164
    "clergy plea" in Massachusetts, 113, 116, 121–122
    groups prohibited from clergy, 7–9
    Massachusetts
        Boston Massacre case, 153–155
        cases of, 135–144
        "clergy plea" and, 113–114
        first use in 1632, 131–132
        implied use of clergy, 145–151
        special cases of, 151–153
    in Plymouth, 121
    slaves and, 43
    Virginia
        abolishment of, 70n60
        by blacks, 89, 90–96
        for children, 84–85
        by race and gender, 71–75, 103–105
        as unsuccessful, 96–103
        by white females, 88–89
        by white males, 79–88
        for women, 85
Bentley, William, 82–83
bigamy
    generally, 9, 27, 28–29
    in Massachusetts, 124–125
    in Virginia, 66–67
Blackstone, W., 1n1
Blair, Elizabeth, 78, 89, 103
Blair, James, 91n119
Blair, Rev. James, 62

blindness, clergy prohibition and, 8–9
Boniface, Archishop, 22
Boniface VIII (Pope), 27n33
Booth, John, 86
Boston Gazette, 133
Boston Massacre, 153–155
Bowen, John, 144
Bradstreet, Simon, 118
branding
    generally, 18, 25, 27n46, 31, 33, 35
    in Virginia, 43, 103
    "well burnt" requirement, 83
Branfbey, Thomas, 65n36
Brett, Maurice, 149, 152
Brittane, James, 151
Brumfield, William, 146
Bryan, Darby, 149
Buckman, Sarah, 149
"buggery," 23, 97–99
Bullard, Henry, 87
burden of proof, in Virginia, 51
burgesses, in Virginia, 41
burglary, in Virginia, 60–61
Burrows, John, 81–82
Butler, Asa, 142–143
Butler, Joseph, 142–143
Button, Jonathan, 44, 100–101

C
Calvinists, in Plymouth, 107–108
capital crimes, increase under Tudors, 22–32
Carter, James, 94–95
Champion, Jane, 89n107
Chapel, David, 88n104
Chapel, Mary, 88n104
Charlemagne (Holy Roman Emperor), 5n17
Charles II (King of England), 33, 35, 122

Charles I (King of England), 79n66
children
    benefit of clergy for, 84–85
    felonies pertaining to, 29n54
    privilege and, 25–26n39
    society stratification in Massachusetts, 114–116
Chubb, Thomas, 141
Clarke, George, 96–97, 161
Clements, Uriah, 150
clergy, defining, 1–16
clericus, tonsuring and, 7–8
Clodd, Robert, 87–88
Clothar II (King of the Franks), 6–7n21
Colcord, Edward, 129
Cole, Peter, 149
Collier, Henry, 86
Colyson, Robert, 17n2
Committee on Law Reform (England), 113
common law, as *lex non scripta*, 162
compurgation, 21n16
Conner, John, 87
constables, 55–56, 59
Constantine (Roman Emperor), 2–3
Constitutions of Archishop Boniface, 22
Cooke, Robert, 141–142
Cooke, Stephen, 141–142
Corey, Giles, 124
Cornish, Joel, 88n104
coroners, role of, 59–60
Cotton, Reverend John, 110n15, 129n91
Council of Trent, 12n41
counterfeiting
    in Massachusetts, 125, 139
    in Virginia, 60
county courts
    in Massachusetts, 119
    in Virginia, 49

Court of Assistants, in Massachusetts, 119, 127
court officials, in Virginia, 55–56, 59
court records
    in Massachusetts, 133–135
    in Virginia, 73–78
Couse (cabin boy), 98–99
Crabb, John, 141
"Criminal Day," 51
Curry, Joan, 102
Curry, John, 102
Cut, Sack, 140

D
Dale, Sir Thomas, 38–40, 47
David, King, 2n5, 13–14
Davies, Thomas, 150
Davis, John, 44
Davis, Richard, 99–100
Davis, Thomas, 149, 153
death penalty
    transportation (exportation) as alternative to, 34–36
    transportation to Virginia as substitute for, 45–49
    in Virginia, 38–40, 42, 53
de Broi, Philip (canon of Bedford), 24–25n36
de Lisle, Thomas (Bishop of Ely), 17n2
Despar, Lambert, 153
dissection, of criminals, 46n41, 53
Dittond, Anthony, 53n85
"double jeopardy," 14–16
Doughty, David, 140
Dowglace, Jonathan, 83–84
Dudley, Joseph, 123
Dudley, Thomas, 118, 123, 135n6
Duell, William, 46n41
due process, origin of, 112
Dunabe, John, 103
Dyer, John, 149

E
East India Company, 79n66
ecclesiastical laws. *see also* benefit of clergy; *individual names of monarchs; individual names of religious leaders*
- in England, jurisdiction lost (1596), 72
- in Massachusetts, 109–111, 122–123
- in Virginia, 44, 62–66

Edict of Clothar, 2n4, 6–7, 15
Edward II (King of England), 17, 20
Edward III (King of England), 7, 17–18
Edward IV (King of England), 17n2, 18
Edward VI (King of England), 9n29, 26–28
Eggington, John, 150
Eldridge, Ezekiel, 140–141
Elizabeth I (Queen of England), 19, 28–31
Endecott, John, 116
England. *see individual names of monarchs*
Ennet, John, 144n42
Evans, Alice, 101
Evans, Robert, 81n72
evidence, convicted felons and, 52
examining courts (Virginia), 42
Executive Journals of the Councils of Virginia, 84–85
exportation, to the Colonies, 31, 32–36

F
Fairfax, George, 150
"farce" ("fiction"), 35n84
felonies. *see also* benefit of clergy; Massachusetts; Virginia; *individual names of crimes*
- in Massachusetts, 122n61, 127n81
- in Virginia, 59–62 (*see also* Virginia)

Ffranke, Daniell, 96–97
Fifth Monarchists, 113
Fignoier, John, 144
Fishbourne, Benjamin, 144

Fitzpatrick, John, 84–85
Fitz Peter, Simon, 24–25n36
Floy, John, 85
Flynt, John, 149
forgery, in Virginia, 61
Frederick II Statimus (Holy Roman Emperor), 1n2
friars, clergy status of, 12
Frost, Nicholas, 146

G
Gabel, Leona, 10, 19n12
gallows, standing in, 144n42
Garrick, Edward, 154–155
Gasket, Joseph, 144
Gatchell, Joseph, 153
Gay, John, 81–82
General Court
    in Massachusetts and Plymouth, 120
    in Virginia, 36n91, 40–41, 54
George I (King of England), 35
Gibbs, Mary, 149
Gibling, Patrick, 52
Gibson, Edmund (Bishop of London), 90–91, 92–93
Goad, Benjamen, 152–153
Godby, Thomas, 82–83
Goldfinch, John, 154–155
Gooch, William, 77–78, 92–93
Gore, William, 18n8
grand larceny, in Virginia, 60, 90
Great Quarter Courts, in Massachusetts, 119, 127
Grinney (Gunney) (slave), 95

H
habeas corpus
    Habeas Corpus Act, 35
    in Virginia, 56
Hanyngton, Sir Edward, 17n2

Harry ("Negro" defendant), 94
Harry (slave), 95–96
Hatch, Margaret, 88–89, 90
Hatch, Pet, 88
Hatch, Thomas, 80n70
Hathaway, John, 146–147, 152
Hawkins, William, 135
Heath, Peleg, 132n1, 135–136, 152
Henry, John, 80n70
Henry, Patrick, 40n17
Henry II (King of England), 12, 14–16
Henry III (King of England), 12
Henry VII (King of England), 18
Henry VIII (King of England), 6, 19, 22–25, 59
Highwood, John, 86–87
Hill, Sarah, 95
Hite, Matthias, 86
Hoffer, P. C., 103–104n154
Holmes, Olvier Wendell, 163
Holmes, Silas, 139
Hooke, Jeremiah, 78, 101
Hopkins, Richard, 121n58, 146
Howell, James, 87–88
Hue, Simon, 137–138
Hulins, Richard, 135
Hunne, Richard, 17n2
Hunting, Samuel, 149
Hurst, James, 86
Hutchins, John, 85
Hutchinson, Chief Justice, 125

I
idolatry, Massachusetts and, 111
incest, in Virginia, 42
indentured servitude
    as criminal sanction, in Virginia, 39
    generally, 32 (*see also* Virginia)

transportation of criminals and, 46
Inglish, Matt, 84–85
Innocent III (Pope), 21n17
Islip, Simon (Archbishop), 21n18

J
Jack (slave), 93–94
Jackson, Benjamin, 81–82
Jacob (slvae), 93n128
James I (King of England), 31–36, 39, 79
Jamestown, early settlement of, 37. *see also* Virginia
Jarvis, Arthur, 101
Johnson, Abigail, 149
Johnson, Arthur, 87
Johnson, Isaac, 118
judges. *see also individual names of courts*
    magistrates compared to, 55
    remuneration of, 55
juries, in Virginia, 50, 51
jurisdiction, of Virginia courts, 54–55, 58. *see also* appeals; examining courts (Virginia); *individual names of courts*
justices of the peace, Virginia, 49–51, 56–58

K
Kesselring, K., 28n51
Keyn, Philip, 148
Kilroy, Matthew, 154–155
Kinchlalius, Andre, 143
King, William, 152
Kingston, Duchess of, 26–27n43
Kirk, Julius, 87
Knowles, Robert, 85

L
labor, convicts transported to Virginia for, 45–49
Lash, Jacob, 143
Latham, Mary, 151

Latham, Robert, 121, 147
Latham, Susanna, 147
Lawes Divine, Morall and Martiall, &c., 165–248
    Alget qui non Ardet (Strachey), 165
    Articles, Lawes, and Orders, Divine, Politique, and Martiall, 170–183
    To the constant, mighty, and worthie friends, the Committies, Assistants (Strachey), 166–169
    defined, 39n12
    Instructions of the Marshall
        for the better inhabling of a Captaine, 212–217
        for the better inhabling of a Corporall, 229–233
        for the better inhabling of a Lieftenant, 218–220
        for the better inhabling of an Ensigne, 221–223
        for the better inhabling of a privat soldier, 234–241
        for the better inhabling of a Serjeant, 224–228
        for better inhabling of the Colonell or Governour, 195–211
    A Praier, 242–248
    The Summarie of the Marshall Lawes, 184–194
Laws and Liberties of Massachusetts, 270–318
    Abilitie, 274–275
    Age, 275
    Ana-Baptists, 275–276
    Arrests, 276
    Bond-Slavery, 276–277
    Capital Lawes, 277–279
    Charges Publick, 279
    Children, 280–281
    Councill, 281–282
    Courts, 282–285
    Deputies for the General Court, 285–286
    Ecclesiasticall, 286–290
    Elections, 290–292
    Fornication, 292
    Freemen, Non-Freemen, 292
    Fugitives, Strangers, 293
    Gaming, 293

General Court, 293–294
Governour, 294
Heresie, 294
Idlenes, 294–295
Impresses, 295–296
Imprisonment, 296
Indians, 296–299
Inditements, 299
In-Keepers, Trippling, Drunkenes, 299–300
Jesuits, 295
Juries, Jurors, 300–301
Justice, 301
Liberties Common, 302
Lying, 302–304
Magistrates, 304–305
Monopolies, 305
Oaths, Subscription, 305–306
Oppression, 306
To Our Beloved Brethren and Neighbours, 270–274
Profane Swearing, 306
Punishment, 306
Schools, 306–307
Strangers, 307–308
Suits, Vexatious Suits, 308, 313
Summons, 308
Tobacco, 308–309, 313–314
Torture, 309, 314
Townships, 309–310, 314–315
Tryalls, 310–311, 315–316
Userie, 312, 317
Votes, 311–312, 316
Witnesses, 312–313, 317–318
lawyers' role, in Massachusetts, 126–130
"lay plea," 20n13, 24
lay trial method, 19n12, 20
Lechford, Thomas, 128–129
Levellers, 113

literacy test, 8n24, 13–14, 30, 41, 71, 77–78, 90, 125
Livermore, Matthew, 139
London Company, 37n1
Lorphelin, Peter, 150–151
Lowe, John, 87
Lowell, John, 144
Ludlow, Roger, 118
Luxford, James, 141
Lyndsey, Eleazer, 139–140
Lynn, Maurice, 94–95

M
Macdonald, John, 138
magistrates
    in Massachusetts, 112, 126
    in Virginia, 42, 55
Major, George, 148–149
manslaughter, in Massachusetts, 125
Marja ("Negro"), 152
marriage laws, in Massachusetts, 112
Martin, Sarah, 88n104
Mary (Queen of England), 28, 42
Massachusetts, 107–130, 131–155. *see also* Laws and Liberties of Massachusetts; Massachusetts Body of Liberties
    abolition of benefit of clergy, 157–164
    benefit of clergy cases, 135–144
    benefit of clergy first used in 1632, 131–132
    Boston Massacre case, 153–155
    court records of, 133–135
    court structure in, 116–120, 123–124, 126–130
    criminal courts and role of lawyers in, 126–130
    early justice system in, 107–120
    exportation to Colonies as punishment, 31, 32–36
    implied use of clergy, 145–151
    legal system as innovative, 132
    Massachusetts Bay Company, 108n4
    original charters and early laws of, 120–126

society stratification in, 114–116
special cases of, 151–153
Massachusetts Body of Liberties, 249–269
   A Coppie of the Liberties of the Massachusets Collonie in New England, 249–258
   defined, 110–111, 112
   as innovative, 132
   Liberties More Peculiarlie Concerning the Free Men, 259–262
   Liberties of Children, 262–263
   Liberties of Forreiners and Strangers, 264
   Liberties of Servants, 263–264
   Liberties of Women, 262
   Off the Bruite Creature, 264
   used in England, 128n86
Mass Court Recs, 133
Mather, Cotton, 129–130
Mathew, Walter, 98
May, Jesse, 87
Mayflower Compact, 107, 121
M'Carty, Dennis, 93–94
McClenahan, Andrew, 78, 102
Medad, 140
Meserere mei Deus (Neck Verse), 12, 35–36
misdemeanors, in Massachusetts, 122n61, 127n81
monks, clergy status of, 12
Montgomery, Hugh, 154–155
Moody, Thomas, 87
Moore, Nathaniel, 97
Morton, Joseph, 95–96
murder
   in Massachusetts, 110
   in Virginia, 60

N
Neal, Robert, 139–140
Necho, George, 139
Neck Verse, 14, 35–36

"Negroes." *see* slaves
Newall, Hannah, 153
Newgate prison (London), 47
Noble, John, 133
Norcott, William, 83–84
Northumberland, Duke of, 26
nuns
    benefit of clergy denied to, 7–8n24
    clergy status of, 12

O
Odo (Bishop of Bayeux), 3n12
Oldham, John, 85, 103, 105
Otis, James, 138
Owen, Thomas, 151
oyer and terminer ("hear and determine") courts, 42–43

P
Packyngton, Robert, 17n2
Paine, Robert, 154–155
Parker, Joseph, 139
Payne, Elizabeth, 150, 152
Peck, Richard, 82–83
peeral benefit claims, 26–27
Pelham, Herbert, 118
"penance," 21
Perkins, Zacheus, 150
Phillis, Alexander, 83
pick-pocketing, in Virginia, 61
"pleading," origin of, 83n78
"pleading the belly," 19, 88–89
Plymouth colony, legal system of, 107, 108–111, 114, 117, 120–121, 123.
    see also Massachusetts
Plymouth Colony Archive Project, 133
Pomeroy, Leonard, 150
Porter, John, 21n20
Postman, Neil, 25–26n39

Pott, John, 82–83
Potts, John, 89n107, 96–97
Praemunire, 18
pressing, 51
Preston, John, 154–155
prisons
    escape from, 67–69
    established by dioceses, 22
    "gaol," defined, 67
    increase of capital crimes under Tudors, 23
privilege, 1–16, 17–36. *see also* benefit of clergy; clerical status
    establishing privilege and early use (325-1066 A.D.), 1–10
    extension of, and increase of capital crimes, 22–32
    extension of privilege and increase of capital crimes, 22–32
    Henry II (King of England) and Beckett, 14–16
    transportation and exportation to the Colonies, 32–36
    validity of claims and plea submission before secular courts, 17–22
    William I (King of England) and, 10–14
privilegium clericus, 1, 6n20, 10–14, 103
privilegium fori ("privilege of the legal forum"), 1–6, 14–15, 23n27, 32–36. *see also* privilege
Privy Council (Westminster), 41, 54, 69–70
Psalm 51, 13–14, 48n47
Pugh, R. B., 21n18
purgation, 21n16

Q
Quakers, in Virginia, 63
Quanset, Jethro, 137–138
Quincy, Josiah, 154–155
Quincy, Samuel, 154–155

R
Ralph, Jeremiah, Jr., 138
Ratcliff, Phillip, 145
Reade, William, 81–82
reading (literacy) test, 8n24, 13–14, 30, 41, 71, 77–78, 90, 125

Records and Files of the Quarterly Court of Essec County, Massachusetts, 1636-1686, 133
Reddish, Edward, 75–76, 99–100, 161
remuneration, of magistrates *versus* judges, 55
Reynor, John, 144
Rice, Gideon, 140
Rigsby, Alexander, 78, 102–103
robbery
    in Massachusetts, 125
    in Virginia, 61
Robert (Bishop of Salisbury), 4
Roberts, Evan, 101
Robins, Sarah, 142
Rogers, Bridget, 89
Round Church, vicar of, 18n8
Rufus (William II) (King of England), 3n12

S
Sachamus, Joshua, 142
Saltonstall, Robert, 128–129
Samson (slave), 94–95
Scarlett, Rofite, 146
Scott, Thomas, 151
Scott, W. B., 103–104n154
Seale, Margaret, 147
Second Council of Lyons, 27n44
"Session of General Jail Delivery of Criminals," 49n55
Sewell, Samuel, 130
sexual offenses/violence
    adultery, 42, 111, 124–125, 149, 151–152
    "buggery," 23, 97–99
    incest, 42
    rape, 139
    Virginia's rulings on, 66–67
Sharpless, Edward, 39–40, 79–81
Shaw, Edward, 147
sheriffs, in Virginia, 55

Shirley, William, 137
Sims, John, 86
Skelton, Samuel, 116
Skousen, L., 23n31
slaves
    benefit of clergy, and race, 71–75, 103–105
    benefit of clergy, in Massachusetts, 134
    benefit of clergy abolished, in Virginia e, 70n60
    benefit of clergy for, in Virginia, 71, 77–78, 89, 90–96
    clergy plea as inconsistent for, 160–161
    oyer and terminer court cases, 43
    societal stratification in Massachusetts, 114–116
Smith, Elizabeth, 144n42
Smith, John, 148
Smith, Sir Thomas, 33n74, 79n66
Smith, Thomas, 85
smuggling, in Virginia, 61
sodomy. *see* "buggery"
soldiers, whipping of, 27
Somerset, Duke of, 26
Spencer, Henry, 150
spirtual cases, spiritual persons *versus*, 10–11
Spotswood, Governor, 90n114
Standlake, Daniell, 147–148
"Starving Time," 45
Statute of Marlborough, 12
Statute of Provisors of Benefices, 17–18
Steale, Margaret, 152
Stephen, King, 4
Stevens, David, 138
Stickey, John, 135
Strachey, William, 165, 166–169
strangers courts, in Massachusetts, 120
Strickland, John, 103
Suffolk Files, 133
Suggit, Edgeworth, 95
Sullivan, Anne, 1–93

Supreme Judicial Court of Massachusetts, 123–124
Sylvester I (Pope), 2n4

T
tonsuring, 7–8
Tool, James, 013
transportation
    to the Colonies, 31, 32–36
    pardons as clergy sentences, 161
    seven-year terms for, 78
    by Virginia, to West Indies, 68–69
    to Virginia, 45–49
Trayes, Robert, 147–148
treason, 24n34

V
vagabonds, branding of, 27n46
Vauden, Nicolas, 148
Vickers, Mary, 83–84, 100–101
Virginia, 37–58, 59–105. *see also* Lawes Divine, Morall and Martiall, &c.
    abolition of benefit of clergy, 157–164
    availability of court records, 73–78
    benefit of clergy in
        by blacks, 89, 90–96
        by race and gender, 71–75, 103–105
        as unsuccessful, 96–103
        by white females, 88–89
        by white males, 79–88
    clericus and non-*clericus* crimes in, 59–70
    criminal courts in, and rule of law, 49–58
    exportation to Colonies as punishment, 31, 32–36
    settlement of, and early law in, 37–45
    transportation to, and benefit of clergy, 45–49
    Virginia Company of London, 37–39, 79–81
Virginia Gazette, 75
Virginia Magazine of History and Biography, 75

W
Wager of War process, 21n16
Walker, John, 147
Walker, Robert, 83–84, 100–101
Ward, Evan, 44, 100–101
Ward, Nathaniel, 112, 118
Warr, Thomas, 101
Washington, Edward, 83–84
Waters, Thomas, 135, 135n6
"well burnt," 83
wergild system, 3n11, 9n34
West, Thomas, 147
Wheeler, William, Jr., 137
White, Samuel, 151
Wihtraed (King of England), 2n4, 9
William I (King of England), 3n12, 10–14
William of St. Calais (Bishop of Durham), 3n12
Williams, Charity, 135n6, 136
Williams, Martin, 153
Williams, Richard (Cornish), 80n70, 97–99
William the Conqueror (King of England), 4n15, 5n17, 10
Windsor, Mercy, 136
Winthrop, John, 107n1, 117n42, 118, 128, 129n30, 145
Wisedom, Jonathan, 101
witchcraft, as unclergyable, 124
Wodeward, William, 17n2
women
    benefit of clergy for, generally, 7–8n24, 33, 85
    benefit of clergy in Massachusetts, 134–135
    benefit of clergy in Virginia, 71, 76–77, 88–89, 103–105
    as convicts transported to Virginia, 48
    peeral benefit claims and, 26–27n43
    "pleading the belly," 19, 88–89
    societal stratification in Massachusetts, 114–116
Woolcott, John, 148
Worcester, Bishop of, 22n22

Wyard, Ellinor, 97
Wyard, Robert, 97

Y
Yardley, Sir George, 96–97

CPSIA information can be obtained at www.ICGtesting.com
Printed in the USA
LVOW03s2314151114

413565LV00001B/1/P